D1483787

# Confronting Appalachian Stereotypes

# Confronting Appalachian Stereotypes

## Back Talk from an American Region

Dwight B. Billings
Gurney Norman
and Katherine Ledford
*Editors*

*Foreword by*
Ronald D Eller

THE UNIVERSITY PRESS OF KENTUCKY

Publication of this volume was made possible in part
by grants from the E.O. Robinson Mountain Fund and the
National Endowment for the Humanities.

Scholarly publisher for the Commonwealth,
serving Bellarmine College, Berea College, Centre
College of Kentucky, Eastern Kentucky University,
The Filson Club Historical Society, Georgetown College,
Kentucky Historical Society, Kentucky State University,
Morehead State University, Murray State University,
Northern Kentucky University, Transylvania University,
University of Kentucky, University of Louisville,
and Western Kentucky University.

*Editorial and Sales Offices:* The University Press of Kentucky
663 South Limestone Street, Lexington, Kentucky 40508-4008

03 02 01 00 99     1 2 3 4 5

Library of Congress Cataloging-in-Publication Data
Confronting Appalachian stereotypes : back talk from an American
region / Dwight B. Billings, Gurney Norman, and
Katherine Ledford, editors : foreword by Ronald D Eller.
    p.    cm.
Includes bibliographical references and index.
ISBN 0–8131–2099–3 (cloth : alk. paper)
    1. Mountain whites (Southern States)—Appalachian Region,
Southern—Ethnic identity.    2. Mountain whites (Southern States)—
Appalachian Region, Southern—Social conditions.    3. Stereotype
(Psychology)—United States.    4. Appalachian Region, Southern—
Social conditions.    5. Mountain whites (Southern States) in
literature.    I. Billings, Dwight B., 1948–    .    II. Norman, Gurney,
1937–    .    III. Ledford, Katherine.
F210.C66    1998
306′.0974—dc21                                                                98–43591

# Contents

## V. Recycling Old Stereotypes: Critical Responses to *The Kentucky Cycle*

# Foreword

Appalachia may likely have replaced the benighted South as the nation's most maligned region. Once disparaged as the "bunghole" of the nation, "the Sahara of the Bozarts,"[1] the South has risen in stature in recent years, and the new "Sunbelt South" now rivals other regions as the symbol of American economic and cultural progress. Not so Appalachia. Always part of the mythical South, Appalachia continues to languish backstage in the American drama, still dressed, in the popular mind at least, in the garments of backwardness, violence, poverty, and hopelessness once associated with the South as a whole. No other region of the United States today plays the role of the "other America" quite so persistently as Appalachia. When my family left West Virginia to migrate to Ohio for a period in the 1950s, most white Southerners were labeled hillbillies; hillbillies in the 1990s are not just Southerners, they are Appalachians.

Perhaps that is why Robert Schenkkan set his 1992 Pulitzer Prize–winning play in eastern Kentucky. An epic tragedy about violence and greed, *The Kentucky Cycle* seeks to recast the American myth as a story of repeated failure and poverty, the failure of the American spirit and the poverty of the American soul. No other region quite symbolizes this countervailing image of America as does Appalachia. With its stereotypical feuds, moonshine stills, mine wars, environmental destruction, joblessness, and human depredation, Appalachia was the place where the American dream had failed, and that idea for Mr. Schenkkan made it "quintessentially American."

Appalachian scholars have long recognized the role that the "idea of Appalachia" has played as counterpoint to the idea of America. As Americans have sought to redefine themselves as a people, Appalachia has become a Janus-faced "other." Throughout much of the nineteenth century Appalachia represented a geographic barrier on the frontier, "a strange land inhabited by a peculiar people"—a people who were at once quaint and romantic and yet a burden to American success. By 1900 a popular image of Appalachia had crystallized that defined the region as "in America but not of America" and spawned a flurry of benevolent efforts that would seek to bring order and development to the mountains.[2] Outside attempts to uplift and "Americanize" the region would last throughout most of the twentieth century.

Until recently, however, the stereotypes and benighted imagery of the "idea of Appalachia" have gone unchallenged. As early as 1921 John C. Campbell wrote that Appalachia was "a land about which, perhaps, more things are known that are not true than any part of our country." Since then the scholarly and non-scholarly material on Appalachia has increased many fold, but the static and savage image of Appalachia has grown and continues to predominate in media, film and other popular views of the region. Only in the last three decades have Appalachian intellectuals and activists begun to challenge these regional stereotypes and resist their perpetuation.

This is a book that shouts Appalachia's challenge to century old images, demeaning portrayals and misleading assumptions about the region and its people. As such it is a symbol of a growing sense of identity within Appalachia and of a new sense of hope and direction. More than just the defensive reaction of an abused people—although defensiveness is an important stage of community building—the response to these popular stereotypes is itself a political act that goes beyond defensiveness, because such images have the power to affect behavior toward the region. Whether government planners, well-meaning missionaries, private corporations, urban journalists, or even local political leaders, those who would do something to and for Appalachian communities have often hidden their interests in the haze of regional stereotypes and the confusion of perceived history.

As the authors of this volume demonstrate, not only do the prevailing images of Appalachia blame the victim for Appalachia's problems, but they trivialize complex political and economic issues facing the region to the level of personality traits and cultural quirks. Moonshiners[3], welfare cheats, coal miners and other Appalachian "types" distance us from the political and economic realities of the region, including our own injustices toward those stereotyped. In the case of Appalachia, such images allow the rest of America to keep the region at arm's length, rather than to confront the systemic problems of a dependent economy, environmental decay, and institutional weakness that challenge mountain communities today.

The "idea of Appalachia," perpetuated in contemporary work such as *The Kentucky Cycle*, not only masks the exploitation of land and people in the region, but it obscures the diversity of conditions, relationships, and cultures within Appalachian society itself—diversity of race, gender and class as well as diversity in religion, education and history. Appalachian scholars have come to recognize that there are many Appalachias, and applying generalizations often contradict local heritage and experiences. Like other American minority groups, Appalachians resist classification. Their culture is dynamic and they are constantly in the process of re-defining their identity.

How we see ourselves, as individuals and as a region, is shaped in part by how others see us. Confronting stereotypes, understanding the motivations and ideologies that generate them, is an important initial step toward self-determination—toward empowerment and the ability to shape an alternative future. This is true for communities across America as we seek to redefine who we are as a people, to respect our diversity, and to confront the burden of our history. In this volume some of Appalachia's leading thinkers and writers have taken it upon themselves to challenge the received stereotypes of the region. In so doing, however, they do more than just slay false images, for they open a new regional conversation about our own distinctiveness. As George Brown Tindall observed about the demise of the myth of the South, "to change is not necessarily to lose ones identity; to change sometimes is to find it."[4]

Ronald D Eller

## Notes

1. H.L. Mencken, "The Sahara of the Bozart" *New York Evening Mail* (1917), quoted in George Brown Tindall, *The Ethnic Southerners* (Baton Rouge, La.: louisiana State Univ. Press, 1979), 47.

2. See Henry D. Shapiro, *Appalachia on Our Mind: The Southern Mountains and Mountaineers in the American Consciousness, 1870–1920* (Chapel Hill, N.C.: Univ. of North Carolina Press, 1978).

3. It is ironic that in spell checking a draft of this document, my word processing software (Microsoft Word Version 6.0) could not locate the word "moonshiners" in its dictionary and recommended that I substitute the word "mountaineers."

4. Tindall, p. 21.

# Acknowledgments

The editors are grateful for the help and encouragement they received in the initiation of this project from George Ella Lyon and the late Jim Wayne Miller. They also thank Richard Angelo, Bill Best, Roslyn Bologh, Patricia Jennings, Karen Tice, and Nanci Unger, for much appreciated advice and assistance.

# I

## (Re)Introducing Appalachia

### Talking Back to Stereotypes

# Introduction

## *Dwight B Billings*

This book began as a series of responses to a play, Robert Schenkkan's *The Kentucky Cycle,* and to the latest round of stereotyping of Appalachian peoples and their cultures that such works exemplify. While the peoples and cultures in the Appalachian Mountains are decidedly plural, outside the region in the arts, the academy, and popular culture, many representations of them now, as for the past one hundred years, are often monolithic, pejorative, and unquestioned. But they are challenged in the region. Appalachian scholars have been engaged in the sustained critique of these stereotypes for many years, and the people of the region "talk back" to stereotypes of themselves by who they are and how they live their lives. This book is intended to bring together these overt and implicit challenges to regional stereotypes and, more generally, to provide insight into the operations of cultural power and ideology in America that such stereotyping signifies.

Perhaps it should not be surprising that the 1990s have witnessed yet another cycle of stereotyping Appalachia and its people. An era of global economic restructuring that has brought insecurity, declining living standards, and cutbacks in benefits and protection to millions of Americans, the nineties have provided fertile ground for anxiety, frustration, and anger as well as for the projection of these emotions onto innocent others. Women and racial and ethnic minorities especially have felt the heat of this anger, and so too have Appalachians. At once quintessential American insiders and archetypal Others, mountain people, it seems, are acceptable targets for hostility, projection, disparagement, scapegoating, and contempt. Here are a few examples from the "Signs of the Times" section of the *Appalachian Journal,* which often takes note of such affronts.[1]

A Republican congressional representative from Indiana, angered over the FBI's deadly treatment of the Branch Davidians in Waco, Texas, states in 1995 that the only law that officials had clearly established as having been broken was that Davidian leader David Koresh "had sex with consenting minors." In addition to offending the Kentucky Domestic Violence Association with his use of the oxymoron "consenting minors," the congressman goes on rhetorically to add, "Do you send tanks and government troops into the large sections of Kentucky and Tennessee and other places where such things occur?"[2]

The mayor of a North Carolina foothills town describes to reporters the cultural difference between the "aristocratic" families who own the local furniture industry and the "rednecks" there who "won't do anything but work in furniture plants." Instead of ballet at the high school, he says, "The majority of the people would rather have rasslin' and hillbilly singin'." "These mountain people are different. You get up here in these mountains, you'll find people that are different than anywhere you'll find in the world. They don't believe in law and order." "They'll handle their own situation. You go up there and cause trouble and they'll kill you. It's just a different breed of people."[3]

In addition to insensitive politicians, some journalists also trade in Appalachian stereotypes as if they were coin of the realm. Thus a *Washington Post* columnist describes the Clinton administration's firing of employees of the White House travel office in 1993 as "shockingly incompetent, replete with the Nixonian use of the FBI and the *hillbillyish* hiring of an ambitious Clinton cousin" (emphasis added). Similarly, a *New York Post* columnist, commenting in 1992 on the image of Republicans after the arrest of the chief justice of the New York Supreme Court for sending lewd and threatening letters through the mail, says in an interview, "Bush isn't out [of office] for six days, and they're acting like crazed Appalachians."[4]

Unfortunately, one cannot escape Appalachian stereotypes simply by avoiding politics and the news; they appear almost everywhere, including leisure and entertainment writings. Increasingly, they are on-line as well. Thus a contributor to *Rock and Ice* describes rock climbing in Kentucky's Red River Gorge by writing, "We drove by clumps of locals who eyed us with smoldering hostility. Hollywood could not have made these guys up. They were the sorriest-looking dudes I'd ever seen." "As I pulled into the trailhead, I noticed Ray's truck wasn't behind me. We waited awhile, hoping they hadn't broken down in front of the cast of *Deliverance*."[5]

Writing about an album recorded by a Swedish band named Rednex, a music critic for *Entertainment Weekly* complains, "Nearly every song is sung in the voice of a drooling, bug-eyed inbred from some imaginary Appalachian trailer park . . . Destined for a Scandinavian version of *Hee Haw*—where they belong."[6]

Finally, a recent article in the *New York Times Magazine* notes that "redneck" jokes are becoming especially popular on computer chat lines. Considering whether this tired avenue of humor is politically correct or not, the article concludes by noting that "the humorous impulse seeks out people who . . . are supposed to be *bad*-reactionary and racist—and thus deserving of all they get.

And there's an added bonus: So few rednecks have computers."[7] However, at least one Appalachian computer user, West Virginia state senator Sondra Lucht, was reportedly not amused by a graphics software program that includes an image of an outhouse as the icon for her home state.[8]

That many Appalachians themselves are not immune to the use of stereotypes, especially when they promise to be profitable, is evident from such cultural events as the annual summer performance of a musical reenactment of the Hatfields and McCoys feud in a West Virginia state park and performances of John Fox Jr.'s *Trail of the Lonesome Pine* in Virginia to the existence of numerous "ma and pa" restaurants, motels, and other small businesses throughout the region that display hillbilly signs and icons to attract tourist attention. Nothing, however, quite equals Pikeville, Kentucky's annual Hillbilly Days festival, a fund-raising event for Shriners children's hospitals in Kentucky and Ohio. A three-day event now more than twenty years old, Hillbilly Days brings nearly one hundred thousand visitors, including representatives from 151 local Shriners "hillbilly" chapters nationally, to this small Appalachian town to dress up and behave like comic book caricatures of mountaineers.[9]

These examples and literally hundreds of others collected in past issues of the *Appalachian Journal* speak worlds about the frequency and impunity of the use of Appalachian stereotypes in everyday writing and publishing in the 1990s. The same is true of other mass media as well. Television networks recycle endless repeats of *The Beverly Hillbillies* and *Dukes of Hazzard* on cable, and not long ago one added a new and especially offensive series to prime time, *Christy,* the story of a famous missionary's efforts on behalf of the benighted people of Appalachian Tennessee. Hollywood has not only brought a new version of *The Beverly Hillbillies* to the big screen but has contributed *Next of Kin* as well, the laughably violent story of eastern Kentuckians who arm themselves with antique firearms and the venomous serpents of their religious rites to go to Chicago to avenge the death of one of their kinsmen at the hands of organized crime. But this is nothing new for Hollywood. Appalachian scholar J.W. Williamson reports that in its early days the film industry made more than four hundred silent movies exploiting the nation's fascination with Appalachian feuds and moonshine making.[10]

Popular media are not the only culprits, though, when it comes to disparaging Appalachians. Academia and the arts follow right in tow. American historians find much to praise in David Hackett Fischer's *Albion's Seed,* an award-winning history of the British cultural influence on early America, but Appalachian scholars, to quote one prominent representative, find Fischer's treatment of the Appalachian backcountry in the days of the early republic to be "a lamentable reinstatement of the hillbilly stereotype—with a vengeance."[11]

Significantly, Fischer grossly oversimplifies the early history of the region by universalizing stereotyped images of one of its population groups, those from northern Britain, as comprising the essence of Appalachian experience and ignoring scholarship of the past two decades on the complexity and diversity of the region that challenges his assumptions.

Essentializing and universalizing Appalachian stereotypes likewise characterize a recent and representative publication in the social sciences by David Cattell-Gordon. Relying primarily on outmoded accounts of Appalachia by popular writers such as Harry Caudill and Jack Weller, Cattell-Gordon interprets the whole of Appalachia as a "traumatized culture" where "withdrawal, depression, inertia, self-blame and resignation" rule. "The effects of [Appalachian] history," he writes, are "bred in the bones of the people of the region" and transmitted across generations. The result is "a culturally transmitted traumatic stress syndrome." Appalachian scholars were prompt to point out that Cattell-Gordon's treatment of the region "overlooks oppositional movements . . . in Appalachia," "relies upon a one-sided reading of Appalachian history," and "incorrectly attributes a unified cultural ethos" to a multicultural region. But it is significant that his article was published in a politically progressive journal that is normally highly sensitive to stereotypes and degrading generalizations.[12]

There are equally troubling cultural expressions in the arts world. The publication of a series of photographs imprudently titled *Appalachian Portraits* by Shelby Lee Adams demonstrates that some Appalachian artists are not hesitant to serve up what mainstream culture expects from the region. A number of the down-and-out subjects displayed by Adams appear to be mentally challenged, such as an adult midget wearing diapers, and quite a few are draped with serpents, yet the book has received praise in reviews from outside the region. Describing several of Adams's portraits as "upon first glance" being "brutal"—"a retired coal miner who is missing an eye, a hog killing, a shirtless man who has received his fifth gunshot wound, youths that look ready to star in a remake of *Deliverance*"—a *Washington Post* critic reports, "Despite this, Adams says, most of those who have seen his photographs can move beyond their initial queasiness. 'A freak show is part of it, just as it's a part of life,' Adams says. 'But if that's all people see, they have a problem, not me.'"[13] Confidently, a critic for the *Chicago Tribune* states, "Photographers long have brought us news of people and places we've never been, but only Adams has delivered such fair, honest portraits of people others might see as freaks."[14]

Interestingly, Adams's photographs received little attention in Appalachian publications, perhaps indicating the uneasiness and confusion they generate.[15] In sharp contrast, however, it cannot be said that Appalachian critics have been silent or hesitant to critique Robert Schenkkan's Pulitzer Prize–winning play, *The Kentucky Cycle*. Indeed, probably no other recent artistic production involving images of Appalachia has received as much attention, or from some quarters as much criticism, as this ambitious but seriously flawed work.

When Robert Schenkkan's play, *The Kentucky Cycle,* won the Pulitzer Prize for drama in 1992, it was notable for being the only play ever to win that award without first being performed in New York. When it did come to Broadway, after runs in Los Angeles and at the Kennedy Center in Washington, D.C., it was most notable for being, at a cost of $2.5 million, the most expensive non-musical ever to open there. Despite breaking box office records at the Mark Taper Forum in Los Angeles and winning five Drama Critics Credits Awards there, *The Kentucky Cycle* flopped in New York. Critics there and in the national press panned it as, in the words of a *New York Times* critic, little more than a "melodramatic pageant."[16] *Newsweek,* the *Nation,* the *New Yorker,* and the *New York Times* each equated it to a television "miniseries" (which, reports say, Kevin Costner is currently planning to produce and star in for Home Box Office), not to good art.[17] So what's the fuss?

Running six and one-half hours in length and involving more than seventy characters, *The Kentucky Cycle* is an ambitious play of epic proportions that covers two hundred years of history in Appalachian Kentucky. Enacted from the standpoint of three interrelated families, two white and one black, the play narrates the endless cycles of violence and betrayal among them—and later, with corporate America—as they struggle over the possession of a small parcel of mountain land. Beginning in 1775 with the murder of Native Americans and the acquisition of their land by Michael Rowen, a greedy indentured servant from Ireland, *The Cycle* traces the tragic fate of Rowen's descendants through the days of Kentucky settlement, slavery, family feuding, the Civil War, the usurpation of the land and coal by outside corporations, the building of a union movement and its corruption, and finally, the Great Society's War on Poverty.

According to the author's note published with *The Kentucky Cycle* and numerous interviews, playwright Robert Schenkkan intended his play as an impassioned criticism of the selfishness of the Bush-Reagan years and especially of the "fracturing along socioeconomic and racial lines" that that political era encouraged as well as the fact, more generally, that Americans "are in denial about our past" and unwilling "to examine [it] and come to terms with it."[18] Schenkkan got the idea of using Appalachia as a metaphor for what is wrong in America when he spent a "day" traveling in Appalachian Kentucky in 1981. Here he encountered "extraordinary" poverty and environmental abuse, "ruin on a grand scale." Schenkkan writes, "The poverty and the environmental abuse I witnessed there were not simply a failure of economics. It went much deeper than that; hence our continual failure to 'social engineer' meaningful changes there. *It was a poverty of the spirit; a poverty of the soul.* What I was a witness to there was a vision of the future" (emphasis added).[19] Ruling out that what he had seen in Appalachia might simply have been the unfortunate but not unusual workings of corporate capitalism on a backstreet of the American economy, Schenkkan determined, instead, to understand more about Appalachia's "poverty of the soul." He thus turned to Harry Caudill's *Night Comes to the Cumberlands.* Reading this popular book, he concluded that the "story of the Cumberland Plateau is a fascinating one, rich with colorful characters and acts of both extraordinary courage and violence. Above all," he says, "it is a quintessentially American story."[20]

Over the years, as he wrote the nine acts of the play, Schenkkan reports that "the play seemed to become less and less about the history of eastern Kentucky or even the history of Appalachia. It was about America," and even more, "about American mythology." In his view, neither family, class, nor social movements are sufficient to "bring an end to these seemingly endless cycles of violence and loss" that Appalachia embodies—only a consciousness of "the whole of nature" is up to that huge task. Believing in the power of myth to explain the rise and fall of civilizations, Schenkkan claims to have written *The Kentucky Cycle* as an exploration of the failed mythology of the American frontier, its "Myth of Abundance" that says our resources are too vast ever to end, and its "Myth of Escape" that says ignore the past and live only for the present. Dramatizing the power of these myths to repress memory and responsibility, Schenkkan puts the following words in the mouth of a twentieth-century descendant of his first villainous Kentuckian, Michael Rowen: "I dream about Hell. Hell is a place where you keep makin' the same mistake over and over again and nobody learns nothin'. It looked a whole lot like Eastern Kentucky."[21]

Schenkkan's stress on the mythic, however, is not to suggest that he denies the historicity of his treatment of Appalachia. Contending that "a bewildering maelstrom of corrupting legacies . . . has trapped the people and the region in recurring cycles of poverty," he expresses hope that *The Kentucky Cycle* "sheds some light on this process." While stressing that the play is fiction, Schenkkan says that "It was very important for me to respect the truth of the people [there]. I wanted to make the events of the region as accurate as possible."[22] And, while "it's not a history," Schenkkan says elsewhere, "I can in perfect honesty support everything I've written in the historical record." He adds that the criticism he has received from Appalachian artists is "ironic . . . because I felt such sympathy with and anger on behalf of that poverty I had seen, of those individuals I had been exposed to. I felt, in my own way, like an advocate for them."[23]

The failure of *The Kentucky Cycle* according to mainstream critics, however, is not the inaccuracy of the history it tells, nor its demeaning portrait of Appalachian people, but the quality of its artistry. The *Nation*'s drama critic,

David Kaufman, perhaps the hardest hitting of national commentators, described the play as "lurid melodrama" that is "dramatically wrong, even vacant." Kaufman contended that, despite its imposing length, *The Kentucky Cycle* is "too brief to develop any of its seventy-odd characters or to sustain any of its themes in anything other than bromidic ways. It's a matter of ambition," he complained, "masquerading as art."[24] Others largely concurred; *The Cycle,* according to the *Washington Post,* was "trivial and mediocre."[25]

Almost universally, and most ironically because none of the national critics voiced surprise or discomfort with the play's stereotypic depictions of Appalachians nor its treatment of Appalachian history, the critics also faulted *The Kentucky Cycle* for being "relentlessly politically correct." According to the *Washington Post,* "the women are all strong and true and the African Americans are all noble and take no nonsense and the Indians are more virtuous than whites." "Except for the violence," the *Post* writer went on, "it is all on the level of a politically correct grade school pageant." While the *New York Times* drama critic complained that Schenkkan's stock African American characters were merely "symbolic ciphers one and all, who are disfranchised by their perfunctory lines as they are by slavery," the same critic expressed no concern that Appalachia was depicted as "a polluted wasteland, a ghost town." Finally, far from being bothered by the fact that *The Kentucky Cycle* works by deploying stock Appalachian characters borrowed as much from *Deliverance* and *Li'l Abner* as from the equally problematic *Night Comes to the Cumberlands,* the *New Yorker* critic simply complained that the play "flounders from overobviousness."[26]

Critics and writers in Appalachia, however, have reacted quite differently. Leading the charge has been eastern Kentucky novelist and story writer Gurney Norman, whose many concerns about *The Kentucky Cycle* were first brought to national attention by another Kentucky writer, Bobbie Ann Mason, in a *New Yorker* article titled "Recycling Kentucky." Faulting Schenkkan for "tromping on real people and the real facts of their history," Norman told Mason in an interview, "I know the story of Appalachia deep in my bones. I have immersed myself in it all my adult life, and to see Robert Schenkkan run roughshod over a whole culture is very upsetting." Observing that the "play imposes the form of classical tragedy—where people bring about their own downfall—on the history of the region," Norman complained that the "play's vision is inaccurate and unjust—it blames the victim." Ironically, he added, the "tradition of citizen participation is greater here than anywhere else I know of." Finally, he said, "America *needs* hillbillies. . . . Mountain people are the last group in America it is acceptable to ridicule. No one would stand for it for a minute if you took any other group—Native Americans, African-Americans, Hispanics, women—and held it up as an example of everything that is low and brutal and mean. But somehow it's O.K. to do that with hillbillies."[27]

Gurney Norman is not the only Appalachian writer to have taken exception to *The Kentucky Cycle*. Nearly six months before Mason's *New Yorker* article appeared, he had been joined by six other writers and artists from the region in critiquing the play for a Lexington, Kentucky, arts publication.[28] Besides Norman, the most outspoken among them were George Ella Lyon and Fred Johnson. Lyon noted that "anyone familiar with the history of outsiders' views of the region will see in *The Kentucky Cycle* the same weary plod through outraged pity, preconceived notions, self-righteous reductionism and psychosocial projection that has been the mark of literary tourism for so long." Still, she asked rhetorically, "how could another dumbshow of stereotypes be lauded and certified and, worse still, guaranteed productions and audiences all over the country? What about the long-term efforts of Appalachian community leaders, writers and artists, teachers, historians and sociologists to battle the very reductive picture Schenkkan reaffirms?"[29] Reflecting upon the irony that Schenkkan's play "seems poised to become a powerful cultural tool in maintaining many of the exploitative relationships his work ostensibly raises its voice against," Johnson raised a number of questions about the possible effects of the play on its audience. Does it, he asked, construct Appalachia as "a place in which people from the urban centers will be more or less likely to continue to dump their toxic waste?" Does the work "continue the vulnerability of the region by displacing images and representations that might make the place more knowable and human, and therefore more difficult to loot[?]" Finally, Johnson asked, "Think of all those people in the cities, sitting around over a cappuccino, trying to figure out what to do with their garbage, with deluded little 'dark and bloody grounds' in their cultural maps of the world. Now what will they do with garbage and toxins?"[30]

Indeed, one of the most troubling aspects of *The Kentucky Cycle*, in part because the author claims to have done "research" on the region in order to write about it and because his account resonates so well with what people expect such research might disclose, is the fact that audiences seem willing to accept the play as a historically factual representation of Appalachia. Thus in a notice that the Theater Arts Guild of Peekskill, New York, would be hosting a reading of the play during the winter of 1996, an announcement in the *New York Times* stated, "The cycle tracks the history of the United States from the perspective of a single family living on a single piece of land in Kentucky from pre-Revolutionary times to the 20th century. . . . The playwright, Robert Schenkkan, researched the history of several families in Kentucky and shaped them into a composite family."[31]

It is ironic that Schenkkan's "research," as he explained in the published version of *The Kentucky Cycle* and as he told Bobbie Ann Mason in her *New Yorker* interview, was guided by Harry Caudill's 1963 publication *Night Comes to the Cumberlands* just when Appalachian scholars were subjecting that work and the rest of Caudill's writings to devastating criticism. And it is doubly ironic that their criticisms of Caudill, written more than fifteen years ago, resemble so closely the criticisms of *The Kentucky Cycle* today. Objecting to Caudill's "patronizing view of the 'folk,'" i.e., a version of "liberal paternalism" that enabled him "to portray the mountain population as unsophisticated and childish, easy game for clever lawyers and land speculators who sought to steal their land and mineral rights," historian Ronald Eller challenged scholars in 1982 "to move beyond Harry Caudill in search of not only a more accurate history of our region but also a more appropriate and just vision of the future."[32] Political scientist Stephen Fisher likewise faulted Caudill for his "unrelieved pessimism" and "hopelessness, cynicism, and despair," as well as for conducting "slipshod and poorly documented" research and writing "sweeping, unqualified generalizations" that portrayed Appalachia as "a region without hope." He was especially critical of Caudill's "failure to acknowledge the extent of citizen resistance in the mountains." Reviewing Caudill's *Theirs Be the Power: The Moguls of Eastern Kentucky,* Fisher most closely anticipated today's critics of *The Kentucky Cycle* by criticizing Caudill for producing "a contemporary American melodrama with lots of bad guys and willing victims" rather than "an incisive, grounded, internally consistent analysis of how our political economy has operated to generate both oppression and struggles against oppression" in Appalachia.[33]

Ignoring or unaware of the criticisms of Appalachian scholars, however, plenty of people around the country seem willing to accept the Caudill/Schenkkan tale of Appalachia as fact. The most compelling—indeed, astonishing—evidence of this unthinking acceptance is provided by a twelve-page "Study Guide" to *The Kentucky Cycle* that was published by the Kennedy Center to accompany its performance of the play. In providing a brief overview of Appalachian Kentucky and its passive victimization at the hands of fate, this guide states unequivocally, "Despite periods of stability, the inhabitants of eastern Kentucky lost control of their land to owners of timber and coal companies. They watched helplessly as the land became scarred and gutted. Poverty has threatened and diminished the lives of the greatest number of them."[34]

An even more remarkable section of the Kennedy Center's guide, reproduced from materials distributed earlier at the Mark Taper Forum in Los Angeles, suggests to its audience that "It is instructive to look at what happened to our first frontier [eastern Kentucky] and consider the lessons that its unhappy history might teach us." Describing the settlers of Appalachian Kentucky as "a fierce and solitary people" who subsequently "lost themselves in the vastness of the wilderness" that they had set out "to subdue . . . with a vengeance," the guide claims that "few strangers visited the region and few new ideas seeped in.

Frontier traditions concealed and locked the mountain people into a perpetual neo-frontier." Consequently, "eastern Kentucky never developed" until outside corporate forces brought "environmental devastation" to the mountains and "virtual economic enslavement" to its people. "Today," as a result, concludes this synopsis of Appalachian History 101, "eastern Kentucky is a welfare state with a degree of poverty and environmental devastation that is unprecedented in the United States." Paradoxically, having thus singled out Appalachia as exceptional, the guide nevertheless proceeds to deploy the region metonomically as the emblem for much that is wrong in America, describing its "dark history" as narrated in *The Kentucky Cycle* as being on a "collision course" with "some of our most cherished national myths."[35]

The contributors to this volume respond to the latest round of stereotyping Appalachia and mountain people in works such as *The Kentucky Cycle* in a variety of ways. A first response is to challenge the historical representations of Appalachia and its population that are so blatantly expressed in the play, the Kennedy Center study guide to the play, and in so many other places. Historian Ronald Lewis provides an excellent overview of recent research on the social and economic history of Appalachia in a lead-off chapter that takes exception to simplistic and monolithic versions of the region's past, especially the commonplace notion that Appalachian culture was the product of continuing frontier isolation.[36]

Beginning at least with the local color literary movement that emerged in the 1870s, it became customary for writers to (re)describe Appalachia as, in the famous words of Will Wallace Harney in 1869, "a strange land and a peculiar people."[37] In sharp contrast to this still lingering perspective, however, Lewis shows that, when viewed from the perspective of nineteenth-century rural development, Appalachia even before the modern era of coal mining and industrialization was not more economically isolated, nor was its population more homogeneous than the populations of other rural sections of the United States. The persistent belief in Appalachian distinctiveness thus results from a persistent way of writing about the mountain region rather than from the region's actual past.

Appalachian scholars have devoted considerable attention to studying this tradition of understanding and writing about the mountain region, i.e., the discourse on Appalachia, that creates the very reality it purports to describe. It is in part the power of this discursive tradition that engenders the assumptions about Appalachia in *The Kentucky Cycle*, even behind the back of its naive playwright, who believes that he is dramatizing real history, and that explains why audiences fail to question the play's "take" on the region. It is this same discourse that long ago emboldened the British historian Arnold Toynbee to declare that Appalachians were "no better than barbarians" who had represented "the melancholy spectacle of a people who had acquired civilization and then lost it," even though, he admitted later, he had never read anything about Appalachia nor studied the region.[38]

In a pioneering work titled *Appalachia on Our Mind,* Henry Shapiro located the social origins of the Appalachian discourse and its myth that the mountain South is "a coherent region inhabited by an homogeneous population possessing a uniform culture" in the writings of local colorists, missionaries, educators, social reformers, and industrialists between 1870 and 1920. David Whisnant likewise examined the politics of cultural preference in mountain settlement-house work and in the mountain music festivals and ballad collecting of the same period. Tyrel Moore has shown the "geographical bias" of early fiction and documentaries that gave preference to certain highly remote sections of Appalachia as representative of the whole. Allen Batteau examined the continuing effects of the discourse on the writings of the depression era, the 1940s and 1950s, and the rediscovery of the region's poverty in the 1960s. J.W. Williamson chronicled Hollywood's enduring fascination and exploitation of hillbilly and mountaineer motifs in popular film.[39]

By probing additional literary sources of contemporary Appalachian stereotypes, the chapters grouped together in "Speaking of 'Hillbillies'" further extend this important dimension of Appalachian cultural studies in new directions. While most studies of the discourse on Appalachia follow Shapiro by concentrating on the postbellum era and afterward, two authors, Katherine Ledford and Kenneth Noe, examine the influence of earlier writings about Appalachia. Ledford locates very early roots of the hillbilly myth in the anxieties and desires that animated seventeenth- and eighteenth-century exploration narratives of the southern mountains. Significantly, she notes that projected images of a wild and untamed state of nature were transferred from the mountains themselves to their earliest inhabitants once upper-class, propertied explorers began to appreciate the value of the region's rich natural resources.

Scholars have shown that representatives of Berea College, especially its president, William Goodell Frost, advanced an influential version of the myth of Appalachia in fund-raising appeals for that college that were pitched to northern benefactors after the Civil War and well into this century.[40] These educational reformers assured northerners that Appalachia had been solidly loyal to the Union during the Civil War and untainted by the sin of slave-holding. Kenneth Noe, whose prior historical research examines how political economy influenced conflicting Civil War loyalties across Appalachia,[41] shows that the Berean myth of Unionist Appalachia displaced an earlier and more realistic understanding of Appalachian sectionalism in his examination of the Civil War era writings of Rebecca Harding Davis. Because prior scholars have not paid attention to Davis as an Appalachian writer, Noe makes an additional contribution by examining the impact of this important (West) Virginia writer on subsequent understandings of the mountain region.

Just as Noe attacks the myth of Unionist Appalachia, John Inscoe, whose prior research has examined the influence of slave-holding on mountain society, dispels the myth of an all-white and non-slave-holding Appalachia.[42] By critiquing the historical assumptions animating two pieces of fiction by William Faulkner that depict the region as both unfamiliar with African Americans and yet virulently racist, Inscoe both challenges assumptions of population homogeneity in Appalachia and provides useful bibliographical references to important new scholarship on the African American experience in the region.

No literary figure more widely influenced national perceptions or has been more closely examined by Appalachian scholars than John Fox Jr., whose fictional accounts of feuding and the early development of the mining economy in the border country of Appalachian Kentucky and Virginia set into play many of the most enduring and pejorative images of the Appalachian mountaineer. Darlene Wilson takes a fresh look at Fox's literary career, including not only his desire for status and money but also what she interprets as his gendered ambition to rescue the degraded reputation of southern white manhood, albeit at the expense of the reputation of the South's mountain population. Kathleen Blee and Dwight Billings compare conclusions from their own historical research on turn-of-the-century Kentucky mountain feuds with the writings of Fox and other popular writers whose depictions of these feuds have been re-animated by Robert Schenkkan for Broadway audiences no more critical of these representations today than were Fox's appreciative readers and audiences of long ago.

Finally, Sandra Ballard examines literary sources of the "hillbilly fool" among nineteenth-century writers such as George Washington Harris, whose Appalachian character, Sut Lovingood, directly influenced contemporary cartoon caricatures of the southern mountaineer by Al Capp (Li'l Abner) and Billy De Beck (Snuffy Smith). By probing the cultural function of the innocent fool as truth-saying Other and social critic from its medieval habitus to current Hollywood, Ballard also shows the potentially subversive appeal of Dogpatch characterizations and, possibly, why hillbilly icons—not to mention the ritualized celebration of Hillbilly Days—often amuse as well as offend mountain people themselves, including Ballard.

In the section titled "Speaking More Personally about Appalachian Stereotypes," six writers, scholars, and activists reflect upon their personal experiences in Appalachia in ways that contradict Appalachian stereotypes. The section begins with an essay by children's writer Anne Shelby, who tries out several answers to the question "What's so funny about redneck jokes?" and ends with a profound reflection upon Martin Scorsese's remake of *Cape Fear* as an expression of the country's uneasiness with—indeed, fear of—mountain people and other southerners and nonwhites.

Next, three writers address the issue of stereotyping more obliquely by simply describing personal experiences of growing up in and near the mountain South and by reflecting upon their personal understandings of family, place, and community that challenge conventional depictions such as *The Kentucky Cycle*. Appalachian novelist Denise Giardina, whose novels *Storming Heaven* and *The Unquiet Earth* rank among the most powerful works of historical fiction ever written about Appalachia, links stories about her ancestors to her personal take on the history of the region, which stands in sharp contrast to the one Schenkkan narrates. Literary scholar Fred Hobson links family traditions about his Quaker and Puritan ancestors in Appalachia to his own memories of growing up in the foothills of North Carolina and visiting grandparents who lived deeper in the mountains. Writer and poet Crystal Wilkinson talks about the ambiguities of identity for African Americans in Kentucky and Appalachia and how coming to terms with her "country" background connects her to a contemporary group of self-identified "Affrilachian poets."

Finally, Stephen Fisher reflects upon his own ambiguous relationship to the region and its hillbilly stigmata as an urban, middle-class youth and upon the ways that his eventual identification as an Appalachian helped to bring focus and commitment to his work as an academic and activist. Eula Hall, a celebrated eastern Kentucky health care activist whose biography is a direct refutation of the stereotype of hillbilly-as-victim, describes her life story as an effort to overcome the disadvantages of rural poverty and to challenge structures of domination in the region.

In his critique of the historicity of *The Kentucky Cycle*, Finlay Donesky points out the "grotesque irony" of a southern California writer portraying Appalachians as "greedy destructive savages" in an era when Appalachian Kentuckians were scoring a stunning political victory by winning passage of a constitutional amendment against certain long-standing abuses by mining companies, while California was suffering acute social and environmental crises. Just as it may be said that Eula Hall's many struggles and victories at the grassroots level in Appalachian Kentucky signify the falsity of the hillbilly-as-victim stereotype, it can also be said that the collective struggles of countless Appalachians to defend their personal rights and communities negate familiar hillbilly caricatures that deny mountain people's agency and adulthood. In the section of this book titled "Sometimes, Actions Speak Louder than Words," several scholars describe these anonymous actions.

In a most appropriately entitled chapter, "The Grass Roots Speak Back," Stephen Fisher documents the wide array of single-issue and multi-issue, membership-driven citizens' organizations in Appalachia and confronts the strengths and weaknesses of such efforts today and in the past. In a new historical investigation, Alan Banks tackles the question of labor militancy and quiescence in Appalachia by taking a close look at the 1922 national coal strike, and the role played in it by Kentucky miners, whose agency and deep involvement were erased even at the time by popular representations. Sally Ward Maggard examines how, more recently, working-class women's labor activism in eastern Kentucky has transformed these women's personal lives and their communities in profound ways.

Literally millions of Appalachian people in recent decades have left Appalachia because of the push of economic insecurity there and the hope for better opportunities elsewhere. Phillip Obermiller documents efforts by urban-based Appalachian advocacy organizations to confront the negative stereotypes that migrants often encounter in their urban destinations as well as attempts to organize politically to demand better educational, economic, health, and social service provisions in cities like Cincinnati, Ohio, where they have won passage of the only human rights ordinance in the nation explicitly protecting the civil rights of Appalachians. Finally, Mary Anglin, an anthropologist, contrasts stories about AIDS and AIDS activism from her own fieldwork and community involvement in the mountains with the pejorative stories of AIDS and Appalachia that circulate in the mass media.

Only in the final section of this book, "Recycling Old Stereotypes," do contributors address Robert Schenkkan's play directly. In quite different ways, each of the four writers included here contend that more than simply dramatizing a set of customary and taken-for-granted representations and interpretations of Appalachia—and despite its intent to critique contemporary life—*The Kentucky Cycle* ends up perpetuating the very myths and ideologies that historically have concealed the real sources of violence and exploitation in American life.

Finlay Donesky provides both a critical summary of the play and a historical analysis of the events it narrates, pointing out in particular how Schenkkan bought into Harry Caudill's tragically deterministic view of Appalachia people without adopting Caudill's accompanying, if contradictory, sense of the effects of class, economics, and history upon the region. Rodger Cunningham asks how the play's portrayal of Appalachia can be taken on its own word to be "progressive" by the liberal media that today claims to be sensitive to multiculturalism. He argues that by ignoring political economy and treating Appalachia as a metaphor of America rather than as one of its causally connected parts, Schenkkan's dramatization remythologizes rather than critiques violence and poverty and thus reproduces the frameworks of power it claims to challenge.

Weaving together political analysis with biographical insights into his own politicization as a young out-migrant from the Ozarks, Herbert Reid critiques *The Kentucky Cycle* as a transient version of New Age Libertarianism that displaces the project of radical democratic politics and obscures the real source of violence and loss in the everyday practices of the corporate capitalist state. He counters Schenkkan's misunderstanding of the sources of American violence and alienation with the articulation of a deeper understanding of American ideology and politics that recognizes corporate capitalist power while enabling place-based, region-related narratives such as his own out of the American Ozarks.

Indeed, according to Gurney Norman, it is the displacement of Appalachian peoples' own narratives and the denial of their rich history of resistance by *The Kentucky Cycle* and the wider national culture-industry apparatus of which it is a part, that explains why the play has troubled him so deeply. Raising important questions about the politics of representation and who claims the authority to speak for and about others, Norman provides a fitting conclusion to this volume by quoting the words of an Appalachian folk song: "Better listen to the voices from the mountains, They might tell you what you just might need to hear."

Not too many years ago, in an insightful comparison of the cultural construct of "Appalachianism" and Edward Said's concept of "Orientalism," Rodger Cunningham expressed his conviction that what Appalachian scholars "are grinding is not an ax but a lens"—a lens, he added, that would enable what Raymond Williams once called "the 'unlearning of the inherent dominative mode.'"[43] The critique of *The Kentucky Cycle* and the reports on how Appalachians talk back in word and deed to such stereotypic representations of them are offered in the same spirit, as a lens on American culture, Appalachian culture, and society's ignorance of and fascination with its hillbilly self.

## Notes

1. I am grateful to Katherine Ledford for help in locating and selecting these examples.

2. Quoted in "Signs of the Times," *Appalachian Journal* (winter 1996) Vol. 23, no. 2: 139.

3. Quoted in "Signs of the Times," *Appalachian Journal* (winter 1996) Vol. 23, no. 2: 144.

4. Quoted in "Signs of the Times," *Appalachian Journal* (fall 1993) Vol. 21, no. 1: 21; and (summer 1993) Vol. 20, no. 4: 348.

5. Quoted in "Signs of the Times," *Appalachian Journal* (summer 1994) Vol. 21, no. 4: 384.

6. Quoted in "Signs of the Times," *Appalachian Journal* (fall 1995) Vol. 23, no. 1: 24.

7. Quoted in "Signs of the Times," *Appalachian Journal* (winter 1995) Vol. 22, no. 2: 139.

8. Quoted in "Signs of the Times," *Appalachian Journal* (fall 1993) Vol. 21, no. 1: 23.

9. "Hillbilly Days Celebrating Its Twentieth Year This Week," *Lexington (Ky.) Herald-Leader,* April 19, 1996, B5.

10. J.W. Williamson, *Hillbillyland: What the Movies Did to the Mountains and What the Mountains Did to the Movies* (Chapel Hill: Univ. of North Carolina Press, 1995).

11. See the complete text of a 1991 Appalachian Studies Association symposium on *Albion's Seed* and David Hackett Fischer's comments in the *Appalachian Journal* 19 (winter 1992): 161–200. The quote is from Gordon B. McKinney, "David Hackett Fischer and the Origins of Appalachian Culture," 165.

12. David Cattell-Gordon, "The Appalachian Inheritance: A Culturally Transmitted Traumatic Stress Syndrome?" *Journal of Progressive Human Services* 1(1) (1990): 55, 47; Karen Tice and Dwight Billings, "Appalachian Culture and Resistance," *Journal of Progressive Human Services* 2(2) (1991): 1.

13. Anonymous, "An Appalachian Eye," *Washington Post Book World,* Jan. 9, 1994, 15.

14. Douglas Balz, "The Eye and the Heart," *Chicago Tribune (Books),* Dec. 5, 1993, 3.

15. For one thoughtful examination in the regional press, however, see the review by Jay Ruby in the *Appalachian Journal* 23 (spring 1996): 337–41.

16. Frank Rich, "Two Hundred Years of a Nation's Sorrows, in Nine Chapters," *New York Times,* Nov. 15, 1993. B1.

17. David Kaufman, "The Kentucky Cycle," *Nation,* Dec. 13, 1993, 740–42; Jack Kroll, "The Bloody Old Kentucky Home," *Newsweek,* Nov. 29, 1993; John Lahr, "Suffering Succotash," *New Yorker,* Nov. 29, 1993, 138–40.

18. Robert Schenkkan, author's notes to *The Kentucky Cycle* (New York: Penguin Books, 1993), 334; second quote from Bobbie Ann Mason, "Recycling Kentucky," *New Yorker,* Nov. 1, 1993, 56.

19. Schenkkan, *The Kentucky Cycle,* 337.

20. Ibid., 335.

21. Ibid., 336, 338; quoted in Lyon, "Another Vicious Cycle," *ACE Magazine: Arts, Commentary, and Entertainment* 4(6) (July 1992), 10. These lines do not appear in the published text of the play but were apparently used in early productions.

22. Quoted in John C. Carr, "*The Kentucky Cycle:* A Study Guide," (Washington, D.C.: The Kennedy Center, 1993), 5.

23. Quoted in Kevin Nance, "The Play Is Not a History: Author Responds to Criticism of 'Kentucky Cycle,'" *Lexington (Ky.) Herald-Leader,* Feb. 11, 1996, F3.

24. Kaufman, "Kentucky Cycle," 740.

25. Lloyd Rose, "The 'Kentucky Recycle': Long, Ambitious, and Oh So Ordinary," *Washington Post,* Sept. 13, 1993, D1.

26. Kaufman, "Kentucky Cycle," 740; Rose, "'Kentucky Recycle,'" D3; Rich, "Two Hundred Years," B4, B1; Lahr, "Suffering Succotash," 139.

27. Quoted in Mason, "Recycling Kentucky," 59, 59–60, 60, 61.

28. See reviews by Jack Wright, Gurney Norman, George Ella Lyon, Fenton Johnson, Jeffrey Lewis, Jo Carson, and Fred Johnson in "The Kentucky Cycle: Essays and Criticism of the Epic Drama," *ACE Magazine: Arts, Commentary, and Entertainment* 4(6): 8–13 (July 1992). Also see Jim Wayne Miller, "The Kentucky (Re) Cycle," *Appalachian Heritage* 21 (spring 1993): 50–62; and John Alexander Williams, "Appalachia Revisited," *Southern Theater* 35(3): 12–14 (1994).

29. Lyon, "Another Vicious Cycle," 10.

30. Fred Johnson, "The Dark and Bloody Ground Indeed," *ACE Magazine: Arts, Commentary, and Entertainment* 4(6): 13 (July 1992).

31. Announcement in the *New York Times (Westchester Guide)*, Feb. 18, 1996. I am grateful to Rosyln Bologh for passing this one to me.

32. Ronald D Eller, "Harry Caudill and the Burden of Mountain Liberalism," in *Critical Essays in Appalachian Life and Culture: Proceedings of the Fifth Annual Appalachian Studies Conference*, ed. Rick Simon et. al. (Boone, N.C.: Appalachian Consortium Press, 1982), 22, 24, 28.

33. Steve Fisher, "As the World Turns: The Melodrama of Harry Caudill," *Appalachian Journal* 11 (spring 1984): 272, 268, 270, 272, 271, 272.

34. Carr, "Study Guide," 2.

35. Ibid., 8.

36. Also see Dwight B. Billings, Mary Beth Pudup, and Altina Waller, "Taking Exception with Exceptionalism: The Emergence and Transformation of Historical Studies of Appalachia," in *Appalachia in the Making: The Mountain South in the Nineteenth Century*, eds. Mary Beth Pudup, Dwight B. Billings, and Altina Waller (Chapel Hill: Univ. of North Carolina Press, 1995), 1–24.

37. Harney's 1869 travel story is reprinted in W.K. McNeil, ed., *Appalachian Images in Folk and Popular Culture*, 2d. ed. (Knoxville: Univ. of Tennessee Press, 1995), which contains other important early writings about Appalachia as well.

38. For a report on Toynbee's exchange with pioneer Appalachian scholar James Brown in the 1940s, see Brown, "An Appalachian Footnote to Toynbee's *A Study of History*," *Appalachian Journal* 6 (autumn 1978).

39. Henry D. Shapiro, *Appalachia on Our Mind: The Southern Mountains and Mountaineers in the American Consciousness, 1870–1920* (Chapel Hill: Univ. of North Carolina Press, 1978), ix; David E. Whisnant, *All That Is Native and Fine: The Politics of Culture in an American Region* (Chapel Hill: Univ. of North Carolina Press, 1983); Tyrel G. Moore, "Eastern Kentucky as a Model of Appalachia: The Role of Literary Images," *Southeastern Geographer* 31(2): 75–89 (Nov. 1991); Allen Batteau, *The Invention of Appalachia* (Tuscon: Univ. of Arizona Press, 1990); and Williamson, *Hillbillyland*.

40. See Shannon H. Wilson, "Window on the Mountains: Berea's Appalachia, 1870–1930," *Filson Club History Quarterly* 64(3): (July 1990), 384–400; also, Shapiro, *Appalachia on Our Mind*. William Goodell Frost's profoundly influential essay of 1899, "Our Contemporary Ancestors in the Southern Mountains," is reprinted in McNeil, *Appalachian Images*.

41. Kenneth W. Noe, *Southwest Virginia's Railroad: Modernization and the Sectional Crisis* (Urbana: Univ. of Illinois Press, 1994).

42. John C. Inscoe, *Mountain Masters, Slavery, and Sectional Crisis in Western North Carolina* (Knoxville: Univ. of Tennessee Press, 1989).

43. Rodger Cunningham, "Appalachianism and Orientalism: Reflections on Reading Edward Said," *Journal of the Appalachian Studies Association* 1 (1989): 132.

# Beyond Isolation and Homogeneity

## Diversity and the History of Appalachia

*Ronald L. Lewis*

Appalachia is a region without a formal history. Born in the fertile minds of late-nineteenth-century local color writers, "Appalachia" was invented in the caricatures and atmospheric landscapes of the escapist fiction they penned to entertain the emergent urban middle class. The accuracy of these stories and travelogues, the dominant idioms of this genre, generated little or no critical evaluation of their characterizations of either mountain people or the landscape itself.

If local color writing in the Appalachian motif must have a beginning, it would be with Will Wallace Harney's 1873 travelogue, "A Strange Land and Peculiar People," published in *Lippincott's Magazine*.[1] His emphasis on physical and cultural isolation was greatly magnified over the next two decades by subsequent writers. The publication in 1899 of Berea College president William Goodell Frost's famous article, "Our Contemporary Ancestors in the Southern Mountains," signified the maturity of the concept of Appalachia as a spatially and culturally remote remnant of a bygone day. From this essay, only one of Frost's storehouse of appeals for support to finance his missionary work in the mountains, came some of the most widely recognized phrases applied to Appalachian mountain dwellers. They were "our contemporary ancestors," our "eighteenth century neighbors" who had just awakened from a long "Rip Van Winkle sleep," pure Anglo-Saxons "beleaguered by nature" in "Appalachian America," one of "God's grand divisions."[2] Frost the publicist certainly knew how to turn a phrase.

"Local color" Appalachia reached its apogee in the novels of John Fox Jr., undoubtedly the most popular author of the genre. Scholars recognize that Fox was a major figure in the creation of Appalachian "otherness," but Darlene Wilson has shown most emphatically how self-serving were Fox's creations. Declaring his writing "deliberate acts of self-creation and self-mythologizing," Wilson's research in family papers reveals the direct linkage between Fox's fictional images and his "role as a publicist for absentee mineral developers" who, along with their agent, Fox's older half-brother James, were involved in the development of the coal industry in central Appalachia. John Fox Jr. perpetrated and then perpetuated the myth of Appalachian otherness to facilitate absentee corporate hegemony by marginalizing indigenous residents economically and politically. In short, for Fox (and how many others?) "Appalachia" was a willful creation and not merely the product of literary imagination.[3]

This fictional representation became accepted and then reified as "history" by subsequent reporters, scholars, and policy makers into what Henry Shapiro has called the "myth of Appalachia." As Shapiro and Allen Batteau show in their work on the "invention" of Appalachia, the idea of Appalachia as a homogeneous region physically, culturally, and economically isolated from mainstream America has its genesis in fiction. In fact, "much of what is believed to be known about the life and people" of Appalachia actually is "knowledge about a complex intertextual reality" that treats the "diverse preindustrial localities in the southern mountains as if each were representative of a single, regionwide folk society."[4] This view has persisted in part because so little formal written history about preindustrial Appalachia exists to provide a measure of empirical authenticity. However, if we examine the region's economic evolution from the perspective of rural nineteenth-century America, without assuming prior knowledge of its fictional existence, or the industrial developments that were to come, it is clear that much of Appalachia was neither unusually isolated, physically or culturally, nor was its population uniformly more homogeneous than that of other sections of rural America.[5]

Acknowledging the risk of exaggeration, much recent scholarship either refutes or greatly revises the standard perspective of preindustrial Appalachia as an isolated frontier. This is particularly true if isolation is understood as the absence of commercial or cultural linkages with regional and/or national markets. Appalachians were not "precapitalist" either, strictly speaking, for even the earliest settlers emigrated from areas where capitalist terms of exchange were well understood. No one generalization holds true for the entire region or over time. Historically, writers have assumed that the conditions they found in the twentieth century were held over from earlier frontier days. In fact, geographer Gene Wilhelm rejects the notion that early Appalachia was a land without commercial or cultural communications with the world beyond the hollow. According to Wilhelm, "the Appalachian region has been an admixture of cultural contact and socioeconomic enterprise rather than a bastion of isolated individuals and a slow sequence of economic development" as numerous new writers have generally insisted. Wilhelm has argued that "the idea that the Appalachian Mountains acted as a physical barrier, either for the people living within the mountain region, or for those individuals trying to cross them, hardly stands up against the evidence at hand."[6] For example, the Blue Ridge Mountains between Front Royal and Waynesboro, Virginia, were marked out by a complex series of trails and trade routes, traversed by Indians for hundreds of years, even before the Europeans came. Before roads were built, horse and wagon trails crossed the mountains north and south, east and west. During the nineteenth century, innumerable public roads and private pikes connected the region internally and externally. Wilhelm correctly points out that animal drovers provide an excellent example of mountaineers who traveled the lines of trade and cultural transmission connecting the mountains with local and urban markets. Cattle dealers journeyed out to the markets and brought back goods, cash, and ideas. Lowland culture bearers, such as lawyers, doctors, seasonal teachers, tax collectors, circuit preachers, peddlers, salesmen, and mailmen, traveled the same avenues of transportation and trade into the mountains. One of the first backward linkages settlers fought for were postal roads to connect them with the lowland population centers. The high level of newspaper and periodical subscriptions, and later catalog circulation, in the mountains suggests an ongoing desire for knowledge of and goods from the broader world. Wilhelm insists that "geographical isolation for the mountain folk is a myth."[7]

Several major works which subsequently dealt with the topic presented variations on Wilhelm's theme. Ronald D Eller agreed with Wilhelm in general but concluded that travel was nonetheless always difficult and ensured a relative isolation.[8] Steven Hahn's study of up-country Georgia between 1850 and 1890 argues that during the antebellum era local farmers were isolated from the external markets and so they relied on community networks, but after the railroad penetrated the region they became increasingly dependent on the cotton export market.[9] Lacy Ford came to a different conclusion in his study of antebellum up-country South Carolina. While yeomen farmers produced a subsistence first, they also participated in the market economy after the arrival of the railroad in 1850.[10] Although Durwood Dunn generally infers that Cades Cove, which is located in the Tennessee Smokies, was isolated and self-reliant during the early years, he emphasizes that "this isolation was always relative" and shows that during the antebellum years Cove people had relatively ready access to regional markets.[11] Most recently, Wilma Dunaway argued that Appalachia was a peripheral region of an emergent world capitalist system and was linked to that system of exchange as a supplier of raw materials from its inception.[12]

Conversely, Altina Waller's Tug Fork, the borderland between Kentucky and West Virginia where the Hatfield-McCoy feud occurred, was isolated in every respect before the area was opened up in 1889 by the railroad. There were no towns, and county seats were physically isolated from even regional markets. Unlike the Blue Ridge, up-country Georgia, or Cades Cove, Tennessee, there was little migration into this section after 1840, and trade beyond the mountains was "almost non-existent."[13] Moreover, Dwight Billings, Kathleen Blee, and Louis Swanson found that Beech Creek residents of eastern Kentucky remained an isolated people "still living a relatively precapitalist life on the eve of World War II." In Beech Creek, "isolation permitted an independent economy to persist in the Appalachian mountains long after it had vanished elsewhere in the United States." Even here, however, national market forces made it increasingly difficult to sustain the local economy.[14]

David Hsiung's study of northeastern Tennessee called for a more critical examination of "isolation" as a conceptual construct and suggested that focusing on the early period between 1780 and 1835 may provide a broader context for measuring Appalachian isolation relative to the rest of backcountry America in the nineteenth century. Not surprisingly, he concluded that isolation was a relative concept both temporally and spatially. In the Revolutionary era residents used the elaborate trail system that fed into the Great Warrior Path and Boone's Trail in northeastern Tennessee. The crude roads made travel and trade difficult and also sparked the creation of new counties so that residents could be closer to the county seat. Residents in these counties were not cut off from the state capital, but clearly they believed themselves to be isolated by poor access to government and the markets. Hsiung noted that it was the "psychic power of physical separation" that motivated county building among the people. By 1820, however, the roads connecting county seats were carrying wagonloads of goods from Philadelphia and other eastern cities into these counties in a brisk interregional trade.[15]

Tracy McKenzie qualifies the development trajectory implied in Hsuing's characterization of northeastern Tennessee. Using 1860 census data, McKenzie has compared the economies of the three grand divisions of western, middle, and eastern Tennessee and found great economic variation among them. Only the mountain counties did not rely on slavery for agricultural production. Even within the three sample Appalachian Tennessee counties (Johnson, Greene, and Grainger) McKenzie found significant differences in their linkages to the regional market. Johnson County farmers "were probably as close to total isolation from the surrounding region as it was possible to be in the nineteenth century," for there were few roads and the railroad did not penetrate the area until the mid-1890s. Grainger and Greene Counties are located in the Valley of East Tennessee. There the land is fertile, and farmers practiced a productive, mixed agriculture.[16] Farmers of Grainger and Greene Counties also were limited by inadequate roads, but they could transport their produce to Knoxville by flatboats down the Tennessee River and its tributaries, or by rail over the East Tennessee Railroad, which was completed through Greene County in the late 1850s.[17]

Similarly, the idea that Appalachia was the land of subsistence farmers until recent times is under serious reevaluation. John Inscoe took direct aim at this notion in *Mountain Masters,* a study of slavery in western North Carolina. Inscoe quotes Olive Dame Campbell's observation in 1925 that "there is no fundamental reason for separating mountain people from lowland people, nor are mountain problems so different at bottom from those of other rural areas in the United States," an unusual insight for the time. Inscoe suggests that much the same could be said of antebellum society in the southern Appalachians generally.[18] On the eve of the Civil War, Inscoe argues, "western North Carolina was far from the backward, isolated area it was later seen to be." In fact, "the variety of situations and the diversity of its populace equaled if not surpassed those of any other rural section of the antebellum South." Furthermore, although the Carolina mountains retained some of the "crude aspects of its frontier origins," the area "constituted a thriving, productive, and even a progressive society."[19]

Scholars of the 1960s broke with the established school of historical approach which focused on universal themes that thread their way through American history, binding the nation together, and became much more interested in the diversity of the American experience. More recently, this shift in focus found expression in Appalachian history as well. The "new" social history, as it was called, has exerted more influence on Appalachian studies than any other branch of history by challenging many of the assumptions (and shibboleths) of American history. One of these challenges in particular, that individualism and capitalism provided the economic foundation of America from earliest colonial origins, is a debate that promises to rewrite what has passed for Appalachian history. Another debate involves the nature of community culture in early America: Was it essentially cooperative or competitive? Were colonial farmers a self-sufficient, precapitalist people who emphasized community harmony over personal self-interest, or were they commercially aggressive, market-oriented, profit-maximizers? In short, were communal farmers initially "modernized" by capitalism into competitive economic men and women, or was capitalism part of their culture from the beginning?[20] Ideology, of course, provided the motive power behind this debate.

Scholars who apply this approach to mountain life are rapidly changing our historical perspective on the relationship of community to market development in preindustrial Appalachia. Historical geographer Robert D. Mitchell's study of frontier Virginia rejects the self-sufficiency thesis. He argues instead that settlers moving west were motivated by economic profit from the beginning.[21]

Robert McKenzie's study of Tennessee directly refutes the oft-repeated view of Ronald D Eller that in preindustrial Appalachia mountaineers owned their own farms, worked the land as a family unit, and employed a strategy of household self-sufficiency that allowed them to avoid reliance on the market economy. Until the industrial transition at the turn of the twentieth century, "few areas of the United States more closely exemplified Thomas Jefferson's vision of a democratic society."[22] McKenzie contends that the isolation of northeastern Tennessee farmers from the markets meant that they were indeed "self-sufficient," but self-sufficiency meant a "precarious" existence at best. He rejects the idea that hardship was offset by the benefits of communal support, strong kinship networks, and particularly, economic independence. While there were social and cultural costs associated with market involvement, he contends that "it is important also not to lose sight of the undeniable economic costs of persistent market isolation."[23] The income disparity among individual farming households in the mountain counties, McKenzie found, "stemmed not from differences in land tenure or slave ownership but in commercial orientation."[24] In any event, self-sufficiency was not inconsistent with production for exchange, and most farmers engaged in both modes of production. Indeed, only those with the smallest farms did not produce anything for exchange. It was neither an aversion to risk nor an indifference to wealth accumulation that discouraged a commercial orientation among them, but rather high transportation costs, low commodity prices, declining soil fertility, and above all, the declining size of farms. McKenzie concludes that agricultural historian Morton Rothstein is correct in observing that self-sufficiency is merely a "delightful euphemism for rural poverty."[25]

Certainly there were isolated sections of Appalachia, such as Beech Creek, Kentucky, where Brown and Schwarzweller, and Billings, Blee, and Swanson have shown that residents continued to rely on household production until well into the twentieth century.[26] Paul Salstrom turns the issue upside down in his book, *Appalachia's Path to Dependency,* contending that, instead of self-sufficiency losing ground to the entrepreneurial ideology, Appalachia followed the reverse pattern. According to Salstrom, declining agricultural production was the primary reason for Appalachia's shift from market production in the 1840s to a subsistence, producer-consumer system as a way to survive under increasingly marginalized economic circumstances—a reversal of the process as it is commonly understood.[27]

Studies of Appalachia that do not attack the self-sufficiency thesis directly have demonstrated by strong implication that a commercial orientation developed early in sections of the region suitable to market production. A wide variety of economic activities have been documented in Appalachia, taking us far beyond the marginal hard-scrabble hill farm stereotype. By far the most significant of these economically and historically was the livestock business. During the antebellum era, Appalachia was the livestock-raising center of the eastern United States. Most recently, Richard MacMaster examined the early cattle industry in western Virginia and found that from the colonial era forward backcountry stock raisers were "remarkable" in their receptivity to new methods, improved breeding stock, and scientific agriculture in a way that most planters were not. They originated the feeder-lot system, were among the first to import pedigreed cattle, and played a major role in the diffusion of the beef cattle industry beyond the Appalachians into Kentucky and Ohio.[28]

Stock raising played a significant role in the upper Shenandoah Valley and Potomac highlands of western Virginia. The South Branch valley was known for its cattle as early as the 1750s, and by the 1780s was a major center for cattle raising and feeding for export to eastern markets. In fact, the modern feeder-lot system has its earliest developmental roots in western Virginia, having evolved in the South Branch of the Potomac River and the Greenbrier River valleys. Cattle from Ohio were sent here to be fattened up for the final leg of the drive to eastern cities. In the 1850s shipment by train took the place of driving, and feeders tracked market prices in order to time the arrival of their stock in the markets at the most advantageous moment. Towns and even small cities grew around the trade as gathering centers developed where local producers could sell their cattle to professional drovers. Lewisburg in Greenbrier County, West Virginia, for example, was one local node in a distribution network that pointed livestock toward the regional center of Covington, Virginia, from which they were shipped by rail to Richmond as early as the 1850s. Winchester, in the Shenandoah Valley, became the regional shipping center for stockmen of the South Branch.[29]

John Inscoe demonstrated that at the southern end of the Great Appalachian Valley in North Carolina "livestock production was the most substantial form of commercial agriculture practiced in the mountains and the primary means of exchange used by merchants and those they dealt with locally and out-of-state." As early as 1800 cattle and hogs were being driven from the Carolina mountains to markets in Charleston, Savannah, Norfolk, and Philadelphia. Although hogs were by far the preferred livestock, cattle, sheep, ducks, and turkeys also were driven over the roads to market. Asheville, located on the Buncombe Turnpike, was the regional center for the western Carolina stock trade, but the traffic significantly increased other related economic activity. Hog drives stimulated corn production among local farmers who also sold their stock to drovers passing on the road. Merchants, innkeepers, and feeding station operators also set up businesses along the pikes to rest and feed the herds and serve the drovers. Inscoe concludes that "most western North Carolinians were involved in this complex trade network" and that "dependence on southern markets was pervasive throughout the mountain counties."[30]

Prominent Appalachian cattlemen were the elites in their world, but most mountain farmers engaged in mixed farming and a range of diverse economic activities in addition to agriculture. Nineteenth-century mountain farmers in eastern Kentucky, for example, spent considerable time hunting and trapping for food and pelts for either the market or to pay taxes. Tyrel Moore found that farm exports from the region included small quantities of ginseng, furs, deer hams, chestnuts, honey, and beeswax. These items were exchanged locally but also exported downstream to the Ohio River valley. Poor roads hindered commercial farming, and many scarce items, such as butter, wool, flax, beeswax, and honey, were produced for home consumption. Cattle and hogs were the preferred livestock and corn the principal grain.[31] Gordon McKinney's study of antebellum western North Carolina leads him to conclude that "the geographic isolation of the North Carolina mountain population was not as great as usually portrayed, and many individuals had substantial dealings with people of the outside world." Even though western North Carolinians attempted to grow much of their own food, they had ceased to be truly self-sufficient by the Civil War at the latest. That they had become dependent on the markets to supply their needs is apparent by the strong demand for finished goods and the suffering that they endured from war-inflated prices.[32]

Economic diversification grew hand in hand with a much greater degree of social stratification than the myth of Appalachia would allow. New studies show that almost from the beginning mountain settlements spawned a commercial elite, and subsequent population growth and the adoption of slavery ensured that mountain society would not only be class-differentiated but heterogeneous as well. Also, it is becoming increasingly clear that different sections of the mountains followed different development patterns. In fact, even within the same county significant variations in social and economic relationships often coexisted. A small but influential middle class of doctors, lawyers, merchants, and politicians who served preindustrial mountain communities were directly linked to, and served as mediators with, the broader market economy.[33] Access to land, however, was the key ingredient to the formation of social stratification in preindustrial Appalachia. Scholarship on this issue has only just begun for Appalachia, but we have much to learn from studies of older settled regions, such as early New England and the Mid-Atlantic colonies. Studies of the western Virginia backcountry during the eighteenth century by McClesky, Hughes, Hofstra, and Rasmussen demonstrate that the best lands were engrossed by a small interrelated elite who either operated on their own or acted as agents for wealthy clients.[34] The acquisition of ever larger landholdings by small select groups continued during the nineteenth century. Mary Beth Pudup's study of antebellum southeastern Kentucky revealed the extent to which land-ownership was one of the key factors in the emergent social stratification in these counties as early as the 1820s. Kinship also was important in facilitating the acquisition of lands by providing another vital strand in the political and economic web that bound together local elites.[35] Robert McKenzie found similar evidence for social stratification in the mountains of Tennessee. On the eve of the Civil War, Tennessee's mountain counties were characterized by a great concentration of wealth, extensive landlessness (42.5 percent average), and great income disparity between a minority of farmers who produced for the market and a poor majority who did not.[36] A similar conclusion was reached by Ralph Mann in his work on four farm communities in Tazewell County, Virginia, between 1820 and 1850. The social structure of these communities confirms Pudup's thesis that the control of local resources and the ability to respond to changes maintained the dominant, and usually earliest, landowning native elite families in a position to retain economic control and political power.[37] The economic stratification suggested in the new studies underscores the dangers of facile generalizations about preindustrial mountain communities and challenges the notion of Appalachia as a Jeffersonian Eden.

It is easy to forget that manufactures related to agriculture served a vital function in the early mountain economy, particularly gristmills, wool-carding mills, sawmills, and tanyards, which grew in relationship to the density of settlement and social complexity that evolved over time. Natural resource industries, although secondary to farming as a means of securing a livelihood in preindustrial Appalachia, also employed an increasing number of people throughout the nineteenth century. It was natural for mountaineers to harvest the forest around them for profit. From the earliest settlement they had used the timber to construct dwellings, barns and outbuildings, mills, and other necessary structures. As demand for wood products increased with the population in the mountains and beyond, timber became a market commodity. From the antebellum era to the end of the nineteenth century, mountain rivers were choked in the spring with rafts of logs heading downstream to the mills. They sent more than raw sawlogs to downstream markets, however, as illustrated in the report of the chief engineer for just one lock and dam on the Little Kanawha River in West Virginia for the period between 1876 and 1877: 388 rafts of logs; 1,162,900 feet of sawed lumber; 3,406,200 oil-barrel staves; 57,749 railroad ties; 343,000 hoop-poles; 45,050 cubic feet of ship timber. Except for the staves, these products were exported to Ohio, New York, Pennsylvania, Maryland, and England.[38]

Salt and iron were among the first industries to develop in the mountains, and both contributed to the development of a nascent coal industry in central Appalachia. The Kanawha Valley of western Virginia became a major supplier of salt for the Ohio River cities and even farther downstream to New Orleans for export. For a half-century after its founding in the early nineteenth century, the salt industry grew and stimulated local development of coal to fire the salt brine boilers, and after the Civil War when the salt industry declined, a vital coal industry took its place as a major employer.[39] Throughout the mountains local blacksmiths plied their trade, but in areas where suitable iron ores were found, the iron industry thrived. During the earliest period charcoal provided the primary fuel for iron furnaces, and a plentiful supply of wood was readily available in the mountains. The charcoal iron industry grew to major proportions in western Maryland, western Virginia, and eastern Tennessee, but charcoal furnaces smelted iron for local markets throughout Appalachia. By the mid-nineteenth century, technology permitted the use of coal to fire iron furnaces. Consequently, the proximity of coal and iron deposits provided the points of concentration for the industry in the mountains, especially in the Cumberland River basin of Tennessee, southeastern Pennsylvania, and northwestern Virginia.[40]

Historians now find a much more politically diversified region as well. Gordon McKinney's study of Appalachian politics from the Civil War to 1900 demonstrates that a significant number of residents in certain sections of the mountains, such as eastern Tennessee, northwestern Virginia, and eastern Kentucky were Unionists in their sympathies.[41] By no means, however, did mountaineers represent a Unionist dagger pointed at the heart of the Confederacy. John Inscoe's study of western North Carolina revises the popular notion that Appalachia was a Union bastion filled with freedom-loving frontiersmen. Indeed, 90 percent of western North Carolinians were not slave owners, and they had waged a protracted and sometimes bitter political struggle with eastern elites. But in the end they marched off in record numbers to join the Confederate armies because they identified themselves as southerners, and their economic interests, forged by the traditionally strong trade ties with Georgia and South Carolina, were tied to the South.[42]

It was the development of trade ties that prompted Southwest Virginia to follow Richmond out of the Union and into the Confederacy, a process that ultimately led to the rending of Virginia and the creation of loyal West Virginia. Kenneth Noe shows how the Virginia and Tennessee Railroad, completed between Richmond and Southwest Virginia in the 1850s, linked the economic fortunes of the mountain section with the eastern tidewater capital of Richmond. The creation of West Virginia, which abolished slavery and forged close commercial ties with the northern markets by trade over the Baltimore and Ohio Railroad as well as by river and road, demonstrates the divisiveness of secession politics in the mountain sections of the slave states.[43] The dismemberment of Virginia also reemphasizes the importance of understanding the history of economic development in the mountains, which often is assumed to have begun only with the industrial transition at the turn of the twentieth century.

The reason northwestern Virginia counties remained with the Union and the southwestern counties followed Richmond into the Confederacy is part of a much larger set of issues, but clearly secession sympathies were directly linked to economic dependencies. Noe states that the commercially-minded in Richmond "unloaded their ideology as well as their goods off the train. Not only did southern modernization and slavery go hand in hand, but the determination to defend slavery and the broader economic and social system it held on its back joined them. . . . The leading factor convincing most southwestern Virginians to don gray and most northwestern Virginians blue in 1861 was the divergence among western Virginians caused by their railroads; where they ran and what they carried, and how economic change caused by railroad building shaped ideology."[44]

There were few slaveholders in western Virginia, but the southwestern and northwestern counties split over the issue of secession from the Union, demonstrating some fundamental differences in the political economy of the mountain districts. Van Beck Hall's study of politics in Appalachian Virginia between 1790 and 1830 documents just how early, vigorous, and universal the push for economic development was at least within some sections of the region. By analyzing voting patterns on key economic development issues in the Virginia Assembly and at state conventions, Hall found that settlers in Appalachian Virginia were more diversified, less fearful of change, and more inclined to use government to accomplish development than were "the more cosmopolitan, longer-settled residents of Virginia counties east of the Blue Ridge."[45]

A cursory examination of western Virginia even during this early period reveals the folly of thinking about the region in simplistic terms even for its early years. Most rural settlements had their own grain mills, tanneries, salt, and iron manufacture. Along with the settlements, numerous small towns and resorts along the Allegheny Front provided local markets for farmers throughout the nineteenth century. Larger towns dotted the western landscape. In fact, Wheeling, Martinsburg, Harpers Ferry, and Wellsburg in present West Virginia were among the fifteen largest towns in the state and represented an evolving urban-commercializing process that increased the political influence of merchants and professionals and the growth of social institutions associated with urban life.[46]

"The growth of these towns created two Appalachias," Hall contends, one composed of counties with growth centers and another made up of rural farm counties, often referred to as "back counties." The counties with growing towns spearheaded the economic diversification of Appalachian Virginia, while the counties without towns failed to develop much commercialization or diversity, according to Hall. Significant differences existed within the western counties, of course, with the residents of towns and more developed counties leading the campaign for economic development and political reform. Westerners stood as one in demands for economic development measures, especially bank charters. But it was the battle over internal improvements that indicates most clearly the economic orientation of western Virginians. Westerners, both rural and urban, almost unanimously supported improvements in transportation. They supported improving navigation of the Potomac in 1795 and constructing a bridge over the Cheat River in 1805, and they backed the James River and Kanawha Canal improvements from 1816 on. Likewise, western support for the improvement and construction of existing roads and turnpikes was nearly unanimous, with little difference between rural and urban counties.[47]

According to Hall, historians have failed to recognize that supposedly backward Appalachian residents "actually backed democratization, the involvement of more individuals in the political process, banks, internal improvements, the protection of the flow of capital and credit, and education and occasionally challenged the institution of slavery." In fact, even the subsistence farmers of the underdeveloped counties voted for programs that many historians associate with progress and modernization. "These actions simply cannot be fitted into the usual portrayal of an Appalachia trapped in a sort of late eighteenth or early nineteenth-century 'time warp' or of a culture and society that was easily manipulated by powerful outside interests," Hall argues. What popular and scholarly writers alike have failed to appreciate, Hall concludes, is that in western Virginia,

> Two Appalachias existed side by side. The one with towns, newspapers, banks, and early industries already differed from the more rural, isolated, farming counties. These counties, much easier to identify with the traditional picture of Appalachia, were less interested in many of the programs backed by their more urbanized colleagues, but even those who lived in the second Appalachia worked much harder for reform and development than did the supposedly more commercial, involved, and aware residents of eastern Virginia. The traditional picture of isolated mountain folk uninterested or uninvolved in outside political questions did not yet exist by 1830.[48]

It is noteworthy that, at the height of local color writing and the reification of the myth of Appalachia, strategic sections of the region were in the throes of a wrenching industrial transition. No section of the mountains was affected by this process more dramatically than central Appalachia. Industrial society advanced into the mountains behind armies of resident and imported laborers who laid the tracks for three major railroad systems. The first to cut its way through the plateau was the Chesapeake and Ohio Railroad, fulfilling a dream dating back to the eighteenth century, when planners of the C and O Canal hoped to connect Virginia tidewater ports with the Ohio River. Armies of laborers invaded the formerly inaccessible New River Gorge country laying the iron rails that would bind Richmond and Huntington in 1873.[49]

The Pocahontas and Flat Top coalfields of West Virginia, southwest of the C and O line, were connected to the national markets by the Norfolk and Western Railroad. This company was organized in 1881 specifically to serve as a coal carrier linking the southern West Virginia and southwestern Virginia coal country with the port of Norfolk and eventually the Great Lakes. The N and W offered financial assistance to investors for the construction of mines and towns along its right-of-way, and in 1883 when the railroad reached Pocahontas, Virginia, on the West Virginia line, the town was already in full operation with large stockpiles of coal ready for immediate shipment. Eventually, the N and W built a major branch line to Big Stone Gap in Wise County, Virginia, and forged ahead with the main line along the Guyandotte River Valley to the Ohio River, and on to the Great Lakes.[50]

While the C and O and the N and W were developing central Appalachia from the east, the Louisville and Nashville Railroad began constructing lines into the Kentucky coalfields from the west. The main line passed along the edge of the plateau running from Louisville to Knoxville. Determined to dominate the eastern Kentucky fields, the L and N constructed a branch line from Corbin, Kentucky, to the Cumberland Gap in the 1880s, but the Kentucky River highlands were not reached by rail until the eve of World War I, when the L and N branch line was completed into Harlan, Letcher, and Perry Counties.[51] Eventually, the entire region was integrated into an elaborate network of main lines, branch lines, feeder lines, and spurs for transporting natural resources extracted from the central Appalachian countryside.

In the southern Appalachians the boom came to the western North Carolina and eastern Tennessee regions with the arrival of the Western North Carolina Railroad at Asheville in 1880 and at the Tennessee state line in 1882. Asheville became a boomtown, and the pioneer developers soon gave way to the large companies, often with operations in several states as the industry was consolidated during the first decade of the twentieth century.[52] Because of its strategic location within the southern mountain region, Knoxville had been an evolving commercial and transportation hub for nearly a century when the convergence of railroads and Cumberland coal and iron elevated the city to the status of regional development hub. From this growth center commercial and modernizing influences reached out into the surrounding mountains. Because Knoxville's coal and iron became locked into a supporting role to the Birmingham coal-steel complex by United States Steel Corporation, and because the city was a major railroad hub, Knoxville's primary industry became light manufacturing, which drew on the surrounding mountain population for its labor force, rather than the black "industrial reserve" of the Black Belt.[53]

The tri-cities of Elizabethtown, Bristol, and Johnson City, Tennessee, held a similar strategic position on the emerging railroad system in the mountains, and they, too, went through a period of development. The tri-cities' industrial expansion attracted immigrants and blacks, but most of them worked in construction and extractive industries. The subsequent development of the tri-cities as a textile manufacturing center provided work primarily for white people in the surrounding countryside, following the southern pattern of a "dual economy" whereby blacks worked in the cotton fields and poor whites worked in the mills.[54]

The enormous capital investment poured into central Appalachian railroads, timber, and coal mining completed the social and economic transition of the region. Trains carried away forest products, but they also returned with manufactured goods such as food, dry goods, household furnishings, farm supplies, and whatever else people ordered out of the mail-order catalogs that supplied the needs of town dwellers and farmers. The railroad connected local communities to the national markets and, as elsewhere in rural America, exerted a profound influence on the way people lived. They were the lines of communication that brought in intellectual and material culture in the form of city newspapers, the telegraph, and the telephone along with incoming manufactured goods.

With the circulation of cash and the virtual explosion in the population of wage earners in the mill and mine towns, merchants were increasingly attracted by the potential for trade beyond the towns in the surrounding countryside.[55] Because of the railroad, for example, the county seat town of Logan, West Virginia, had banks, a newspaper, running water, sidewalks, fire hydrants, and a fire department even before there was a single coal mine in the county. Logan was not urban, according to David Corbin, "but the people were neither isolated nor wholly ignorant of industrialization or capitalism. No longer was the area, as a journalist covering the Hatfield-McCoy feud a few years earlier sensationalized, 'as remote as central Africa.'"[56]

Coal operators entering central Appalachia found few of the supporting services required to sustain a workforce, and so the railroads also hauled in the equipment operators required to build their own. The unincorporated company town became one of the defining features of life in the region. Its very nature militated against the development of those civic ideals that became the catechism, if not the practice, of enlightened corporate capitalism elsewhere in America. The company constructed the town's physical plant, became the miners' landlord, provided the police force, built the churches and stores, and provided any other service that the towns required. Of course, there were great differences among company towns, ranging from crude coal camps erected on "gob piles" to model towns with all the modern conveniences and a benevolent owner-operator. All of them, however, were privately owned entities, not sovereign political jurisdictions.[57]

Pioneer industrialists not only had to build their own towns, but a scarcity of labor in the region also necessitated the importation of a workforce. The central Appalachian districts dominated by the coal industry experienced the greatest demand for labor and, therefore, the greatest importation of workers. Consequently, the population of the central Appalachian plateau grew dramatically between 1880 and 1920 from under two hundred thousand in 1870 to over 1.2 million in 1920. However, growth did not proceed uniformly, nor was it evenly distributed. The West Virginia plateau grew rapidly throughout the era, with the population of its southern counties nearly quintupling from 93,174 to 446,051. Kentucky's plateau counties, which already contained a sizable population on the eve of industrialization, grew sporadically from 216,883 to 538,350 during the same period. Virginia's central Appalachian counties, however, grew moderately but steadily from 55,349 to 155,405. The several plateau counties of northern Tennessee contained the smallest population, and over the course of this forty-year period they doubled their population from 45,375 to 96,063.[58]

The preindustrial African American population of central Appalachia was relatively small, totaling only 14,360 in 1870, but by 1890 that figure had more than doubled to 30,226 and quadrupled to 64,251 by 1910. During the decade of World War I, the number of blacks in the region continued to climb, reaching 88,076 by 1920 and 108,872 by 1930 when the immigration ended. Most of this increase was associated with the rise of the coal industry. In 1870 only 36 percent of the African American population of central Appalachia resided in the sixteen major coal-producing counties of the fifty-six-county region. By 1920, however, 96 percent of the blacks living in central Appalachia resided in those sixteen coal counties. By far the greatest increases in the black population came in southern West Virginia, where 69 percent of the region's African Americans (totaling 60,488) and 62 percent of the state's black miners (totaling 17,799) resided by 1920. Here the scope of industrial transformation was greatest and, correspondingly, the demand for labor was strongest as well.[59]

In the coalfields blacks met and mingled with a bewildering array of peoples and cultures. As the immigrants poured into industrializing America during the late nineteenth century, bureaus were established to help deploy (for a fee) the newly arrived laborers to states where employers sought their services. The number of immigrant miners in the region grew dramatically between 1880 and 1920. Although there are no precise estimates for central Appalachia, the number of immigrants must have reached at least one-quarter of the mine workforce, and in some locations, much higher. In West Virginia, the number of foreign miners among the mine labor force was less than one thousand in 1870. By 1907 their number had reached nearly sixteen thousand, and on the eve of World War I (1915), after the flow of new immigrants had stopped and

Table 1. African American Black Population of Central Appalachia, 1880–1990

| Year | Kentucky | Tennessee | Virginia | West Virginia | Totals |
|------|----------|-----------|----------|---------------|--------|
| 1880 | 6,734 | 2,570 | 4,242 | 5,781 | 19,327 |
| 1890 | 7,444 | 3,653 | 6,552 | 12,577 | 30,226 |
| 1900 | 7,602 | 3,609 | 7,056 | 21,584 | 39,851 |
| 1910 | 10,222 | 4,415 | 7,669 | 41,945 | 64,251 |
| 1920 | 15,692 | 2,943 | 8,953 | 60,488 | 88,076 |
| 1930 | 18,286 | 2,129 | 7,616 | 80,841 | 108,872 |
| 1940 | 18,662 | 1,918 | 7,709 | 85,465 | 113,754 |
| 1950 | 14,284 | 2,941 | 6,659 | 86,421 | 110,305 |
| 1960 | 10,240 | 2,884 | 4,083 | 64,613 | 81,820 |
| 1970 | 7,232 | 2,718 | 2,585 | 44,956 | 57,491 |
| 1980 | 6,506 | 3,253 | 2,688 | 42,277 | 54,724 |
| 1990 | 5,602 | 3,413 | 2,446 | 35,004 | 46,465 |

Source: U.S. Bureau of the Census, Characteristics of the Population for the decennial censuses 1880 through and including 1990.

Note: Counties included within the central Appalachian subregion: (Kentucky) Bell, Breathitt, Carter, Clay, Elliott, Estill, Floyd, Harlan, Jackson, Johnson, Knott, Knox, Laurel, Lawrence, Lee, Leslie, Letcher, Magoffin, Martin, Menifee, Morgan, Owsley, Perry, Pike, Powell, Rockcastle, Rowan, Wayne, Wolfe, and Whitley; (Tennessee) Anderson, Campbell, Claiborne, Morgan, and Scott; (Virginia) Buchanan, Dickenson, Lee, Russell, Tazewell, and Wise; (West Virginia) Boone, Braxton, Clay, Fayette, Kanawha, Lincoln, Logan, McDowell, Mercer, Mingo, Nicholas, Raleigh, Summers, Webster, and Wyoming.

at least half of the immigrants had returned to their native lands, immigrant coal miners in West Virginia still totaled almost thirty-two thousand. These immigrants, representing nearly all of the nations of Europe, came to the Appalachian coalfields in much the same manner that immigrants came to other areas of America during this period. Some were deployed from Ellis Island by labor agents who worked the port towns as representatives of either states or companies. Many followed the typical chain migration pattern whereby family and friends established a "beachhead" for others from the region who joined them later.[60]

In the coalfields, native whites, African Americans, and foreign immigrants lived and worked in company towns where they usually were segregated into sections designated as "Colored Town," "Hunky Hollow," or "Little Italy." Generally, there was discrimination in the kinds of jobs available to each group in the mine as well, with natives or British immigrants serving as bosses or in the technical positions, and blacks and immigrants in the harder, more dangerous, and most unsteady jobs. Still, blacks and immigrants were attracted by relatively high wages. Underground the men worked together, but even on the surface the rigid segregation often became blurred in company towns, and with-

Table 2. Race and Ethnic Origins of West Virginia Coal Miners by County, 1909

| | Fayette | Raleigh | Mercer | McDowell | Totals |
|---|---|---|---|---|---|
| Mines Reporting | 96 | 24 | 17 | 70 | 207 |
| Native/White | 5,724 | 1,062 | 907 | 3,217 | 10,910 |
| Black | 2,949 | 455 | 927 | 4,419 | 8,750 |
| Italian | 978 | 137 | 398 | 1,648 | 3,161 |
| Hungarian | 392 | 83 | 227 | 1,056 | 1,758 |
| Polish | 319 | 67 | 42 | 179 | 607 |
| Lithuanian | 46 | 10 | - | 5 | 61 |
| Swedish | 9 | 2 | - | 20 | 31 |
| English | 122 | 26 | 7 | 21 | 176 |
| Austrian | 70 | 3 | - | 10 | 83 |
| Russian | 77 | 30 | 17 | 416 | 540 |
| German | 108 | 15 | 6 | 36 | 165 |
| Scottish | 93 | 15 | - | 4 | 112 |
| Litvitch | 24 | 12 | - | 4 | 40 |
| Greek | 5 | 61 | - | 130 | 196 |
| Irish | 14 | - | - | 15 | 29 |
| Slavish | 155 | 40 | 33 | 401 | 629 |
| Syrian | 15 | - | - | - | 15 |
| Romanian | 9 | - | - | 120 | 129 |
| Unknown/Other | 1,750 | 801 | 369 | 2,894 | 5,814 |
| Totals | 12,859 | 2,819 | 2,933 | 14,595 | 33,202 |

Source: West Virginia Department of Mines, Report of the Chief Inspector (Charleston, 1909), 94–95.

Note: The number of blacks and Hungarians would be considerably larger if figures for the Virginia portion of the Pocahontas field were available, because one of the largest employers of black and Hungarian miners in the field was located just across the state line.

out other employment opportunities, the workers came to focus on their common economic interests in the United Mine Workers of America, the one organization in the coalfields they could control.[61]

Industrializing Appalachia was a matrix of cultural interaction among very diverse races and cultures. Coal operators sought a "judicious mixture" of native whites, blacks, and foreign immigrants to balance the dissonant cultural traits that were seen as weaknesses by the operators. Like workers elsewhere in America before work was mechanized and control was shifted to the owners of production, mountaineers tended to take time off from work for hunting and fishing, planting, harvesting, family reunions, weddings, and other family affairs. Recognizing "blue Monday" by staying in bed after a weekend drinking bout was common throughout industrializing America.[62] Most immigrants in the coalfields were from southern and eastern Europe, and their Catholicism itself provided striking contrast to the austere Protestantism found among most of the indigenous residents. One Catholic priest observed of the southwestern Virginia coalfields around Norton in the 1920s: "As to the nationalities that make up the vast congregation at present . . . there are only four American born families in the whole section; Roda is all Hungarian, Inman half Hungarian and half Slavs, in the other camps the Catholics are about evenly divided between Poles and Slavs . . . and at occasions like First Communion, Confirmation or dedication of a new church, the outpouring of Catholics is quite a revelation and one would imagine to live for the time in a village of the former Austrian-Hungarian Empire."[63] The extent of cultural exchange and eventually intermarriage among this extremely heterogeneous population usually is unappreciated even by regional scholars. All of these groups carried their own cultural traditions with them into the mountains and influenced others by their presence.

The transition to industry in central Appalachia produced the most dramatic example of development of racial and ethnic diversity within the region, but we should not lose sight of the fact that African Americans and the racially mixed Melungeons had resided in southern Appalachia since the earliest settlement days, and Native Americans from time immemorial.[64]

Until recently, writers have accepted the long-standing assumption that, because of geographical isolation, rural Appalachia had functioned in the past as a subculture that was essentially autonomous from mainstream society. Accordingly, its culture was regulated by traditional values they associated with the frontier, such as traditionalism, individualism, familism, and fundamentalism. Many believed that Appalachia's traditional values, insulated by geographic and cultural isolation, were barriers that explained the "backward" economy found in the mountains and sustained by a "culture of poverty."

The belief in a distinct, regionwide Appalachian subculture resistant to economic development was shaped by a large body of literature that accepted uncritically a fictional Appalachia invented by local color writers of the late nineteenth century. A review of this literature, however, reveals remarkably little empirical evidence for the proposition that Appalachian culture was the product of continuing frontier isolation. Recent historical research challenges the fictional Appalachia by demonstrating that, when viewed from the perspective of the preindustrial era, Appalachia was not much different from other regions of nineteenth-century rural America. Therefore, the pervasive assumption that modern economic problems in the region somehow stem from Appalachia's long physical and cultural isolation must be reconsidered.

## Notes

1. Will Wallace Harney, "A Strange Land and Peculiar People," *Lippincott's Magazine* 12(Oct. 1873): 430–31.

2. William Goodell Frost, "Our Contemporary Ancestors in the Southern Mountains," *Atlantic Monthly* 83(March 1899): 311–19, quotations on 311.

3. Darlene Wilson, "The Felicitous Convergence of Mythmaking and Capital Accumulation: John Fox Jr. and the Formation of An(Other) Almost-White American Underclass," *Journal of Appalachian Studies* 1(fall 1995): 8, 6, 7.

4. Henry D. Shapiro, *Appalachia on Our Mind: The Southern Mountains and Mountaineers in the American Consciousness, 1870–1920* (Chapel Hill: Univ. of North Carolina Press, 1978); Allen W. Batteau, *The Invention of Appalachia* (Tucson: Univ. of Arizona Press, 1990); Dwight B. Billings, Mary Beth Pudup, and Altina L. Waller, "Taking Exception with Exceptionalism: The Emergence and Transformation of Historical Studies of Appalachia," in *Appalachia in the Making: The Mountain South in the Nineteenth Century*, ed. Mary Beth Pudup, Dwight B. Billings, and Altina L. Waller (Chapel Hill: Univ. of North Carolina Press, 1995), 3.

5. The line between preindustrial and industrial Appalachia is sharply drawn at the turn of the twentieth century by some scholars. See, for example, Ronald D Eller, *Miners, Millhands, and Mountaineers: Industrialization of the Appalachian South, 1880–1930* (Knoxville: Univ. of Tennessee Press, 1982). Others argue that the critical changes were already taking place in the 1850s. See, for example, Kenneth W. Noe, *Southwest Virginia's Railroad: Modernization and the Sectional Crisis* (Urbana: Univ. of Illinois Press, 1994).

6. Gene Wilhelm Jr., "Appalachian Isolation: Fact or Fiction?" in *An Appalachian Symposium*, ed. J.W. Williamson (Boone, N.C.: Appalachian State Univ. Press, 1977), 77–78.

7. Ibid., 79–80.

8. Eller, *Miners, Millhands, and Mountaineers*, 100.

9. Steven Hahn, *The Roots of Southern Populism: Yeoman Farmers and the Transformation of the Georgia Upcountry, 1850–1890* (New York: Oxford Univ. Press, 1983). See also Steven Hahn, "The 'Unmaking' of the Southern Yeomanry: The Transformation of the Georgia Upcountry, 1860–1890," in *The Countryside in the Age of Capitalist Transformation*, ed. Steven Hahn and Jonathan Prude (Chapel Hill: Univ. of North Carolina Press, 1985), 179–203.

10. Lacy K. Ford Jr., *Origins of Southern Radicalism: The South Carolina Upcountry, 1800–1860* (New York: Oxford Univ. Press, 1988), 219–77.

11. Durwood Dunn, *Cades Cove: The Life and Death of a Southern Appalachian Community, 1818–1937* (Knoxville: Univ. of Tennessee Press, 1988), 85, 99, 115, 143, 145.

12. Wilma Dunaway, *The First American Frontier: Transition to Capitalism in Southern Appalachia, 1700–1860* (Chapel Hill: Univ. of North Carolina Press, 1996), 10, 198–99, 204–11.

13. Altina L. Waller, *Feud: Hatfields, McCoys, and Social Change in Appalachia, 1860–1900* (Chapel Hill: Univ. of North Carolina Press, 1988), 103, 20–23.

14. Dwight Billings, Kathleen Blee, and Louis Swanson, "Culture, Family, and Community in Preindustrial Appalachia," *Appalachian Journal* 13(winter 1986): 155, 161.

15. David C. Hsiung, "How Isolated Was Appalachia? Upper East Tennessee, 1780–1835," *Appalachian Journal* 16(summer 1989): 336–49. See also Hsiung's *Two Worlds in the Tennessee Mountains: Exploring the Origins of Appalachian Stereotypes* (Lexington: Univ. Press of Kentucky, 1997), 1–73.

16. Robert Tracy McKenzie, *One South or Many? Plantation Belt and Upcountry in Civil War-Era Tennessee* (Cambridge: Cambridge Univ. Press, 1994), 3–4.

17. Robert Tracy McKenzie, "Wealth and Income: The Preindustrial Structure of East Tennessee in 1860," *Appalachian Journal* 21(spring 1994): 262–63.

18. John C. Inscoe, *Mountain Masters, Slavery, and the Sectional Crisis in Western North Carolina* (Knoxville: Univ. of Tennessee Press, 1989), 11; Mrs. John C. [Olive Dame] Campbell, "Flame of a New Future for the Highlands," *Mountain Life and Work* 1(1925): 9.

19. Inscoe, *Mountain Masters*, 12–13.

20. The essay that touched off this debate is James A. Henretta, "Families and Farms: Mentalité in Pre-Industrial America," *William and Mary Quarterly* 35(Jan. 1978): 3–32. See also Christopher Clark, *The Roots of Rural Capitalism: Western Massachusetts, 1780–1860* (Ithaca, N.Y., Cornell Univ. Press, 1990); Allan Kulikoff, *The Agrarian Origins of American Capitalism* (Charlottesville: Univ. Press of Virginia, 1992); Winifred Barr Rothenberg, *From Market-Places to a Market Economy: The Transformation of Rural Massachusetts, 1750–1850* (Chicago: Univ. of Chicago Press, 1992).

21. Robert D. Mitchell, *Commercialism and the Frontier: Perspectives on the Early Shenandoah Valley* (Charlottesville: Univ. Press of Virginia, 1977), 8.

22. Eller, *Miners, Millhands, and Mountaineers*, 3–38, quote on 3.

23. McKenzie, "Wealth and Income," 270–71.

24. Ibid., 271.

25. Ibid., 273–74, 272; Morton Rothstein, "The Antebellum South as a Dual Economy: A Tentative Hypothesis," *Agricultural History* 41(1967): 375.

26. Billings, Blee, and Swanson, "Culture, Family, and Community," 154–70. For Beech Creek, see also Harry K. Schwarzweller, James S. Brown, and J.J. Mangalam, *Mountain Families in Transition: A Case Study of Appalachian Migration* (University Park: Pennsylvania State Univ. Press, 1971).

27. Paul Salstrom, *Appalachia's Path to Dependency: Rethinking a Region's Economic History, 1730–1940* (Lexington: Univ. Press of Kentucky, 1994).

28. Richard K. MacMaster, "The Cattle Trade in Western Virginia, 1760–1860," in *Appalachian Frontiers: Settlement, Society, and Development in the Preindustrial Era*, ed. Robert D. Mitchell (Lexington: Univ. Press of Kentucky, 1991), 127–49. See also Paul C. Henlein, *Cattle Kingdom in the Ohio Valley, 1783–1860* (Lexington: Univ. of Kentucky Press, 1959); John E. Stealey III, "Notes on the Ante-Bellum Cattle Industry from the McNeill Family Papers," *Ohio History* 75(winter 1966): 38–47, 70–72; Eugene J. Wilhelm, "Animal Drives: A Case Study in Historical Geography," *Journal of Geography* 66(Sept. 1967): 327–34.

29. MacMaster, "Cattle Trade," 132–49; Stealey, "Notes on the Ante-Bellum Cattle Industry," 38–47, 70–72; Wilhelm, "Animal Drives," 327–34; Henlein, *Cattle Kingdom*, chap. 1.

30. Inscoe, *Mountain Masters*, 45–52, quotations on pp. 45, 52. See also H. Tyler Blethen and Curtis W. Wood, "A Trader on the Western Carolina Frontier," in *Appalachian Frontiers*, Mitchell, 150–65.

31. Tyrel G. Moore, "Economic Frontiers: Settlement, Society, and Development in the Preindustrial Era," in *Appalachian Frontiers*, Mitchell, 223, 227.

32. Gordon B. McKinney, "Economy and Community in Western North Carolina, 1860–1865," quote on 168, in *Appalachia in the Making*, Pudup, Billings, and Waller, 171–72.

33. Ibid., 166.

34. Turk McClesky, "Rich Land, Poor Prospects: Real Estate and the Formation of a Social Elite in Augusta County, Virginia, 1738–1770," *Virginia Magazine of History and Biography* 98(July 1990): 449–86; Sara Shaver Hughes, *Surveyors and Statesmen: Land Measuring in Colonial Virginia* (Richmond: Virginia State Library, 1979); Warren Hofstra, "Land Policy and Settlement in the Northern Shenandoah Valley," in *Appalachian Frontiers*, Mitchell, 105–26; Barbara Rasmussen, *Absentee Landowning and Exploitation in West Virginia, 1760–1920* (Lexington: Univ. Press of Kentucky, 1994); Wilma A. Dunaway, "Speculators and Settler Capitalists: Unthinking the Mythology about Appalachian Landholding, 1790–1860," in *Appalachia in the Making*, Pudup, Billings, and Waller, 50–75.

35. Mary Beth Pudup has written on social stratification in "Social Class and Economic Development in Southeast Kentucky, 1820–1880," in *Appalachian Frontiers*, Mitchell, 235–60; "The Boundaries of Social Class in Preindustrial Appalachia," *Journal of Historical Geography* 15(April 1989): 139–62; and "The Limits of Subsistence: Agriculture and Industry in Central Appalachia," *Agricultural History* 64(winter 1990): 61–89; "Town and Country in the Transformation of Appalachia," in *Appalachia in the Making*, Pudup, Billings, and Waller, 270–96. See also Dwight B. Billings and Kathleen M. Blee, "Appalachian Inequality in the Nineteenth Century: The Case of Beech Creek, Kentucky," *Journal of the Appalachian Studies Association* 4(1992): 113–23.

36. McKenzie, "Wealth and Income," 175.

37. Ralph Mann, "Diversity in the Antebellum South: Four Farm Communities in Tazewell County, Virginia," in *Appalachia in the Making*, Pudup, Billings, and Waller, 137–62.

38. Chief of Engineers Report, *Index to the Executive Documents of the House of Representatives*, 45th Cong., 2d sess., vol. 3, part 1 (Washington, D.C.: Government Printing Office, 1878), 664.

39. John E. Stealey III, *The Antebellum Kanawha Salt Business and Western Markets* (Lexington: Univ. Press of Kentucky, 1993).

40. Moore, "Economic Frontiers," 230; Ronald L. Lewis, *Coal, Iron, and Slaves: Industrial Slavery in Maryland and Virginia, 1715–1865* (Westport, Conn.: Greenwood Press, 1979); Lester J. Cappon, "Iron-Making: A Forgotten Industry of North Carolina,"

*North Carolina Historical Review* 9(Oct. 1932): 331–48; R. Bruce Council, Nicholas Honerkamp, and M. Elizabeth Will, *Industry and Technology in Antebellum Tennessee: The Archaeology of Bluff Furnace* (Knoxville: Univ. of Tennessee Press, 1992).

41. Gordon B. McKinney, *Southern Mountain Republicans, 1865–1900: Politics and the Appalachian Community* (Chapel Hill: Univ. of North Carolina Press, 1978), chap. 2. See also Dunn, *Cades Cove*, chap. 5.

42. Inscoe, *Mountain Masters*, 209–57.

43. Kenneth W. Noe, *Southwest Virginia's Railroad: Modernization and the Sectional Crisis* (Urbana: Univ. of Illinois Press, 1994), 6–8.

44. Ibid., 7–8. For similar influences and conclusions for East Tennessee see W. Todd Groce, "The Social Origins of East Tennessee's Confederate Leadership," in *The Civil War in Appalachia: Collected Essays,* eds. Kenneth W. Noe and Shannon H. Wilson (Knoxville: Univ. of Tennessee Press, 1997), 30–54.

45. Van Beck Hall, "The Politics of Appalachian Virginia, 1790–1830," in *Appalachian Frontiers*, Mitchell, 166.

46. Ibid., 169. For similar conclusions for a slightly earlier period in the Virginia backcountry, see Warren R. Hofstra and Robert D. Mitchell, "Town and Country in Backcountry Virginia: Winchester and the Shenandoah Valley, 1730–1800," *Journal of Southern History* 59(Nov. 1993): 619–46.

47. Hall, "Politics of Appalachian Virginia," in *Appalachian Frontiers*, Mitchell, 172–73. See also Charles Henry Ambler, *Sectionalism in Virginia from 1776 to 1861* (Chicago: Univ. of Chicago Press, 1910).

48. Hall, "Politics of Appalachian Virginia," 186, in *Appalachian Frontiers*, Mitchell, 186.

49. Ronald L. Lewis, *Black Coal Miners in America: Race, Class, and Community Conflict, 1780–1980* (Lexington: Univ. Press of Kentucky, 1987), 122; Charles Bias, "The Completion of the Chesapeake and Ohio Railroad to the Ohio River, 1869–1873," *West Virginia History* 40(summer 1979): 393–403.

50. Lewis, *Black Coal Miners*, 123; Joseph T. Lambie, *From Mine to Market: The History of Coal Transportation on the Norfolk and Western Railway* (New York: New York Univ. Press, 1957), chap. 1–2.

51. Eller, *Miners, Millhands, and Mountaineers*, 140–53; Maury Klein, *History of the Louisville and Nashville Railroad* (New York: Macmillan, 1972), 23.

52. Eller, *Miners, Millhands, and Mountaineers*, 101; Ina Woestermeyer Van Noppen, *Western North Carolina since the Civil War* (Boone, N.C.: Appalachian Consortium Press, 1973).

53. John H. Stanfield, "The Sociohistorical Roots of Black/White Inequality in Urban Appalachia: Knoxville and East Tennessee," in *Blacks in Appalachia*, eds. William H. Turner and Edward J. Cabbell (Lexington: Univ. Press of Kentucky, 1985), 133.

54. Margaret Ripley Wolfe, *Kingsport, Tennessee: A Planned American City* (Lexington: Univ. Press of Kentucky, 1987), chaps. 2, 4; V.N. Phillips, *Bristol, Tennessee/Virginia: A History, 1852–1900* (Johnson City, Tenn.: The Overmountain Press, 1992), chaps. 10, 12.

55. For the impact of railroads on American society see, for example, Albro Martin, *Railroads Triumphant: The Growth, Rejection and Rebirth of a Vital American Force*

(New York: Oxford Univ. Press, 1992). For their impact in the Appalachians see also Allen W. Trelease, *The North Carolina Railroad, 1849–1871, and the Modernization of North Carolina* (Chapel Hill: Univ. of North Carolina Press, 1991); William Price McNeel, *The Durbin Route: The Greenbrier Division of the Chesapeake and Ohio Railway* (Charleston, W.Va.: Pictorial Histories, 1985); Mary Verhoeff, *The Kentucky Mountains: Transportation and Commerce, 1750–1911* (Louisville, Ky.: Filson Club, 1911).

56. Corbin, *Life, Work, and Rebellion*, 7.

57. There are divergent interpretations on the nature of coal company-owned towns. One view grants exceptions to the rule, but holds that generally they oppressed their inhabitants. See Eller, *Miners, Millhands, and Mountaineers*, chap. 5; Corbin, *Life, Work, and Rebellion*, chap. 3. The opposing view also grants exceptions, but generally argues that life was better in company towns than what their inhabitants had known before. See Crandall A. Shifflett, *Coal Towns: Life, Work, and Culture in Company Towns of Southern Appalachia, 1880–1960* (Knoxville: Univ. of Tennessee Press, 1991). For the Americanization movement see John C. Hennen Jr., *The Americanization of West Virginia* (Lexington: Univ. Press of Kentucky, 1995).

58. U.S. Census of Population, 1880–1920; Randall G. Lawrence, "Appalachian Metamorphosis: Industrializing Society on the Central Appalachian Plateau" (Ph.D. diss., Duke Univ., 1983), 51–52; Ronald L. Lewis, "From Peasant to Proletarian: The Migration of Southern Blacks to the Central Appalachian Coalfields," *Journal of Southern History* 55(Feb. 1989): 81.

59. Lewis, "Peasant to Proletarian," 82; Joe William Trotter Jr., *Coal, Class, and Color: Blacks in Southern West Virginia, 1915–32* (Urbana: Univ. of Illinois Press, 1990), chap. 3.

60. Margaret Ripley Wolfe, "Aliens in Southern Appalachia: Catholics in the Coal Camps, 1900–1940," *Appalachian Heritage* 6(winter 1978): 45; Kenneth R. Bailey, "A Judicious Mixture: Negroes and Immigrants in the West Virginia Mines, 1880–1917," in *Blacks in Appalachia*, Turner and Cabbell, 118–120.

61. Lewis, *Black Coal Miners*, 156.

62. See Herbert G. Gutman, *Work, Culture, and Society in Industrializing America* (New York: Vintage Books, 1977), 3–78.

63. Anonymous observation quoted in Wolfe, "Aliens in Southern Appalachia," 43. For an example of cross-cultural exchange see Barry O'Connell, "Doc Boggs, Musician and Coal Miner," *Appalachian Journal* 1–2(autumn-winter 1983–84): 44–57.

64. See, for example, Dunaway, *First American Frontier*; N. Brent Kennedy, *The Melungeons: The Resurrection of a Proud People* (Macon, Ga.: Mercer Univ. Press, 1994); John R. Finger, *The Eastern Band of Cherokees, 1819–1900* (Knoxville: Univ. of Tennessee Press, 1986).

# II

## Speaking of "Hillbillies"

### Literary Sources of Contemporary Stereotypes

# A Landscape and a People Set Apart

## Narratives of Exploration and Travel in Early Appalachia

### Katherine Ledford

We don't have to look hard to find a hillbilly today. Turn on the television, open a newspaper, watch a movie, listen to political debate, or attend a performance of a Pulitzer Prize–winning play and there he is—drinking, feuding, and fornicating. But how has this character, the one who leading national publications such as the *Washington Post* have no trouble accepting as sociological fact, gotten here? Where do we begin searching for the "first" hillbilly, the ancestor of respectable Americans' dangerous and degenerate country cousin? In *Appalachia on Our Mind* (1978) Henry D. Shapiro identifies the rise of magazines such as *Lippincott's* and the related local color movement of the late nineteenth century as sources of this characterization of Appalachian people.[1] Subsequent scholarship has focused on historical, sociological, and economic reasons for such late-nineteenth-century characterizations, influencing analysis of the hillbilly stereotype in the twentieth century. For example, J.W. Williamson in *Hillbillyland* (1995) analyzes the stereotype's popularity in the twentieth century through the medium of motion pictures, a phenomenon reminiscent of the nincteenth-century rise of popular magazines and their literary exploitation of the Appalachian region and its people.[2]

Recent advances in the understanding of colonial and antebellum Appalachia, however, offer the opportunity to investigate earlier manifestations of the hillbilly image that, I argue, predate the appearance of northern journalists in southern Appalachia. If we accept that every culture creates an Other in some fashion, examining the forces that determine which groups become thus marginalized can define basic concerns of the dominant cultures. Why have Appalachian people, instead of the residents of the Virginia tidewater or New England or the Rocky Mountains, been the subject of an enduring and, I will argue, an increasingly popular national myth of cultural, moral, and biological

degeneracy? Analysis of Appalachian exploration and travel narratives is helpful for addressing this question. Throughout the colonial and antebellum periods I see evidence of a deepening association of Appalachian frontiersmen and
residents with the mountainous landscape that they inhabited, an equation
that says more about the explorers and travelers and their cultures than it does
about either the geographic reality of the Appalachian Mountains or the people
who inhabited them.[3]

Exploring the Appalachian Mountains on horseback—part of the journey,
sometimes necessarily, on foot—or later, traveling through them in a wagon or
carriage was no easy feat in colonial times or during the early Republic. These
mountains are some of the most rugged terrain east of the Mississippi River,
and it is not surprising to find descriptions of frightening precipices, impenetrable laurel thickets, and encounters with wolves, bears, and rattlesnakes. What
is interesting to me are the descriptive patterns that emerge when narratives
from across different time periods are read together, even while accounting for
some common descriptive tendencies. Marjorie Hope Nicolson in *Mountain
Gloom and Mountain Glory* (1959) traces the representations of mountains
from the Greeks to the English Romantics, noting the propensity of human
beings across cultures and times to characterize mountains as both horrific
and sublime.[4] While it is important to acknowledge such tendencies, they are
not mandates. Explorers and travelers describe the landscape and their encounters with it through a complex system of public and private concerns. Nothing
says that the Appalachian Mountains must always be described as frightening,
dangerous places or as sublimely beautiful. Many explorers and travelers comment habitually on sheltering valleys, luxuriant vegetation, and good water—
all relatively mundane, but necessary concerns—to the exclusion of more dramatic descriptions. Some people traveling through the area, such as Henry
Timberlake in 1765 or Francis Asbury in 1789, seldom, if ever, describe the
mountains. I read narratives not for an "accurate" description of the mountains and the people, but for the dynamics in the hegemonic culture revealed
by the descriptive choices writers make.

One such dynamic is a process of cultural assignment engaged in by some
Appalachian explorers and travelers as they addressed anxieties about changing social and economic boundaries. Utilization of the mountains and eventually the mountain people to work through national economic and class concerns—
a process well documented in the late nineteenth and twentieth centuries—is
evident in three early phases of Appalachian exploration and travel. To sketch
the trajectory of this function for early Appalachia, I will examine narratives
from European colonial exploration (1660–1720), the first systematic
commodification of the mountains (1720–1800), and sustained settlement of
the region (1800–50).

During the first colonial explorations, men persistently characterized the mountains as adversarial, unnatural, and out of control, a descriptive choice that offers insight into the social landscape of colonial America. As seen in John Lederer's 1669–70 exploration narrative, anger, resentment, and confusion marked men's experiences on the Appalachian frontier.[5] Circumstances of travel and camp life necessitated that men from different social classes in Lederer's party—officers, wealthy elites, laborers, frontiersmen—associated intimately and for prolonged periods of time. This social intimacy was at odds with the growing antagonism between frontiersmen and coastal elites that developed in the colonies from the 1660s to the 1740s. As these groups journeyed across the frontier and into the Appalachian Mountains beyond, they placed themselves in an environment that was the domain of neither party. Explorers' reactions to the landscape became a site for expression of social anxieties that such a circumstance fostered.

Later, during the first widespread and systematic commodification of the Appalachian Mountains, parts of the region were settled and the possibility of exploitation of the region's natural resources became more plausible. Wealthy men who ventured into remoter areas of the region, such as William Byrd II, again adapted their response to the landscape according to changing social and economic concerns. The mountains harbored riches, altering the region's primary identity from a barrier to expansion to a valuable commodity. As the land became economically important, characterization of the mountains reflected this change. Byrd's narratives reveal an uneasiness about settlers' proximity to the increasingly valuable land and the implications this development had for the economic and social relationship between frontiersmen and coastal elites.

Unlike Lederer, Byrd did not consistently describe the mountains as dangerous. Anxiety over clashes between social groups manifested itself differently in these two phases of Appalachian exploration. When members of contentious social groups met on a landscape considered a barrier to desirable westward expansion, explorers characterized the mountains as dangerous. But when that landscape turned into a valuable commodity and settlers were a potential barrier between the explorers and exploitation of natural resources, the mountains became beautiful and desirable while the inhabitants became adversarial, unnatural, and out of control.

Finally, as the region became more substantially settled and major trade and travel routes were established through the mountains, travelers continued to address social and class issues through an association of the mountain landscape with mountain people. This time, however, depictions of the land and the people emphasized the fluidity of positive and negative characteristics. The developing economic and cultural complexity of the region combined with travel patterns that placed different classes of people in closer proximity with each other influenced these depictions. Travel narratives by Timothy Flint (1826) and James Kirke Paulding (1816) include passages in which backwoodsmen are alternately demonized and glorified. As the men travel through the region, they similarly describe a mountainous landscape that shifts between danger and beauty. This landscape of extremes, coupled with the often difficult circumstances of travel in the mountains, created an atmosphere in which travelers' anxieties about class difference in the early Republic became manifest.

In the rest of this essay, I will discuss exploration and travel narratives from each of the three phases I have outlined, paying particular attention to the intersection of national economic and class concerns with the descriptive choices writers make. I do not try to determine through these narratives an accurate picture of the geographical terrain that explorers and travelers encountered. Furthermore, recognizing that anecdotal evidence about any people is subjective, I do not use these texts as evidence for a more accurate representation of Appalachian people. The explorers' and travelers' attitudes contained in these texts intrigue me, not the veracity of their comments. Stephen Greenblatt's critical engagement of New World exploration narratives proves a helpful model for my own analysis. Greenblatt asserts that an account of the Other tells us more about the writer of the account than about the party described.[6] I use his theory of anecdotal significance for my analysis of Appalachian explorers' and travelers' representations of the mountains and people.

Hernando de Soto was the first European to enter the Appalachian region as he explored what is now the southern United States from 1539 to 1543. Systematic exploration of the mountains, however, did not begin until about 120 years later, after Europeans had established permanent settlements on the East Coast. By the 1660s, established towns dotted the seaboard while widely scattered settlements and solitary farms pushed inland. The mountains were far beyond the frontier. Repeating a town/country split evident in European society, social division developed along lines of settlement between frontiersmen and town aristocrats. The parceling out of huge land grants near the coast by aristocratic government authorities to other favorites of the Crown forced men of lower social standing into the frontier area where they were vulnerable to political and territorial reprisals. Fearing Indians, who sometimes responded violently to the increasing pressure settlers put on them, frontiersmen considered themselves without friends on either side. Increasingly, frontiersmen came to resent aristocrats as they were squeezed between landed elites on the east and hostile Indians on the west. The southern colonies of Maryland, Virginia, and the Carolinas, far from exhibiting a spirit of adventure and expansionism, suffered under the constant fear of a class insurrection as a result of the resentment this forced westward push bred.[7]

From the middle of the seventeenth century, a growing staple economy with a related plantation system shaped a stratified social system made up of extremely wealthy elites, a comparatively small middle class, a large white tenant class, and a massive number of slaves. According to Gary Nash, violence in the 1660s and 1670s originated in a formidable class of "landless, impoverished, socially blocked, and armed freemen."[8] As the frontiersmen's relations with wealthy aristocrats became more strained, interaction with Indians reflected social conditions in the colonies in which the "colonizers of the South were more continuously, intimately, and violently involved in exploiting the Indian societies of their region than were their counterparts in New England or the Mid-Atlantic."[9] Confrontation over land finally broke into violence in Bacon's Rebellion of 1676. Howard Zinn characterizes this rebellion as anti-aristocrat and anti-Indian, a case of frontiersmen fed up with being forced west and then not being protected by their colonial government taking up arms in the company of slaves and servants.[10] In this atmosphere of social inequity and unrest, the first colonial explorations of Appalachia, the region beyond the pale, took place under the sponsorship of the colonial government and the aristocrats who controlled coastal land. Recognizing that a growing population could not reside peacefully for very long in the physically limited Piedmont, colonial officials sought an answer beyond the Appalachian Mountains, an answer that seemed illusive during the late seventeenth century as explorers reported rugged terrain to the west with no end in sight.

Colonial officials and their superiors in Britain, increasingly uneasy about class struggles for land, also appreciated the danger posed by rival colonial powers across the mountains. Spain controlled much of the land south and west of the Appalachian range, and if the British wished to secure land for settlement beyond the mountains, speedy discovery of a reliable route west was imperative. Also, the mountains formed a barrier to possibly rich western farmland that could provide an opportunity for successful small-scale farming. Characterization of the Appalachian Mountains from the 1660s to the 1720s reflects this time of intrasocial and intracolonial strife, highlighting the concerns coastal elites had about the frontier and the uncertainty and danger it represented socially and politically.

Many published exploration narratives had their origins in government-sponsored expeditions. Leaders of these expeditions were often members of the coastal elite or had been hired by colonial government officials. These affiliations with the colonial aristocracy influenced the explorers' relationships with the frontiersmen and Indians whom they hired as guides. Many expeditions placed all of the contentious social groups together: coastal elites (or their representatives), Indians, frontiersmen, and often, slaves. With strained relationships between these groups throughout the colonies necessitating a quick solution to fermenting problems, explorers' characterizations of the geographical terrain that was so vital to all their interests are productive places to examine these anxieties. John Lederer's three expeditions in 1669 and 1670 to the Virginia Blue Ridge address these concerns.

John Lederer was one of the first colonists to explore the Appalachian Mountains, and his description of the landscape emphasizes danger and uncertain natural order, conditions both realistically and symbolically prominent in increasingly strained class relations from the 1660s to the 1720s. On a commission from Governor William Berkley of Virginia, Lederer made three journeys into the region from 1669 to 1670, and in London in 1672, he published a record of his experiences. Lederer was a native of Germany and had been well educated before his arrival in Virginia in 1668. His position as an emissary of the governor and his education placed him in a social class different from that of his frontier guides. Members of different races and classes accompanied Lederer on his three journeys, but the only men Lederer identifies by name, besides military officers, are the three Indians who accompanied him on his first expedition; he refers to the frontiersmen only as "men."

In describing all three of his expeditions, Lederer characterizes the landscape as inaccessible and dangerous, a terrain "unpassable, being both steep and craggy." From a distance the "rocks seemed . . . to resemble eggs set up on end."[11] He finds it impossible to ascend one of the mountains on horseback because of the extraordinary thickness of the vegetation, so he progresses on foot. As he climbs the mountain, the first precipice he encounters is "so steep, that if I lookt down, I was immediately taken with a swimming in my head."[12] He finally reaches the summit and, instead of seeing the Indian Ocean as he expects, he sees higher mountains behind him, a wall of barriers to the rich lands and waterways he believes are beyond.[13] On one occasion, having left his horse and one of his Indian guides at the foot of the mountain, Lederer searches alone on a snow-covered summit for a pass, but the cold air in late March drives him back without success. The mountains present a host of dangers, from air that is "very thick and chill" to the "waters issuing from the mountainsides" that are "of a blue colour, and allumish taste." At another time, he travels over "a continuous marish overgrown with reeds, from whose roots sprung knotty stumps as hard and sharp as flint" and worries that his horse will be lamed. Lederer presents a terrain of extremes where he is "almost swallowed in a quicksand" and travels through a "barren sandy desert."[14] He asserts that he would have died if he had not found an Appalachian oasis, a pool shaded from the sun by oak trees.

This dangerous landscape frustrates Lederer's attempts—and symbolically, the colonial government's attempts—to successfully move through the region.

In a colony troubled by the agitation of frontiersmen in the Piedmont and the hostility of Indians beyond them, Lederer finds a difficult landscape that he characterizes as dangerous and uninviting, a serious physical barrier that the colonial government would have to contend with as it faced waves of disgruntled frontiersmen and hostile Indians. This atmosphere of uncertainty and growing danger appears in Lederer's characterization of the mountains as a dangerous, inhospitable, impenetrable place.

Further emphasizing the danger of the mountains, Lederer's descriptions contain numerous references to peculiar vegetation and frightening animals. He laments the laurel thickets that make his journey more difficult. He suffers hunger, "finding little sustenance for man or horse for these places are destitute both of grain and herbage." Lederer tells his readers that "the Apalataean mountains . . . are barren rocks, and therefore deserted by all living creatures but bears, who cave in the hollow cliffs." He kills a "rattle-snake of an extraordinary length and tickness [sic], for I judged it two yards and a half or better from head to tail, and as big about as a mans arm." He believes the snake to be pregnant until he slices it open and finds a whole squirrel in its stomach, a feat snakes accomplish, he assures his readers, through charming squirrels out of trees "by fixing their eye steadfastly upon them" or by surprising squirrels in their nests and dropping on them from higher branches. The mountains harbor a variety of other dangerous animals. An Indian guide shoots a wild cat that turns "with a terrible grimas at us; but his strength and spirits failing him, we escaped his revenge." Lederer sees bears "crashing mast like swine" and hears "leopards" and wolves howl.[15] He is afraid the wolves will devour his horses even though they are tied to the tree under which he sleeps. In Lederer's view, the mountains and all they contain are hostile.

Lederer's account of his exploration of the mountains is valuable not for its veracity but for its negative characterization of the landscape. Undoubtedly, the mountains were a dangerous place. Precipices and extreme cold are real. But so are sheltering valleys and clear streams. Lederer's anecdotes of Appalachia, from egg-shaped rocks to charming snakes, have a wider cultural function than simple relation of curiosities. Greenblatt identifies anecdotes as important elements of a culture's categorization of the present and an attempt to create a larger, encompassing whole: "anecdotes then are among the principal products of a culture's representational technology, mediators between the undifferentiated succession of local moments and a larger strategy toward which they can only gesture."[16] Anecdotal representation of the Appalachian Mountains is culturally significant, systematically chosen information that signifies both an attempt to mediate a local experience—traveling over geographical terrain—and a desire to negotiate larger social and political encounters through the landscape. Lederer's characterization of the mountains as a harsh, cruel environment represents colonial anxieties about growing hostilities among frontiersmen and coastal elites over land-ownership and settlement patterns.

The rigors of journeying into the mountains on horseback for weeks at a time took its toll on Lederer's expeditions. His anecdotal evidence shows an uneasy, sometimes mutinous relationship among different social groups. The mundane, necessary details of camp life prove ground for strife: "The air in these parts was so moist, that all our biscut became mouldy, and unfit to be eaten, so that some nicer stomachs, who at our setting out laughed at my provision of Indian-meal parched, would gladly now have shared with me: But I being determined to go upon further discoveries, refused to part with any of that which was to be my most necessary sustenance." Traveling over an unknown terrain also invites contention among the party. Unsure of how to proceed west when they find no gap, Lederer and his party ask local Indians for directions. The Indians advise heading south, a prospect unpleasant to members of the party intent on finding a passage west through the mountains. Lederer relates that his "English companions, slighting the Indians directions, shaped their course by the compass due west. . . . Thus we obstinately pursuing a due west course, rode over steep and craggy cliffs, which beat our horses quite off the hoof."[17] Dissenting from the group decision, Lederer chooses to follow the Indians' directions when he travels with only one Indian as guide later in the second expedition.

Lederer's second expedition, which contains the largest number of frontiersmen, is marred by rebellion within the expedition's ranks. When the party reaches the banks of the James River in Virginia, Lederer wants to cross and march on, "but the rest of the company were so weary of the enterprise, that crying out, one and all, they had offered violence to me, had I not been provided with a private commission from the Governor of Virginia to proceed, though the rest of the company should abandon me; the sight of which laid their fury." An officer, Major Harris, chooses to return with the frontiersmen and gives Lederer a gun before he leaves, believing Lederer to be "a lost man, and given up as a prey to Indians or savage beasts." This second expedition broke not only at the level of the frontier masses but also between representatives of the coastal elite. Lederer asserts that Harris's conviction that he would perish in the wilderness "made him the bolder in Virginia to report strange things in his own praise and my disparagement, presuming I would never appear to disprove him. This, I suppose, and not other, was the cause that he did with so much industry procure me discredit and odium; but I have lost nothing by it, but what I never studied to gain, which is popular applause."[18] In a note to the reader, William Talbot, Lederer's translator from Latin, identifies setting the record straight as a reason for publishing an account of the expeditions. Harris had accused Lederer of mishandling government funds. When the factional parties of the 1660s and 1670s came together, mutiny and character defamation, at least from Lederer's perspective, ensued.

Toward the middle of Lederer's account of his expeditions is a passage that foreshadows the next phase of characterization of the mountains and their inhabitants. After noting the presence of mineral-bearing rock, Lederer speculates that "many other rich commodities and minerals there are undoubtedly in these parts, which if possessed by an ingenious and industrious people, would be improved to vast advantages by trade." This brief observation, quickly passed over by Lederer, becomes a driving force for a shift from negative descriptions of the mountains representing social and economic anxiety to negative descriptions of Appalachian people as representative of those cultural forces.[19] As exploitation of the region's natural resources for economic gain became less of a passing remark and more of a reason for serious pause, positive descriptions of the Appalachian Mountains became a necessity. Social and economic anxiety did not disappear, just a negative geographical terrain for mapping anxiety as that land became desirable. Another site had to take its place. This time, Appalachian settlers became the physical entity for transference of social and economic unease. William Byrd II proved adept at making this cultural switch.

William Byrd's accounts of his explorations of the Piedmont and Appalachian regions of Virginia and North Carolina from the 1720s to the 1730s demonstrate a change in the characterization of the mountains and their inhabitants. As Byrd discovers the value of the mountain land, his descriptions of the settlers who were beginning to inhabit the land become increasingly negative. On his expeditions, Byrd often negotiated lodging and dining in the houses of settlers and servants who were occupying the land in ever-increasing numbers. As a member of the privileged, landholding elite, Byrd had every reason to be concerned about the acquisition of potentially valuable lands by settlers of a different class. Whereas early explorers could transfer their uneasiness about social intimacies and political quagmires onto the mountains, that option is complicated for Byrd because of the growing awareness of the economic value of the land. As the land's value rose, Byrd characterized the mountains in a more positive way to reflect that commodification. Backwoods inhabitants filled a similar role for later explorers as the mountains did for earlier ones: they became sites for addressing anxieties about social and economic order. Byrd's writings reveal a further development of this transference process. Descriptions of backwoods people reflect growing concerns about socio-economic boundaries. The result is a first step toward the hillbilly stereotype, a characterization that has, on one level, been used to justify economic exploitation of the mountains and mountaineers for over two hundred years.

Byrd's position in the upper class explains some of his class antagonisms, but his private relationships and living conditions reveal social and economic anxieties that found an outlet in characterization of others. Though born in Virginia, Byrd was educated and spent a great deal of his life in England. Shuttling back and forth between Europe and the colonies, Byrd strove to reach a social position that was ultimately beyond him. He lobbied unsuccessfully throughout his life for the governorship of Virginia and courted a series of women whose social and economic positions were far beyond his. He followed this pattern both before and after his marriage to Lucy Parke, a woman whose father exhibited the kind of political success that Byrd sought. Byrd's marriage was a contentious one, marked by frequent fighting and cautious reconciliation. Kenneth Lockridge attributes Byrd's misogynistic private writings to feelings of inadequacy in both the public and private realm.[20] Byrd kept a commonplace book—a collection of paraphrased or transcribed writings that the compiler considers rhetorically important—while in London from about 1721 to 1726. His collection contains a series of anecdotes about reproduction, lascivious women, and sexually inadequate men. Lockridge contrasts Byrd's frank hatred and fear of women in his private writings with his more subtle expressions of misogyny in "The Female Creed," an essay written concurrently and intended for the public. Lockridge's analysis of Byrd's private and public writings and the impact his personal anxieties had on representations of women offers a model of critical engagement for my investigation of Byrd's representation of frontier people.

As a learned gentleman in the eighteenth century, Byrd wrote for both a public and a private audience throughout his life. The different responses to a given subject, such as women or the mountains, provide a point of comparison that is often fruitful for determining a cultural meaning in Byrd's writings. Byrd's characterizations, some would say caricatures, of North Carolinians and frontiersmen in the mountains have often been taken as an accurate representation of these people. While dispelling stereotypes is necessary work, analyzing what cultural function those stereotypes fulfilled is equally important. Byrd's writings are an important place to begin because his characterization of frontier/mountain people as lazy, dirty, and socially backward was the first such focused critique. The changing economic value of the western land settlers inhabited influenced this characterization.

During most of the eighteenth century, travel into the Appalachian Mountains remained an activity that, in many parts of the region, could still be considered exploration. By 1790 frontiersmen had only sparsely settled the Tennessee Valley and the north central Bluegrass region of Kentucky. Vast tracts of land unpopulated by whites stretched through present-day West Virginia, eastern Kentucky, and western North Carolina.[21] When Byrd traveled into the mountains of North Carolina and Virginia in the 1720s to 1730s, the eastern slopes of the Blue Ridge were still largely unpopulated by whites with only a few colonists having established small farms in the foothills. Two fundamental changes had occurred since Lederer's time that impacted Byrd's response to the geographical terrain: Economic value of the land had increased and settlers were beginning, however slowly, to occupy the land.

Two of Byrd's private essays, "A Journey to the Land of Eden" and "Progress to the Mines," show his growing awareness of the economic value of the land.[22] While the purpose of the "journey" as stated in the text is to examine tracts of land that he and his companions have already acquired and survey unclaimed land that they may find desirable, the prospects of mineral wealth constantly sidetrack Byrd on this journey. Byrd and his company pay a visit to Colonel Stith and examine a copper mine worked by a servant and two slaves. It "showed but a slender vein, embodied in a hard rock of white spar," but Byrd sees about "one peck of good ore above ground, and that promised to be very rich." From another mine they see "some pieces of copper ore . . . which seemed full of metal." "This mine," Byrd relates, "has a better show than any yet discovered," and "there are so many appearances of copper in these parts, that the inhabitants seem to be all mine-mad, and neglect making of corn for their present necessities, in hopes of growing very rich hereafter." Byrd presents the inhabitants of the region as obsessed with discovering productive mines. Frontiersman John Butcher "set a mighty value on the mine he fancied he had in his pasture, and showed us some of the ore, which he was made to believe was a gray copper, and would certainly make his fortune. But there is a bad distemper rages in those parts, that grows very epidemical. . . . As you ride along the woods, you see all the large stones knocked to pieces." Unwilling to believe himself struck by the same distemper, Byrd nevertheless comments on river stones that "by their weight and color, promised abundance of metal" and "marble, of a white ground, with streaks of red and purple." Byrd asserts that "it is possible the treasure in the bowels of the earth may make ample amends for the poverty of its surface."[23]

In "Progress to the Mines" Byrd's purpose for exploring the region is acquisition of natural resources. In the company of other landholders, Byrd finds a site where a small amount of iron ore "gave us not great encouragement to search deeper, nor did the quantity appear to be very great." Nevertheless, for Byrd's "greater satisfaction" he "order[s] a hand to dig there for some time this winter." He tells a settler and prospector, Mr. Chiswell, that he has "come to spy the land, and inform [him]self of the expense of carrying on an iron work with effect." Chiswell offers advice about determining if a mine will prove profitable. Byrd visits an ironworks and the majority of the essay consists of his accounts of the operation of the works and instructions about how to successfully run such an operation. The proprietor of the works tells Byrd that he has found iron in several parts of his forty-five-thousand-acre tract of land.[24]

Byrd's journeys focus on the possibility of opening mines and ironworks, a prospect that Lederer only alluded to in his exploration narrative. The feasibility of extracting profit from the eastern slope of the mountains colors Byrd's characterization of the landscape. Plentiful timber, full rivers, and good access routes into the region are imperative for successful mining and for operation of ironworks. These features of the landscape captivate Byrd's attention on his expeditions. Throughout the texts, he praises large trees, swift streams, and a hilly terrain that is relatively easy to cross. Frequent rainstorms, while an annoyance to campers, keep the rivers full. Economic factors clearly mark the geographic terrain Byrd explores. In her study of European travel writing, Mary Louise Pratt locates in the eighteenth century the "inauguration of a new territorial phase of capitalism propelled by searches for raw materials." "It is the task of the advance scouts for capitalist 'improvement,'" Pratt asserts, "to encode what they encounter as 'unimproved' and . . . available for improvement."[25] Byrd's exploration narratives, exhibiting these concerns, are filled with speculations about the suitableness of sites for dwellings. He travels over terrain that "formed very agreeable prospects and pleasant situations for building" and discovers an island that "would make an agreeable hermitage for any good Christian, who had a mind to retire from the world." He also finds a "delightful situation for the manor house."[26]

Byrd mentions plants and animals mainly in conjunction with some type of human use, not as curiosities. His Indian hunters kill bears, deer, and buffalo, the only mention of these animals, and Byrd keeps a sharp lookout for ginseng and other medicinal plants. Byrd's geographic terrain is significant only for what can be used or sold from the land, a quality of description that places Byrd in company with explorers of South America and Africa during the eighteenth century. Pratt notes that the "European improving eye produces subsistence habitats as 'empty' landscapes, meaningful only in terms of a capitalist future and of their potential for producing a marketable surplus." Presented as an empty landscape, significant only for its capitalist potential, the mountains "must be represented as uncontested" to fulfill European aspirations.[27] With vested interests in the commodification of the region's minerals, plants, and waters, Byrd sees the mountains in a congenial light. Concern over landownership on the frontier and acquisition of mineral rights manifests itself in negative descriptions of settlers, themselves a source of social and class anxiety because of their association with the potentially rich land.

On his journeys into the mountains, Byrd often relies on the hospitality of settlers on the frontier to feed and shelter him. These same people were claiming land, building houses, and opening mines—all capitalist activities that Byrd also planned. Pratt asserts that when an expansionist capitalist economy moves onto frontier lands, "it is not only habitats that must be produced as empty and unimproved, but inhabitants as well."[28] Byrd characterizes the settlers he encounters and sometimes boards with as slovenly, lazy, unfit for living on the land: "there was one poor dirty house, with hardly anything in it but children, that wallowed about like so many pigs. It is a common case in this part of the country, that people live worse upon good land; and the more they are befriended by the soil and the climate, the less they will do for themselves." Byrd is most disgusted when forced to associate too closely with these people. He complains that he along with "ten or a dozen people" were "forced together in a room" for the night and "were troubled with the squalling of peevish, dirty children into the bargain."[29]

Byrd's most famous characterizations of backwoodsmen and frontiersmen occur in *The History of the Dividing Line*. Often anthologized, this description was given the status of sociological study for many years:

> Surely there is no place in the World where the Inhabitants live with less Labor than in N Carolina. It approaches nearer to the Description of Lubberland than any other. . . . The Men, for their Parts, just like the Indians, impose all the Work upon the poor Women. They make their Wives rise out of their Beds early in the Morning, at the same time that they lye and Snore, till the Sun has run one third of his course. . . . Then, after Stretching and Yawning for half an Hour, they light their Pipes, and, under the Protection of a cloud of Smoak, venture out into the open Air; tho', if it happens to be never so little cold, they quickly return Shivering into the Chimney corner.[30]

In many other writings Byrd characterizes backwoodsmen in much the same light, but nowhere is an anecdote more fully developed. *The Secret History of the Dividing Line*, a seemingly logical place for an even more vitriolic account of those worthless Carolinians, only has one negative description of the people in common: they eat too much pork. All other denouncements of character in the *History* are missing in the *Secret History*. Whatever Byrd's private feelings, he clearly saw a need for a negative image of North Carolinians and backwoodsmen during a colonial struggle for land-ownership and for control of capitalist resources such as the Roanoke River. Through anecdote, Byrd engaged in a powerful cultural process of representation that had ramifications for generations to come. The power of such anecdotes, according to Stephen Greenblatt, is that "any given representation is not only the reflection or product of social relations but . . . it is itself a social relation, linked to the group understandings, status hierarchies, resistances, and conflicts that exist in other spheres of the culture in which it circulates."[31]

The process of culturally encoding anecdotal evidence about Appalachian frontiersmen served not only Byrd's personal capitalist ventures but also the capitalist aims of colonial government. Byrd's characterizations of frontiersmen, however casually observed, as Greenblatt notes, retain significance: "if anecdotes are registers of the singularity of the contingent . . . they are at the same time recorded as *representative* anecdotes, that is as significant in terms of a larger progress or pattern." As economic and social explorer, Byrd's characterizations function in the unique cultural space of anecdote: "a purely local knowledge, an absolutely singular, unrepeatable, unique experience or observation, is neither desirable, nor possible, for the traveler's discourse is meant to be useful, even if the ultimate design in which this utility, will be absorbed remains opaque."[32]

Byrd's descriptions of the frontier terrain and its inhabitants reflect capitalist intentions. Parting from an earlier tradition of describing the mountainous landscape as dangerous, impenetrable, and frightening, Byrd inaugurates a new cultural relationship with the mountains. He reacts to them primarily as a capitalist, inventorying what can be extracted for economic gain. Thus blocked from transferring anxieties about land-ownership and class changes onto the landscape, as did earlier explorers, Byrd and those capitalists who entered the mountains after him found human subjects for that process. The hillbilly stereotype has its misty origins in colonists' relationships to the land. In the first half of the nineteenth century, the stereotype began to be more clearly drawn as the mountains were more thickly settled and more nonresidents had reasons to go there, such as traveling through them to the new western frontier beyond, visiting the spas that developed around mineral and hot springs, and moving trade goods to and from the region. Nineteenth-century travel narratives display a continuing concern about class in the early Republic and the antebellum period that gets worked out on the mountainous landscape of Appalachia and through the mountain people themselves.

Following a trend common in the travel narrative format, nineteenth-century men and women who visited the mountains and who had the leisure and interest to write about their journeys spent a great deal of time analyzing, categorizing, and defining the landscape and the people they encountered, drawing analogies to help explain new scenes and objects. More often than not, their descriptions of the mountainous landscape break down into the horrific and the sublime. While such reactions are not surprising, the parallels that emerge in many of these texts between negative/positive descriptions of the landscape and similarly marked descriptions of the inhabitants of that landscape are intriguing. In text after text, travel writers characterize the mountains and the mountaineers in strikingly similar ways. On a landscape that, as Marjorie Hope Nicolson has noted, invites description through a positive/negative dichotomy, travelers simultaneously addressed a social dichotomy that had concerned the nation from colonial times—the backwoods/Atlantic Coast split. As earlier, the Appalachian Mountains and mountain people became a site for working through national social concerns.

The propensity to glorify the mountains was indulged by many travelers. In an 1826 account of her tour to health spas in the Virginia mountains, Anne Newport Royall noted this tendency and declared her intention to steer clear of it:

> I have little partiality for mountains; I have suffered too much amongst mountains; they are splendid objects to look at, and sound well in theories, but nothing wears worse than mountains, when you take up your abode amongst them. True, you can have a delicious phesant, a venison, or a trout now and then, but these delicacies are greatly overbalanced by the cold blasts of the winter, killing your lambs and calves by dozens, chilling vegetation, overwhelming every thing with snow, and a thousand other inconveniences. . . . I confess I cannot admire mountains as I hear many do.[33]

All her stoical resolve is put to the test, however, when her carriage rounds a bend and she sees a spectacular vista: "what a scene this for the fancy and pen of a poet! while I have neither leisure nor talents to exhibit it in simple prose."[34] Royall's acknowledgment of the descriptive choices writers make serves to highlight the constructedness of other travelers' accounts of the landscape and points to the range of possible responses to that terrain.

The line between positive and negative descriptions of the mountains often becomes preciously thin. Thomas Ashe, traveling through Appalachia in 1806, found himself alone on a mountaintop trail with night fast approaching and no welcoming cabin in sight. Afraid that if he should advance on the unknown trail "a sudden and rapid death was unavoidable; or if [he] remained where [he] was, wolves, panthers, and tiger cats, were at hand to devour [him]," Ashe weighs his options and chooses to stay where he is for the night. He watches fog rise from the valley as the moon shines "caprisiously," "exhibit[ing] various fantastic forms and colours," making the "'darkness visible,' conveying terror and dismay."[35] Ashe's horrific landscape, as he is nearly overcome with fear, instantly changes into one of almost indescribable beauty:

> such apprehensions were gaining on my imagination, till an object of inexpressible sublimity gave a different direction to my thoughts, and seized the entire possession of my mind. The heavenly vault appeared to be all on fire. . . . through which the stars, detached from the firmament, traversed in eccentric directions, followed by trains of light. . . . Many meteors rose majestically out of the horizon: and having gradually attained an elevation of thirty degrees,

suddenly burst; and descended to the earth in a shower of brilliant sparks, or glittering gems. This splendid phenomenon was succeeded by a multitude of shooting-stars, and balls and columns of fire.[36]

Ashe falls to his knees, crying, "offering to the great Creator of the works which [he] witnessed, the purest tribute of admiration and praise." This sublime land-scape is not stable for long as "the profound silence maintained during the luminous representation, was followed by the din of the demon of the woods."[37] Owls screech; wolves and panthers howl. Ashe's story is a vivid example of the instability of the mountain landscape as described in many nineteenth-century travel narratives, a landscape that can be at once horrific and sublime.

This landscape of extremes is, in many travel narratives, inhabited by a people of extremes, an anecdotally significant situation when read with an eye to social anxieties at play in the nation. In *Letters from an American Farmer* (1782), J. Hector St. John de Crevecoeur establishes clear distinctions between people based on where they live in the new nation: "it is natural to conceive that those who live near the sea, must be very different from those who live in the woods; the intermediate space will afford a separate and distinct class." He goes on to claim that "men are like plants; the goodness and flavor of the fruit proceeds from the peculiar soil and exposition in which they grow." The "great woods" and the frontier contain the most degenerate class: "there, remote from the power of example, and check of shame, many families exhibit the most hideous parts of our society."[38] This classification of people according to the land they live on continued to resonate with Americans during the early nine-teenth century. Travel narratives by Timothy Flint and James Kirke Paulding show that Appalachia functioned as a site for addressing those national class concerns.

Timothy Flint traveled with his family overland to Pittsburgh and Wheel-ing from New England and then by river to Louisville as they made their way west to the Mississippi River where he was to begin a career as a minister. Re-flecting on the journey some years later, Flint recalls that his family had heard tales of the backwoods and that they felt like "strangers in a strange land" as they crossed the mountains. For them, "the interior of Ohio" was "a name which yet sounded in our ears like the land of savages." He asserts that "the people in the Atlantic states have not yet recovered from the horror, inspired by the term 'backwoodsman.'" He and his family were so terrified by the tales they had heard about these backwoodsmen that they "mistake" a herd of cattle and swine on the road from Ohio for a pack of wolves in their "unnatural shagginess, and roughness." The drover, "a man as untamed and wild in appearance, as Robinson's man, Friday," does not inspire much confidence in them either. With hindsight, Flint admits that his family's fears were unfounded. They find the backwoodsmen that they live among as law-abiding, sober, and congenial as the general population back east, noting that "the gentlemen of the towns, even here, speak often with a certain contempt and horror of the backwoodsmen."[39]

James Kirke Paulding also had preconceived notions of who and what he would find in the backwoods. On a pleasure tour through the mountains of Virginia, stopping often at mineral baths and hot springs, Paulding encounters the nation's backwoods nightmare. Caught out after dark far from public lodging, he knocks on a cabin door only to have it answered by a hulking man at least seven feet tall. Ushered into the kitchen, he finds the man's six equally gigantic sons sitting around the kitchen table: "Hereupon, at sight of this most picturesque group, all the stories I had ever read of people being killed, wounded, and thrown into a ditch, in traversing lonely heaths, or desert mountains, rushed upon my memory. I fully determined to look at the sheets to see if they were not bloody, before I went to bed. . . . I did not like the looks of three or four rifles, displayed rather ostentatiously over the chimney."[40] In a scene reminiscent of Thomas Ashe's horrific/sublime landscape split, Paulding listens to the men talk of "the day's work they had just gone through, and of the task of the morrow, when they were going to reap a field of oats—and at once all apprehensions subsided." Paulding assures his reader that "the industrious farmer, even in the wildest recesses of the mountains, is ever a harmless, honest being, with whom the lonely stranger may eat, and drink, and sleep in safety." In this reversal of fortune, Paulding's bloodthirsty robbers become "cultivators of the land" who "constitute the real wholesome strength and virtue of every civilized country." "These are the lads to go in front of the great caravan of man, in his progress to the west—to clear the lands, to hunt the deer, to war against the wild beasts, and cope with the savage, equally wild."[41]

On the mountain landscape—and according to Crevecoeur, because of the mountain landscape—national anxieties over class coalesce and fall apart as the landscape itself shifts between danger and beauty. By the middle of the nineteenth century, the Appalachian Mountains had already begun to function as a site for addressing national anxieties over economic and social concerns. The intersection of colonialism, capitalism, and human characterization is not unique to the Appalachian region of North America. J.M. Coetzee has investigated the representation of Boers (European "Afrikaners") in South Africa and has identified a similar process of cultural description connected to the land. For new colonial immigrants and travelers, "the true scandal of the nineteenth century was not the idleness of the Hottentots [Khoi] . . . but the idleness of the Boers." Reminiscent of the description of Appalachian frontiersmen, writers characterize Boers as slothful, dirty, and stupid. This refrain "is taken up by every traveler who penetrates into the back country and encounters farmers living in mean dwellings set on vast tracts, barely literate, rudely clad, . . . disdainful of manual labor, content to carry on subsistence farming in a land of potential plenty." Coetzee recognizes that such anecdotal evidence frames a dilemma faced by the colonizers: "the spokesmen of colonialism are dismayed by the squalor and sloth of Boer life because it affords sinister evidence of how European stock can regress after a few generations in Africa." Invested in a system that privileges the colonizer as a "better steward of the earth than the native," travelers through the region see the Boers' contentment to "scratch no more than a bare living from the soil" as a betrayal of the colonial mission.[42] Similar condemnations of European settlers also occurred among the Dutch in the Caribbean and the Spanish-American Creoles in the southern United States.[43]

By the end of the nineteenth century writers such as Mary Noailles Murfree and John Fox Jr. could draw on the hillbilly stereotype for their literary needs. Backwardness, superstition, and ignorance, or innocence, simplicity, and kindness—the hillbilly embodied it all. But this hillbilly did not step fully formed out of post–Civil War America. Elements of Li'l Abner, Jed Clampett, and their *Deliverance* kin—and the purposes they serve—formed during the colonial, early Republic, and antebellum periods, coalescing out of struggles over land, money, and class. And when we find hillbillies today in movies, newspapers, and plays, their presence still reflects the nation's struggle over the uneven ground of economics and class.

# Notes

1. Henry D. Shapiro, *Appalachia on Our Mind: The Southern Mountains and Mountaineers in the American Consciousness, 1870–1920* (Chapel Hill: Univ. of North Carolina Press, 1978), 3–31.

2. J.W. Williamson, *Hillbillyland: What the Movies Did to the Mountains and What the Mountains Did to the Movies* (Chapel Hill: Univ. of North Carolina Press, 1995).

3. I am concerned here with characterizations of European settlers of the mountains. While native peoples are described in many early texts, their characterizations according to European racial and cultural assumptions necessitate an analysis different from the one based on geography and class that I develop in this essay.

4. Marjorie Hope Nicolson, *Mountain Gloom and Mountain Glory: The Development of the Aesthetics of the Infinite* (Ithaca, N.Y.: Cornell Univ. Press, 1959).

5. John Lederer, *The Discoveries of John Lederer, In Three Several Marches from Virginia to the West of Carolina, and Other Parts of the Continent: Begun in March 1669, and Ended in September 1670*, trans., Sir William Talbot (Rochester, N.Y.: George P. Humphrey, 1902).

6. Stephen Greenblatt, *Marvelous Possessions: The Wonder of the New World* (Chicago: Univ. of Chicago Press, 1991), 14.

7. Howard Zinn, *A People's History of the United States* (New York: Harper Collins, 1980), 39.

8. Gary Nash, *Race, Class, and Politics: Essays on American Colonial and Revolutionary Society* (Urbana Univ. of Illinois Press, 1986), 15.

9. Ibid., 17.

10. Zinn, *A People's History,* 39.

11. Lederer, *Discoveries of John Lederer,* 13.

12. Ibid., 12.

13. In the text's dedication to Lord Ashley, William Talbot, Lederer's translator, notes that following Lederer's expedition the "long looked-for discovery of the Indian Sea does nearly approach." He equates the Appalachian Mountains with "the prodigious wall that divides China and Tartary" and believes they "deny Virginia passage into the West Continent."

14. Lederer, *Discoveries of John Lederer,* 11, 20, 22.

15. Ibid., 13, 6, 9, 10, 11.

16. Greenblatt, *Marvelous Possessions,* 3.

17. Lederer, *Discoveries of John Lederer,* 14, 13.

18. Ibid., 13, 13, 14, 14.

19. Ibid., 19–20; Lederer leaves the observation thus: "But having tied myself to things onely that I have seen in my travels, I will deliver no conjectures." 20.

20. Kenneth A. Lockridge, *On the Sources of Patriarchal Rage: The Commonplace Books of William Byrd and Thomas Jefferson and the Gendering of Power in the Eighteenth Century* (New York: New York Univ. Press, 1992).

21. Robert D. Mitchell and Milton B. Newton Jr., "The Appalachian Frontier: Views from the East and the Southwest," *Historical Geography Research Series* 21 (1988): 4–64.

22. William Byrd, *A Journey to the Land of Eden and Other Papers,* ed., Mark Van Doren, (n.p.: Macy-Masius, Vanguard Press, 1928).

23. Ibid., 269, 274, 304–5, 287.

24. Ibid., 316, 324, 340.

25. Mary Louise Pratt, *Imperial Eyes: Travel Writing and Transculturation* (London: Routledge, 1992), 61.

26. Byrd, *Journey,* 298–99, 316, 284.

27. Pratt, *Imperial Eyes,* 61.

28. Ibid.

29. Byrd, *Journey,* 306, 303.

30. William Byrd, *William Byrd's Histories of the Dividing Line Betwixt Virginia and North Carolina,* ed. William K. Boyd (Raleigh: North Carolina Historical Commission, 1929), 92.

31. Greenblatt, *Marvelous Possessions,* 6.

32. Ibid., 3, 3.

33. Anne Newport Royall, *Sketches of History, Life, and Manners in the United States* (New Haven, Conn. 1826), n.p., 20.

34. Ibid., 21.

35. Thomas Ashe, *Travels in America, Performed in 1806* (London: W. Sawyer, 1808), 16.

36. Ibid., 16.

37. Ibid., 17.

38. J. Hector St. John de Crevecoeur, *Letters from an American Farmer* (London: J.M. Dent and Sons, 1926), 44, 45, 47.

39. Timothy Flint, *Recollections of the Last Ten Years* (Boston: Cummings, Hilliard, and Co., 1826), 11, 9, 174, 9, 175.

40. James Kirke Paulding, *Letters from the South* (New York: James Eastburn, 1816), 174.

41. Ibid., 174–75.

42. J.M. Coetzee, *White Writing: On the Culture of Letters in South Africa* (New Haven: Yale Univ. Press, 1988), 29–31.

43. Pratt, Imperial Eyes, 63.

# "Deadened Color and Colder Horror"

## Rebecca Harding Davis and the Myth of Unionist Appalachia

### *Kenneth W. Noe*

"When the civil war came," Berea College president William Goodell Frost confidently wrote in 1899, "there was a great surprise for both the North and the South. Appalachian America clave to the old flag. It was this old-fashioned loyalty which held Kentucky in the Union, made West Virginia 'secede from Secession,' and performed prodigies of valor in east Tennessee, and even in the western Carolinas."[1]

Most students of Appalachia[2] are aware that one of Frost's great legacies is the mature incarnation of the mountain stereotype. While earlier generations of local colorists and missionaries had publicized and profited from the alleged "strangeness" and "otherness" of southern mountain society, it took Frost's 1899 essay, "Our Contemporary Ancestors in the Southern Mountains," to place firmly and finally in the national imagination, just in time for the twentieth century, the fully developed stereotype of a large, homogeneous, backward, and isolated "other" America he christened "Appalachian America." What largely has been forgotten is that an essential component of Frost's original argument that southern mountaineers were Americans' "contemporary ancestors" was their "Revolutionary patriotism," which allegedly reawoke as Unionism in 1861 after decades of dormancy. To Frost and many of his contemporaries, mountaineers' all-but-universal opposition to slavery and secession was a central component of Appalachian imagery, one of the few positive factors that made an otherwise ignorant and backward population deserving of gratitude, assistance, and uplift.[3]

As with the better-known elements of the Appalachian stereotype, broad descriptions of mountain Unionism such as Frost's have been rejected recently by modern Appalachian historians, although the tradition of a totally Unionist Appalachia survives in the popular mind, even among many mountaineers who disparage the rest of the hillbilly myth.[4] Starting in the late 1970s, historians concerned with the period before mountain industrialization began to put to rest the notion that Appalachia was an antislavery, Unionist monolith that "clave to the old flag" with "old-fashioned loyalty." Some rediscovered the region's slaves and slave-owners, and maintained that the peculiar institution was not only important to mountain masters but also absolutely vital to the psyche of many nonslaveholders. Others began to relate the tragic wartime divisions and escalating violence between fluid groupings of Confederate sympathizers, Unionists, and those who rejected both ideologies in a futile attempt to avoid the horrors of war. While Unionism certainly was a dominant creed in places such as East Tennessee and West Virginia, they contend, support for secession and the Confederacy reigned supreme elsewhere, as in Southwest Virginia or western North Carolina. The residents of still other mountain sections defy such easy categorization altogether, so confused and volatile was the real situation. The end results of such heterogeneity were localized "inner civil wars" characterized by division, fear, privation, and the violence of guerrilla warfare.[5]

If division rather than Unionist consensus truly characterized the southern mountains during the Civil War, how then did the fictional Unionist monolith propagated by commentators such as Frost, the "Myth of Unionist Appalachia," take root in America's collective memory? In what manner were the southern mountains' slaves and Johnny Rebs swept under the nation's intellectual rug, and why?[6] Henry D. Shapiro came closest to answering those questions in 1978 in his seminal discussion of Appalachian imagery. While largely concentrating on the other degrading aspects of the stereotype, Shapiro did consider the Unionist myth. He explained it as the end result of a two-stage process that largely had to do with attracting northern dollars to the mountains. During the first phase, which lasted from 1865 until 1883, writers downplayed sectionalism and ignored the war as much as possible in hopes of attracting northern investment and Yankee immigrants. In the reunited Union, reminders of the mountains' Confederate past were at best irrelevant and at worst stumbling blocks to industrialization, development, and modernization. In such a climate, accurate memories of wartime divisions and especially mountaineers in gray were liabilities. Thus, of the thirty-nine popular works concerning the region that were published between Appomattox and 1883 and considered by Shapiro, only nine mentioned the Civil War in any way. Moreover, of those nine, essays such as Edward King's "The Great South: Among the Mountains of North Carolina" and Edward A. Pollard's "The Virginia Tourist" dismissed the topic in a few sentences. The Civil War was a theme to be avoided for most chroniclers of Appalachia in the immediate postwar period.[7]

Then in 1883, according to Shapiro, an abrupt about-face occurred. Spearheaded by one of Frost's Berea predecessors, Professor Charles Fairchild, northern-born mountain missionaries enthusiastically embraced war themes. Confronted with the fact that sectional wounds had not healed and that as a result many potential donors still balked at donating to "southern" causes, missionaries like Fairchild manipulated the very real fact of mountain Unionism so as to "de-southernize" the mountains entirely and make them a separate region in the American mind. Heroic depictions of mountain patriots and martyrs, one piled atop another, cumulatively suggested that all mountaineers had been loyal Unionists and therefore deserved northern financial assistance, preferably funneled through an institution such as Berea, founded before the war by abolitionists.[8] By the time Frost took over the college, Fairchild's 1883 assertion that "this whole section was loyal in the battle for a united country unstained by slavery" was a major fund-raising ploy at Berea and an accepted truth in northern religious and literary circles.[9]

While Shapiro's explanation remains important, more recent scholars interested in Appalachia's Civil War have called for modifications that taken as a whole suggest the need for a reconsideration of the myth's genesis. John C. Inscoe, for example, evaluated a literary genre heretofore ignored—at least by Appalachian scholars—that dealt squarely with the region's Civil War, the memoirs of Union veterans who escaped from Confederate prisons into the mountains. Such memoirs highlighted mountain Unionism and moreover contained a strikingly positive general assessment of mountain society that today provides a refreshing contrast to the all-too-familiar degrading stereotype. Importantly, however, few of the twenty-five writers discussed by Inscoe—including the nine who published before Fairchild's 1883 article—asserted that all mountaineers were Unionists. Indeed, much of the book's drama—or melodrama—grew from the seemingly universal conviction on the part of the authors that no white mountaineer could be trusted at first. A highlander was just as likely to be a dangerous Confederate sympathizer as a Lincolnite, more likely if a white male, hence the danger and excitement inherent in an escape. The overall portrait is of a region in ideological confusion and compassed with danger, rather than an enclave united in its Unionism.[10]

Another student of the region, Shannon H. Wilson, has rejected Shapiro's contention that the founding fathers of Berea College drastically reversed course and took up the bloody shirt only in 1883. Rather, Wilson demonstrates conclusively that before and during the Civil War, the founders of Berea College already had planted in the American mind the notion of loyal, antislavery mountaineers, a concept that at least northerners of abolitionist leanings apparently found reassuring if successful fund-raising serves as a useful guide. Immediately after Appomattox, the Unionist myth went to work as a stock tool of the college's fund-raisers, and from 1865 until 1883 Berea hammered away at the theme for all who would pay attention. Fairchild's assertion that Appalachia was a Unionist monolith "unstained by slavery," then, was no new departure at all, but instead was merely business as usual. Indeed, Fairchild said next to nothing that had not already been printed regularly in the college's own publications and fund-raising literature.[11]

Both Inscoe and Wilson, in other words, call into question parts of Shapiro's explanation. A third difficulty emerges as well. Like other students of Appalachia, Shapiro glanced over at least three authors, writing during and just after the war, who like Inscoe's veterans dealt with the mountain conflict in a manner radically different than that found in the publications of Berea College. In several widely read magazine articles, all but one works of fiction, their dissenting voices addressed the war and its horrors squarely, depicting a tragically divided and often bloody Appalachia in which Confederate sympathizers seemed to either equal or outnumber Unionists. All called American readers' attention to Appalachia's Civil War, and the last of the works clearly provided a needed transitional framework for the myth to follow. That such a counterinterpretation existed in addition to the prison narratives studied by Inscoe means that the myth of Unionist Appalachia did not emerge from a vacuum of avoidance in 1883, but rather in opposition to contrary voices who provided truer descriptions of wartime mountain divisions.

Who were these dissenters? The earliest, and certainly the most important, was Rebecca Harding Davis. Largely forgotten, except as the mother of dashing turn-of-the-century journalist Richard Harding Davis, she recently has been rediscovered by several scholars of women's studies. Far from unimportant in her own right, Rebecca Harding Davis was in fact one of the most popular and prolific writers of fiction and nonfiction in the second half of the nineteenth century. Revolutionary in her realistic depictions of women, she also became one of the most talented local colorists, and many of her stories and essays concerned the southern mountain region. It was an area she knew well. Although born in Pennsylvania in 1831 and for a short time an Alabamian, young Rebecca Harding grew up largely in Wheeling, [West] Virginia. She burst onto the national scene in April 1861—along with the Civil War—with her powerful and acclaimed short story "Life in the Iron Mills," one of the first examples of American realism and today her best-remembered work. A mountain Unionist, a sincere abolitionist, and a friend to federal general John C. Frémont and his talented wife Jessie as well, she nonetheless sympathized with southerners and particularly maintained that the southern states had a constitutional right to secede. With her own loyalties confused and friends serving on both sides, Davis quickly came to view the war as nothing more than a horrible tragedy that had divided homes and communities and unleashed brutal and needless violence. She had little patience for the rhetoric of nobility or causes, a sentiment that came across dramatically in her fiction.[12]

Davis's initial story depicting Appalachia's Civil War—probably the first work of fiction on the war written by anyone—was "John Lamar," a tale published in April 1862 in *Atlantic Monthly*. Set in the author's native western Virginia like all of the wartime stories, "John Lamar" is the powerful story of the title character, a Confederate officer; Captain Charley Dorr, Lamar's Unionist kinsman and an old friend; and Lamar's slave, Ben. As the story opens, Dorr is holding Lamar prisoner on their grandfather's farm, now "a strong point for the Federal troops . . . a sort of wedge in the Rebel Cheat counties of Western Virginia." Determined to escape, Lamar has arranged for Ben to saw into his jail, a shed, and aid his flight. Ben, however, begins to have second thoughts. Overhearing a conversation between Dorr and Lamar in which neither advocates black freedom—Dorr in fact insists that "this slavery question must be kept out of the war"—Ben abandons hopes for his own freedom in the North. "He understood enough the talk of the white men," Davis writes, "to know that there was no help for him,—none. Always a slave." Further confused by Dave Hall, an Illinois soldier and ardent abolitionist who delivers a lay sermon calling for vengeance against the South—but then offers no real help—Ben ultimately saws into the shed only to murder Lamar and escape northward into the hills. Left to guard the body, Hall worries that his fiery antislavery rhetoric was responsible for the crime but finally convinces himself that all Americans share guilt for the war and are to be scourged by God for their sins. "The day of the Lord is nigh . . . ," Hall says, "it is at hand; and who can abide it?"[13]

In many respects, "John Lamar" could have been set just as easily elsewhere in the occupied Confederacy. Davis's overarching theme of a nation's collective guilt and her specific condemnation of those who sought to use Christianity to justify man enslaving or killing man was hardly confined to Appalachia. Indeed, most of the characters were not even mountaineers: Hall is from the Midwest, Ben is a Georgia field hand in the hills by chance, and Lamar is a western Virginian only in heritage. What makes "John Lamar" particularly important to mountain scholars are the accurate details concerning the Federals' West Virginia campaign against Gen. John B. Floyd's Confederates, and more important, the author's depiction of the everyday brutality of Appalachia's Civil War. Crisscrossing in the background throughout the narrative are various bands of Unionist guerrillas, "Snake-hunters," and their Confederate "Bushwhacker" counterparts, killing each other without mercy or seemingly even cause in a region heavy with "stagnation . . . deadened color and . . . colder horror." For Lamar and Dorr, that horror literally comes close to home; their grandfather, as well as a neighbor's young daughter, are killed by "Secesh" bushwhackers and the homestead burned. Cruelly, Lamar's captors even take him to the site, "to the wood-pile to show him where his grandfather had been murdered, (there was a red mark,) and buried, his old hands above the ground." Bitterly, Davis adds that the mountaineers themselves bear relatively little of the responsibility for the bloody mountain war. "Both armies used [mountaineers] in Virginia as tools for rapine and murder," she has Lamar conclude.[14]

A few months later, Davis followed up "John Lamar" with another short story set in West Virginia, "David Gaunt." Published in *Atlantic Monthly* like the first tale, "David Gaunt" also depicts a region where war has tragically divided friends and family, with terrible consequences. The title character is a young, itinerant Methodist minister, originally from the Virginia Tidewater, who at length has decided to join the Union army. Gaunt is convinced that the North's cause "was God's cause, holy: Through its success the golden year of the world would begin on earth." His views run counter, however, to those of his only real friend, Joe Scofield. An older man whose son George died in Confederate service at Manassas, "Scofield was a Rebel in every bitter drop of his heart's blood." One winter night, the two men set out to a meeting of Unionists to be held at a local Methodist church. Neither tells the other his true purpose: Gaunt plans to enlist, while Scofield hopes to confirm rumors of a Federal attack on a party of nearby Rebels and then warn the Confederates.[15]

On the way, the pair encounter Douglas Palmer, the local Unionist captain and a man absolutely convinced of the righteousness of his cause: "he accepted it, in all its horror, as a savage necessity."[16] Palmer had been George Scofield's closest friend, and when encountered, is on the way to Scofield's cabin to woo Scofield's daughter Dode. The chance meeting leaves Gaunt shaken, for he too loves Dode and as a result hates Palmer. The Yankee captain rides on to the cabin, where Dode rejects him, surprisingly not for his ideology but rather because of his religious skepticism. Returning to the church to lead the planned attack, he is surprised to learn that Gaunt has joined his band, but has a friendly chat with Scofield, who for his part has been spying the entire time.

"David Gaunt" ends with expected melodrama. Scofield rides off in the snow to warn the Rebels, but the old man moves slowly enough that the blue column catches him. Lieutenant Jim Dyke, an Ohioan who "had quit the hog-killing for the man-killing business," orders Gaunt to shoot a figure seen moving ahead in the road.[17] The victim turns out to be Scofield; Gaunt has knowingly killed his dearest friend for the sake of an ill-defined ideology. Palmer is wounded in the ensuing melee, but a guilt-ridden Gaunt rescues him, takes him back to Scofield's cabin, and marries the two lovers for good measure before laying down his gun forever and going west to serve as a nurse. Palmer and his new bride also abandon political causes and turn the Scofield farm into a hospital open to all.

Above all, "David Gaunt" is an antiwar story. War, in Davis's mind, was an abomination that not only divided friends and family but also perverted the true message of the Prince of Peace, turning ministers into murderers and churches into military headquarters where killing is planned.[18] That the story is something of a religious polemic is made even clearer on the first page, where the author compares her characters to John Bunyan's virtues personified in *Pilgrim's Progress:* Gaunt is "Christian," Scofield "Rebellion," and Dode "Infidelity," and the characters literally encounter "Evil" in an Appalachian "Valley of Humiliation."[19]

Again, however, Davis realistically depicts an Appalachia violently at war with itself in a feeding frenzy of murder and retaliation. Not only is one circle of friends divided, but so is the neighboring community. Both the ambushed Confederates and the attacking Yankees are local men, former friends, and fellow communicants of the same church, while the loafers on the church steps cynically cheer for both the Union and Jefferson Davis. The local war is brutal as well. Danger is everywhere: "rebel guerrillas lurked behind every tree, and every woman in the village-shanties was ready to risk limbs or life as a Rebel spy." Another woman "had found her boy's half-charred body left tied to a tree by Rebel scouts."[20]

Davis saves her greatest criticism for the soldiers who callously burned homes and made war on women and children. Those enemies of domesticity "had work to do on the road back: the Rebels had been sheltered in the farmer's houses near; the 'nest must be cleaned out': every homestead but two from Romney to the Gap was laid in ashes. It was not a pleasant sight for the officers to see women and children flying half-naked and homeless through the snow, nor did they think it would strengthen the Union sentiment; but what could they do? As great atrocities as these were committed by Rebels. The war, as Palmer said, was a savage necessity."[21] That this description of an atrocity so much resembles a real event in January 1862, Col. George Crook's Chapman's Store–Gardinier's Store Raid, suggests that Davis, as often was the case, was spurred by a real incident.[22]

In 1863, Davis married and moved to Philadelphia, where she spent much of the rest of the war years grappling with illness (hers and others'), pregnancy, depression, and financial problems that increasingly forced her to churn out more and more stories of lesser quality. Intellectually, she moved on as well. While she still used West Virginia as a setting for other short stories, the locale and the mountain war itself became more and more incidental after 1862; clearly Davis had said most of what she had to say about the conflict raging in her backyard. Sometimes, as in "The Promise of Dawn: A Christmas Story" and "The Luck of Abel Steadman," the region furnished nothing more than familiar scenery for tales that might have been set anywhere. Likewise, West Virginia's Civil War is merely background for the first half of "Paul Blecker," an ambitious and melodramatic love story in three parts in which the title character, a Union doctor, finally gets the girl after her cruel Confederate husband is mortally wounded at Fredericksburg. Ranging from Harpers Ferry to Broadway via the celebrated battlefields of Virginia, "Paul Blecker" asserts the primacy of faith, love, and home over the political ideologies that create wars and make "machines" of men.[23]

At other times, West Virginia's Civil War functioned as an abstract, otherworldly symbol. During the second half of the war, Davis curiously published two ambitious versions of "Ellen," based on the true story of a simple young Michigan woman searching for her soldier brother in western Virginia. The second, expanded version is much darker than the first, but in both, the real war ultimately is incidental to an existential plot. Appalachia is Ellen's personal "heart of darkness," the final destination of a terrifying personal journey that takes her deeper and deeper into danger and toward madness. The antithesis of Ellen's quiet fishing village, West Virginia is a sort of domestic version of the stereotype of darkest Africa. In the later version, published in 1865, Davis describes the area as "the border region, where the war was breaking ground, with all its dull, gross reality of horrors, to which the farther South and North were strangers; the broken talk in the cars was . . . of quiet farmers murdered in cold blood, of pillaging and outrage, of anticipated insurrections among the slaves, and vengeance for their wrongs." At least, mountain people (including a thinly disguised author) retain their humanity in both "Ellens" and, like the kindly Yankee civilians encountered north of the Ohio, largely help the bewildered traveler. It is a cruel northern woman, a sutler affiliated with a Federal regiment, who puts Ellen in her greatest peril when the woman dismisses Ellen's tale and accuses her of spying. In the first version, published in 1863, Ellen finally triumphs; she not only finds brother Joe but true love as well with a Yankee lieutenant. The two siblings return to domestic bliss in Michigan. There is no happy ending in the later version, however, as Ellen vanishes into the dark void of West Virginia's Civil War, never to be heard from again. As late as 1863, it seems, Davis had hopes that the American family could survive the war. By 1865 she was no longer sure.[24]

For nearly a decade after the revised publication of "Ellen," Davis largely remained silent on Appalachia's conflict and wrote little in general about the war. So did others. As several scholars have written, most Americans shied away from the Civil War as a literary theme during the first decade after Appomattox. Veterans "hibernated" according to Gerald Linderman and allowed their emotional wounds to heal. Meanwhile, as Nina Silber maintains, noncombatant northerners proclaimed "forgetfulness," or "historical amnesia," to be a virtue that demonstrated one's high-minded character and progressive nature.[25]

Writers interested in the mountain South, such as Davis, were no exception. Thus, the theme of a divided wartime region beset with localized guerrilla violence reemerged in postwar popular literature in full force only in 1873, in one of the most cited (and damned) early local color depictions of the south-ern mountains, Will Wallace Harney's short story "A Strange Land and Peculiar People." Henry Shapiro borrowed Harney's title for the entire concept of Ap-palachian "otherness," and one certainly can find much of the nascent moun-tain stereotype in Harney's infamous narrative. Yet, ultimately, "Strange Land" is really about the Civil War, and in that respect at least it is decidedly nonstereotypical.[26]

As the unnamed southern narrator and his sickly bride pass through south-eastern Kentucky, the former relates two tales of the war. The first concerns the young, noble Lassie, torn between loyalty to her Confederate brother and love for her "Captain Cophetua," an old friend of the brother who has joined the Union army. When Lassie's neighborhood is occupied by Federal troops, her lover returns to marry her. Then, the brother delivers under a flag of truce Mrs. G_____, ostensibly a southern lady seeking the body of her late husband. Lassie's simple mountain charms cannot compete with Mrs. G_____'s elite refinement, and soon the Federal captain is smitten. It is a near-fatal error. Mrs. G_____ turns out to be a Rebel spy, and the lover is arrested for treason. Only the last-minute interdiction of the two women at the captain's Louisville court-martial saves the unfortunate soldier from the gallows.

All ends well for Lassie and her beau—they marry and live happily ever after—but lest the reader view the entire mountain war benignly, Harney ap-pends a second, starker tale, of which the lesson is "War is a bad thing always, but when it gets into a simple neighborhood, and teaches the right and duty of killing one's friends, it becomes demoniac. . . . Up in the poor hills they could only kill and burn, and rob the stable and smoke-house." Shorter and without any recognizable protagonists, the second story describes the deaths of thirty Confederate soldiers ambushed and killed at a dance by six former neighbors turned Unionist guerrillas. Harney's imagery is brutal: "with shrieks and groans, and deep, vehement curses, the rapid reports of pistols fill the chambers. The beds, the floors, the walls, are splashed with blood, and the chambers are cum-bered with dead and dying men in dreadful agony."[27]

One year after the publication of "A Strange Land and Peculiar People," journalist Edward King also rediscovered a divided Appalachia. Dispatched by *Scribner's Magazine* president Roswell Smith to play up the South's economic potential and promote sectional reconciliation, King considered the southern mountain region in two installments of a series. Having all but ignored the Civil War in his essay on western North Carolina, the Massachusetts-born jour-nalist makes the conflict a central theme of "The Great South: Southern Moun-tain Rambles in Tennessee, Georgia, and South Carolina." In the latter essay,

King describes in great detail the fighting around Chattanooga. More important, he implies that most mountaineers along the Georgia-Tennessee border supported the Confederacy. Even that celebrated bastion of Unionism, East Tennessee, was politically "difficult to classify," according to King. "There were . . . hosts of uncompromising Union men in Eastern Tennessee," he writes, "so there were, also, many committed to the interests of the Confederacy, and both classes were much broken in fortune." Overall, King asserts that the great themes of Appalachia's Civil War were the bitter divisions between Unionists and secessionists—the now-familiar cliche of "brother against brother"—and the tremendous privation resulting from plundering armies. In other words, King advanced a thesis strikingly similar to that of recent historians, but markedly unlike that of the myth to come.[28] That his observations on widespread mountain support for the Confederacy were made in a series designed to stimulate "good feeling between the lately hostile sections" adds to their import.[29]

More important, Rebecca Harding Davis finally returned to the theme of a divided, war-torn Appalachia at the same time as Harney and King. Curiously, her tentative and somewhat disappointing initial foray was a story for children, "Our Brothers: A Story of the War," which appeared at the end of 1873 in *The Youth's Companion*. More than King's essay, "Our Brothers" was a blatant plea for sectional reconciliation. In the story, young Bob, an eager listener to adventure stories of the war, is "discomfited" by a less-than-glorious tale from his usually taciturn grandfather, Charles Hooper. Investigating reports of depredations against local civilians in Virginia's Shenandoah Valley, Hooper had been lured into a trap by Mrs. Vance, the widow of a Rebel soldier, only to be saved by an unlikely, Davisesque coincidence. The woman learns that Hooper not only had befriended her husband while the latter was a prisoner, but finally had buried the unfortunate man in the Hooper family cemetery in Pennsylvania. Shaken, she warns him just in time to escape from a Confederate ambush. Little Bob, who already had taken on the task of caring for Vance's grave, places a flower on it, having learned "the difference between his *brothers* and beasts of prey." Clearly, the other "Bobs" who read *The Youth's Companion* were to come to the same conclusion.[30]

As in her earlier Civil War stories, Davis proclaims the supremacy of Christian love and family ties over the rhetoric of ideological causes. Yet, the most notable attribute of "Our Brothers," at least in terms of Appalachia's Civil War, is Davis's surprising lack of concern for realism. Not only does she have Robert E. Lee's Army of Northern Virginia operating in the Shenandoah Valley, a surprising gaffe that by itself would suggest a story scribbled hastily for a well-paying serial,[31] she also denies the horror of the war described so vividly in her earlier stories. The mountain war has become orderly, bloodless, and benign in

"Our Brothers." The reported depredations turn out to be largely unfounded, and even the treacherous widow agrees that "The country hadn't had such order kep' up for years"[32] thanks to the gentlemanly Federal occupiers. Conceivably, Davis put sectional reconciliation ahead of her earlier regard for accuracy. Perhaps more likely, the western Virginia of "John Lamar" and "David Gaunt" remained too ugly for the eyes of young people.

That Davis had lost none of her edge became apparent soon after with a much darker story intended for an adult audience, "The Rose of Carolina." A reportorial study of elite mountain women not from West Virginia, but rather Buncombe County, North Carolina, it was published in 1874 and like King's piece appeared in the slightly prosouthern *Scribner's*. "The Rose of Carolina" begins with the image of a woodcut of Confederate General P.G.T. Beauregard placed next to a photograph of Rose's eldest brother, apparently killed in battle at Chattanooga, dressed in Confederate uniform. Rose's father, a slave owner identified only as the "Colonel," also served the Confederacy, losing an arm at Appomattox. Davis relates the family's hardships during the war and then, after stimulating sympathy for the family, turns to Rose's older sister, who "used to keep watch . . . upon the house of a poor farmer, whose sons were Union men hiding in the mountains for three years." One night, after seeing the sons return, Rose's sister alerted the home guards. "When she heard the shots an hour after, and the terrified negroes rushed in to tell her that the men, her neighbors all her life, lay dead, outside the very door, she cooly bade them go help to bury them, as though it had been dogs or mountain boomers she spoke of." After the war, the coldly calculating sister hypocritically keeps up appearances by paternalistically doting on the Unionists' widowed mother, "and when the old woman is sick makes her nice little dishes, for she stays with her at night, leaving her baby to the nurse."[33]

Davis's major themes of political division and the horrors of a local war first reemerged in "The Rose of Carolina." However, the story ultimately acts only as a prologue for the best and by far the most crucial of Davis's stories of wartime Appalachia, her classic "The Yares of the Black Mountains." Published in 1875 in *Lippincott's Magazine,* "The Yares" also was set in western North Carolina and, like the two tales called "Ellen," concerns a young woman's journey into the unknown represented by Appalachia. It is a journey into light, however, rather than into darkness. "The Yares" begins as the young, sad, and simple New York widow Mrs. Denby, her sickly son Charley, and Miss Cook, a condescending writer and dilettante, travel past where "Civilization stops" and on toward Asheville. Mrs. Denby has been advised by her doctor that the only chance of saving the child's life is to "journey to the balsam mountains . . . Charley must have mountain-air." In Asheville, much to Cook's dismay, she hires a seemingly brutish local hunter named Jonathan Yare to take her farther "among the balsams." Before she leaves, Denby is warned by Cook that the Yares have "a terrible history" and "live like wild beasts."[34]

In the mountains, the young northerner finds neither madness nor despair, as Ellen Carrol did, but rather salvation. At the man's home, a simple cabin, the mother and child are taken in immediately by the "peculiar" but "courtly" Yare family and treated with unaccustomed kindness. Despite the dirty squalor, a constant in Davis's mountain stories, Charley recovers in the care of the Yares, "a family born with exceptionally strong intellects and clean, fine instincts." The Yares turn out to be not brutes, but rather untutored saints; the father resembles "some ancient knight." At the end of the tale, Davis concludes: "She lived in their hut all summer. Her baby grew strong and rosy, and the mountains gave to her also their goodwill and comfort."[35]

By that conclusion, however, one cares less about Charley than his knightly benefactors, for it becomes apparent that Davis's real concerns are neither the local colorist Cook nor the mother, but rather the Yares themselves. Like the young widow, the reader is led deeper into the mountains, away from a familiar civilization and along a bewildering path, to discover not only the Yare's Christian virtue, but also their tragic secret. That is revealed one night when Mrs. Denby mentions the warnings of the family's "terrible history," leading the family's matriarch to explain, "It was not their fights with wolves and bears that turned the people at Asheville agen the name of my boys and their father. They were the ony men anigh hyar that stood out for the Union from first to last. They couldn't turn agen the old flag, you see, Mistress Denby."[36]

The family's history indeed had been "terrible." Just after the war began, Federal soldiers brutally killed all the male members of the nearby Granger family, including an eight-year-old boy "with nine bullets in his breast." Sickened, the Yare sons refuse to join Federal regiments despite their support for the Union cause. Instead, the mother explains, "My sons' work in them years was to protect an' guide the rebel deserters home through the mountings . . . an' to bring Union prisoners escaped from Salisbury and Andersonville safe to the Federal lines in Tennessee."[37]

These Unionist activities make the Yares targets of Confederate authorities. Stymied in their attempts to capture the men, Confederates arrest first their sister Nancy, who had been taking food to her brothers in the mountains, and then the aged father. Nancy is locked up in Asheville, and the old man is imprisoned in Richmond's infamous Libby Prison. To save the others, the Yare sons turn themselves in. Refusing a last chance to put on the gray, they are sentenced to die. However, when Jonathan displays "pluck" by crying out, "By God, I am a Union man!" the honorable Rebel captain allows the men to live.[38] Two weeks later, Lee surrenders.

Mrs. Denby trembles with emotion. Her late husband David had escaped from Salisbury Prison during the war. "He might have slept in this very bed where the child lay. These people might have saved him from death." She later pleads with the family "to come out of their solitude to the North. 'There are hundreds of men there,' she said, 'of influence and distinction whose lives your sons have saved at peril of their own. Here they will always pass their days in hard drudgery and surrounded by danger.'"[39] Mother Yare refuses, however, sagely realizing that the family would be lost beyond their beloved hills.

In one sense, "The Yares" was not a major departure from Davis's other tales of the Civil War in Appalachia, nor for that matter did it present a starkly different moral than did King or Harney. The mountaineers beyond Asheville were divided in sympathies, and the Unionist Yares remain the exceptions in a region dominated by mountain people loyal to the Confederacy. We are not yet in Unionist Appalachia. There is, however, a crucial shift in emphasis that ultimately makes "The Yares" very different from the author's earlier stories. In "The Rose of Carolina" Unionists are sketchily described victims of a wealthy slave owner's petty cruelty. In "John Lamar" and "David Gaunt" Unionists and Secessionists are equals ostensibly, but in truth the latter elicit more sympathy from both the author and the reader. "Gaunt"'s Joe Scofield is a brave old man, while Douglas Palmer is an atheist devoid of feeling until the love of a southern woman redeems him.

In contrast, Unionist mountaineers clearly are the heroes of the mountain war in "The Yares." Davis, who like many other local colorists that often wrote with political reform and social justice in mind, had a point to make. Northerners had to return to the mountains and provide their noble former comrades with protection, education, and better lives. Unionist mountaineers were the Jonathans to the North's Davids, beloved friends who deserved thanks, and not the animals depicted by the Miss Cooks of American letters. Since they refused for good reason to leave the land—to "come to the North"—the North had to go to them. Here then was the basic, transitional framework for the myth of Unionist Appalachia. Mountain Unionists were no longer deluded cogs in a senseless war machine, as in Davis's earlier stories, "tools" of outsiders, but rather heroes subsequently and shamefully abandoned by a North too willing to forget.[40]

Thus, while Rebecca Harding Davis's greater role in Appalachian myth-making surprisingly remains sadly unappreciated if not ignored by mountain scholars—certainly "The Yares" greatly influenced Mary Noailles Murfree's early work, and John Fox Jr. was a family friend—the Yares of the Black Mountains clearly were the archetypal Unionist mountaineers of popular literature. All that remained was for other writers to reassure the northern public that the noble Yares were not representatives of a noble minority, as Davis more realistically maintained, but rather typical mountaineers. At that moment, writers such as the founders of Berea College stepped forward to tell the literate and monied northeast exactly what it now wanted to hear.[41]

# Notes

1. William Goodell Frost, "Our Contemporary Ancestors in the Southern Mountains," *Atlantic Monthly* 83 (1899): esp. 313–14. The present essay is a greatly expanded version of my earlier, preliminary exploration of these themes, "Toward the Myth of Unionist Appalachia, 1865–1883," *Journal of the Appalachian Studies Association* 6 (1994): 67–74. I am grateful to Kenneth J. Bindas and John C. Inscoe for their comments on that earlier work, which informed the present study.

2. "Appalachia" clearly is a presentist term that was all but unknown in the period under discussion. Nonetheless, for the sake of clarity, I will use the term interchangeably with "southern mountains" or "southern mountain region" throughout.

3. Frost, "Our Contemporary Ancestors"; Henry D. Shapiro, *Appalachia on Our Mind: The Southern Mountains and Mountaineers in the American Consciousness, 1870–1920* (Chapel Hill: Univ. of North Carolina Press, 1978), 68, 119–32, 275; Allen W. Batteau, *The Invention of Appalachia* (Tucson: Univ. of Arizona Press, 1990), 5, 74–79, 84–85, 195.

4. For an example see James G. Branscome and James Y. Holloway, "Nonviolence and Violence in Appalachia," in *Appalachia Inside Out: A Sequel to Voices from the Hills*, ed. Robert J. Higgs, Ambrose N. Manning, and Jim Wayne Miller, vol. 1, *Conflict and Change* (Knoxville: Univ. of Tennessee Press, 1995), 309. For a discussion of various definitions of "myth" and "tradition," see Michael Kammen, *Mystic Chords of Memory: The Transformation of Tradition in American Life* (New York: Alfred A. Knopf, 1991), esp. 17–39.

5. Notable examples include Martin Crawford, "Confederate Volunteering and Enlistment in Ashe County, North Carolina," *Civil War History* 37 (March 1991): 29–50, and "Political Society in a Southern Mountain Community: Ashe County, North Carolina, 1850–1861," *Journal of Southern History* 55 (Aug. 1989): 373–90; Durwood Dunn, *Cades Cove: The Life and Death of a Southern Mountain Community, 1818–1937* (Knoxville: Univ. of Tennessee Press, 1988); several works by John C. Inscoe, notably *Mountain Masters, Slavery, and the Sectional Crisis in Western North Carolina* (Knoxville: Univ. of Tennessee Press, 1989); Ralph Mann, "Family Group, Family Migration, and the Civil War in the Sandy Basin of Virginia," *Appalachian Journal* 19 (summer 1992): 373–93, and "Mountains, Land, and Kin Networks: Burkes Garden, Virginia, in the 1840s and 1850s," *Journal of Southern History* 58 (Aug. 1992): 411–34; James B. Murphy, "Slavery and Freedom in Appalachia: Kentucky as a Demographic Case Study," *Register of the Kentucky Historical Society* 80 (spring 1982): 151–69; Kenneth W. Noe, *Southwest Virginia's Railroad: Modernization and the Sectional Crisis* (Urbana: Univ. of Illinois Press, 1994); Philip Shaw Paludan, *Victims: A True Story of the Civil War* (Knoxville: Univ. of Tennessee Press, 1981); Jonathan D. Sarris, "Anatomy of an Atrocity: The

Madden Branch Massacre and Guerrilla Warfare in North Georgia, 1861–1865," *Georgia Historical Quarterly* 77 (winter 1993): 679–710; Peter Wallenstein, "Which Side Are You On? The Social Origins of White Union Troops from East Tennessee," *Journal of East Tennessee History* 63 (1991): 72–103. See also Kenneth W. Noe and Shannon H. Wilson, eds., *The Civil War in Appalachia: Collected Essays* (Knoxville: Univ. of Tennessee Press, 1997).

6. Not all twentieth-century purveyors of popular culture, of course, fully accepted the Unionist myth. Native Kentuckian D.W. Griffith, for example, made a divided Civil War Appalachia the locale of films such as *The Fugitive*, and John Fox Jr. depicted a divided Appalachia in his *Little Shepherd of Kingdom Come* (New York: Scribners, 1903). See Jack Temple Kirby, *Media-Made Dixie: The South in the American Imagination* (Baton Rouge: Louisiana State Univ. Press, 1978), 1–17, 39–43.

7. Edward King, "The Great South: Among the Mountains of North Carolina," *Scribner's Monthly* 7 (March 1874): 513–44; Edward A. Pollard, "The Virginia Tourist," pt. 1, *Lippincott's Magazine* 5 (May 1870): 487–97; Shapiro, *Appalachia on Our Mind,* 311–14.

8. Shapiro, *Appalachia on Our Mind,* 16, 85–91, although the inelegant term "desouthernize" is mine.

9. Charles Fairchild, "Address of Professor C.E. Fairchild," *American Missionary,* n.s., 36 (Dec. 1883): 393.

10. John C. Inscoe, "Moving through Deserter Country: Fugitive Accounts of the Inner Civil War in Southern Appalachia," in Noe and Wilson, *Civil War in Appalachia,* 158–86.

11. Shannon H. Wilson, "Window on the Mountains: Berea's Appalachia, 1870–1930," *Filson Club History Quarterly* 64 (July 1990): 384–400; and "Lincoln's Sons and Daughters: Berea College, Lincoln Memorial University, and the Myth of Unionist Appalachia, 1866–1910," in Noe and Wilson, *Civil War in Appalachia,* 242–64.

12. Rebecca Harding Davis told her own life story in *Bits of Gossip* (Boston: Houghton Mifflin, 1904). Spurred by Tillie Olson, ed., *Life in the Iron Mills and Other Stories* (New York: Feminist Press, 1972; revised and expanded ed., 1985), a Davis renaissance happily has begun. Two notable recent biographies are Sharon M. Harris, *Rebecca Harding Davis and American Realism* (Philadelphia: Univ. of Pennsylvania Press, 1991), esp. 20–166, 208–55; and Jane Atteridge Rose, *Rebecca Harding Davis* (New York: Twayne, 1993), esp. 1–56. Neither approaches Davis from an Appalachian perspective, however. One older work that does stress the mountain connection, albeit briefly, is Arthur Hobson Quinn, *American Fiction: An Historical and Critical Survey* (New York: Appleton-Century-Crofts, 1936), 181–90. The best sources, of course, are Davis's works. See Jane Atteridge Rose, "A Bibliography of Fiction and Non-Fiction by Rebecca Harding Davis," *American Literary Realism* 22 (spring 1990): 67–86.

13. [Rebecca Harding Davis], "John Lamar," *Atlantic Monthly* 9 (April 1862): 411–23; quotes on 411, 417, 419, 421. For the assertion that the story was the first American work of fiction on the Civil War, see Quinn, *American Fiction,* 184; and Rose, *Rebecca Harding Davis,* 52. Olson, *Life in the Iron Mills,* 97, called it "the most chilling and perfectly executed of her stories."

14. [Davis], "John Lamar," 412, 413; Harris, *Rebecca Harding Davis*, 76–81, interprets the story somewhat differently. Focusing on Ben and Hall, she explains it as Davis's radical criticism of those naive abolitionists who refused to see that their pie-in-the-sky abolition rhetoric might (and perhaps should) lead to bloodshed and revolution. Jan Cohn, "The Negro Character in Northern Magazine Fiction of the 1860s," *New England Quarterly* 43 (1970): 582–84, also stresses the importance of Ben, noting that the story was perhaps the first with a black protagonist.

15. [Rebecca Harding Davis], "David Gaunt," parts 1 and 2, *Atlantic Monthly* 10 (Sept./Oct. 1862): 257–71, 403–21, quotes on 261, 259.

16. Ibid., 404.

17. Ibid., 403.

18. In one notable passage, Gaunt purifies the church by removing an American flag, although "he hardly knew why he did it. There were flags on every Methodist chapel, almost: the sect had thrown itself into the war *con amore.*" [Davis], "David Gaunt," 407. For other comments, see Harris, *Rebecca Harding Davis*, 92–94; Olson, *Life in the Iron Mills*, 102; and Rose, *Rebecca Harding Davis*, 53–55.

19. [Davis], "David Gaunt," 257.

20. Ibid., 405, 404.

21. Ibid., 411.

22. For Crook's raid, see Kenneth W. Noe, "'Exterminating Savages': The Union Army and Mountain Guerrillas in Southern West Virginia, 1861–62," in *Civil War in Appalachia,* Noe and Wilson, 116–17. Davis might well have heard details of the incident, for her home was just across the street from Union headquarters. See Olson, *Life in the Iron Mills*, 89.

23. [Rebecca Harding Davis], "The Promise of Dawn: A Christmas Story," *Atlantic Monthly* 11 (Jan. 1863): 10–25; idem, "Paul Blecker," parts 1 and 2, *Atlantic Monthly* 11 (May/June 1863): 580–98, 677–91, quote on 684; part 3, *Atlantic Monthly* 12 (July 1863): 52–69; and idem, "The Luck of Abel Steadman," *Atlantic Monthly* 16 (Sept. 1865): 331–41. For Davis's problems and new interests see Olson, *Life in the Iron Mills*, 114–29; Rose, *Rebecca Harding Davis*, 56–65, as well as Harris, *Rebecca Harding Davis*, 103–27, 143.

24. [Rebecca Harding Davis], "Ellen," *Peterson's Magazine* 44 (July 1863): 38–48; idem., "Ellen," *Atlantic Monthly* 16 (July 1865): 22–34, quote on 29. In the earlier version, Davis again makes a direct connection to *Pilgrim's Progress* to remind readers that her characters—and I believe even the setting—were symbolic. Harris, *Rebecca Harding Davis*, 126–27, and Rose, *Rebecca Harding Davis*, 41–42, 47–48, 89, point out that the two "Ellens" led to charges of plagiarism and a rather weak reply from a pregnant and exhausted Davis.

25. Gerald F. Linderman, *Embattled Courage: The Experience of Combat in the American Civil War* (New York: Free Press, 1987), 266–97; Nina Silber, *The Romance of Reunion: Northerners and the South, 1865–1900* (Chapel Hill: Univ. of North Carolina Press, 1993), 2–12, 61–63. See also Kammen, *Mystic Chords of Memory,* 13, 101–31.

26. Will Wallace Harney, "A Strange Land and Peculiar People," *Lippincott's Magazine* 12 (Oct. 1873): 429–38. For Shapiro's comments, see *Appalachia on Our Mind*, 3–5, 267–68.

27. Harney, "Strange Land," 435, 436–37.

28. Edward King, "The Great South: Southern Mountain Rambles in Tennessee, Georgia, and South Carolina," *Scribner's Monthly* 8 (May 1874): 5–33, quote on 19–20. For information on King, see Robert Underwood Johnson, *Remembered Yesterdays* (Boston: Little, Brown, 1923), 96–97; Silber, *Romance of Reunion,* 45, 73; and Anne Rowe, *The Enchanted Country: Northern Writers in the South, 1865–1910* (Baton Rouge: Louisiana State Univ. Press, 1978), xi–xx.

29. Johnson, *Remembered Yesterdays,* 97.

30. Rebecca Harding Davis, "Our Brothers: A Story of the War," *Youth's Companion,* Dec. 25, 1873, 417–18, quotes on 417, 418. Davis, who had become a regular contributor to the publication, also wrote of the war for young people—but the war beyond the mountains—in stories such as "Hard Tack," *Youth's Companion,* Jan. 5, 1871, 46–47. For Davis and juvenile literature, see Harris, *Rebecca Harding Davis,* 152, 164, 165, 167, 242, 248, 294; and Rose, *Rebecca Harding Davis,* 91, 113, 144. See also an earlier story for adults curiously set in wartime Missouri, "Captain Jean," *Peterson's Magazine* 56 (Nov. 1896): 351–59.

31. Harris, *Rebecca Harding Davis,* 165, 248.

32. Davis, "Our Brothers," 417.

33. Rebecca Harding Davis, "The Rose of Carolina," *Scribner's Monthly* 8 (October 1874): 723–26, quotes on 725–26. While the older sister hardly is an attractive character today, she may have seemed more so to Davis's original audience. As Nina Silber pointed out, the stock character of the hostile, hate-filled southern woman was giving way during the period in question to another stereotype, the "innocent creature" or "sympathetic victim" whose anger could be explained away as irrational feminine emotion or at least contrasted with more admirable qualities, notably her determination to hold her head high through defeat and deprivation. See Silber, *Divided Houses,* 26–29, 49–51.

34. Rebecca Harding Davis, "The Yares of the Black Mountains," *Lippincott's Magazine* 16 (July 1875): 35–41, quotes on 38, 41. Davis reprinted the story in her only contemporary collection, *Silhouettes of American Life* (New York: Scribners, 1892). Silber, *Romance of Reunion,* 66–73, notes that the sickly northerner looking for a healthy climate was very much a stock character for the local colorists. Silber even titles one chapter "Sick Yankees in Paradise."

35. Davis, "Yares," 43, 47.

36. Ibid., 44.

37. Ibid.

38. Ibid., 46.

39. Ibid., 45, 46.

40. For local colorists and reform, see Grace Toney Edwards, "Emma Bell Miles: Feminist Crusader in Appalachia," in *Appalachia Inside Out,* Higgs, Manning, and Miller, vol. 2, *Culture and Custom* 709–10. Harris, *Rebecca Harding Davis,* 250–51, concentrates on Davis's use of vernacular. Rose, *Rebecca Harding Davis,* 114–16, underplays the reform implications of the story and interprets it rather as a "story of spiritual homecoming" in which nature and the domestic bonds of family heal victims of modern

society and teach the rejuvenating value of domesticity. To be sure, Davis often used "simple" characters to teach life's "great lessons," notably a brain-damaged and physically deformed former mill worker named Yare in her novel *Margret Howth* (Boston: Ticknor, 1862).

41. Harris, *Rebecca Harding Davis*, 251. Scholars of Appalachia inexplicably have ignored Davis. Batteau, *Invention of Appalachia*, does not mention her at all, while Shapiro, *Appalachia on Our Mind*, 6, only lists her as one of many writers who visited western North Carolina. Much remains to be done.

# The Racial "Innocence" of Appalachia

## William Faulkner and the Mountain South

*John C. Inscoe*

Yoknapatawpha County, Mississippi, is a long way from southern Appalachia, and William Faulkner has never been noted as a chronicler of the mountain experience. But in at least two instances he did write of southern mountaineers, and in both he emphasized their isolation from the rest of the South, and in particular, from its black populace. In an early and little-known short story, "Mountain Victory," and in what is arguably his finest novel, *Absalom, Absalom!*, Faulkner related the initial encounters of nineteenth-century highlanders with African Americans. In "Mountain Victory," it is a black man who intrudes upon an Appalachian family's home. In *Absalom, Absalom!*, it is a mountaineer who leaves his native environment and discovers in its lowland setting the peculiarities of the "peculiar institution." The differences in these situations are considerable, and yet it is the similarities that are more revealing. For both scenarios involve white mountaineers traumatized by their first interracial confrontations and the drastic actions to which they are driven as a result.

Probably no other American novelist has left us with as rich a body of work dealing with the subtleties, complexities, and ambiguities of southern race relations as has William Faulkner. According to Joel Williamson in his 1993 study of Faulkner as a southern historian, "race was central, integral, and vital." This was particularly true of Faulkner's fiction of the 1930s, works that "remain probably the ultimate indictment not merely of the injustices of the racial establishment in the South in and after slavery, but in its capacity for the often subtle, always brutal reduction of humanity, both black and white."[1]

Faulkner's two attempts to apply these themes to the mountain South indicate that he was intrigued by what was probably the only group of southerners who he believed had never known blacks and whose lives had been untouched by the basic biracial character of the rest of the South. In applying this "brutal reduction of humanity" to mountaineers suddenly exposed to members of a second race, Faulkner provided some not-so-subtle insights into the anomaly of what he perceived as the racial "innocence" of southern Appalachia. This essay is an analysis of how Mississippi's greatest writer dealt with that anomaly in his fiction and of the array of early-twentieth-century sources from which he drew his assumptions of the racial dynamics of this southern region so different from his own.

"Mountain Victory" first appeared in the *Saturday Evening Post* in December 1932 and was included two years later in Faulkner's first short story collection.[2] It is the story of a Confederate major, Saucier Weddel, who returns at the Civil War's end from service in Virginia to his Mississippi plantation. Accompanied by Jubal, his black body servant, he approaches the cabin of a Tennessee mountain family and asks to spend the night. The rest of the story addresses the mixed reactions of the five-member family to the two strangers: the fanatical hatred of the eldest son, Vatch, a Unionist veteran who bitterly resents both "rebels" and "nigras"; his unnamed sister's strong sexual attraction to this refined uniformed officer; the awe of his young brother Hule; and the wary distance and more muted hostility maintained by both of their parents. When his sister's lust hardens Vatch's resolve to murder both of the unwanted guests, his father warns them to leave immediately. But Weddel, though probably aware that a delay could cost him his life, refuses to leave until his black companion, temporarily immobilized by potent mountain corn whiskey, can go with him. When the two finally attempt a hasty retreat off the mountain the next morning, Vatch and his father ambush and kill them as well as young Hule, who is caught in their range of fire as he makes a last desperate effort to save his new hero.

Despite the story's intriguing premise and literary merit (Irving Howe called it "Faulkner's best piece of writing about the Civil War"[3]), "Mountain Victory" has been all but overlooked by most critics. The few attempts at analysis have recognized as major themes either the clash between lifestyles of the plantation aristocrat and the poor white mountaineer;[4] the contrasting loyalties between family members and between master and servant;[5] or the most obvious source of tensions between the Tennesseans and their visitors, their opposing sympathies toward the Union and the Confederacy.[6]

But a more subtle and perhaps more important catalyst for the ensuing tragedy is the racial hostility of the Tennesseans toward their guests. Faulkner conveys the highlanders' unfamiliarity with blacks by the primate associations Jubal's appearance evokes. They see him as "a creature a little larger than a large monkey" and "crouched like an ape in the blue Union army overcoat." The initial dismay of the family as they watch the two men approach—they stare as if they have seen "an apparition"—takes on new meaning when well into the narrative, it becomes apparent that they think Major Weddel is a black man, too. When Vatch calls him "you damn nigra," Weddel recognizes the real source of the Union sympathizer's hostility. "So it's my face and not my uniform," he replies. "And you fought four years to free us, I understand." The sister broaches the question directly to his servant, whose disdain for what he calls "deseyer igntunt mountain trash" is heightened by such an assumption. "Who? Him? A nigger? Marse Soshay Weddel?" Jubal exclaims. "It's caze yawl aint never been nowhere. Aint never seed nothing. Living up here on a nekkid hill whar you cant even see smoke. Him a nigger? I wish his maw could hear you say dat."[7]

It is only when the father confronts Weddel about his racial makeup that the source of the confusion is revealed. Weddel explains that his father was part French and part Choctaw Indian, which accounts for his own appearance, described by Faulkner as "a half Gallic half Mongol face thin and worn like a bronze casting."[8] Compounding the mountain family's confusion as to Weddel's race is his kind treatment of his black servant. Because Jubal is ill, the major allows him, his companion and protector since childhood, to ride his horse and to wear his coat.[9] This close relationship between master and former slave, along with a certain "uppitiness" on the part of the latter, adds to the family's suspicions of Weddel's racial identity and their distaste over not only the presence of both men but the connection between them. Their lingering uncertainty becomes a crucial factor in sealing the pair's tragic fate because of the daughter's lust for the Mississippi soldier. Though never before conceived as a possibility, such a biracial union (though an erroneous perception) proves to be as strict a taboo for these mountain men as for most other southerners and thus provides the added impetus for their deadly ambush. Ultimately, though, it is Faulkner's penetrating and subtle depiction of the variety of responses to these outsiders—from revulsion to attraction, from fascination to contempt, all stemming from their unfamiliarity with either blacks or interracial relationships—that makes that theme the heart of the story and the most basic explanation for its violent denouement.

In *Absalom, Absalom!*, published four years later in 1936, Faulkner perpetuated and expanded these themes of highland racism, but with interesting variations. In this version of the clash between cultures, it is the mountaineer who becomes the outsider. Only late in the novel does Faulkner reveal the background of the central character, Mississippi planter Thomas Sutpen, and the incident which sets the novel's plot in motion. Sutpen was born in 1808 in the mountains of what would much later become West Virginia. When he was ten, his mother died and his father, for reasons never fully ascertained, took him and his sisters back to resettle in Tidewater Virginia, near the mouth of the James River. "The whole passel of them . . . slid back down out of the mountains, skating in a kind of accelerating and sloven and inert coherence like a useless collection of flotsam on a flooded river." The narrative of this section is subtly transferred to Sutpen's young eyes, and his uninitiated impressions of plantation life are among Faulkner's most perceptive passages. The account begins with the statement that "Sutpen's trouble was innocence."[10] While much of his naïveté is based on his youth, Faulkner quickly makes it apparent in his fullest description anywhere of southern Appalachian society that young Sutpen represents a regional innocence as well:

> he was born where what few other people he knew lived in log cabins with children like the one he was born in—men and grown boys who hunted or lay before the fire on the floor while the women and older girls stepped back and forth across them to reach the fire to cook, where the only colored people were Indians and you only looked down at them over your rifle sights. . . . Where he lived the land belonged to anybody and everybody and . . . only a crazy man would go to the trouble to take or even want more than he could eat or swap for powder or whiskey. . . . So he didn't even know there was a country all divided and fixed and neat because of what color their skins happened to be and what they happened to own, and where a certain few men not only had the power of life and death and barter and sale over others, but they had living men to perform the endless repetitive personal offices . . . that all men have had to do for themselves since time began. . . . So he had hardly heard of such a world until he fell into it.[11]

While perpetuating the standard stereotypes of a slovenly primitive lifestyle, Faulkner stresses even more the egalitarian, nonmaterialistic, almost utopian communal nature of mountain life. In describing this undeveloped, idyllic society, he imbued it with a moral superiority over the more sophisticated and "civilized" caste system of the plantation South. The image of the family sliding down out of the mountains suggests not only a geographical descent, but a social, economic, and moral backsliding as well. Faulkner clearly implied that the critical factor in making the journey that Melvin Backman has called "the unhappy transition from frontier independence to sharecropping subservience" is the black presence in the flatlands and the inherent racism based on that presence.[12] Thus it is the awakening of such feelings in Sutpen on which this episode centers and which makes it, in turn, central to the novel's meaning.

Faulkner described the first black man seen by these mountain children as "a huge bull of a nigger . . . his mouth loud with laughing and full of teeth like tombstones" as he carries their inebriated father out of a tavern "over his shoulder like a sack of meal." Soon afterward, his sister is nearly run over by a carriage driven by a "nigger coachman in a plug hat shouting 'Hoo dar, gal! Git outen de way dar!'" In observing this new and foreign landscape and in finally settling with his family in a cabin on the edge of a plantation "where regiments of niggers with white men watching them planted and raised things that he had never heard of," young Thomas Sutpen learns the difference "not only between white men and black ones, but . . . between white men and white men" as well. That awareness only fully registers in a personal sense about two years later when Sutpen delivers a message from his father to the plantation owner on whose land they live. Knocking on the mansion's front door, he is met by a house servant who, without even hearing the purpose of his errand, instructs him to use only the back door. That reprimand by a man he describes as a "monkey nigger" with a "balloon face"—in terminology reminiscent of "Mountain Victory"—sends the boy running from the house in shock and confusion.[13]

This rebuff becomes a traumatic turning point for Sutpen, as he at once discovers his innocence and loses it. For it is at this instant that he is first made conscious of his own status within this newly discovered racist and class-distinctive world. "He had never thought about his own hair or clothes or anyone else's hair or clothes until he saw that monkey nigger, who through no doing of his own happened to have had the felicity of being housebred in Richmond maybe, looking . . . at them." His shame at the slave's contempt for his patched jeans and lack of shoes leads the boy to the further humiliating realization that the plantation owner, "the rich man (not the nigger) must have been seeing them all the time—as cattle, creatures heavy and without grace, brutely evacuated into a world without hope or purpose for them, who would in turn spawn with brutish and vicious prolixity."[14]

Out of his humiliation and his sense of helplessness to retaliate for the insult inflicted on him, Sutpen, only thirteen or fourteen years old, resolves that in order to live with himself and to challenge the superiority of the planter class and those they own, "you have got to have what they have that made them do what the man did. You got to have land and niggers and a fine house to combat them with."[15] With that goal firmly implanted in his mind, he leaves the cabin and his family in the middle of the night, never to see them again. He somehow manages to get to the West Indies and eventually to Mississippi, where he begins his rise to wealth and power as a planter, a course that ultimately leads to his own and his children's tragic downfall, brought on by miscegenation, interracial marriage, and murder.

Thus, in two very different contexts, Faulkner portrays the innocence of the southern mountaineer confronting the biracial character of the rest of the South along with the bewilderment and hostility toward a heretofore unknown entity: a black man. In both cases that contact leads to traumatic overreactions of significant consequence. For a writer whose work was constantly attuned to the variations and complexities of race relations in the South, it is easy to see why the premise explored in these two works so intrigued Faulkner. And one can readily trace the sources of his interest and information regarding the southern highlands, a region he would not see firsthand for many years to come.

Faulkner's own family traced its roots back to late-eighteenth- and early-nineteenth-century residents of Haywood County, North Carolina, which at that time covered much of the area west of Asheville to the Tennessee border. His great-great-grandfather, Joseph Falkner, was born and raised in western North Carolina just after the Revolutionary War, his father having moved there from South Carolina during that conflict.[16] Joseph married Caroline Word of Surry County, and in 1825 they began a westward trek to Missouri. They got only as far as Knoxville when she delivered William Clark Falkner, whose first name his literary great-grandson would bear. That migratory pattern from the Carolinas to the frontier wilds of the Old Southwest, of which his own family was a part, provided the basis for the backgrounds of his fictional families, the Sartorises and the Compsons, as well as Calvin Burden, and of course, Thomas Sutpen, despite his more circuitous route via Tidewater Virginia and Haiti.[17]

Much more immediate influences on the highland depictions of "Mountain Victory" and *Absalom, Absalom!* were literary sources. An Irvin S. Cobb story, relating the ambush and murder of a homeward-bound Confederate veteran by Tennessee mountaineers, provided the bare bones for Faulkner's short story.[18] But the theme of both of Faulkner's works—racism made all the more virulent by mountain innocence—seems to have been shaped as much by three fictional works on southern Appalachia inscribed by Faulkner and added to his library in September 1932, just a month before he submitted "Mountain Victory" to the *Saturday Evening Post*. They were Emmett Gowen's *Mountain Born* and Grace Lumpkin's *To Make My Bread*, two recently published novels, and George Washington Harris's 1867 classic collection of stories and sketches, *Sut Lovingood*, the tone of which is set by its subtitle, *Yarns Spun by a "Nat'ral Born Durn'd Fool" Warped and Wove for Public Wear*.[19]

Faulkner once listed *Sut Lovingood* as one of his favorite literary creations, and it remained one of the select volumes that he kept most accessible throughout his life in a bookcase next to his bed.[20] Though race relations remained peripheral to Harris's tales of East Tennessee, blacks on occasion served as subjects of the racist derision typical of nineteenth-century regional humorists. There are casual references as well to the contempt mountaineers had for blacks as part of the outside world. Harris wrote of one particularly colorful but stereotypical backwoods moonshiner: "He hates a circuit rider, a nigger, and a shot-gun—loves a woman, old sledge [a card game], and sin in eny shape."[21]

More pervasive in Harris's "yarns" is the sense of that unstructured and carefree society that Faulkner envisioned. Lovingood's philosophy of life sounds strikingly like Faulkner's description of Sutpen's birthplace: "Men were made a-purpus jus' to eat, drink, an' fur stayin' awake in the early part of the nites: an wimen were made to cook the vittles, mix the spirits, an' help the men do the stayin' awake. That's all, an' nothin' more, unless it's fur the wimen to raise the devil atwix meals, an' knot socks atwix drams, an' the men to play short cards, swap hosses with fools, and fite fur exercise, at odd spells."[22] Faulkner seems to have extracted much of that description for his own use, but he leaves behind the satiric disdain in which Harris had wrapped it. In his romanticized twentieth-century interpretation, mountain "innocence" is taken far more seriously and treated with considerably more respect than Harris, a native East Tennessean, could ever muster for it.

More in tune with Faulkner's tone is Emmett Gowen's *Mountain Born*. Despite its focus on feuding Tennessee families, Gowen assigns much the same sense of virtue and purity to mountain society, which a New York executive and homesick highland expatriate describes as "beautiful and Arcadian." Its residents, he says, "can't read, but their hearts are full of poetry and their heads full of fine thought."[23] But of these three works it is Grace Lumpkin's proletariat novel, *To Make Our Bread*, that provided Faulkner with the most basic inspiration for the Thomas Sutpen story. Like Faulkner, Lumpkin focused on a mountain family who moves out of the hills and finds their innocence shattered when faced with the hard realities of a racist and class-conscious society in the flatlands. Driven from their South Mountain home in North Carolina by encroaching lumber companies around the turn of the century, the McClures are forced to settle in a piedmont industrial community (modeled on Gastonia, North Carolina) where they eventually become involved with the labor unrest in its textile mills in the 1920s.

Their initial interracial contacts were only incidental to Lumpkin's themes, but she conveyed both the curiosity and surprise of the mother and daughter and the contemptuous avoidance of the former's elderly father when they first see black children on entering a mill town. "They're niggers," he informs the women. "White and black don't mix." The McClure women's reactions bring to mind Faulkner's description of the Sutpen girls who, along with "the other white women of their kind," have a "certain flat level silent way . . . of looking at niggers, not with fear or dread but with a kind of speculative antagonism." Even more incidental, but possibly an influence on Faulkner's short story, is the elderly McClure's reference, in relating his experiences in the Civil War, to a "rich man's son" who serves in the army with a slave to care for him, who stays on even after he knows he is free.[24]

Although Faulkner once stated that he "never read any history,"[25] he wrote these stories in the wake of a number of historical treatments of southern Appalachia that contributed greatly to the popular image of the region as monoracial in its makeup. From the 1890s on, a variety of published works contributed to the dual assumptions upon which Faulkner based these two works— the absence of blacks in the mountains and the strong animosity mountain residents felt toward them. In 1897, a journalist wrote admiringly of the north Georgia mountains, "Nowhere will be found purer Anglo-Saxon blood." In 1901, an ethnogeographer echoed these sentiments for another part of the region.

Kentucky mountaineers have not only kept foreign elements at bay; they have "still more effectively . . . excluded the Negro. This region is as free of them as northern Vermont."[26]

As for hostility toward blacks, East Tennessee seems to have generated more commentary than other parts of the mountain South, perhaps because of the lengthier Union occupation it endured during and after the Civil War. In a seminal and widely used document collection on Reconstruction first published in 1906, Walter Fleming included several passages illustrating the irony of the fact that the South's most ardent Unionists were also among its most intense racists. From northern journalist J.T. Trowbridge's observations in 1865, Fleming singled out the quote, "East Tennesseans, though opposed to slavery and secession, do not like niggers." He also drew from congressional testimony of Freedman's Bureau officials in 1866 the statement, "It is a melancholy fact that among the bitterest opponents of the Negro in Tennessee are the intensely radical loyalists of the mountain district—the men who have been in our armies."[27] Whether or not Faulkner ever read these specific passages, the same concept—that mountain Unionists could also be rabid racists—comes through so clearly in "Mountain Victory" that it seems hardly coincidental that he set his story in East Tennessee.

By far the most popular treatments of the region, Horace Kephart's *Our Southern Highlanders* (1913 and 1922) and John C. Campbell's *The Southern Highlander and His Homeland* (1921), were still in wide circulation in the early 1930s. Their pronouncements on the racism and racial demographics of the mountain South represent a culmination of contemporary thought on highlanders' attitudes, past and present, and were perhaps the most accessible of nonfictional corroborative sources for Faulkner's interpretation of the antebellum mountaineer at the time he was writing.

Kephart notes that "the mountains proper are free not only of foreigners but from negroes as well." In many mountain settlements, "negroes are not allowed to tarry," he writes, explaining that the mountaineers' dislike of blacks is simply an instinctive racial antipathy, plus a contempt for anyone who submits to servile conditions.[28] Campbell echos these conclusions. While acknowledging variations in racial demographics and attitudes in the region, he stresses that even in his own time there were mountain counties "without a single Negro inhabitant and where it was unpleasant if not unsafe for him to go." He tells of a terrified child who beholds a black man for the first time and calls him a "no-tail bear."[29]

Such examples are certainly exceptional, but it is in such instances that perception most deviates from reality. Though there were certainly pockets of extreme isolation and alienation throughout the southern highlands, the depictions of racial "innocence" are far too simplistic, romanticized, and exaggerated a notion to apply to the region and its people as a whole. The black presence in many parts of southern Appalachia was considerable, and slaveholding was by no means as foreign to much of the area as Faulkner and his sources implied.

Only within the past decade and a half have historians and sociologists fully embraced the reality of an African American presence in the southern highlands, particularly for the antebellum period. We know that slavery existed in every county in southern Appalachia in 1860, and despite considerable shifts in the region's racial demographics after the Civil War, there was never a point at which an all-white population characterized the region.[30] We now have a variety of local and regional studies on the impact of both the presence and the multiple functions of slaves throughout Appalachia. We have also recognized and documented the class distinctions created because of the presence of those slaves, and the considerable economic and political influence wielded by those mountain masters who owned them.[31]

Countering the idea of racial hostility among mountain residents are indications that many opposed slavery on humanitarian grounds, that those who owned slaves treated them more leniently, that there were several strongholds of abolitionism in East Tennessee and Kentucky, and that the highlands served on occasion as safe havens for slaves escaping oppression and cruelty elsewhere. The rampant Unionism of much of the region during the Civil War and the Republicanism afterward also led more distant observers to equate such sentiments with racial liberalism.[32]

While those trends too were as much perception as reality, Faulkner never showed any interest in these alternative facets of highland race relations. It was the darker side of the white Appalachian mindset—their latent but volatile racism—that most intrigued him. His application of the term "innocence" to his fictional highlanders did not imply any benign sentiments or lack of prejudice toward blacks simply because they were unknown entities; rather it suggested only an ignorance of African Americans and of the multitiered society their presence imposed on the rest of the South.

Yet it wasn't even that innocence or the single-race vacuum in which it was bred that most inspired Faulkner's treatment of the mountain South. In both "Mountain Victory" and *Absalom, Absalom!,* it was the consequences of that innocence challenged from which problems arose and plots emerged. Once exposed to the reality of that second race, mountaineers experienced what Joel Williamson termed a "brutal reduction of humanity." For the Tennessee hosts of Major Weddel and the Sutpen family who "slid back down" out of the Virginia highlands into Tidewater plantation society, their initial interactions with blacks ended in tragedy. Faulkner's genius is most evident in his ability in these cases to portray his highlanders as both victims and perpetrators of their respective tragedies. Men and boys not only lost their innocence, they found their humanity brutally reduced as well.

Faulkner owed much to current literary and historical treatments of the Appalachians in his depiction of an exclusively white society unencumbered by the stratification and oppression of the plantation South and yet as racially prejudiced as, if not more than, almost any other segment of the South. The basis for this assumption had been alive and kicking for over a century by the time it drew Faulkner's attention, and it was by no means on the wane when he discovered it. Five years after the publication of *Absalom, Absalom!*, W.J. Cash gave it even more widespread credence when, in *The Mind of the South*, he concluded, like Kephart, Campbell, and Faulkner, "Though there were few slaves in the mountains, [the mountaineer] had acquired a hatred and contempt for the Negro even more virulent than that of the common white of the lowlands, a dislike so rabid that it was worth a black man's life to venture into many mountain sections."[33]

One cannot say whether Faulkner's work was among those that helped shape Cash's views. But even if not a direct influence on Cash, Faulkner's depictions of the racial innocence of the mountain South would ensure the viability of such assumptions for years to come. The fact that Faulkner reached a far more vast readership throughout the rest of the twentieth century than did most of the contemporary or preceding mountain chroniclers on whom he drew gave their views far greater and longer-lasting exposure through his work than they would probably otherwise have enjoyed. As with many of the myths of southern history, the very adaptation by William Faulkner of this concept of Appalachian racism infused it with new levels of meaning, dramatic force, and even credibility.

## Notes

This chapter is an expanded version of an essay that first appeared in the *South Atlantic Quarterly* (Summer 1991): 244–53.

1. Joel Williamson, *William Faulkner and Southern History* (New York: Oxford Univ. Press, 1993), 7.

2. William Faulkner, "Mountain Victory," *Saturday Evening Post*, Dec. 3, 1932; later reprinted in Faulkner, *Doctor Martino and Other Stories* (New York: H. Smith and R. Hass, 1934).

3. Irving Howe, *William Faulkner: A Critical Study* (Chicago: Univ. of Chicago Press, 1975), 264.

4. Ibid.

5. Dorothy Tuck, *Crowell's Handbook of Faulkner* (New York: Crowell, 1964), 171.

6. Philip Momberger, "A Critical Study of Faulkner's Early Sketches and Collected Stories," (Ph.D. diss., Johns Hopkins Univ., 1970), 244–50. Momberger's is the most thorough analysis of "Mountain Victory."

7. William Faulkner, "Mountain Victory," *Collected Stories* (1950; reprint, New York: Random House, 1977), 746, 753, 747, 751, 763, 756.

8. Ibid., 762. Weddel's background is established in another Faulkner short story, "Lo!" in *Collected Stories*, 381–403.

9. Faulkner may well have based the relationship between Weddel and Jubal on that between his own great-grandfather Col. William Clark Falkner and his body servant, Nate. For full accounts of Colonel Falkner's Civil War career, see Joseph Blotner, *Faulkner: A Biography*, vol. 1 (New York: Random House, 1974), 20–32; Williamson, *Faulkner and Southern History*, chap. 2; and Daniel J. Singal, *William Faulkner: The Making of a Modernist* (Chapel Hill: Univ. of North Carolina Press, 1997), 22–27.

10. William Faulkner, *Absalom, Absalom!* (1936; reprint, New York: Random House, 1951), 223, 220. Sutpen's past is reconstructed by Quentin Compson and his Harvard roommate, based on Compson's grandfather's version of what Sutpen had told him. For an analysis of Thomas Sutpen as a mountaineer, see Lynn Dickerson, "Thomas Sutpen: Mountain Stereotype in *Absalom Absalom!*" *Appalachian Heritage* 12 (spring 1984): 73–78.

11. Faulkner, *Absalom*, 221–22.

12. Melvin Backman, *Faulkner: The Major Years, A Critical Study* (Bloomington: Indiana Univ. Press, 1966), 98.

13. Faulkner, *Absalom*, 225, 231, 226–27, 232.

14. Ibid., 232, 235.

15. Ibid., 238.

16. Blotner, *Faulkner*, vol. 1, 8–9. See also his genealogical chart in vol. 2, 222–23. The family's named was spelled without a "u" until the author himself added it. For his explanation of the new spelling, see Leland H. Cox, ed., *William Faulkner: A Biographical and Reference Guide* (Detroit: Gale Research Co., 1982), 4.

17. William Faulkner, *Sartoris* (1929; reprint, New York: Random House, 1956), 9; *The Sound and the Fury* (1929; reprint, New York: Random House, 1966), 404; *Light in August* (1932; reprint, New York: Random House, 1967), 228.

18. Howe, *William Faulkner*, 264.

19. Joseph Blotner, *William Faulkner's Library: A Catalogue* (Charlottesville: Univ. Press of Virginia, 1964), 34–36, 41. See also Dickerson, "Thomas Sutpen," 74. Though each of the three books have inscriptions in Faulkner's handwriting dated September 1932, this did not necessarily mean that he had only then acquired these volumes. His copy of *Sut Lovingood* was one owned long before by his grandfather. Milton Rickels, *George Washington Harris* (New York: Twayne Publishers, 1965), 128.

20. Jean Stein, "William Faulkner: An Interview," in *William Faulkner: Three Decades of Criticism*, eds. Frederick J. Hoffman and Olga W. Vickery (East Lansing: Michigan State Univ. Press, 1951–60), 79; Rickels, *George Washington Harris*, 128. Indeed, one wonders if Faulkner derived the name Sutpen from Lovingood's first name.

21. George W. Harris, "The Knob Dance: A Tennessee Frolic," in *High Times and Hard Times: Sketches and Tales by George Washington Harris*, ed. M. Thomas Inge (Nashville: Vanderbilt Univ. Press, 1967), 46.

22. Quoted in F.O. Matthiessen, *American Renaissance: Art and Expression in the Age of Emerson and Whitman* (New York: Oxford Univ. Press, 1941), 642.

23. Emmett Gowen, *Mountain Born* (Indianapolis: Bobbs-Merrill Co., 1932), 235–36.

24. Grace Lumpkin, *To Make My Bread* (New York: Macauley, 1932), 144–45, 230, 86.

25. Robert Cantwell, "The Faulkners: Recollections of a Gifted Family," in *William Faulkner*, Hoffman and Vickory, 57.

26. William Brewer, "Moonshining in Georgia," *Cosmopolitan* 23 (June 1897), 132, quoted in Nina Silber, *The Romance of Reunion: Northerners and the South, 1865–1900* (Chapel Hill: Univ. of North Carolina Press, 1993), 144; Ellen Churchill Semple, "The Anglo-Saxons of the Kentucky Mountains: A Study in Anthropogeography," in *Appalachian Images in Folk and Popular Culture*, 2d ed., ed. W.K. McNeil (Knoxville: Univ. of Tennessee Press, 1995), 151. For a fuller discussion of this issue, see John C. Inscoe, "Race and Racism in Nineteenth-Century Appalachia: Myths, Realities, and Ambiguities," in *Appalachia in the Making: The Mountain South in the Nineteenth Century*, eds. Mary Beth Pudup, Dwight B. Billings, and Altina L. Waller (Chapel Hill: Univ. of North Carolina Press, 1995), 103–31.

27. Walter Lynwood Fleming, *A Documentary History of Reconstruction*, vol. 1 (Cleveland: A.H. Clark, 1906–7), 81–82.

28. Horace Kephart, *Our Southern Highlanders* (New York: Outing, 1913), 453–54.

29. John C. Campbell, *The Southern Highlander and His Homeland* (New York: Russell Sage, 1921), 94–95.

30. On the racial demographics of Appalachia, see Robert P. Stuckert, "Black Populations of the Southern Appalachian Mountains," *Phylon* 48 (June 1987): 141–51; and James B. Murphy, "Slavery and Freedom in Appalachia: Kentucky as a Demographic Case Study," *Register of the Kentucky Historical Society* 80 (1982): 151–69.

31. See, for example, Richard B. Drake, "Slavery and Antislavery in Appalachia," *Appalachian Heritage* 14 (winter 1986): 25–33; John C. Inscoe, *Mountain Masters: Slavery and the Sectional Crisis in Western North Carolina* (Knoxville: Univ. of Tennessee Press, 1989); Kenneth W. Noe, *Southwest Virginia's Railroad: Modernization and the Sectional Crisis* (Urbana: Univ. of Illinois Press, 1994); Robert Tracey McKenzie, "Wealth and Income: The Preindustrial Structure of East Tennessee," *Appalachian Journal* 21 (spring 1994): 260–79; Mary Beth Pudup, "Social Class and Economic Development in Southeastern Kentucky, 1820–1880," in *Appalachian Frontiers: Settlement, Society, and Development in the Preindustrial Era*, Robert D. Mitchell (Lexington: Univ. Press of Kentucky, 1991), 235–60; and Martin Crawford, "Political Society in a Southern Mountain Community: Ashe County, North Carolina, 1850–1860," *Journal of Southern History* 55 (Aug. 1989): 373–90.

The breadth of scholarship on race in Appalachia is reflected in two essay collections: William H. Turner and Edward J. Cabbell, eds., *Blacks in Appalachia* (Lexington: Univ. Press of Kentucky, 1985); and John C. Inscoe, ed., *Appalachia in Black and White:*

*Historical Perspectives on Race Relations in the Mountain South* (Lexington: Univ. Press of Kentucky, forthcoming).

32. Recent explorations of these views include Turner and Cabbell, *Blacks in Appalachia,* 21, 201; Drake, "Slavery and Antislavery in Appalachia"; Inscoe, *Mountain Masters,* chap. 5; Inscoe, "Race and Racism in Nineteenth Century Appalachia," 108–12, 116–18; David W. Bowen, *Andrew Johnson and the Negro* (Knoxville: Univ. of Tennessee Press, 1989), 15–16; Kenneth W. Noe, "Toward the Myth of Unionist Appalachia, 1865–1883," in *Appalachian Adaptations to a Changing World,* ed., Norma Myers, *Journal of the Appalachian Studies Association* 6(1994): 73–80; and Durwood Dunn, *An Abolitionist in the Appalachian South: Ezekiel Birdseye on Slavery, Capitalism, and Separate Statehood in East Tennessee, 1841–1846* (Knoxville: Univ. of Tennessee Press, 1997).

33. W.J. Cash, *The Mind of the South* (New York: Alfred A. Knopf, 1941), 219.

# A Judicious Combination of Incident and Psychology

## John Fox Jr. and the Southern Mountaineer Motif

*Darlene Wilson*

Midway through 1894, Theodore Roosevelt had not yet been challenged by the exigencies of either war or presidential succession and still had time to indulge his considerable passion for history, anthropology, and literature. Into his ever-growing circle of American men of letters, he welcomed a new writer, a central Kentucky native named John William Fox Jr. (1862–1919), whose romantic fiction set in the southern Appalachian Mountains was featured in three installments by a national magazine that summer. Samples of correspondence between Fox and his new admirer survive; one letter from Roosevelt, dated June 21, 1894, especially illustrates the tone of their budding friendship:

> What you said in your letter (about Southern mountaineers) . . . was so interesting that last night I read it to Cabot Lodge and Henry Adams, with whom I was dining. If you ever come up through Washington I want you to meet both of them. We will have a dinner with them. . . . Mrs. Lodge, however, emphatically objected to your statement that "if the women took baths and the men didn't shoot each other in the back," they would be first class characters, on the ground that she saw no earthly reason why you should apparently condone the offense of the men not taking baths, or think that cleanliness was essential to only the one sex.[1]

Thus we find one nonchalant route for the easy dissemination of Appalachian, or "southern mountaineer," stereotypes.

Scholars of southern literature and in the Appalachian studies movement have long been alert to John Fox Jr.; a typical analysis is that he possessed minor talent as a fiction writer but enjoyed phenomenal success as the result of fortuitous timing.[2] A beneficiary of the "local color" literary trend that swept

America in the late nineteenth century, Fox capitalized on the success of Mary Noailles Murfree (aka Charles Egbert Craddock) and others to offer his self-described "scientific analysis" of Appalachian, or southern mountaineer, exceptionalism. In his many lectures and readings between 1894 and 1910, Fox revealed talents for singing, banjo playing, mimicry, and dramatic staging and was praised in press accounts for his entertaining, if demeaning, renditions of mountain speech and structures of feeling. While Fox, solely on his own, did not invent the stereotypical "hillbilly" that prevailed soon after the turn of this century, as the essays in this volume vividly demonstrate, he indeed popularized, or situated in the emergent national consciousness, a "docufictional" exposition of Appalachian culture that has had remarkable longevity.[3]

Elsewhere, I have argued that, given his personal interest in exploiting the coal and other resources of Kentucky and Virginia, Fox may best represent "the felicitous convergence of mythmaking and capital accumulation."[4] Fox's literary longevity has been remarkable, echoing Roosevelt's prediction in 1894 that his work had "in it the element of permanence."[5] Seventy-five years after his death, the University Press of Kentucky continues to print two of his short novels, *Little Shepherd of Kingdom Come* (1903) and *Trail of the Lonesome Pine* (1907), as well as a collection of allegedly true accounts of life, law, and regional tensions in Kentucky, *Bluegrass and Rhododendron* (1901).[6] The Fox shelf totals ten lean volumes, featuring self-contained novels and collections of short stories and essays. Several, already in second and third printings, were reissued following his death from pneumonia in 1919 at the age of fifty-six; a Revolutionary War novel then in progress was finished and released in 1920 by his two sisters.[7] Throughout the last decade of his life, Fox negotiated with copyright attorneys, agents, playwrights, scriptwriters, producers, and other representatives of an emerging American film industry who all recognized the broad market appeal of his plotlines. For his *Southern Mountaineer Filmography*, Jerry Williamson located synopses of plots and/or surviving prints of thirteen movies between 1914 and 1961 that were attributed to a story, plot, or title by John Fox Jr. From data for other entries on that fascinating list, one could easily argue that another fifty or more films were inspired by the recurrent themes popularized by Fox, and most were produced during the silent-film years, the critical phase, according to Williamson's analysis, in the re-presentation of popular stereotypes about mountain people. The result was that set of embodied sight gags—a buxom, scantily dressed, mountain she-cat and her lazy, unkempt male relatives clutching either a Revolutionary War–era firearm, a jug of moonshine, a flea-covered hound, or any combination of the three—that would, along with the banjo and outhouse adorned with the quarter-moon, become such fixtures of Appalachian identity in the national consciousness.[8] Instantly recognizable caricatures for mass consumption, these hillbillies are thus assigned a totemic value—always lower in class or status—such that white Americans wanting desperately to believe in a three-class (or more) structure could breathe a sigh of relief. "See," they could say, "that's the bottom for white folks and we're not like that at all," thus confirming their idealized middle-class self-positioning. An intriguing chicken-or-egg dilemma should be of interest to historians, anthropologists, and sociologists: that is, which came first? Marginalization or misbehavior?

Of Fox's popularity, other intriguing questions can be immediately identified. The first—why white Americans in 1894 seemed so desperately to need Fox's reassuring messages confirming their (and his own) middle-class status and respectability—has been asked and, to some extent, answered. Over the last two decades, many historians and other cogent critics have come to agree that, between 1880 and 1920, white, native-born Americans experienced several severe social and economic traumas. The period from Reconstruction to World War I witnessed rapid industrialization and a phenomenal growth in the number and size of major metropolitan areas fed by intense if cyclical migration from the rural South as well as from eastern and southern Europe. Within those metropolitan areas and elsewhere, white Americans could not escape the fallout from the resultant prolonged labor conflicts, political scandals, and populist agitation for major economic reforms to redistribute both wealth and access to the opportunities for economic advancement. Out of these crises of identity and purpose, whites fashioned legislative remedies, such as anti-immigration laws and the institutionalization of "Jim Crow." They also fashioned culture-drenched economic bandages for social control, such as extralegal labor practices that enforced rigid gender differentiation and race segregation. Whites conducted "100% Americanization" campaigns in the schools and neighborhoods of European immigrants, African Americans, and southern mountaineers. Together these corrective measures acted to purge Americanism of any taint of otherness. Homogeneity topped the agenda; some white-enough men (including several so-called "race leaders" of mixed African American ancestry) were allowed into the inner circle, but women, as well as dark(er)-skinned Americans, Asian immigrants, and Hispanics, remained categorized as "others." Many were also contained in "domestic spheres," ghettos, shantytowns, and barrios that remained outside the boundaries of polite male-class(ed) America. By 1920, Appalachia, at least superficially, had come to better resemble the national norm of a society with two classes—men and not-men—and two castes—people of color and the uncolored.[9]

The second question presents a regional twist on the question of need. What utility did the hillbilly stereotypes pose for residents of Kentucky, Virginia, Tennessee, and other partly mountainous states? When did southern mountaineers rebel against the hillbilly motif and resituate its physical and psychic traits onto residents of eastern Kentucky? For Kentuckians elsewhere, did the Kentucky mountaineer stereotype not serve a similar purpose of reinforcing middle-class consciousness, taking into consideration that class identity is often rendered in oppositional terms: i.e., what one (or one's class) is not? The production of Robert Schenkkan's *The Kentucky Cycle* on the campus of the University of Kentucky (and his 1992 Pulitzer Prize for the same) suggests that the hillbilly-Other remains available for exploitation and expropriation by needy whit(ened) elites within the state and beyond its borders.[10] Asked later to explain his "immediate" literary and performing success, Fox reflected that he had used his musical talents to build a foolproof sense of continuity within and among his compositions. In a statement laden with ominous undertones for Fox's literary career *and* his "southern mountaineer," he prescribed a foolproof recipe for successful stereotyping that mixes echoic and cyclical dimensions critical to thematic reinforcement:

> Now I had always been able to twang or thump an instrument by ear and I noticed that every song or waltz always went back to the key in which it started. I noticed too that if I was interrupted at the piano and left it hurriedly, I had to go back and sound the dominant note of the key in which I had been playing—*the emotional circuit had to be completed*. I wondered if that idea would not be a good one for short stories so I wrote the stories . . . as practices in condensation and after that musical idea. [Emphasis added.][11]

This essay explores, in the case of John Fox's own emotional circuitry, the creation and perpetuation of stereotypes as the outcome of fortuitous timing and psychological need. A recent interpretation by Altina Waller explored relevant aspects of Fox's role but fell short of an astute analysis due to incomplete research.[12] She and others have suggested that a Kentucky variant of New South boosterism motivated Fox to calculate a popular rendition of mountain cultural stereotypes and encouraged his readers to accept his interpretation as authoritative.[13] In another reading, a particularly astute one for gender, he can be located as a practitioner-in-fiction of "the romance of reunion," a popular gendered discourse, expressly sexual, in late-nineteenth-century literary efforts that aimed to bury the bloody shirts of the Civil War and Reconstruction.[14] While these interpretations indeed launch a critical analysis, neither approaches the full complexity of Fox's role and significance in the creation of southern mountaineer stereotypes.

I argue that, in contrast to the fiction of Mary Noailles Murfree, dismissed by one critic for her "excessive" appreciation of some "ancient mountain Arcady," Fox chose his subject material out of a more gendered ambition to rescue the degraded national reputation of southern white manhood. More explicitly, he sought to celebrate white gentlemen from the incomparable Bluegrass region of central Kentucky who had suffered an emasculating loss of integrity among both Northerners and Southerners for their Civil War stance of neutrality. Initially dismissed by editors and most critics, Fox achieved literary success by his choice of the "southern mountaineer" men and women as the culprits most responsible for the decline in status for southern (and Kentucky) manhood, by his presumption of the need for an "interpretation" of "mountain dialect" and by his self-appointment to the role of cross-cultural translator. Unlike Murfree, Fox asserted—and allowed others to assert on his behalf—that his interpretations of life in the southern Appalachian mountains were "factual," "borne of personal experience," "case histories," "scientific analyses," "anthropological," and a "great boon to the new field of sociology."[15] His overweening ambition to succeed as a literary figure and cultural commentator was complicated by sustained periods of malnutrition, debilitating prostate disease, and a complex personal quest for popularity and social security. Fox was tormented by matters of class; among the themes that lurk in his private correspondence and within his literary efforts are the Fox family's chronic poverty, his failure to make good on their sacrifices in sending him to Harvard, his own poor health and mounting medical expenses, and the Panic of 1893 that for Fox, his father, and seven brothers came as no greater burden due to their long string of unsound financial ventures and social reverses.

Out of this intriguing combination of incident and psychology would come Fox's southern mountaineer motif, a sort of reliable field guide to the spotted hillbilly, which demanded from the audience a predictable response to easily detectable features of mountain people and culture. Dirt, deception, darkness, drunkenness, defiance, and all-around moral degradation figure prominently in Fox's fiction and in his allegedly true treatments of mountain culture and natives.

The Fox motif remains popular among sight-seeing tour directors looking for the authentic Appalachian experience for their clientele of American senior citizens and foreign tourists. In 1994, the new, conservative governor of Virginia, George Allen, designated the summer production of *Trail of the Lonesome Pine* to be an official state drama, pleasing some residents and merchants in the town of Big Stone Gap. Known as the Gap, the town is located in the southwest corner of Wise County, Virginia, on the other side of Black and Pine Mountains from the Kentucky counties of Letcher, Harlan, and Bell. Since the mid-1960s, local Fox memorialists and tourism boosters have staged this production; although its script has been tinkered with for years, it remains loosely based on Fox's novel *Trail of the Lonesome Pine*. The outdoor drama has always depended upon tour bus traffic for sufficient audience revenue but on local residents and summer in-migrants, mostly volunteer, for its cast and crew. Centering on the town's traditional claim to Fox as its most famous, pseudo-native son, drama boosters perpetuate the myth first cast in advertising for the book and for its author's lectures and readings—that is, that his characters were drawn from real people living near the Gap in the last decade of the nineteenth century.

Promotional materials claim that Fox's novel and the script taken from it should be interpreted by the audience as more true than not, a "documentary" presentation of Big Stone Gap's history.[16] Although one might argue that *Trail* represents the corporate-sanctioned version of that history, nowhere in Fox's private papers nor in his nonfiction texts can one locate the means for substantiating his own or subsequent claims to authenticity or historical veracity. Yet, even today, some historians, too many journalists, and assorted in-country missionary types persist in treating Fox's novel and his other afflicted texts as primary source material without critical analysis. The latest author is, of course, Robert Schenkkan—the handout distributed at the University of Kentucky's production of *The Kentucky Cycle* listed John Fox Jr. as one of several authoritative sources recommended for audience members seeking validation of the *Cycle*'s historical veracity. Schenkkan admitted to having read John Fox's novel *Trail of the Lonesome Pine* alongside Harry Caudill's *Night Comes to the Cumberlands*. Caudill, in that and other writings during the 1960s and '70s, had also overly relied on Fox's tales and essays to explicate Kentucky's mountain culture.

In the *Trail* novel, Fox's fictional heroine, June Tolliver, is a beautiful but rarely washed mountain lass living near the Gap, a nature(d) child-sprite (possibly prepubescent) with the voice of a songbird, who falls in love with suave Jack Hale, a visiting mining engineer of a higher social class. All in all, it is a hopeless, feud-complicated situation until Hale arranges to have her transported out of the mountains to be cleaned up, educated, and civilized in the real world of Louisville, Kentucky, and New York City. Meanwhile, back at the Gap, her lover degenerates while trying in vain to save his high-risk mining venture, which has been threatened by the ancient unfathomable feud in which June's family figures prominently. Hale's classy exterior collapses as he comes to resemble June's male kinfolk and thwarted suitors: a whiskey-guzzling, ill-dressed, bad-smelling mountaineer prone to sneaky gunplay, or so Fox describes the male population. Upon June's return to the mountains, she is able to rescue Hale from his degraded state and declining fortunes by first getting him clean and sober(ed) and then marrying him, thereby securing his access to her father's remaining coal lands. More important, she returns in time to remind him (and her huge, ill-washed family) of the "civilized world" he almost lost by going native. Thus her first task at home is to establish a "clean," flower-bedecked, 100 percent American household, according to the Bluegrass and blue-blood models of higher culture that she has been taught to recreate anywhere, even "imprisoned" at home in impoverished "mountain fastnesses." This synopsis, I argue, is the Fox motif in a nutshell, although it is appropriate to note that the modern script performed in the summer of 1995 in the Gap contained less references to body odor and more to alleged mountain habits of incest than did the original text.

From Roosevelt's dinner-table repartee to the nation's collective ear, then, the Fox motif thrives and remains visible, only slightly modified a century later in hillbilly iconography and in stereotype-drenched reinterpretations of contemporary Appalachia.[17] The tenor of the Fox-Roosevelt correspondence, and even the dinner party at which Fox's views were shared, is more comprehensible if we recall that all shared the Harvard connection and, in their various writings, a self-consciously white, patriarchal propensity for theorizing about matters of class, gender, and race. Although there is no evidence that John Fox ever got his promised dinner with Lodge or Adams, his career as an author was indeed given a boost by his collaborative friendship with Roosevelt, who recommended Fox's ideas and forwarded his queries to literary acquaintances. One was Owen Wister, a Philadelphia lawyer and author of *The Virginian*—the type of white-winged, manly fiction the future president admired. Wister read "young Fox" and immediately wrote an admiring note of congratulations, predicting the Kentuckian would "prove to be a judicious combination of incident and psychology."[18]

I consider Wister's casually scribbled remark to be prophetic. Certainly Fox's financial situation and social status were immediately enhanced by his new social acquaintances: at the very time that his correspondence with Roosevelt began, Fox was involved in court proceedings over his family's substantial debts, and, throughout his life, he contrived to obscure the fact that his Harvard education had been provided by the Garth Fund for Poor Boys in Bourbon County, Kentucky. Within months of their first exchange of letters, Roosevelt invited him to join his Rough Riders in the excursion against Spain in Cuba, but Fox had to decline since he couldn't afford to buy the required horse and gear. With Roosevelt's intervention, however, he managed to secure a last-minute "speculative" assignment as a journalist for *Harper's Weekly* when that journal's first-choice, Casper Whitney, received a late, better-paying offer from a rival periodical before the convoy sailed from Tampa.

Suffering only a persistent case of unpleasant but nonlethal "campaign fever," Fox returned from Cuba to resume his literary career newly enthused by the righteousness of Euro-American racism and expansionism. Also significant (both socially and professionally) was the overtly militaristic camaraderie he shared for the rest of his life with Roosevelt and with his campaign "bunkmates," author/journalist Richard Harding Davis and artist Frederick Remington. Davis once telegraphed Fox to "hurry on with a blue serge suit" to be a groomsman at his wedding and later gave him one of two job offers he had received to "report" the Russian-Japanese War in 1904–1905 for British and American readers. Remington regularly referred to Fox and himself as "Bunkies" and even offered to illustrate one of Fox's mountaineer stories if he could write one with "no damned women."[19]

Fox has been described as the "ideal summer man," a pleasant and entertaining houseguest "adored" by his hostesses. His letters to family members between 1894 and 1910 show that he was judiciously adept at stretching out visits to his new friends for several months.[20] According to several existing accounts, for both his for-fee and for-free (hostess-pleasing) performances, Fox simply added the now ubiquitous banjo to the content of his literary "act"— "true" anecdotes he pretended to have personally witnessed in his mountain travels, and a large repertoire of witty caricatures offered as interpretations or translations of southern upcountry speech, social stratification, and sexuality.[21] Letters of appreciation and newspaper clippings in the Fox family scrapbooks suggest that his live performance constituted a sort of white-tie minstrel show that offered confirmation of class identity for elitist audiences who responded eagerly to Fox's style of genteel titillation.

Fox's eldest brother, James, later claimed to be one of two models for the character of Jack Hale in *Trail of the Lonesome Pine.*[22] Since 1878, James had steadily drawn the entire family—including his stepmother, "The Madame," and two half-sisters—into his web of dreams to control the infant bituminous coal industry in Northeast Tennessee, eastern Kentucky, and Southwest Virginia. In 1890, James relocated his recently bankrupted parents and six of nine younger siblings from central Kentucky to the site of Three Forks, Virginia. Located strategically at the larger of two gaps in Stone Mountain and one gateway to the famous Powell Valley and Cumberland Gap, Three Forks was a small but established Euro-American community that, for centuries before resettlement circa 1800, was well known and inhabited, according to their cultural terms, by Native Americans and their mixed-heritage descendants. If anything, according to early-nineteenth-century resistance leaders among the Shawnee and Cherokee and later to observers on both sides of the Civil War, the area was too well known for its abundant water and mineral riches, not to mention its proximity to Cumberland Gap and the peak of Pine Mountain at Pound Gap on the Kentucky-Virginia border. Hardly isolated from the "chariot-wheels" of civilization, as Fox would later claim, the area's inhabitants, I argue, were often on the leading edge of socio-cultural fusion, confusion, and diffusion.[23]

Yet Three Forks was erased from social memory and formally renamed Big Stone Gap after 1888 by absentee rail and coal investors working through a cadre of trusted southerners who were on the ground in Southwest Virginia, upper East Tennessee, and eastern Kentucky. Several in this cadre, including

James, were from Lexington or Louisville, Kentucky. After his graduation from Harvard in 1883, John himself became an integral absentee player in promoting interest and continued investment in schemes involving the Gap and its surrounding wealth of bituminous coal and timber. Both brothers preferred to live in or near New York while allowing their father and younger brothers to oversee matters in the mountains. Despite his claims to authenticity, John's experiences in the mountains and with mountain people were strictly self-limited—he despised his family's home as "commonplace" and retreated there only when his pockets were empty, his presence was required for his own bankruptcy or other court proceedings, or when more interesting invitations were not at hand. With the exception of some brief early visits (mainly in the summer of 1882) and one two-week business trip for his brother, John avoided the mountains and gleaned his material from James, his younger brothers still living at home, and other coalfield speculators. In fact, James or one of his partners personally viewed and edited John's earliest "sketches," which were written and offered to the New York-based commercial newspapers as vital components of an aggressive marketing campaign seeking investments for coal and timber exploitation in the southern Appalachian region. Later, his "true" lectures and essays were also submitted for approval to his brother and certain close business associates.

Working from their accounts of prospecting for mineral rights in the postbellum upcountry, where male residents still expressed deep alienation from mainstream southern manhood, Fox toyed sporadically from 1886 with a short story titled "A Cumberland Vendetta." He wanted then to write plays and act himself and, I would argue, developed his stories with that goal clearly in mind. In plot and action, the story mimicked other popular melodramas with themes of "feuding families" reminiscent of Shakespeare's *Romeo and Juliet*, but was thought sufficiently unusual by editors at *Century* for serialization in 1894. The first installment introduced the combatants and forlorn lovers from opposing families, the Stetsons and the Lewallens. Fox's cast was composed of manly, mischievous men and winsome women (in want of a good wash) whose queer culture and dialect were rendered more intelligible via the narrator's rearticulation. Earlier drafts were far less readable, according to *Century* editor R.W. Gilder, who sent the story back to Fox for the second time on April 12, 1893, citing "still too much talky-talk by the author" and a "tendency to expressions" and "trite sentimentalities" often found in "amateur fiction." He also sounded a warning about Fox's written rendition of what Gilder described as "southern" speech: "Please let up a little on the dialect! . . . This 'hit' business is getting to be a little tiresome. It is not understood by most readers, and it actually takes one's breath away. There is a reaction against dialect anyway, and the less of it the better."[24]

Grudgingly Fox made some of the changes suggested by Gilder but argued to keep some "mountain dialect in the dialogue." This dialect, he had learned from a sound authority, was "of late proven to be distinctly Chaucerian in origin," a "colonial relic" that had become imprisoned in mountain speech patterns. Gilder asked for still more revisions, but the author was abed ill, convalescing from an attack of his chronic prostate problem, so the draft that went to the printers offered straight English narration interspersed with dialogue that was described in promotional literature as "authentic representations of Chaucerian-era speech." This last draft, as it appeared in print, so excited Theodore Roosevelt that he wrote immediately to Fox on stationery borrowed from his employer, the U.S. Civil Service Commission. "I hope you will excuse this informality in address, coming from a fellow-Harvard man who wishes to congratulate you most heartily. . . . I am glad you have avoided the dialect pit. . . . Dialect is a good adjunct for a feast, but it is very poor as a feast itself."[25]

C.E.L. Wingate, another Harvard connection (like Fox, a member of the Class of 1883), was the managing editor of the *Boston Journal* when his old classmate's story appeared. He too reported his delight in Fox's story for its "simplicity of narrative and strength of sentimental interest."[26]

The following year, the story re-appeared as a book which was offered as "authentic" and "true experiences," the same terms used to promote Fox's si-multaneous, self-promotional reading tour for the Southern Lyceum Bureau. An extensive, carefully mounted collection of clippings from this tour and the book's reception are preserved in the Fox family scrapbooks in archives at the University of Kentucky. These clippings provide an intimate glimpse of the family's delight in Fox's growing popularity but also offer the modern reader bittersweet insight into a widespread willingness among newspaper staffs across the growing nation to accept his renditions as accurate depictions of reality. One Chicago newspaper assured its readers that, unlike other mountain-based fiction, *A Cumberland Vendetta* was "the history of the famous Stetson-Lewallen feud." The *Buffalo Express* recommended this "quasi-fictional treat-ment of well-authenticated cases . . . one of those strange family feuds in which sire and sons live for little else than to kill off the men of some neighboring family."

Approving critics extrapolated idly from the title that the story was set on either side of the Cumberland River; in the Cumberland Mountains of either Kentucky, eastern Tennessee, or West Virginia; or on the Cumberland Plateau of Kentucky. Their summaries rained praise upon Fox's "true descriptions" of these sites as dangerous "border lands" whose "rude and unlettered" inhabitants feared "furriners" from the "settlements" and shared a common indigenous bent for "sly-ness," and other "crudities and oddities." While geographic confusion was wide-spread, no one publicly challenged Fox's claims to authenticity. The *Christian*

*Register* of Boston thought Fox's readers got a "sense of reality" from "this sketch of mountains and morals as they influence conduct among the mountaineers of the Cumberland *Valley*." The *Rochester (N.Y.) Herald* termed it a "believable and vigorous story . . . picturing life among the 'pore white trash' in the *Cumberland hill country* . . . [where] there are no large events so family feuds and neighborhood jealousies take the place of questions of state, the settlement of which require skill in handling firearms, rather than the mastery of diplomacy." From Boston, a reader reported to the *Herald* his shock in learning that "under cover of our civilization there are yet remote places where the white heat of passion knows no legal restraints" and worried that these Cumberland mountaineers might well represent "an ineffaceable component element of American life." The *New York Review of Reviews* found it appropriate that a *journalist* like Fox could find "social value" in his "explorations and study of the lawless mountain regions of the *Southwest*," a curious geographic placement indeed.

A unique critique was offered by Graham Jones of Chicago, who was so impressed after two readings of Fox's story that he proposed adapting it for a "truly American (U.S. of North American!) opera."

> There is the elementary, rugged, barbaric simplicity about the mountaineer . . . with the background of his native wild hills and black ravines, and the melancholy tone of his folk song affords a sombre dramatic quality, which softened by an idealized atmosphere of love, can be made to mirror with rare beauty the heart of man . . . that would leave the audience with a feeling of renewed hope in life and let them go home with a sweet taste in their mouths . . . a work of art, yet one which shall appeal to the masses.[27]

To be fair, Fox's first book received a very mixed set of reviews. One editor charged (and others echoed the indictment) that "by means of thick paper and very broad margins" a long story had been made into "a fair-sized book" but "the publishers would have been treating their customers with more fairness had they included two stories at the price." Several critics chided the author for plowing old ground with worn-out plotlines and tired styling, but others admired his flair for describing the natural beauty of the region while faithfully rendering the gritty lifestyle of its rude residents. The *St. Louis Christian Advocate* thought *Vendetta* "fell far short of the standard set by Miss Murfree," although the *Boston Watchman* thought her arena of expertise had been "invaded and exploited by a completely successful rival."

The *Pittsburg (Pa.) Bulletin* found *Vendetta* to be a refreshing departure from Miss Murfree's "artistic survivals of long-lost Arcady." By contrast, the Pittsburg reviewer wrote, Fox's characters were "just plain ruffians, bloodthirsty and ignorant to a degree that may inspire some gentle Japanese reader with a 'call' to come over and convert the savages of Kentucky and Tennessee." Mountain humanity could only be salvaged when old generations died out and new ones were trained to civilization, or so the reviewer argued. After all, Fox's hero was "a step upwards, for he only wants to murder when his own life is in danger," and the heroine was still "a trifle bovine but also an improvement on her parents."

Not all readers shared an appetite for the dialect, but many offered assessments of Fox's approach to its textual representation. The *New York Outlook* found that "like Miss Murfree, he reproduces dialect to an extent that becomes wearisome." On the other hand, the *Bee* of Omaha, Nebraska, found Fox's minimalist approach to dialect quite superior to Murfree's: "It is a dialect that, like Uncle Remus' negro talk, may be easily understood." A new acquaintance, J.B. Aldrich of Boston, promised to take the book "with me on the yacht" and "fight it out to the finish" with the dialect. Another new friend, R.U. Johnson of New York, shared the book with his houseguests, Mr. and Mrs. Rudyard Kipling, and invited John to meet and dine with them in order that the great Kipling could satisfy his longing to hear the dialect read aloud by a true "expert" such as Fox.[28]

Fox had quickly sketched a sequel to *A Cumberland Vendetta* to be released simultaneously with the stretched-out novel. For "The Conviction of Isom Stetson," he disregarded Gilder's advice and employed a first-person narrative device for the character of young Isom, the "near-idiot yet saintly" adolescent member of the feud-loving Stetson clan. Portrayed as albino-like and thus a genuine "other," Isom so suffered from bouts of feud fatigue and remorse that he was "convicted" to discontinue the next generation's turn of family warfare. Fox's rendition of Isom as a mountain "oddling" or nature child allowed to speak in his own voice was to serve as an adjunct dish, but the feast remained the *Vendetta* feud, even in its declining state. According to an initial rejection letter from Gilder, the sequel was "written in a literary falsetto" and "lacked the clarity of interpretation" that had recommended the final draft of *Vendetta*.[29]

Thus, Fox's career was shaped since he ever afterward retreated to a handful of portable plotlines, all bearing his own "fungible motif": the benevolent outsider or narrator essentially acting as mediator or interpreter for the southern mountaineer, to explain away odd speech patterns, irregular behavior, and quaint customs.[30] The emotional circuitry was always distinct. In fiction and in allegedly true essays, he argued that this interpretation was necessary because mountain folk were so bereft of hope and bewildered by modernity that they were virtually mute. Not only did mountain people seem incapable of self-agency, even had they recognized the concept they were sure to screw up the pronunciation. So, for the mountaineers' own sake and in the interests of rapid assimilation and speedy acquiescence to the new order of aggressive capitalism that had seized the southern Appalachian coalfields, Fox declared himself ready for the role of interpreter. In the words of James Lane Allen, another Kentucky author and an intimate friend of Fox's brother James, "never before had a primitive people been so in need of benevolent interpretation" such as that "Fox was uniquely qualified to provide" on the lecture circuit and in his fiction.[31] As one unidentified reader wrote in a review pasted into a family scrapbook, the reader followed Fox's storyline "not only to be amused at his characters but longing to be helpful to them." Following his personal appearance and reading on campus, students at Vassar College were so overwhelmed with sympathy for Fox's mountain characters—"silent and pathetic remnants of the pioneer days"—that a scholarship fund was gotten up for a "superior-speaking mountain girl," if one could be located. Meanwhile the author was invited to become an honorary member of Vassar's Southern Club.[32]

Gabrielle Marie Jacobs, writing for *Scribner's*, caught up with the author on his 1895 tour and conducted a personal interview. She praised his soulful empathy for his mountaineer subjects, which she understood to be "pale, listless, melancholy creatures—the dust from the chariot-wheels of colonial civilization—thrown high upon the hills more than a century ago" until the arrival of their benevolent interpreter, John Fox, who "broke the monotony of the lives of their women and children with such conversation as their stunted minds and starved souls could comprehend." Of his claim to having developed an innovative approach to local color and story gathering, she wrote: "With ready tact, and the wisdom born of his journalistic training, he threw aside his university polish of speech and manner and the boyish, brown-haired, blue-eyed 'furriner,' seemingly too guileless to be a revenue officer, was welcomed everywhere. . . . With *pardonable duplicity,* he played a different role with the mountaineers, assuming their garb, drawl, and mannerisms so successfully as to win their hearts" (emphasis added).[33]

A Fox family scrapbook contains an 1898 brochure from the Southern Lyceum Bureau of Louisville, Kentucky, promoting Mr. John Fox as available for "Lecture: *The Southern Mountaineer* for Schools, Colleges, and Anthropological Societies" and for "Talks: *The Kentucky Mountaineer,* Mountain Feuds, Dialect, Humor, Traits of Character, etc." The brochure offered reprints from various newspaper clippings, including one from the *Louisville Courier:* "His rendering of the mountain dialect is simple and unaffected and rings as true as Mr. [Thomas Nelson] Page's negro talk." An accidental meeting with Page in New York in the early 1880s resulted in a lifelong friendship, so Page was always glad to recommend Fox and is also cited: "He understands the dialect of the mountaineers of Virginia and Kentucky as no one else . . . and he is perfectly natural." Another commentator offered this tribute: "[Fox] relates his stories with more vigor, rush, and determination than does Miss Murfree but like her lets his characters speak in their own dialect, thus coloring their relentless hatred and their open quarrels with an intensity that would weaken in power were it interpreted by a foreign tongue."

Audiences were encouraged to expect a "realistic" or "real" interpretation of culture and dialect from both Fox the lecturer and Fox the storyteller. Following his premiere in that city, the *Boston Journal* devoted a long column to the evening's entertainment: "He is able to give to all his sketches a realistic interpretation that brings before the minds of the hearers the quaint personages whom he describes and imitates. His stories deal for the most part with the mountaineers of Kentucky, whose unique ways of life, striking peculiarities of speech, and odd methods of thought and action proved a revelation." The Boston reporter also noted that some stories had "bits of song" which "were crooned by the author pleasingly."

Fox's oral renditions of mountaineer 'langua-lect' served as a source of enlightenment to audiences outside the region. The *Augusta (Ga.) Chronicle* trumpeted his triumph as "a delineator of the character, customs, and dialect of the Kentucky mountaineer" and praised his "fine voice and complete mastery of the dialect." The *Washington Post* thought Fox's reading before the Washington Club "the most enjoyable affair in Washington this winter" and cited his success in "giving very accurate impressions of the quaint characters . . . [who] seemed, for the moment, to be present in the flesh, so capital was Mr. Fox's imitation of the dialect and the peculiar drawl." Similarly, the *Atlanta Constitution* noted his first appearance before that city's "cultured class" for his "unconventionality" and "classically chiseled profile, a splendid brow, a good Grecian nose, and the self-reliant heaviness about the chin." His voice was "musical and deep-chested" and "could be drawn into a resonant twang when he dropped into the mountaineer dialect," but the audience could easily trace, in his "revelations" about the mountaineers, both his "secret fund of fun" and "a subtle strain of pathos on a sub-strata of rough humor."

Programs for Fox's lectures and readings survive in family scrapbooks along with several texts he used for these performances. In his public readings, he drew from his own attempts at fiction and that of Murfree and then offered a "scientific analysis of the Southern Mountaineer." After establishing that species markings, he analyzed the Kentucky subspecies. Arguing with the force of convictions that had grown in intensity since his years at Harvard (1880–1883), he protested that Kentucky's Civil War history of neutrality had caused white manhood of Bluegrass Kentucky to be falsely portrayed as "flaccid" or "flabby." He claimed that this portrayal followed from widespread confusion over the differences between the "real Southern manhood" of the Bluegrass and those unpredictable, "unknowable" residents of the mountain South whose deeds and culture had so wrecked Southern solidarity and abetted the Northern cause.

His audiences apparently accepted this argument as valid—and why not? Few of them had actually been to Kentucky and fewer subsequently aspired to go there. Thirty years after war's end, Fox repositioned the southern mountaineer type as only slightly ahead of the "uppity negro" and the new(er) immigrant as a threatening cultural and economic stereotype, but because they were almost-white, almost-men, the mountaineers posed the greatest danger as potential saboteurs of true North-South reconciliation. In this respect, I find that Fox's text resembles other pleas extant for subduing populist opposition to the goals of New South boosters.

However Fox's strongest arguments were reserved to rescue Kentucky from her decline in status among states. To do so, he reinforced the dichotomous stereotype of twin Kentuckys—mountain Kentucky, signified by its profuse undergrowth of rhododendron in which hid sneaky, murderous moonshiners, versus the Bluegrass, the civilized "outer-world" of the rest of the state. Contrary to popular press images in the 1890s, it was not Fox's chivalry-drenched Bluegrass Kentucky that was prone to political feuding in its courthouses and gun-blazing duels between well-liquored men astride fine horseflesh. No, the mountaineers were the lawless feudists, he swore, as he pointed toward the mountains and offered a guided tour of mineral lands available for purchase for a limited time via options held by either himself or his brother. Kentucky could be restored to its proper "state of manhood" only after the savage barbarians of its mountainous eastern region were properly subdued under a new economic and political order.[34]

The solution, he had concluded, was the multifaceted force for civilization that was even then, under his steerage and his family's tutelage-by-example, intruding upon this "fossilized" population in the form of railroads, coal and iron ore exploitation, timber clear-cutting, courthouse relocations, and settlement schools. The options for a national or state policy to salvage the mountain population, according to Fox's "scientific analysis," were few: assimilation if possible, depopulation when expedient, but—just in case the natives continued to prove ignorant, reluctant, or hostile to their own economic conversion—there had already occurred a few successful applications of other forms of persuasion. He pointed to state troops bringing in "the power of the outside world," judicial and police intervention in property disputes, changes of venue to "civilized courts," arbitrary use of incarceration, and even the judicious imposition of martial law and spectator punishments.

To illustrate his argument, Fox pointed to several cases of "well-earned hangings" after "the law awoke even in the mountains." One of these was the September 1892 hanging of Talt Hall in Wise County, Virginia, which took place after the new economic order of the Gap formed a "Police Guard" of Bluegrass "gentlemen" for the express purpose of "protecting private property," declared "martial law," occupied the county seat, and ensured the public spectacle of hanging a local "bad guy." The story of the hanging of Talt Hall would appear in subsequent Fox texts of various forms—in news articles, in short stories, and in his nonfiction essays.[35]

In the year before Hall was hanged, John had managed to avoid the mountains. But he arrived home to pick up his mail just in time to interpret the hanging as a cultural event for the outside world. A week later, safely back in New York City, he reported in a letter to his brother James on September 9, 1892: "Eyes gone bad on me, can't write anymore. On the hanging of Talt Hall, I had two columns in the NY Herald, one column in the NY Sun, one and half columns in the NY World and one half column in the Louisville Commercial." The recurrent tone of these columns, carefully preserved in the family's scrapbooks, is echoed in his subsequent fiction and nonfiction texts. To wit: Fox, his brothers, and other manly types from the Bluegrass had been hard-pressed to tame the mountainous regions, but with the help of a friendly set of governors, willing bankers, and pliant lawmakers, they would—armed with Winchesters, police whistles, and a strong rope—continue to protect the property of all absentee investors against the spotted hillbilly, mute and threatened but far from extinct and prone to "playing possum." The emotional circuitry of the Fox motif, I submit, remains unbroken.

From within the region, challenges to Fox's rendition(s) were swift, but these did not receive equal treatment by newspaper editors, commentators, or audiences, a situation that persists today. In 1895, a Cincinnati journalist recorded the comments of mountain-born students in Berea's student choir who had witnessed John's telling of his "true" adventures and considered his performance "insulting . . . [and] an affront" to some mountain family's hospitality. He had "proven" himself "anything but a gentleman" and the Berea students promised that "henceforth, Mr. Fox would be a most unwelcome visitor" in their home neighborhoods. One offered tar and feathers for emphasis, thus giving the reporter an excuse for portraying the Berea students as potentially dangerous.[36] Fox took the warning seriously and until 1910 avoided traveling in the Kentucky mountains if at all possible.

There was at least one literary response in opposition to Fox, a delightful, small book entitled *The Mountaineers; or, Bottled Sunshine for Blue Mondays*, published in 1902 in Nashville, Tennessee. The author is "Jean Yelsew," a pen name that inverted the real middle name of the author, one J. Wesley Smith, D.D., who stated in his introduction that he wrote "with an honest desire to do simple justice to a much maligned but noble people."

> The best-advertised people for their deficiencies and the worst maligned
> for their virtues are the so-called mountaineers. A great deal has been said,

and much has been written, about that class of our fellow-citizens whose homes are on or among the mountains . . . to one who has traveled among and lived with these people, how strange the stories we see in the newspapers and magazines! How little truth and how unlike the very characters they have undertaken to describe! Of course these writers found what they were sent to get—"a man of Straw"—and like the patent medicine man, what they did not have on hand they could easily make. Do you know of a book or a novel descriptive of mountain character, life, or dialect but what is a fabrication, whose foundation is the merest shadow or semblence of the truth? But such writers deserve a great deal of credit, for they have made more out of less material than almost any other class of writers I have read after.

A close reading of the surrounding text shows Yelsew/Smith to be a regular Methodist circuit rider in Southwest Virginia and a native mountaineer who is vexed by Fox and his ilk. His views deserve extended reproduction here:

How soon we turn missionary, and not only dilate on the magnitude, superiority, refinement, and wealth of the people in that "land of corn and wine" we left behind us, but we belabor our neighbors for their want of progressiveness, lack of enterprise, their ignorance, illiteracy, and the poverty and degradation of its people as compared with "our own." . . . So many of the stories told to the detriment of these mountaineers . . . were born in a distorted and prefilled imagination. . . .

In fact there is as much gentility, refinement, and, I may say, education among these mountain people in proportion to population, all things considered, as you will find in the valleys, village, or city. There may not be that glamour of dress, the polish of polite speech or manners which is largely made by rubbing constantly one against another in city or village . . . but there is a freedom of speech and manner that betokens the kindliness and real gentility of the lady or gentleman. . . .

Yet it is unfair—yea, unjust—to measure the whole community of mountaineers by a few feeble-minded illiterates that may be found here and there and to chide these good people with failings they do not possess. . . . But the enterprising Yankees and their colaborers, the magazine and newspaper critics, have wasted a great deal of artificial sympathy and shed a great many very salty and hypocritical tears over these unfortunate "dwellers of the Alps." When these benevolent philanthropists find "the ignorant, illiterate native" with large boundaries of untouched forests of valuable timber lands undergirded with rich veins of black diamond coal, they deplore his uncultured intellect and covet his undeveloped wealth. They long to improve his mind and to secure his property. Of course their actions are based on the "law of benevolent assimilation." Their motives are (hardly) impersonal and unselfish. . . . It's not to improve their minds, but to cabbage their mines; not to save their souls, but to secure their soil.

There are other hidden transcripts, similarly neglected, but jangling discordantly and contradicting the emotional circuitry required by American elites to maintain their illusions of superiority and their faith in aggressive capitalism. The evocative cycle, wherever encountered, must be disrupted to give these voices our ear.

## Notes

1. Roosevelt to Fox, June 21, 1894, Collection #157, Fox, John, 1863–1919, and Fox family papers, 1852–1962, at the Univ. of Kentucky, Lexington, Division of Special Collections and Archives, Margaret I. King Library. There are thirty-seven letters from T. Roosevelt to John Fox in the collection. Hereinafter cited as Fox-UK.

2. For relevant, critical analysis, see Cratis Williams, "The Southern Mountaineer in Fact and Fiction," (Ph.D. diss., Columbia Univ., 1961, "John Fox Jr., A Belated Romantic," 888ff.); Don Askins, "John Fox Jr.: A Re-Appraisal; or With Friends Like That, Who Needs Enemies?" in *Colonialism in Modern America: The Appalachian Case,* eds. Helen Lewis et al (Boone, N.C.: Appalachian Consortium Press, 1978); Henry D. Shapiro, *Appalachia on Our Mind: The Southern Mountains and Mountaineers in the American Consciousness, 1870–1920* (Chapel Hill: Univ. of North Carolina Press, 1978); Ronald D Eller, *Miners, Millhands, and Mountaineers: Industrialization of the Appalachian South, 1880–1930* (Knoxville, Tenn.: Univ. of Tennessee Press, 1982); David Whisnant, *All That Is Native and Fine* (Knoxville, Tenn.: Univ. of Tennessee Press, 1981); Allen Batteau, *The Invention of Appalachia* (Tucson: Univ. of Arizona Press, 1990); and Rodger Cunningham, "Signs of Civilization: *The Trail of Lonesome Pine* as Colonial Narrative," *Journal of Appalachian Studies Association* 2 (1990).

3. For a comprehensive treatment that raises several important issues for students of history and cultural politics, see Jerry Williamson, *Hillbillyland: What the Movies Did to the Mountains, What the Mountains Did to the Movies* (Chapel Hill: Univ. of North Carolina Press, 1995). I am borrowing this usage of "docufictional" from Williamson.

4. See Darlene Wilson, "The Felicitous Convergence of Mythmaking and Capital Accumulation: John Fox Jr. and the Formation of An(Other) Almost-White American Underclass," in *Journal of Appalachian Studies* 1:1 (fall 1995). This article summarizes some of the conclusions I have reached over four years of research into the Fox family archives at the University of Kentucky and further explores some of the themes mentioned here. My dissertation, "On the Trail of a Silver-Tongue Fox," seeks to identify which of three Fox men—John Senior, or his sons, James and Johnny—achieved the greatest long-term significance or notoriety in the history of southern Appalachia.

5. Roosevelt to Fox, August 11, 1894, in Fox-UK.

6. Indeed, the same university press acquiesced to this writer's thesis and in November 1996 republished Fox's 1913 novel, *Heart of the Hills.* See my Foreword to that volume for my view that this novel represents Fox's attempt to make amends to his mountain-based subjects and to fulfill his promise to his dying father to bring attention to the growing environmental catastrophe that accompanied deforestation, railroad

building, and exploitation of water courses near coal mines during the period from 1890 until 1912.

7. Fox, *Erskine Dale: Pioneer* (New York: Scribner's, 1920).

8. Williamson, *Hillbillyland*.

9. The literature is vast and still growing. The starting place for most is still Robert H. Weibe, *The Search for Order, 1877–1920* (New York: Hill and Wang, 1967); but for more recent studies, the reader might consider Elizabeth Ewen, *Immigrant Women in the Land of Dollars: Life and Culture on the Lower East Side, 1890–1925* (New York: Monthly Review Press, 1985); Susan A. Glenn, *Daughters of the Shtetl: Life and Labor in the Immigrant Generation* (Ithica, N.Y.: Cornell Univ. Press, 1990); Robyn Muncy, *Creating a Female Dominion in American Reform, 1890–1935* (New York: Cambridge Univ. Press, 1991); Kathleen M. Blee, *Women of the Klan: Racism and Gender in the 1920s* (Berkeley: Univ. of California Press, 1991); Patricia Morton, *Disfigured Images: The Historical Assault on Afro-American Women* (New York: Praeger, 1991); Anne Firor Scott, *Natural Allies: Women's Associations in American History* (Champaign: Univ. of Illinois Press, 1992); W. Fitzhugh Brundage, *Lynching in the New South: Georgia and Virginia, 1880–1930* (Champaign: Univ. of Illinois Press, 1993); Eileen Boris, *Home To Work: Motherhood and the Politics of Industrial Homework in the United States* (New York: Cambridge Univ. Press, 1994); Mary E. Odem, *Delinquent Daughters: Protecting and Policing Female Sexuality in the United States, 1885–1920* (Chapel Hill: Univ. of North Carolina Press, 1995); Nancy F. Cott, "Giving Character to Our Whole Civil Polity: Marriage and the Public Order in the Late Nineteenth Century," in Kerber, Kessler-Harris, and Sklar, eds., *U.S. History as Women's History: New Feminist Essays* (Chapel Hill: Univ. of North Carolina Press, 1995), 107 passim. An excellent review of the broad implications of these themes can be found in Teresa Amott and Julie Matthaei, "Race, Class, Gender, and Women's Works," in *Race, Gender and Work: A Multi-Cultural Economic History of Women in the United States* (Boston: South End Press, 1996). Some insight into my own research into the intersections of race, class, and gender in Appalachian history may be gleaned on-line, via: <http://pluto.clinch.edu/appalachia/melungeon/dw_proj1.htm>

10. For a theoretical discussion worthy of consideration on the issue of self-representation and the power of seductive assimilation, see Robert Cantwell, *Ethnomimesis: Folklife and the Representaion of Culture* (Chapel Hill: Univ. of North Carolina Press, 1993).

11. See unpublished autobiographical essay in the Fox family papers.

12. Altina Waller, "Feuding in Appalachia: Evolution of a Cultural Stereotype," in Mary Beth Pudup et al, *Appalachia in the Making: The Mountain South in the Nineteenth Century* (Chapel Hill: Univ. of North Carolina Press, 1995), 347 passim. Waller fails to acknowledge Johnny's poverty or that of his family and completely ignores the role of elder brother James Fox. She also ignores James's intimate involvement with Henry Watterston of the *Louisville Courier-Journal* (another major player in her interpretation) and James's reliance on Johnny as a paid publicist for his own coal and railroad ventures.

13. See, e.g., Eller, Whisnant, Batteau, cited in note 2 above.

14. Nina Silber, *The Romance of Reunion: Northerners and the South, 1865–1900* (Chapel Hill: Univ. of North Carolina Press, 1993).

15. All quotes here were found in clippings preserved in Fox family scrapbooks, Fox-UK.

16. See *Trail of the Lonesome Pine* program, produced and printed by *The Post*, Big Stone Gap, Virginia, an NPI Media Services newspaper, also published as an insert for the *Coalfield Progress*, Norton, Virginia, in June 1994, June 1995, June 1996, and June 1997. In an article included in the 1994 program, "The Truth about the Trail," an anonymous writer asserts, "*The Trail of the Lonesome Pine* is a delightful documentary of the development of law and order and industry and the life of the folk who lived in the mountains."

17. Recent stereotype-drenched reinterpretations that lean heavily on the Fox motif include Robert Schenkkan's 1992 play, *The Kentucky Cycle*, discussed elsewhere in this volume, and the recent "sermonette" by Anthony Salatino, *Will Appalachia Finally Overcome Poverty?* (Kuttawa, Ky.: McClanahan Publishing, 1995).

18. Owen Wister to John Fox Jr., dated "Wednesday, May 8," no year given but probably 1895, in Fox-UK.

19. For these and other letters from Remington, Davis, and others, see correspondence files, Fox-UK.

20. For "ideal summer man" quote, see anonymous introduction written and delivered at one of Fox's lectures, in file labeled "Biographical Materials" in Fox-UK. Also see correspondence between Fox and Thomas Nelson Page, whose wife designated a bedroom as "always ready for dear Johnny" Fox at their Virginia mansion as well as at their Rock Harbor summer estate in Maine; also see letters from Mrs. Page and her daughter Florence, Edith and Alice Roosevelt, Cecil Davis, and other grateful hostesses.

21. See Fox family scrapbooks for letters of condolence from Roosevelt's widow and daughter, following Fox's sudden death from pneumonia in 1919. Also see scrapbooks for 1894–1905 for reviews of his lectures. These scrapbooks, assembled by the family, underwent several revisions, and many of the clippings are undated.

22. The other was R.C. Ballard-Thruston of Louisville, Kentucky.

23. Darlene Wilson, "Multi-Cultural Mayhem and Murder in Virginia's Backcountry: The Case of Pierre-Francois Tubeuf, 1792–95," *Journal of Appalachian Studies* 4:1 (spring 1998).

24. R. Gilder to John Fox Jr., April 12, 1893, in Fox-UK correspondence files; also see scrapbook labeled "Cumberland Vendetta."

25. Theodore Roosevelt to John Fox Jr., June 4, 1894; reprinted in *The Letters of Theodore Roosevelt, vol. 1, The Years of Preparation, 1868–1898*, (Cambridge, Mass.: Harvard Univ. Press, 1951), 384.

26. Fox family scrapbook #2, in Fox-UK.

27. Fox family scrapbook #2, in Fox-UK.

28. Aldrich and Johnson letters in correspondence files, 1895, in Fox-UK.

29. R.W. Gilder to John Fox Jr., August 3, 1894, in Fox-UK.

30. Use of the term "fungible motif" rests on my understanding of the term as used by University of Kentucky political theorist Herbert Reid in "Global Adjustments,

Throwaway Regions, Pulitzer Prizes: Resituating *The Kentucky Cycle* on the Postmodern Frontier," 1995, revised version elsewhere in this volume.

31. From promotional brochure, in Fox family scrapbook, in Fox-UK.

32. Clippings from Vassar College reading in Fox family scrapbook, in Fox-UK.

33. Fox's claim to having conducted undercover research cannot be substantiated. In fact, his encounters with so-called mountain folk are relatively unremarkable prior to 1885, or so we must surmise. After 1895, he avoided the mountains of eastern Kentucky and some corners of Southwest Virginia; not until after 1910 would he attempt to travel freely through the mountains, and even then Fox was cautious about revealing his true identity to mountain folk. I have found one verifiable autograph (now in my personal collection) by Fox written for a "mountain resident"; it is scribbled on the back of an L&N train schedule and reads: "John Fox Jr. 1903– *Guilty* of 'Hell-fer' Sartin' and other stories of home-life in the *South*" (Fox's emphasis).

34. In January of 1900, this rendition was afflicted by the actual assasination of William Goebel, 1899 gubernatorial candidate (and soon to be confirmed as the new but dead governor) as he approached the steps of the state capitol in Frankfort, supposedly in the more-civilized Bluegrass. The election had been strongly contested with railroad interests who stood firmly in opposition to Goebel's agenda for regulating their affairs and underwrote the resistance to his confirmation. Not surprisingly, mountain men were implicated in fact and fiction. See John Fox Jr.'s *The Heart of the Hills* (New York: Scribner's, 1912; reprint, Lexington: Univ. Press of Kentucky, 1996).

35. See John Fox Jr., *Bluegrass and Rhododendron,* essays titled "The Hanging of Talton Hall," "The Red Fox of the Mountains," "Civilizing the Cumberland," and "The Southern Mountaineer." Also, *Trail of the Lonesome Pine,* in both drama and novel forms, draws from the same incidents. Family papers show that Johnny Fox was more concerned with interviewing the "doomed criminal" in order to secure a "confession." Hall refused to confess to the crime for which he was being hung, although he coyly suggested to Fox that the Guard had made a "poor choice" of cases to push. In Fox-UK, box 12.

36. Cincinnati clipping in Fox family scrapbook, in Fox-UK.

# Where "Bloodshed Is a Pastime"

## Mountain Feuds and Appalachian Stereotyping

*Kathleen M. Blee and Dwight B. Billings*

A persistent concern among Appalachian writers, activists, and scholars remains the challenge of responding to pervasive stereotypes regarding the
peoples, cultures, and communities found—or imagined—in the central and
southern sections of the Appalachian Mountains.[1] A landmark text in this ongoing process of refutation is, of course, Henry Shapiro's brilliant intellectual
history of the idea of Appalachia, *Appalachia on Our Mind*. In this familiar
work, Shapiro did much to deconstruct the "mythic system" that interprets
Appalachia as "a coherent region with a uniform culture and homogeneous
population" by showing how mythical versions of Appalachia were produced
in late-nineteenth-century local color fiction as well as in the accounts of early-
twentieth-century educators and social workers, many of whom depicted Appalachia as "a strange land and a peculiar people."[2]

The great contribution of Shapiro's work was to show that "Appalachia" is
not simply something that is immediately "out-there" in the southern mountains. Rather, much of what we take to be "Appalachia" is a complex, multi-
layered, and intertextual reality. In other words, it is a social construction
produced and reproduced—often without much interference or assistance by
locals—in an ongoing set of discourses about the actual place and its peoples,
i.e., a body of interpretation and discussion that routinely occurs in journals
and newspapers, at conferences, on stage or in film and television, and in numerous other scholarly, artistic, and popular media. The powerful and long-
lasting effects of this discourse about social life and culture in the Appalachian
Mountains remain with us long after many of its original contributors are forgotten or are no longer read, thus making their version of "Appalachia" appear
all the more objective and factual as the traces of their construction activities
fade. Perhaps it is the ambiguity of the original depiction of Appalachians as
simultaneously an "us" and a "them,"—"our contemporary ancestors," yet a
"peculiar" other inhabiting a "strange" place—that explains why, as John Reed

remarks, the Appalachian hillbilly remains the only acceptable "ethnic fool" still safe to disparage in American popular culture.[3] American audiences, in fact, have recently been treated to several new cultural productions that rely on crude and essentialistic stereotypes to depict hillbillies as either silly and foolish or violent and sinister. Thus in a recent movie-length remake of *The Beverly Hillbillies,* mountain people are depicted as lovable but silly, and in the 1992 Pulitzer Prize–winning play, *The Kentucky Cycle,* and the movie *Next of Kin,* they are depicted as unmitigatedly violent.

In *Culture and Imperialism,* a work that attempts to reconnect seemingly "innocent" works of American and European narrative fiction with their rightful "position in the history and world of empire," Edward Said argues that culture is not a pure and disinterested realm of aesthetics but rather "a sort of theater where various political and ideological causes engage one another."[4] This insight into culture as power and as shaped by power is obvious from the standpoint of *The Kentucky Cycle* and *Next of Kin,* both of which depict endemic violence as the essence of social life in the Cumberland Mountains. In *The Kentucky Cycle* the irredeemable greed and violence of succeeding generations of east Kentuckians, including within that cycle their exploitation by corporate America, function as a metaphor for the corruption of American life in general. Though presented as a progressive critique of contemporary capitalism's degradation of humanity and the environment, this tragic dramatization of Harry Caudill's dark vision of Appalachian Kentucky is profoundly reactionary because of its use of simplistic and essentialized images of Kentuckians.[5] The same is true of *Next of Kin,* although the political sympathies of this Reagan-era comedy are quite different from those of *The Kentucky Cycle,* and its portrayal of Appalachians is more sympathetic. Here, the violence of eastern Kentuckians is celebrated, including their use of primitive squirrel rifles, crossbows, and even a venomously modern snakemobile, in a plot that turns on the failure of policing in the post-Miranda state to provide justice and the eventual necessity of a Rambo-like invasion of Chicago by hillbillies from Perry County, Kentucky, in the defense of family values.[6]

Despite the very different ideological pretensions of *The Kentucky Cycle* and *Next of Kin,* both fictional narrations work by universalizing common stereotypes of hillbillies and implying that these images represent all that is essential about Appalachian peoples—black and white, straight and gay, rural and urban, rich and poor.[7] By reducing a complex regional society that is peopled by diverse groups to a set of simplistic caricatures, many of today's cultural producers, regardless of their pretensions, do little more than dust off the old, familiar stock characters of hillbilly fiction and make them available once again for whatever aesthetic and political purposes their animators happen to choose.

Similarly, appropriations of old, readily-at-hand stereotypes also persist in current academic scholarship. Indeed, many of the turn-of-the-century assumptions about Appalachia that were popularly recycled by authors such as Jack Weller and Harry Caudill a generation ago can be found cropping up once again in contemporary academic publications. Thus in *Albion's Seed*, a study of early American regional formations that has been highly praised and critically acclaimed by those unfamiliar with recent Appalachian scholarship, David Hackett Fischer depicts the nineteenth-century southern backcountry of Appalachia, including its violent feuds, in an astonishingly essentialized fashion. Taking no note of the vast body of research by Appalachian scholars that has discredited the scholarship upon which he relies, Fischer describes the region as if it were little more than the New World survival of archaic Scotch-Irish culture.[8]

Another instance of the stereotype recycling project that seems to be afoot in the 1990s is provided by the example of a social science study that literally interpreted all Appalachians as suffering from a regionwide case of "post-traumatic stress syndrome." Published in a politically progressive journal and purportedly sympathetic to Appalachians as the shell-shocked "victims" of capitalist exploitation, the author of this article described the people of the region as characterized by a "tangle of contrary tendencies." Appalachians are "warm and hospitable, yet . . . suspicious of outsiders[;] proud . . . yet uncertain . . . [;] determined to fight injustice but . . . suspicious and alienated[;] resourceful . . . but . . . depressed, helpless."[9] In a rejoinder, Karen Tice and Dwight Billings critiqued the author's simplistic view of culture as a bag of psychological traits and showed how stereotypes that constitute Appalachians as passive victims render as reactionary what the author undoubtedly intended as a critique of the system. Further, they recounted the rich history of struggle and resistance in Appalachia to illustrate the agency and efficacy of mountain people and grassroots organizations that often go unseen and unreported.[10]

What Tice and Billings did not point out is how remarkably similar are the terms, especially those posed as dualities, in the article they criticized to similar tropes found in the writings of John Fox Jr., the influential turn-of-the-century Kentucky essayist and novelist who, more than anyone else, inscribed the mythic image of the Kentucky mountaineer that endures to this day.[11] In his profoundly influential essay "The Kentucky Mountaineer," published in 1901, Fox described Appalachian mountaineers as being "proud, sensitive, kindly, obliging in an unreckoning way that is almost pathetic, honest, loyal, in spite of their common ignorance, poverty, and isolation." Further, he assured readers, "they are naturally capable, eager to learn, easy to uplift." Such, according to Fox, were "the best features of mountain life and character." But Fox also pointed out a darker side of the mountaineer that must have simultaneously fascinated and repulsed his middle-class readers. He wrote, "It is only fair to add, however, that nothing that has ever been said of the mountaineer's ignorance, shiftlessness, and awful disregard for human life, especially in the Kentucky mountains, that has not its basis, perhaps, in actual fact."[12]

Published nearly a century apart, the profound similarities of these two highly essentialized and universalized representations of the hypothetical mountaineer, like the recent works of stage and film, attest to the persistence of Appalachian stereotypes. Because John Fox Jr.'s mountaineer inhabits newly refurbished quarters among the pages of 1990s academic publications, and occasionally even struts about onstage at the Kennedy Center for the Performing Arts, we must continue to examine the early social construction of Appalachia and the lasting influence of that discourse on today's understanding of the southern mountain region.

In this chapter, we explore how the depictions of the southern mountains as a violent subculture gained currency in the popular and scholarly accounts of Appalachian feuds that were written at the end of the nineteenth century and at the beginning of the twentieth.[13] As Shapiro pointed out, naming functioned as explaining in the process of identifying and understanding social problems in the southern mountains.[14] Turn-of-the-century reportage of violence there represents a good example of this phenomenon. Community conflicts were used by nonlocal writers to help define "Appalachia" and, once constructed, the idea of "Appalachia" was used to explain the forms of violence that erupted there.[15]

As part of a larger study of the social origins of poverty and political oppression in Appalachian Kentucky, we have investigated one of the longest and most widely reported of the feuds at the turn of the century—an outbreak of violent disputing in Clay County that lasted nearly sixty years. Clay County's violence, dubbed a "feud" by outsiders, but locally known as a "war," pitted against each other the county's most prosperous and politically prominent families—the Whites and the Garrards—along with their allies, their employees, and in antebellum years, their slaves. The most notorious period of violence occurred between 1897 and 1901, causing the dispatch of state troops to maintain order in the county on two occasions and costing at least seventeen lives.

The tensions that set the White and Garrard families on a collision course were rooted in economic and political factors. From the settlement of the county in the first years of the nineteenth century, the two families competed for control of the county's industry and commerce, first as salt manufacturers in antebellum times, and later as merchants and timber and coal developers. Economic competition fueled conflict over control of the county's political machinery, which alternated between the Whites and the Garrards through much of the nineteenth century.[16]

Conflict flared between the Whites and the Garrards throughout the nineteenth century, but the period of greatest violence began in 1897, following a bitter race for sheriff between Gilbert Garrard and B.P. White. Tension soon spread to allies of the two families, sparking a series of violent ambushes, arsons, and murders. By 1898, violence was so widespread that Judge A.H. Clark opened the February term of circuit court by warning that "the lawlessness in this county should be put down if it required half the population to do it."[17] His words went unheeded. In June, the county sheriff, William White, was murdered by Tom Baker, a longtime associate of the Garrards. Fearing a complete collapse of civil order, the county judge pleaded with the governor to dispatch state troops to preserve order and secure arrests. The governor complied, but violence continued in the county, with a series of arsons and ambush killings that marked and intensified polarization in the county.

The following year, state troops were again ordered to Clay County to monitor the trial of Tom Baker for the killing of Sheriff White. Despite the presence of the state guard, Baker was shot and killed in the courthouse yard by a bullet fired from the home of the late sheriff's brother. Following this, a number of deadly battles broke out across the county, involving families more and more remote from the original protagonists. Tensions began to subside in the northern section of the county in 1899 when the antagonists in the area jointly agreed to establish the Oneida Baptist Institute as a college for the children of feudists, but tensions continued to be heated elsewhere in the county. The arrival of nonpartisans in the county, however, created additional pressure to end the hostilities. In 1901 a gun battle between Garrards and Whites in front of the courthouse so outraged a new county judge that he forced both sides to negotiate a peace treaty and the conflict subsided.

Violent community conflict like that in Clay County was widespread throughout not only the post-Reconstruction South but also the developing West, the industrial North, and the increasingly interracial environments of urban America in the late nineteenth century. Throughout the nation, such conflicts expressed new tensions but relied upon traditional and often violent forms of direct action, including riots, mob action, labor struggles, vigilantism, racial and ethnic harassment, regulation, rebellion, and, most rarely, outright civil war, that have existed in American society from colonial times to the present, from the Boston Tea Party and Shays's Rebellion to the most recent riots in Los Angeles. Despite such good company within the annals of America's history of violent conflict, the Cumberland Gap region of Kentucky came to be singled out as "one of the few dark spots on the map of the United States" and the Kentucky mountaineer as "a man of blood, governed more by hate than by justice."[18]

In this chapter, we scrutinize the building of popular understandings of Appalachia and Appalachian violence by examining newspaper, scholarly, and popular magazine accounts of this violent dispute and others like it. We seek to understand how Kentucky's feuds were presented to national audiences and how this attention shaped understandings of the mountains and the mountaineer. Below, we contrast how nonlocal writers described mountain feuding with some of the principal findings from our study of Clay County violence in the nineteenth century.

## Myth #1: Violence was overwhelming.

Nothing captures the popular imagination—then or now—like images of violence. Turn-of-the-century journalists and local color writers were highly adept at satisfying their audiences' appetites for stories of blood and gore. In the accounts of Kentucky's violence, blood was a constant leitmotif. The southern mountains, it seems, were steeped in violence and savagery. Readers across the nation were horrified and titillated by images of southern mountaineers as a people for whom "the lust for human blood has become a malignant disease." "By birth, tradition, and environment," these stories warned, the Kentuckian is "taught to regard the taking of human life with as little concern as he would feel in removing a stone from his path." The feudist was "a man of blood, and governed more by hate than by justice."[19]

Typical of this genre was an account published in 1902 in *Frank Leslie's Popular Monthly*. The author, E. Carl Litsey, was dispatched by the magazine's editor to "the dark and bloody ground" of Kentucky to bring back "first-hand information" on the state's feuds. Having made his way into Clay County, "the heart of the feudists' country," Litsey cautioned readers that the region's notorious reputation was well deserved. "If [Kentucky's history] is tinged with the blood of the innocent, and blackened by reasonless deeds of hate, I cannot mitigate or cleanse, for these things are true. . . . The mountain feudist . . . stalks somberly across the page of history and his footsteps are marked with blood."[20]

A year later, *Munsey's Magazine* similarly exposed its readers to southeastern Kentucky, "[a] region of the United States in which bloodshed is a pastime and cruel and cowardly murder goes unpunished." In breathless detail, the magazine related the story of a "primitive" land where "the lust for human blood has become a malignant disease." Among Kentucky's feuds "one finds only the sickening story of bloodshed told over and over again, the cowardly attack from behind, the shooting of unarmed men." By another account, "there is scarcely an acre within the county boundaries that does not hold a spot where some member of the populace has been shot from ambush, and in most instances left to die unattended, as often as not in total ignorance of the identity of his slayer."[21]

In reality, feuding violence was far more episodic and usually less dramatic than portrayed by these writers. In the most intensive period of violence in Clay County's feud, in the late 1890s, fewer than two dozen killings are documented. Arson, ambush, and shooting were not uncommon in the county, but incidents of these were far less frequent than these outsider accounts suggest. When Litsey and his companion set off for Clay County "armed [he] with a kodak and I with a note book,"[22] they cast themselves as fearless adventurers entering a zone of combat, but the reality of life in Clay County did not match this image. For several brief periods, local governance was overwhelmed by conflict between the county's most politically powerful families and the county required state intervention to regain civil order. But most of the time, even during the most acute periods of feuding, there was little to distinguish Clay County from other rural communities of the period. Property was bought and sold, lawsuits adjudicated, children sent to school, and elections held. Violence lurked in the background of daily life in Clay County, as it did elsewhere, but rarely to the extent presented by outside writers.

## Myth #2: Feuds were rooted in poverty, ignorance, and isolation.

Those who descended on Clay County in search of its violent atrocities delighted in descriptions of the region as impoverished and isolated and of its people as ignorant. A former member of the United States Geological Survey recounted a Kentucky mountain home in which "[t]wo rough benches served as seats for the adults of the family, while the children with the exception of the two youngest who were held by the women, were obligated to stand." Mountain food was described in no less primitive terms, as consisting of "cabbage which had been converted into a species of sauer kraut by being soaked in water until it had fermented. Then it was boiled and put into the bowl, and over it was poured molasses and grease obtained from frying some rancid pieces of 'sow bosom' as the 'natives' snickeringly dub the fat salt pork which constitutes their principle article of diet in the meat line." The mountaineer, this writer concluded, was "an ill-nourished lot, unkempt and ignorant."[23]

Others contributed similar images, describing mountain dwellers "thinly clad in homespun jeans, without overcoats," scraping out a living in a region that provided "practically no opportunity for education or enlightenment." In his description of Kentucky mountains titled "Beyond the Gap: The Breeding Group of Feuds," C.T. Revere painted a stark portrait of mountain dwellers who "have never come in contact with the world, and are amazingly ignorant of anything which happens outside their immediate neighborhood."[24]

These images of poverty and isolation easily wafted into accounts of feud violence, leaving the impression that it was penury and seclusion that fueled local warfare. In an article in the *Cosmopolitan* titled "Romance and Tragedy of Kentucky Feuds," for example, J. Stoddard Johnston wrote that the southern mountaineer had been "caught in an eddy, and have stood still or retrograded." Others were even more forthright in their judgments, arguing that the county's civic and moral "regeneration" would come "only through the introduction of outside influences." The *New York Times,* although acknowledging the roots of feud violence in conflicts between wealthy and well-connected local elites, reverted back to issues of poverty and isolation when it proclaimed that Clay County needed "the civilizing railroad" to end its violence. "It has been too much by itself," the paper insisted. "Little wonder that a part of the population, and that an ignorant part, has been provoked to commit murder as an outgrowth of the resentments of rival families."[25]

In contrast to these images of poverty, isolation, and ignorance, our study finds that the principals in the Clay County conflict were highly educated and politically connected local leaders from whose ranks came numerous county magistrates, judges, sheriffs, legislators, state officials (including a secretary of state), and members of Congress (including a speaker of the United States House of Representatives). The main feuding families also were immensely wealthy and controlled Clay County's economy from its earliest years. James White, a Virginian whose estate was valued at two million dollars when he died in 1838, began purchasing land and manufacturing salt in Clay County in cooperation with his brother Hugh (and Hugh's sons), who moved to Clay County during the first decade of the nineteenth century. By 1860, the White family owned more than twenty thousand acres of land in Clay and other mountain counties. James Garrard, the second governor of Kentucky, patented more than forty-five thousand acres of land in Kentucky before and after Kentucky's statehood, including thousands of acres in the Kentucky mountains, and sent his son Daniel to Clay County to establish salt wells and furnaces there early in the century. Daniel Garrard and his sons acquired at least an additional ten thousand acres in southeastern Kentucky before the Civil War. The Whites and the Garrards, along with a few other families, thus established economic and political dynasties in Clay County based on slave labor, salt manufacturing, commerce, and large-scale farming that persisted throughout the antebellum and early postbellum periods and, in some cases, even into the modern era.

Further, far from cultivating ignorance, these feud leaders expended great efforts to educate their children in the nation's finest schools. Laura White, daughter of feud leader Daugherty White, for example, was one of the first female graduates of the University of Michigan (then Michigan University), where she earned a degree in mathematics before matriculating to Massachusetts Institute of Technology (MIT) in Boston and the Sorbonne in Paris to study architecture.

Moreover, the economic history of Clay County betrays the myth of total isolation. The manufacture and sale of salt, produced by slave labor and shipped on flatboats down the Kentucky and Cumberland Rivers or by wagon through the Cumberland Gap, linked that locality to central Kentucky and more distant markets in Virginia and Tennessee from the earliest decades of the nineteenth century until the Civil War. Far from being an island of self-sufficiency, Clay County boasted one of antebellum Kentucky's most important industries more than one hundred years before railroads reached Manchester. Ironically, in fact, the tensions that led to permanent hostility within the county's manufacturing elite first emerged when the local effects of the national depression of 1839–42 were being most sharply felt in the commercial sector, suggesting that the notion of integration rather than isolation better captures that locality's even most distant economic past. Because of the importance of its local industry, some of the earliest public investments by the Commonwealth of Kentucky were made in Clay County to facilitate the salt trade, including improvements on the Kentucky River and the establishment of three turnpikes during the antebellum period to help pay for local road building. As a result, no other county in Kentucky in 1908 had as many roads per square mile as Clay.[26]

## Myth #3: Feuding was casual violence, a residue of a distant, savage past.

A corollary to the assumption of the geographical isolation of the feud country was the assumption of the primitiveness of its population. Virtually every popular account characterized the southern mountains as "one of the most primitive regions of the United States," or as "a savage, primeval country" with blood feuds "beside which the Italian vendetta is a childish thing, almost humane in comparison." *Collier's Weekly* introduced a 1913 article titled "Children of the Feudists" with a sentence that situated its readers and Kentucky's feudists in decidedly different eras: "[a]ccidently we seem to have mislaid some three million Americans for a hundred years or so in the mountains of Kentucky." Others stressed the peculiar migratory routes that Kentucky's mountain pioneers were said to have followed as an explanation for the dearth of civilization in the region. "Most of these mountain folk are descendants of Anglo-Saxon pioneers from Virginia and the Carolinas to whom the savage, inaccessible wilderness appealed, and of criminals who were driven out of the older settlements because jails were few, or who sought asylum in the mountains to escape sudden justice. The taint of this lawless ancestry is over the whole of the Land of Feuds."[27]

Primitiveness, in writings about feuds, went hand in hand with unfettered violence. A particularly colorful metaphor for feuding was that adopted by Hartley Davis and Clifford Smyth in their article "The Land of Feuds." They described it as a "relic of medievalism upon which have been grafted the atrocities of modern war politics; and the hybrid is a horrible thing." Most writers used a similar logic, arguing that in such an antiquated population "resort to violence required little provocation." Feuds thus represented a cultural expression of earlier, even Old World, behaviors and antagonisms. As Johnston put it, Kentucky's conflicts "have every earmark of the Scotch feuds among the clans, and no more than in the savage custom of waylaying and killing from ambush."[28]

The notion that the Appalachian Mountains were settled predominantly by Scotch-Irish immigrants who carried feuding traditions with them from the Old World, a thesis endorsed recently by as notable a historian as David H. Fischer, rests upon dubious historical evidence. Not only is this carryover unlikely—because feuds had vanished from Scotland nearly two centuries before Appalachian Kentucky's earliest settlements[29]—but also the ethnic composition of Appalachia's early population remains in doubt, consisting of some unknown composition of English, German, French, Dutch, Welsh, and Scotch-Irish settlers. Ethnic diversity is especially apparent among families involved in the Clay County feuds, including the feuds' most prominent participants, the Garrards and the Whites. Thus while the Whites were, indeed, descendants of Scotch-Irish immigrants, the Garrards were descendants of French Huguenots. Consequently, the attribution of feuding to a Scotch-Irish inheritance is highly misleading.

In keeping with the notion of mountain dwellers as primitive, most accounts of the feuds also portray their violence as casual, even random. Davis and Smyth's conclusion that "[h]uman life is the cheapest thing in the land of the feuds" is typical. "The mountaineer host who slept on the floor so that the visitor might have his bed, and refused any payment, will calmly waylay and kill the same visitor later in the day for twenty dollars or less. There are hundreds of men in the Land of Feuds who can be hired out for two dollars a day to lie out in the open for 3 months, if necessary, to kill any one pointed out to them—providing, of course, that the victim does not belong to their clan."[30]

Although feuds were often portrayed in the popular press as irrational responses to petty conflicts, we found that they are better understood as series of conflicts structured by the antagonisms between Clay County's most powerful families and by the economic dependency that compelled allegiance to these families from the rest of the populace. For most of the early decades of white settlement in Clay County, life revolved around two very different systems of production: subsistence-oriented agricultural production (known as "forest farming"), based predominantly on family labor, that was practiced by the vast majority of the population; and a smaller, slave-based manufacturing economy controlled by a few wealthy families, particularly the Whites and the Garrards. The result of this dual system was a highly stratified community. The top ten wealthiest individuals in Clay County in 1860—all of them slave owners—

averaged personal estates worth $45,890 in a county where the mean estate was worth only $859, or fifty-three times less. In fact, the wealthiest individual, salt manufacturer Francis Clark, was two hundred times richer than the mean, with an estate worth $175,000 in 1860.

At the peak of the salt industry's influence, entrepreneurs from Clay County outlined a bold scheme to the Kentucky legislature that proposed a $10 million interstate canal, lock, and dam system that eventually would have linked Clay County's saltworks to the Atlantic Coast. But the Panic of 1837 and related economic setbacks, not to mention opposition from railroad interests, relegated this plan to a footnote in Kentucky history. Soon thereafter, the Clay County salt industry began to decline as salt manufacturing elsewhere, in regions with better locational advantages, prospered.

As Clay County's economy sagged, its most prosperous citizens found new avenues for profit-taking. The most successful of these was as the indigenous agents of outside capital in the late-nineteenth-century exploitation of local labor, land, timber, and coal resources. B.P. White and John White thus served as land agents for the massive real estate speculation of the New York and Kentucky Land Company in the 1890s, while the Garrards made staggering sums by selling land to outside timber and railroad companies.

At the same time that many of the county's wealthy families prospered from the increasing commercialization that was taking place in Clay County during the last decade of the nineteenth century, the standard of living fell dramatically for many of the county's farm families. As we have shown elsewhere,[31] economic contradictions of low accumulation, population increase, intergenerational farm subdivision, soil depletion, and land shortages produced great strain in the subsistence farming system. These factors not only contributed to the development of an underemployed labor pool that could be utilized cheaply in the expanding railroad, timber, and mining industries but also provided dependent and readily deployable human resources for the lethal battles that raged at the turn of the century in Clay County. When conflict among elites turned to violence, those who were bound by economic ties to the feud protagonists could be pressed into service as foot soldiers in battles between wealthy Garrards and Whites.

## Myth #4: Feuding was due to the absence of law.

Feuding was also attributed to the essentially lawless quality of social life in the Cumberland Mountains. Regardless of how implausible it was to imagine a people successfully reproducing their way of life outside of law and norms, Davis and Smyth wrote of the southern mountains that "[f]or a hundred years the isolation of these people has been almost complete. They have lived a wild, free life, governed only by such laws as it pleased them to observe." Litsey also located law within the individual rather than in the community, noting that in the mountains "men are governed by a medieval idea of right and wrong, and each man's mind is his own court and judge."[32]

The journalistic assessment of the lawlessness of the Kentucky mountains found backing among the nation's most influential social scientists. Ellen Churchill Semple, an eminent geographer, later a president of the American Association of Geography, argued in a 1901 article in the *Geographical Journal* (reprinted in 1910 in the *Bulletin of the American Geographical Society*) that the "remoteness" and "necessary self-reliance" of southern mountain life had led to an "intense spirit of independence," shown in their "adherence to the blood-feud which inculcates the duty of personal vengeance for a wrong." In a 1901 article in the prestigious *American Journal of Sociology,* S.S. MacClintock similarly concluded that "it was a long time before the wild animals and Indian disappeared and law and order became established . . . each man had been a law unto himself too long to be able to forget it immediately and look to civil law for protections." B.H. Schockel, writing in the *Scientific Monthly* in 1916, elaborated this point, noting that feuding "survived among the isolated valleys of the mountains, where it was fostered by folk-song, the flaring resentment of the Indian fighter and pioneer, and the habits of thought natural in isolated communities where for a long time there was neither sheriff nor jury, and where, even to this day, the government hardly has been able to inspire confidence or dread."[33]

Against the assumption that Appalachians turned to violent means to resolve disputes because they were unfamiliar and inexperienced with the use of civil and criminal courts, we found that so-called feudists were consistent and intense litigators throughout the nineteenth century. Civil cases involving feuding groups constituted between one-fifth and one-third of all such cases filed in the Clay County Circuit Court during the periods of peak feuding activity (1845–49 and 1896–1900) and represented a high proportion of the docket during periods of quiescence as well. Thus besides being lawyers and lawmakers, Clay County's feudists routinely and consistently turned to local courts to redress grievances and resolve disputes. The local court and legal system did break down briefly during both periods of conflict, yet in both instances, those breakdowns were consequences, not causes, of political violence aimed at capturing local government.

## Myth #5: Women were behind/outside the conflict.

To the journalists, essayists, and social scientists who flocked to Clay County at the end of the nineteenth century, mountain women were the most peculiar of this "peculiar people." In his trip to Clay County in the summer of 1901, Litsey seemed to take his readers on a human safari, directing attention to what he saw as the uncivilized state of women and children in this remote place. In words that echoed contemporary depictions of so-called primitive peoples elsewhere on the globe, he recalled that "Now and again we would pass a small hut. . . . Wild and poorly clad forms would appear in the low doorways; faces almost expressionless would stare at us in a kind of apathetic wonder. Women's and children's faces for the most part; the men were away."[34] Mountain women generally were portrayed as far removed from the world of politics, law, and business, as operating entirely within the web of familial and domestic relationships. Those who reported tales of Clay County's feud built upon and elaborated these images.

In the feud, women generally were described as in the shadows, literally and figuratively. They rarely were portrayed as venturing from the home, thus seldom were they portrayed as involved in actual fighting. But mountain women, feud accounts concurred, could be treacherous, deceptive, and sly. Major-General O.O. Howard, the founder of Lincoln Memorial University in the mountains of eastern Tennessee, wrote of the feuds that "there is a reverence for women and children and they are spared. Yet mothers and sisters, wives and sweethearts, frequently urge on the contest." Writing in the journal of Berea College at the edge of the Kentucky mountains, Elijah Dizney concluded that if "it was the role of these wars everywhere not to molest women, children, or old people," nonetheless, "[w]omen have figured in all these feuds, sometimes as the precipitating cause, always in the capacity of an efficient and loyal retainer." Other commentators also insisted that women acted as provocateurs behind the scenes of feud violence, that "many of the women added fuel to the feud fires by gossip and by insults and by encouraging others to fight."[35]

Litsey was swept up in his own sense of adventure and images of the guile of even the youngest mountain females as he traveled "deeper and deeper into the mountains . . . [into] feudists' country, where the sun set crimson and the moon rose red." "I asked a tousle-headed, brown-faced little maid where her father was. . . . A change came over the child's face, and she backed away in distrust; the guile of the serpent crept up and flamed in her foxlike eyes, and she answered quickly, and with a furtive glance around, 'I don't know!' . . . Duplicity and cunning were bred in her bone, and had been fostered year by year as she grew."[36]

Little wonder, then, that accounts of the feud cast women as steely, ominous figures. As C.T. Revere wrote in *Outing Magazine* after a visit to a mountain family mourning the shooting of a young son, "[t]he women were dry-eyed and vindictive. I did not hear one word of regret, to say nothing of grief over the death of the boy, but there were threats enough to have given the murderer shivers if he had heard them." Mountain women were sufficiently callous, Revere concluded, that "[a]dmirers of feminine beauty would do well to hunt elsewhere for objects upon which to bestow their admiration."[37]

Given women's purported behind-the-scenes feud activity, they seldom appeared in feud reportage, except as widows. In these accounts, they were always "prostrate," dragged from sites of death. Typical is Tom Baker's grieving widow, always described as bent over her assassinated husband's body. Even in mourning, however, Baker's widow looked toward vengeance, swearing her twelve sons to a blood oath to avenge their father's death. "Each day," she is said to have declared, "I shall show my boys the handkerchief stained with his blood, and tell them who murdered him!"[38]

These images of mountain women as afflicted but treacherous, as peripheral yet ominous, profoundly shaped the perception of women's role in nineteenth-century mountain life, riveting attention on women in family dramas and slighting them outside of that context. For those chronicling the Clay County feud, as well as for their readers far removed from the Appalachian Mountains, such accounts served to validate the perception that it was the alliances, politics, and economic stakes of mountain men—not mountain women—that were the key to understanding mountain violence and mountain life as a whole. No reporting on the feud suggests that women were involved in the county's political or economic life, or that they might have monetary grievances that would involve them in the conflicts of Clay County's feud.

However, many mountain women played much more prominent roles in Clay County life than outside chroniclers were prepared to understand. This was true particularly of women of the county's elite families, many of whom pursued educational and financial opportunities with the same vigor as their male kinfolk.

Although until 1892 Kentucky law did not allow married women to control their own property, a number of prominent Clay County women found ways to evade these restrictions. An example was Ellen C. (Jett) Lyttle, married to David Yancey Lyttle, a lawyer, farmer, and Democratic state senator. In 1879, Ellen and David jointly filed a lawsuit stipulating that Ellen had property from her father's estate and that she "be empowered to use, enjoy, sell and convey, for her own benefit any property that she may now own or hereafter acquire free from the choice of her husband." The court granted the petition, allowing Ellen to "make contracts as a single woman, sue and be sued, to trade in her own name, to dispose of her property by will or deed free from the control of her husband and in regard to the disposition of her property has all the rights and privileges and powers of a femme sole." Ellen exercised her newly acquired independent legal status to deal in real estate. When she died in 1890, her estate included landholdings in four counties.[39]

Martha Coldiron Hogg, who donated land to establish Oneida Baptist College as part of a turn-of-the-century peace treaty, was another financial figure in late-nineteenth-century Clay County. Her first husband died in 1892, leaving Martha with a sizable estate that she determined to retain and manage herself. When she decided to marry Stephen P. Hogg, the county judge of a neighboring county, she convinced him to sign a prenuptial agreement stating that she would retain ownership of all her real and personal property and have the ability to transact financial matters on her own, and then had herself declared a "femme sole." Martha wielded her property to become a major power broker in Clay County. Like her male counterparts, she increased her fortune considerably by foreclosing on property and by buying undervalued real estate at court-ordered auctions to resell for a profit.[40]

Even Martha's grant of land to Oneida Baptist College, which made her a legendary figure in the feud truce for northern Clay County, reflected painstaking efforts to control the disposition of her property. In two separate deeds in 1899, she conveyed one-quarter acre valued at twenty-five dollars to the college for the construction of a school building, but specified that the school building must be worth not less than six hundred dollars, that it must be built within two years, and that the college must use the house only for school or church purposes. Martha also donated an additional ten acres worth one thousand dollars, stipulating that the college must erect a school building worth not less than five thousand dollars within ten years, that the building must open onto a street fifty feet wide, and that no other buildings could be built on the land. Moreover, Martha retained a lien on the land and specified that the property would revert to her if the school closed.[41]

Few people outside the Kentucky hills were watching, or cared, in the early decades of the nineteenth century when the Garrards and the Whites began their struggle to dominate Clay County, Kentucky. But a half-century later, when the control of such timber and mineral-rich counties became a matter of great importance, national attention was riveted on the region and its people. Through the lens of those who rushed to the southern mountains to chronicle the region, it was a curious people who inhabited the land of newfound riches. Whether portrayed as savage, primitive, treacherous, or bloodthirsty, mountaineers were definitively cast as the other, radically and essentially different from the rest of American society.

Such characterizations of the mountains and its inhabitants spawned an abiding ideological and political legacy. "The power to narrate," according to Said, "or to block other narratives from forming and emerging, is very important to culture and imperialism, and constitutes one of the main connections between them."[42] By creating an impression of the southern mountain region as a dark zone of chaos and violence in desperate need of "civilizing" influences from the outside, feud narratives gave American readers a framework through which to view the profound changes that were taking place at the turn of the century in Appalachian Kentucky and the spasm of violence that was accompanying its industrialization.

It would be nice if we could conclude by arguing that the Kentucky mountain feuds were nothing more than a product of fantasy and misrepresentation, but we cannot. Undoubtedly, the writings on feuds were often erroneous, exaggerated, and self-serving, yet the modern era of political life in Appalachian Kentucky was nonetheless ushered in by widespread and sometimes fatal conflicts in many mountain counties. Appalachians have at times both challenged misreporting and sought in tourism and outdoor drama, for instance, to profit from the commodification of feud imagery. Outdoor dramatizations of the Hatfields and McCoys and John Fox Jr.'s *Trail of the Lonesome Pine,* for example, have been performed now in West Virginia and Virginia for roughly twenty-five years. What remains to be done, however, is for Appalachians to come to terms with the long-term impacts of discursive stereotyping by outsiders and of the reality of their history of protracted violent conflict on public life, politics, and policies in modern life.

## Notes

1. Jean Haskell Speer, "From Stereotype to Regional Hype: Strategies for Changing Media Portrayals of Appalachia," *Journal of the Appalachian Studies Association* 5 (1993): 12–19.

2. Henry D. Shapiro, *Appalachia on Our Mind: The Southern Mountains and Mountaineers in the American Consciousness, 1870–1920* (Chapel Hill: Univ. of North Carolina Press, 1978), 265, 3. In "Signs of Civilization: The Trail of the Lonesome Pine as Colonial Narrative," *Journal of the Appalachian Studies Association* 2 (1990), Roger Cunningham criticizes Shapiro for treating the interpretation of Appalachia as a purely cognitive problem devoid of the play of power. As a remedy, Cunningham, p. 22, wisely recommends reading Shapiro in relation to Edward Said's *Orientalism* (New York: Random House, 1978): "No Appalachian scholar can read *Orientalism* without being irresistibly reminded that 'Appalachia on America's Mind' is a function of 'Appalachia in America's hands.'"

3. John Shelton Reed, *Southern Folk, Plain and Fancy* (Athens: Univ. of Georgia Press, 1986), 43. According to Edward Said in *Culture and Imperialism* (New York: Vintage Books, 1994), xxv, the "identity thought" that constructs such categories as "us" and "them" to designate other societies and peoples is a "hallmark of imperialist cultures."

4. Said, *Culture and Imperialism,* xii, xiii.

5. For a brief discussion of the impact of reading Harry Caudill's *Night Comes to the Cumberlands* and taking a day trip through eastern Kentucky on the author of *The Kentucky Cycle* see Robert Schenkkan, author's note in *The Kentucky Cycle* (New York: Penguin, 1993), 333–38.

6. For a discussion of how Appalachian storyteller and artist Andrenna Belcher experienced performing a minor role in *Next of Kin* and her inability to challenge ste-

reotypes during its filming, see her "Relatively Strange: On the Set of *Next of Kin*," *Now and Then* 8 (fall 1991): 22, 25–26.

7. On essentialism in writings by and about Appalachians, see Alan Banks, Dwight Billings, and Karen Tice, "Appalachian Studies, Resistance, and Postmodernism," in *Fighting Back in Appalachia: Traditions of Resistance and Change*, ed. Stephen L. Fisher (Philadelphia, Pa.: Temple Univ. Press, 1993), 283–301.

8. David Hackett Fischer, *Albion's Seed: Four British Folkways in America* (New York: Oxford Univ. Press, 1989). For critiques of this work by Appalachian scholars see the *Appalachian Journal* 19(2) (winter 1992): 161–200.

9. David Cattell-Gordon, "The Appalachian Inheritance: A Culturally Transmitted Traumatic Stress Syndrome," *Journal of Progressive Human Services* 1(1): 44 (1990).

10. Karen Tice and Dwight Billings, "Appalachian Culture and Resistance," *Journal of Progressive Human Services* 2(2): 1–18 (1991).

11. For a deeply penetrating analysis of Fox's most important novel about Appalachia, *Trail of the Lonesome Pine*, as a colonialist narrative, see Cunningham, "Signs of Civilization."

12. John Fox Jr., "The Kentucky Mountaineer," in *Blue-Grass and Rhododendron: Out-Doors in Old Kentucky* (New York: Charles Scribner's Sons, 1901), 52. Images of darkness in the writings of Fox and his contemporaries signify Appalachia's place in the savagery/civilization dualism that, according to Said in *Orientalism*, is a constant feature of western colonialist discourse. More than a half-century after Fox, Harry Caudill effectively cashed in on this semiotic legacy in his various book titles such as *Night Comes to the Cumberlands, A Darkness at Dawn*, and *The Watches of the Night*.

13. For an excellent historical overview of Kentucky feuds see James C. Klotter, "Feuds in Appalachia: An Overview," *Filson Club Historical Quarterly* 56 (1982): 290–337.

14. Shapiro, *Appalachia on Our Mind*, especially his chapter "Naming As Explaining: William Goodell Frost and the Invention of Appalachia," 113–32.

15. For a discussion of how the *New York Times* confused early labor violence in southern West Virginia with Appalachian feuding, see Allen W. Batteau, *The Invention of Appalachia* (Tucson: Univ. of Arizona Press, 1990), 111–12.

16. Kathleen M. Blee and Dwight B. Billings, "Violence and Local State Formation: A Longitudinal Case Study of Appalachian Feuding," *Law and Society Review* 30(4) (1996): 671–705.

17. John Jay Dickey, *Diary*, roll 3, entry for February 8, 1898; Ruth B. Carr, transcriptionist, 1933.

18. C.T. Revere, "Beyond the Gap: The Breeding Ground of Feuds," *Outing Magazine* (Feb. 7, 1907), 610; E. Carl Litsey, "Kentucky Feuds and Their Causes," *Frank Leslie's Popular Monthly* 53(3):292 (Jan. 1902).

19. Hartley Davis and Clifford Smyth, "Land of Feuds," *Munsey's Magazine* 30(2): 162 (Nov. 1903); Litsey, "Kentucky Feuds," 287, 292.

20. Litsey, "Kentucky Feuds," 183, 187.

21. Davis and Smyth, "Land of Feuds," 161, 162; James M. Ross, "The Great Feuds of Kentucky: II-The Baker-Howard Feud," *Wide World Magazine* 140(24): 191 (Dec. 1909).

22. Litsey, "Kentucky Feuds," 283.

23. Revere, "Beyond the Gap," 612, 621.

24. J. Stoddard Johnston, "Romance and Tragedy of Kentucky Feuds," *Cosmopolitan* 27(5): 553 (Sept. 1899); Litsey, "Kentucky Feuds," 291; Revere "Beyond the Gap," 612.

25. Johnston, "Romance," 552; Davis and Smyth, "Land of Feuds," 172; *New York Times*, Dec. 3, 1899, 17.

26. The classic study is Mary Verhoeff, *The Kentucky Mountains Transportation and Commerce, 1750–1911: A Study in the Economic History of a Coal Field* (Louisville, Ky.: John P. Morton, 1911). Also see Tyrel G. Moore, "Economic Development in Appalachian Kentucky, 1800–1860," in *Appalachian Frontiers: Settlement, Society, and Development in the Preindustrial Era,* ed. Robert D. Mitchell (Lexington: Univ. Press of Kentucky, 1991), 222–34. In our own demographic study of Clay County, we found surprisingly low rates of population persistence from 1850 through 1910, suggesting that the stereotype of early rural Appalachia as stable and isolated is wrong on both counts. See Billings and Blee, "Family Strategies in a Subsistence Economy: Beech Creek, Kentucky, 1850–1942," *Sociological Perspectives* 33(1): 63–88 (1990); Thomas Clark, "Salt, A Factor in the Settlement of Kentucky," *Filson Club History Quarterly* 12(1): 42–52 (Jan. 1938); John Smith, "The Salt-Making Industry of Clay County, Kentucky," *Filson Club History Quarterly* 1(3): 134–41 (April 1927); Roy R. White, "The Salt Industry of Clay County, Kentucky," *Register of the Kentucky Historical Society* 50(172): 238–41 (July 1952). An occurrence during Clay County's earliest period of feuding offers anecdotal evidence that this locality was not closed off culturally or geographically from the wider world. Shortly before the trial of Dr. Abner Baker in 1844 for charges of murder, a judicial event that first set feuding families against each other, Dr. Baker was missing. His father attempted to notify him of the need to return to Clay County to stand trial by advertising notices in the New York, Charleston, and New Orleans newspapers. Baker was found vacationing in Cuba. See C.W. Crozier, *The Life and Trial of Dr. Abner Baker, Jr.* (Louisville, Ky.: Prentice and Wessinger, 1846); Verhoeff, *The Kentucky Mountains,* 176.

27. Davis and Smyth, "Land of Feuds," 161, 162, 172; Bruce Barton, "Children of the Feudists," *Collier's Weekly,* Aug. 23, 1913, 7.

28. Davis and Smyth, "Land of Feuds," 161; Johnston, "Romance," 553.

29. Jenny Womald, "The Blood Feud in Early Modern Scotland." in *Disputes and Settlements,* ed. John Bossy (New York: Cambridge Univ. Press, 1983) 101–44.

30. Davis and Smyth, "Land of Feuds," 162.

31. Dwight Billings and Kathleen Blee, "Agriculture in the Kentucky Mountains," 233–69 in *Mountain Life and Work: Preindustrial Appalachia and Its Transformation,* eds. Mary Beth Pudup, Dwight B. Billings, and Altina Waller (Chapel Hill: Univ. of North Carolina Press, 1995); Billings and Blee, "Family Strategies."

32. Davis and Smyth, "Land of Feuds," 172; Litsey, "Kentucky Feuds," 287.

33. Ellen Churchill Semple, "The Anglo-Saxons of the Kentucky Mountains," *Bulletin of the American Geographical Society* 42(8): 580, (1901; reprint, Aug. 1910); S.S. MacClintock, "The Kentucky Mountains and Their Feuds II," *American Journal of Soci-*

*ology* 7(2): 171 (Sept. 1901); B.H. Schockel, "Changing Conditions in the Kentucky Mountains" *Scientific Monthly* 3(2): 126 (Aug. 1926).

34. Litsey, "Kentucky Feuds, 284.

35. Major-General O.O. Howard, "The Feuds in the Cumberland Mountains," *The Independent,* April 7, 1904, 788; Elijah Dinzey, "Mountain Feud-by a Mountain Man," *Berea Quarterly* 13(1): 13 (April 1909).

36. Litsey, "Kentucky Feuds," 284.

37. Revere, "Beyond the Gap," 611, 621.

38. *New York Times,* "A Kentucky Vendetta," June 12, 1899, 1. See also A.L. Lloyd, "Background to Feuding," *History Today* 2(7): 451–57 (July 1952).

39. *J.R. Burchell vs. Ellen C. Lyttle's heirs,* Clay County Circuit Court, 1890; *J.R. Burchell vs. B.P. White and David Hobbs,* Clay County Circuit Court, 1890. Although not herself directly involved in feud violence, one of Ellen's children married Beverly White Jr., a farmer who was assassinated in 1921, and one of her stepchildren co-owned land with James Garrard.

40. Prenuptial agreement in Clay County Deed Book R, p. 262, March 2, 1894. Darrell C. Richardson, *Mountain Rising,* (Oneida, Ky.: Oneida Mountain Press, 1986); Private communication from Jess Wilson, Clay County; *William L. White vs. H.C. Coldiron, J.W. Wright, and Martha Hogg,* Clay County Circuit Court, 1898.

41. Clay County Deed Book U, 440, Aug. 1,1899, and July 25, 1899.

42. Said, *Culture,* xiii.

# Where Did Hillbillies Come From?

## Tracing Sources of the Comic Hillbilly Fool in Literature

### Sandra L. Ballard

> Come and listen to a story 'bout a man named Jed. Poor mountaineer, barely kept his family fed. Then one day when a critic called him "fool," up from the ground came a bubbling feud. Black eye, that is. Stereotype. Fightin' words.

Because I grew up in western North Carolina, graduated from Appalachian State University and the University of Tennessee, live in East Tennessee, and have no qualms about identifying myself as a native of Appalachia, some people expect me to object to the comic image of "hillbillies" depicted in syndicated television shows such as *The Beverly Hillbillies*. But I happen to like *The Beverly Hillbillies*.

I grew up laughing at the six-foot, sixth-grade graduate Jethro Bodine and the Clampett family who struck oil and moved from a cabin in the mountains to a Beverly Hills mansion with a "cement pond." I view these characters as the exaggerations that they are, while some critics view the show as a slap in the face to the integrity of Appalachian people.

But I haven't always held the view that I have now. When I first read James Branscome's essay "Annihilating the Hillbilly: The Appalachians' Struggle with America's Institutions," I found myself nodding in agreement with his complaint about the early-1970s CBS Tuesday-evening lineup of *The Beverly Hillbillies*, *Green Acres*, and *Hee-Haw*. When he described such programming as "the most intensive effort ever exerted by a nation to belittle, demean, and otherwise destroy a minority people within its boundaries,"[1] I thought he was absolutely right. "If similar programs even approaching the maliciousness of these were broadcast today on Blacks, Indians or Chicanos," he said, "there would be an immediate public outcry from every liberal organization and politician in the country.... But ... America is allowed to continue laughing at this minority group because on this, America agrees: hillbilly ain't beautiful."[2]

He has a point—a number of points: Mountaineers are a marginalized population, Americans do laugh at them, and no stigma inhibits the laughter.

But Branscome's charge of "maliciousness" bothers me. Such criticism falls short of recognizing that at least some of the comedy of shows like *The Beverly Hillbillies* comes from the characters' naïveté or from the upper hand they gain over "city folks" and city ways. After all, if the show were truly malicious, would I recognize that the Clampetts brought with them from the hills all of their good traits, too—family loyalty, honesty, trust, fair treatment of others, and generosity?

Horace Newcomb, in his essay "Appalachia on Television: Region as Symbol in American Popular Culture," agrees that "the simpler values of the Clampetts win out over the morally deficient swindlers. What appeared to be simple-mindedness turns out to be deep wisdom simply expressed." But then he goes on to explain that *The Beverly Hillbillies* offers "no fully developed adult characters who can be associated with the positive values. . . . Their goodness is the simple goodness of children."[3]

The central problem, therefore, according to Newcomb, is that, despite their virtues, the mountain people are depicted as mere children. Of course, Jethro's behavior often seems "infantile," but Newcomb overstates his case when he claims that Granny is "childlike in her near senility," and Jed "seems zombie-like . . . and is rarely alert enough to exert his will."[4] While Granny is comic, excitable, and loud, her herbal remedies, "rheumatis' medicine," and home-made dinners are offered in the spirit of generosity, not "near senility." And Jed Clampett, who often shows wisdom in his silence, acts as an ironic observer of his family's antics, an active participant who exerts quiet control, ensuring that fairness and positive values prevail.

Recognizing the essential "goodness" of the Clampetts makes me more comfortable with *The Beverly Hillbillies* than some people from the region are. But even now, when I tune in to watch reruns, my analytical mind cautions, "You really shouldn't laugh—this show shamelessly portrays mountain people as comic fools. Do you want to be a part of perpetuating this stereotype that continues to stigmatize you and your neighbors today?" I just can't help myself. I still smile every time one of Jethro's bone-headed ideas causes Jed to declare, "Someday, I got to have a long talk with that boy."

Because of my mixed reactions to the comic stereotype, I set out to examine the sources of comic hillbillies. From medieval images and Renaissance jesters to modern American literature and culture, we can trace images that connect with the southern Appalachian "hillbilly fool."[5] Reexamining fools in their historic context offers us another way of looking at them—as mockers, truth-tellers, and mirrors of culture, subversive identities that overlap and intertwine.

The fool is traditionally an outsider. Like the Clampett family in Beverly Hills, fools are almost always set apart, "alienated, if not outcast." Wylie Sypher in "The Meanings of Comedy" explains that the fool is "the detached spectator who has been placed, or has placed himself, outside accepted codes. From this point 'outside'—this extrapolated fulcrum—he takes his leverage on the rest of us."[6] In other words, if we dismiss the "hillbilly fool" and assign him a place to "lean" on the edge of American culture, he has the potential to be in a position of power.

The power to mock authority may derive from the outsider's status of feeling inconsequential and having little to lose. The word "fool" derives from the Latin *follis*, meaning a pair of bellows or a windbag. The noun "fool," according to the *Oxford English Dictionary*, usually fits one or more of these descriptions: "deficient in judgment or sense, one who . . . behaves stupidly, a silly person, a simpleton"; "one who professionally counterfeits folly for the entertainment of others, a jester, a clown"; or in Biblical terms, a "vicious or impious" person. By examining these definitions together, as psychologist William Willeford does in his insightful study, *The Fool and His Scepter*, we see the fool as one who is as free and unpredictable as the wind, a blowhard, one whose words are apparently empty, absurd, or alarming.[7] However, when fools express ideas that can be dismissed as silly nonsense, they may be speaking dangerous truths.

A fairly traditional example of this type of fool is one who challenges God. Medieval fools, often cast in the role of disputers with a deity or with a secular source of power, appear in drawings alongside texts of Psalms 14 and 53, where the psalmist wrote, "The fool has said in his heart, There is no God." Psalters from the thirteenth to the fifteenth centuries contain illustrations that show the fool arguing with God, with devils, or with a monk. Images of the fool reveal his rustic, ragged poverty—his clothes barely cover him, or he is naked to the waist.[8] His nakedness may be interpreted as an outward sign of his truth or authenticity.

In contrast to images of wealth and power, the fifteenth-century fool wears bells and multicolors, apparently to create a distracting visual clash with the norm. Gifford explains that "in most cases [he] seems to try and underline the lack of symmetry which goes with lack of reason." He holds a weapon—a club or stick in one hand.[9] While such an obvious, direct challenge to the deity may cause anxiety and discomfort for a believer or a wary observer, honest truth-seeking believers recognize the chaos that prompts such defiance.

Fools boldly raise questions and call attention to truths and contradictions that many dare not voice. As J.W. Williamson points out, "the medieval state caught on fast that . . . sanctioning such folly was the best way to limit it. Hence the institution of All Fools Day, allowed on one day a year and no more." Encouraging people to wear fools' motley and inviting challenges and parodies of every authority—from the sacred to the secular—did not signify freedom, but its opposite.[10] The one-day event gave people only the illusion of freedom.

The official, authentic fool, the clown jester, of course, enjoyed a role that made him truly free throughout the year.

Shakespeare's fools enjoy similar sanctioned exemptions that allow them to be truth-tellers. Willeford explains that the fool is an "idiotic or mad person"—one with genuinely crazed wits (a natural fool) or one who "professionally counterfeits folly" (an artificial fool). "In the time of Elizabeth I, . . . either could serve as a jester or clown." Shakespeare creates professional fools, such as Touchstone in *As You Like It* and Feste in *Twelfth Night*, and the natural fool in *King Lear*. While in the forest of Arden, away from court, Touchstone parodies court manners and cleverly describes the relative merits of court and country life. He contrasts sharply with the fool in *Lear*, "who understands Lear's folly as no one else can. . . . In a sense, he is totally fearless, despite Lear's continual references to the whip, by which the fool could be officially chastised." *Lear's* fool, unlike Touchstone, is a more complete outsider, who becomes the king's "ritual scapegoat," though he offers Lear sound philosophical and moral advice. Because the fool acts "completely outside the social hierarchy, he is free to speak and to act without constraint."[11] His function is to speak truth to power.

In general terms, then, one way to look at the "hillbilly fool" is as a "ritual clown" who mocks power by challenging God or some other authority figure. According to Maurice Charney's *Comedy High and Low*, ritual clowns are "the most humble of creatures, the lowest on the social scale, completely anonymous and insignificant. Yet as truth-speakers they are endowed with a terrifying power. They are not, of course, aware that they are anything so exalted as truth-speakers. They merely act their role according to the prescribed forms and in an unsophisticated and unselfconscious way."[12] The hillbilly fool may get his way without trying because his actions are based on common sense and honesty, exposing the base ignorance and greed of someone with more power who considers himself superior.

Fools especially mock the power of those who fool themselves about their own lives. In the sixteenth-century work "The Praise of Folly," for instance, Erasmus identifies "fool" to mean "Everyman in the presence of God." He contends, "if I *recognize* someone as a fool, I am in the act of assuming that I am a non-fool; and in thinking *that*, I become a fool in fact."[13] As Williamson explains, "in other words, the fool could be thought of as a mirror image of power's absurd possibilities, a funhouse mirror image set up for medicinal purposes."[14]

In fact, fools function so well as mirrors that they create a kind of double vision. Medieval fools and Renaissance court jesters often carry small heads on sticks as a visual reminder of our divided selves, our vanity, and our unclear self-knowledge. European artists depict fools literally holding mirrors, so that they can examine themselves, the image of someone else, or a glimpse of ourselves. In one of Holbein's illustrations of Erasmus's *Praise of Folly*, a fool looks at himself in a handheld mirror, and the image in the mirror seems to mock the fool by sticking out its tongue.[15]

A tarot card from Austria (1453–57) carries the inscription "Female joker. Looking at her grinning idiot's face in the mirror." The problem is that the face in the mirror is not smiling, though the woman holding the mirror clearly is, and the angle at which she holds the mirror makes it seem more likely that the mirror reflects the face of the onlooker than that of the female joker.[16] The mirror literally and symbolically reflects the interplay between the fool and ourselves, illusion and reality, deception and self-awareness.

Artists depict the German fool/trickster Till Eulenspiegel with an owl and a mirror. The name "Eulenspiegel" combines "owl" (*eule*), a symbol of wisdom, with "glass" (*spiegle*). According to Williamson, "Both owl and mirror had been symbols of self-knowledge and wisdom, but Till's wisdom came in knowing folly." With the character posing as a jester, he allows the owl to look into the mirror, "which is once again aimed at the reader: 'To get wisdom, look into this folly and see yourselves.'"[17]

When a fool shows us ourselves, if we trust what we see, that fool can be called an *eiron*. Tracing the long heritage of the fool from European art to American literature becomes easier with Northrop Frye's discussion of classic comedy in the *Anatomy of Criticism*, which offers terminology to name observable relationships between the fool and others. According to Northrop Frye, the *eiron* is self-deprecating;[18] he recognizes that "human beings won't change or can't change and therefore we make the best of our situation by laughing at ourselves and others." The *eiron* "reflects a comic view of life" and functions "to puncture the illusion of the *alazon*."[19] The *alazon*, Greek for "imposter," is "someone who pretends or tries to be something more than he is."[20]

The *eiron* hillbilly "takes for granted a world which is full of injustices, follies, and crimes, and yet is permanent and undisplaceable... What is recommended is conventional life at its best: a clairvoyant knowledge of human nature in oneself and others, [and] an avoidance of all illusion." Frye describes such an *eiron* as "a rustic with pastoral affinities" and aligns him with "the kind of American satire that passes as folk humor, exemplified in the Biglow Papers, Mr. Dooley, Artemus Ward, and Will Rogers."[21] These figures have in common their proclivity for exposing illusions by deflating arrogance and pretensions.

In American literature, William Byrd II is one of the best eighteenth-century examples of the *alazon*, the pompous one who assumes a superior stance to the Carolinians in *The History of the Dividing Line, Between Virginia and North Carolina as Run in 1728–29*. Byrd, a native Virginia aristocrat, describes North Carolina as "Lubberland," a prototype of Dogpatch, USA: "Surely there is no place in the World where the Inhabitants live with less Labour than in N Carolina. It approaches nearer to the Description of Lubberland than any other, by the great felicity of the Climate, the easiness of raising Provisions, and the Slothfulness of the people."[22] Throughout his backwoods surveying trek, Byrd, the *alazon* authority figure, clearly assumes himself superior to the rustic North Carolinians. According to Byrd, the rustics are particularly shiftless fools.

> They make their Wives rise out of their Beds early in the Morning, at the same time that they lye and Snore, till the Sun has risen one-third of his course, and disperst all the unwholesome Damps. Then, after Stretching and Yawning for half an Hour, they light their Pipes, and, under the protection of a cloud of Smoak, venture out into the open Air....
>
> Thus they loiter away their Lives, like Solomon's Sluggard, with their Arms across, and at the Winding up of the Year Scarcely have Bread to Eat.
>
> To speak the Truth, tis a thorough Aversion to Labor that makes People file off to N Carolina, where Plenty and a Warm Sun confirm them in their Disposition to Laziness for their whole lives (record of March 25 1841).[23]

The aristocratic Byrd is among the first in American literature to caricature agrarian people as crude, lazy drinkers of homemade liquor. He describes Lubberlanders who drink rum that "is not improperly called 'kill-devil' . . . distilled there from foreign molasses, which, if skillfully managed, yields near gallon for gallon."[24] His portrayal of North Carolinians does not allow them to become true *eirons* in this work because he never gives them the chance to speak for themselves.

Byrd contrasts their lack of industry with his own expectations, however, not with their necessity. Though he ridicules their lack of industry, he plainly describes them as self-sufficient people who live with little labor because they can. Because the North Carolinians wisely chose to reside in a place that easily provided for their needs, their actions suggest that Byrd failed to see them (and himself) clearly.

One of the best nineteenth-century examples of an American frontier *eiron* is George Washington Harris's character Sut Lovingood. "Sut was a rambunctious, hell-raising, and unconventional character out of the mountains of Tennessee who told his fantastic yarns in his own language and reflected on the hypocrisies, inequities, and absurdities of human nature."[25] Sut, with more vulgarity than many later hillbilly fools, challenges every kind of authority—from his own father, who's chased by hornets, to the "law" and the preacher. We admire his ability to mock authority, to cut right through dishonesty, and to expose our illusions about others and ourselves.

As an American *eiron*, Sut casts a long shadow across the nineteenth century and into the twentieth. Thomas Inge, editor of the facsimile edition of *Sut Lovingood Yarns*, points out that after Mark Twain reviewed the book in 1867, he showed immense, lifelong admiration for the work, and that William

Faulkner owned a copy of the book which he kept by his bed. "Erskine Caldwell's poor white trash, Al Capp's denizens of Dogpatch, or television's Beverly Hillbillys [sic] and Dukes of Hazard [sic] are all a part of the tradition. . . ." In fact, Inge, contends that Sut directly influenced cartoonist Billy De Beck to relocate Barney Google's racetrack to the Appalachian Mountains and, as long as he was alive, to give "carefully researched authenticity" to the comic strip. "It was only after a thorough reading and rereading with increasing admiration of *Sut Lovingood Yarns* that he created Snuffy Smith."[26] The comic strip character of Snuffy Smith, however, changed dramatically when taken over by De Beck's assistant, Fred Lasswell. Stephen Becker, author of *Comic Art in America*, described Snuffy Smith and his clan as "no realer than Al Capp's Yokums, but their dedication to illicit moonshine whisky and their general belligerence brought them much closer to the archetypal idea of the American hillbilly."[27]

Unlike Snuffy Smith, however, Sut Lovingood is a self-effacing fool who doesn't fool himself. Sut shows enough self-awareness to call himself a "nat'ral born durn'd fool" and to ask readers, "did yu ever see sich a sampil of a human afore?" Sut could not be more self-deprecating when he sees himself as a man with no soul: "I haint got nara a soul, nuffin but a whisky proof gizzard."[28]

As "a nat'ral born durn'd fool," Sut raises subversive and dangerous questions about human nature. He challenges God's representatives (bishops and elders), and his worldview mirrors his own observations about the human appetite for power: "Whar thar ain't enuf feed, big childer roots littil childer outen the troff, an' gobbils up thar part. Jis' so the yeath over: bishops eats elders, elders eats common peopil; they eats sich cattil es me, I eats possums, possums eats chickins, chickins swallers wums, an' wums am content tu eat dus, an' the dus am the aind ove hit all."[29] Sut holds no illusions about human nature, and he holds nothing sacred but the here and now—as he says, dust is the end of it all. As Appalachian studies scholar Robert J. Higgs points out, "he raises the question who is the bigger fool—Sut, who acknowledges his condition, or those of us who refuse to recognize our own predatory ways and pretensions?"[30] Sut, an unparalleled *eiron*, asks us to take a look at our own place in the Great Chain of Being.

Sut Lovingood inspired the hillbilly fools in the funny papers. When Al Capp introduced the world to Mammy, Pappy, and Abner Yokum in his comic strip *Li'l Abner* in 1934, the idea came from Capp's memories of a hitchhiking trip through Kentucky and from the popularity of "hillbilly" music in a vaudeville show and on the radio.[31] Capp, who blended "yokel" and "hokum" to create the name of Yokum, was the first cartoonist to use hillbillies as his principal characters.[32]

Capp described his rawboned rustics as a "family of innocents" who learn that the world outside their native Dogpatch, Kentucky, is a treacherous place: "This innocence of theirs is indestructible, so that while they possess all the homely virtues in which we profess to believe, they seem ingenuous because the world around them is irritated by them, cheats them, kicks them around. They are trusting, kind, loyal, generous and patriotic. It's truly a bewildering world in which they find themselves." Story lines, particularly during the first few years of *Li'l Abner*, contrasted the innocent, rustic Yokums with city folks who did not adhere to the basic fairness and decency that ruled in Dogpatch. Yet, Dogpatch is "ultimately . . . the simple and therefore often astounding reflection of the world surrounding it. We most laugh at Dogpatch when it most closely mimics our own society, and the denizens of Dogpatch are never funnier than when they reveal through their foolishness our own absurdities."[33]

In the "'Zoot Suit' Yokum" episode, for example, Al Capp slaps at the inanity of commercialism and American capitalism. Mr. J. Colossal McGenius, an advertising executive who makes ten thousand dollars per word of advice, hires Li'l Abner to wear a zoot suit and "to do kind deeds and perform stupendous feats!!" Abner agrees, "Thass fine!!—ah loves t'do kind deeds—an' ah already got stupendous feets—see?" Abner, like Jethro on *The Beverly Hillbillies*, also claims to have "th' intelly-gunce t'handle this job!—wal, jest lissen t'this! two an' two is three; three an' three is fo'. . . ."[34]

With Abner as the Zoot Suit Hero demonstrating "incredible, foolhardy courage" that attracts media attention, zoot suit sales soar, and the nation seems to have gone crazy. Newspaper headlines announce (with eerie prescience) that a media celebrity is "Offered Nomination for Presidency!!" The other clothing manufacturers unite to discredit Abner by hiring a convict double, Gat Garson, to do despicable acts that ruin the reputation of zoot suits.[35] Manipulated by the rich and powerful, Abner is clearly a fool—but so are Americans who blindly trust advertisers and the media.

Despite his fame as the best-known comic strip hillbilly fool, Li'l Abner Yokum has a complex identity. He is a hero because "somehow he does not become debased . . . Abner maintains his basic goodness and incorruptibility" and at the same time, he is an antihero. "After all," as Arthur A. Berger explains in his *Li'l Abner: A Study in American Satire*, "he is a fool, he has no profession, and he is embarrassingly uninterested in women. He is a man without qualities in a world that is without order, without sanity, and in moral and political chaos. He is a continual refutation of the American dream of rising from rags to riches—for he is always in rags and seems to be happy there."[36] Abner's foolishness is laughable, but when we look closely at those who dupe him, we see either that we are smarter and more capable of dealing with villains of higher social class and power or that we prefer Abner's trust in other people's goodness to the cynical alternative.

Most people perceive Li'l Abner as "a fool—because of the things he says and does—" but, according to Berger, "they are not quite sure what kind of fool he is." Abner's role as a pawn of rich and successful city people makes him, as Berger points out, "a victim who diverts the wrath of the gods (and, who makes the reader feel better by being so obviously a stupid and inferior person)."[37] When we laugh at this hillbilly fool, we laugh at ourselves.

Capp's satire in *Li'l Abner* holds up a mirror to a society more willing to laugh at itself in a comic strip than in an editorial. *Li'l Abner* leads us to see such contradictions in human nature as our tendency to trust people, but to doubt appearances; to live freely, but occasionally to oppress others; to manipulate, and to be manipulated. "If . . . Capp gets us to see what hypocrites we are, and yet doesn't make us completely despise ourselves for being what we are, he is indeed teaching us something."[38] (When Al Capp became increasingly conservative near the end of his life, I think he tended to teach us less.)

Finally, by studying the hillbilly fools in *Li'l Abner* in the first half of this century, we have the opportunity to learn about other hillbilly icons in late-twentieth-century popular culture—the slouch-hatted, bib-overalled, barefooted hillbilly image sold on cards and plaques in tourist shops from Gatlinburg, Tennessee, to Little Rock, Arkansas; from Blowing Rock, North Carolina, to Bluefield, West Virginia.

When J.W. Williamson, editor of the fine regional studies review *Appalachian Journal*, poses the question, "Who buys these icons of negative identity?" his answer is "not the upwardly-sashaying urban class, the managers, the professionals, the office warriors." Williamson believes that "hillbilly souvenirs do not go into condos but into countryside homes where ground sense is acknowledged and accommodated. Stuck-working people buy them, the purely-salaried buy them, and they get the joke. The hillbilly takes his durn ease right in the middle of all these working people. He gives the horse-laugh to middle-class respectability. He's absurdly and delightfully free."[39] Those who think these consumers merely endorse the stereotype by purchasing hillbilly souvenirs may be missing the point: the real fool is the deluded one who believes the image—not the one who gets the joke and carries it home.

So what does all of this "fool" history have to do with *The Beverly Hillbillies*? As agrarian people in an urban setting, the Clampetts, like many Appalachian people, are outsiders in American culture. In ragged clothes, reminding us of the raggedness of medieval fools, the Clampetts are free—free to decide not to get "above their raising" with fancy clothes, sports cars, and unfamiliar "city ways."

Though the oil discovered on their property made them millionaires and they moved from a cabin in the Ozarks to a Beverly Hills mansion, they haven't changed much. Though their money gives them the freedom to expose the greed of banker Milburn Drysdale, as well as the excesses of American capitalism, they don't fool themselves about who they are. They know they are ignorant of city ways, but they also know they learned about everything they value before they ever left the mountains.

Like Sut Lovingood, they enjoy life, and in their encounters with everyone, from police officers to clergy, physicians, and college professors, they challenge figures of authority with honest questions. As Al Capp said of his Yokums in Dogpatch, the Clampetts have refreshingly "indestructible" innocence, and "they reveal through their foolishness our own absurdities."[40] They are fools who hold up mirrors to us when they speak the truth. The hillbilly fool may get his way without trying because his actions are based on common sense and honesty, exposing the base ignorance and greed of someone with more power who considers himself superior. The Clampetts remind me that I don't have to defer to those in positions of authority who violate my trust or common sense. If they didn't ever lead me to see myself a bit more clearly, I'd be angry to see hillbilly fools on television and on postcards on wire racks at the corner gas station. But now that I place these "fools" in line with their kin, I finally get the joke.

## Notes

1. James Branscome, "Annihilating the Hillbilly: The Appalachians' Struggle with America's Institutions," *Katallagete* 3 (winter 1971): 25.

2. Ibid.

3. Horace Newcomb, "Appalachia on Television: Region as Symbol in American Popular Culture," in *Appalachian Images in Folk and Popular Culture*, 2d ed., W.K. McNeil (Knoxville: Univ. of Tennessee Press, 1995), 322, 323.

4. Ibid.

5. I gratefully acknowledge J.W. Williamson, author of *Hillbillyland: What the Movies Did to the Mountains and What the Mountains Did to the Movies* (Chapel Hill: Univ. of North Carolina Press, 1995), for his generosity in sharing parts of his *Hillbillyland* manuscript with me before publication. From his book I collected many of the examples to which I refer, though his work contains still others as well as a wonderful collection of illustrations.

6. Wylie Sypher, "The Meanings of Comedy," in *Comedy* (Garden City, N.Y.: Doubleday Anchor, 1956), 234.

7. William Willeford, *The Fool and His Scepter: A Study in Clowns and Jesters and their Audience* (Evanston, Ill.: Northwestern Univ. Press, 1969), 10.

8. D.J. Gifford, "Iconographical Notes towards a Definition of the Medieval Fool," in *The Fool and the Trickster*, ed. Paul V. Williams (Totowa, N.J.: D.S. Brewer, Rowman, and Littlefield, 1979) 31, 20.

9. Ibid., 19.

10. Williamson, *Hillbillyland*, 26.

11. Maurice Charney, Comedy High and Low: An Introduction to the *Experience of Comedy* (New York: Oxford Univ. Press, 1978), 10, 173, 173.

12. Ibid.

13. Willeford, *Fool and His Scepter*, 10.

14. Williamson, *Hillbillyland*, 27.

15. Willeford, *Fool and His Scepter*, 35.

16. Ibid., 39.

17. Williamson, *Hillbillyland*, 27, 28.

18. Northrop Frye, *Anatomy of Criticism: Four Essays* (1957; reprint, Princeton, N.J.: Princeton Univ. Press, 1971), 40.

19. Robert J. Higgs, "Loyal Jones: Calvinist Eiron." (paper, presented at Loyal Jones's retirement celebration, Berea, Ky., 1994), 4. (I appreciate Jack Higgs's sharing his work with me.)

20. Frye, *Anatomy of Criticism*, 39.

21. Ibid., 226, 227.

22. William Byrd II, "The History of the Dividing Line . . .," in *Anthology of American Literature*, vol. 1, 2d ed., eds. George McMichael et al, (New York: Macmillan, 1980), 205.

23. Ibid.

24. Ibid., 206.

25. Thomas Inge, introduction to *Sut Lovingood: Yarns Spun by a Nat'ral Born Durn'd Fool,*" by George Washington Harris (Memphis: St. Lukes Press, 1987), not paginated.

26. Ibid.

27. Stephen Becker, *Comic Art in America* (New York: Simon and Schuster, 1959), 94.

28. Harris, *Sut Lovingood*, 172.

29. Ibid., 228.

30. Robert J. Higgs, "Versions of 'Natural Man' in Appalachia," in *An Appalachian Symposium: Essays Written in Honor of Cratis D. Williams*, ed. J.W. Williamson (Boone, N.C.: Appalachian State Univ. Press, 1977): 161.

31. Becker, *Comic Art in America*, 188, and Catherine Capp Halberstadt, introduction to *Li'l Abner: Dailies, Vol. One*: 1934–35 (Princeton, Wisc.: Kitchen Sink Press, 1988), 4.

32. Edwin T. Arnold, "Al, Abner, and Appalachia," *Appalachian Journal* 17 (spring 1990): 264, 266.

33. Ibid., 266–67, 274.

34. Al Capp, "Innocents in Peril." *The World of Li'l Abner* (1952); rpt. *Li'l Abner: Dailies, Volume One: 1934–35* (Princeton, Wisc.: Kitchen Sink Press, 1988), 5.

35. Al Capp, *From Dogpatch to Slobbovia: The World of Li'l Abner*, (Boston: Beacon, 1964), n.p.

36. Arthur Asa Berger, *Li'l Abner: A Study in American Satire* (New York: Twayne, 1970), 92, 163.

37. Ibid., 90, 91.

38. David Manning White, "The Art of Al Capp," in *From Dogpatch to Slobbovia: The World of Li'l Abner* (Boston: Beacon, 1964), n.p.

39. Williamson, *Hillbillyland*, 3.

40. Arnold, "Al, Abner, and Appalachia," 266, 274.

## Bibliography

Arnold, Edwin T. "Al, Abner, and Appalachia." *Appalachian Journal* 17(3) (spring 1990): 262–95.

Becker, Stephen. *Comic Art in America*. New York: Simon and Schuster, 1959.

Berger, Arthur Asa. *Li'l Abner: A Study in American Satire*. New York: Twayne, 1970.

Branscome, James. "Annihilating the Hillbilly: The Appalachians' Struggle with American Institutions." *Katallagete* 3 (winter 1971): 25–32.

Byrd, William, II. "The History of the Dividing Line . . . " In vol. 1 of *Anthology of American Literature*, 2d ed., ed. George McMichael et al., 195–99. New York: Macmillian, 1980.

Capp, Al. "Innocents in Peril." *The World of Li'l Abner*. 1952. Reprint, Princeton, Wisc.: Kitchen Sink Press, 1988.

Charney, Maurice. *Comedy High and Low: An Introduction to the Experience of Comedy*. New York: Oxford Univ. Press, 1978.

Frye, Northrop. *Anatomy of Criticism: Four Essays*. 1957. Reprint, Princeton, N.J.: Princeton Univ. Press, 1971.

Gifford, D.J. "Iconographical Notes towards a Definition of the Medieval Fool." In *The Fool and the Trickster*, ed. Paul V. Williams, 18–35. Totowa, N.J.: D.S. Brewer, Rowman, and Littlefield, 1979.

Harris, George Washington. *Sut Lovingood: Yarns Spun by A "Nat'ral Born Durn'd Fool,"* ed. M. Thomas Inge. Memphis: St. Luke's Press, 1987.

Higgs, Robert J. "Loyal Jones: Calvinist *Eiron*." Berea, Ky. 1994.

———. "Versions of 'Natural Man' in Appalachia." In *An Appalachian Symposium: Essays Written in Honor of Cratis D. Williams*, ed. J.W. Williamson, 159–68. Boone, N.C.: Appalachian State Univ. Press, 1977.

Newcomb, Horace. "Appalachia on Television: Region as Symbol in American Popular Culture." *Appalachian Journal* 7(1–2) (autumn-winter 1979–80): 155–64; rpt. in *Appalachian Images in Folk and Popular Culture*, ed. W.K. McNeil, 315–29. Knoxville: Univ. of Tennessee Press, 1995.

Sypher, Wylie. "The Meanings of Comedy." In *Comedy*. Garden City, N.Y.: Doubleday Anchor, 1956.

White, David Manning. "The Art of Al Capp." *From Dogpatch to Slobbovia: The World of Li'l Abner*. Boston: Beacon, 1964.

Willeford, William. *The Fool and His Scepter: A Study in Clowns and Jesters and Their Audience*. Evanston, Ill.: Northwestern Univ. Press, 1969.

Williamson, J.W. *Hillbillyland: What the Movies Did to the Mountains and What the Mountains Did to the Movies*. Chapel Hill: Univ. of North Carolina Press, 1995.

# III

# Speaking More Personally

## Responses to Appalachian Stereotypes

# The "R" Word

## What's So Funny (and Not So Funny) about Redneck Jokes

### Anne Shelby

◈　　◈　　◈　　◈◈　　◈　　◈　　◈

If you happen to be from eastern Kentucky, as I am, then other people's stereotypes of the place you are from are as much a part of your landscape as the hills themselves. They can loom as large and seem as permanent. You have to find your way over or around them. But unlike the mountains, which can be seen from some distance, stereotypes jump out at you in ambush—at parties and meetings, at dinner with friends, from movies, from magazines and newspapers, from your favorite TV show. Even in college classes.

"And this group," a University of Kentucky professor says of the eastern Kentucky population in a study of television viewing habits, "probably doesn't even know how to turn on their sets." I think about Lillie Fae, my neighbor, who has a party every New Year's Eve. There's no drinking at Lillie Fae's, but there is a lot of eating—shuck beans, corn bread, dried apple stack cakes—and lots of homemade music. "Great party," I tell her. "You can watch it anytime you want to," she says. "I've got the last eight New Years on videotape."

The down-and-out neighbors on *The Drew Carey Show* ask him to give them a fake job reference by saying they were his interior decorators. "Right," he says. "And I'll hire an Appalachian family to do my garden." I think about my own neighbors' gardens, about perennial beds bordered with river rock, carefully tended rose bushes, late patches of greens, and ripe corn and tomatoes ready to put up for the winter.

The fifth-grade teacher is introducing me to her class at a private school in Louisville. "This is Anne Shelby, our visiting author," she says. "She lives in the middle of nowhere." No, I protest, I live in the middle of somewhere, a real place. Maybe that's the trouble. We live in a real place that other people see as a symbol. And in the wide gap between the reality and the symbol—we have to live there, too. Being Appalachian means being presented throughout one's life with images of Appalachia that bear little or no resemblance to one's own experience. The difference between the image and the reality creates dissonance, a contradiction to be resolved, and people try to do that in different ways.

When I was a young teenager and photographs from the War on Poverty began to appear in the media, some of them from the area where I lived, I understood that the people in the pictures lived in Appalachia. It was the first time I had heard the word outside of geography class, where it referred to a chain of mountains, like the Rockies or the Poconos. But now it seemed to mean something else, a place where dirty children sat listlessly on the porches of old shacks, a place that existed only in black and white. I had seen people and houses like the ones in the pictures, but not many, not in comparison to most of the people and houses I saw in eastern Kentucky. So I figured Appalachia must be in West Virginia. Much later I had a student from West Virginia who said he'd always thought they must be talking about East Tennessee.

Many people resolve the contradiction between image and reality in this way, which enables them to escape the stereotypes without the trouble of questioning them. The "real hillbillies," whoever they are, are hard to find. They're always over the hill somewhere, or on up the holler, one county over and one class down.

Another response is just to go along. For every briar hopper joke they tell you, tell them two. "Why did they build a bridge across the Ohio River?" "So the hillbillies could swim over in the shade." Yuck it up. Pretend not to be all that bright. Manufacture and exaggerate your hillbilly credentials. I have a friend who practices this method and recommends it highly. "You're pulling their leg all the time," he says. "And they don't even know it."

But a more common response to the stereotypes is anger. If you hang around long enough and the subject comes up, you will see it. It can come across as mere testiness or oversensitivity, but it is the product of a thousand insults, small and large. In this huge and diverse region, it is, perhaps more than anything else, what we have in common.

For no matter which response we choose, the problem presents itself to be solved again and again. Appalachians have been objecting to the stereotypes for well over a century now, seemingly to no avail. The images keep coming because the rest of the country seems to need and enjoy them, and because the perception on which they rest remains unshaken, the perception of Appalachia, not as one region in a country made up of regions, but as a symbol. What it is seen as a symbol of, depends, of course, on who's doing the looking. And it doesn't matter so much what they're looking at as what they're looking for.

Particular landscapes—mountains, deserts, bodies of water—seem to suggest certain meanings. We approach such places with expectations. Mountains seem to suggest something hidden in those labyrinthine folds, like a secret truth tucked in the labyrinth of the mind. In the late nineteenth century, an America questioning "progress" took an interest in mountains and other areas supposedly "untouched by civilization." Later folk revivals saw the region as a repository for American and British folklife. Less nostalgic eras took a more jaundiced view, seeing Appalachians as relics, humorous or dangerous, of a barbarous past. From noble mountaineers to quaint charming folk to hillbillies to victims to genetic freaks, our stock keeps falling. Now the word "hillbilly" is often the first in the phrase "hillbilly redneck poor white trash."

Stop me if you've heard these. Please. Stop me. How to tell you're a redneck: You go to a family reunion to pick up dates. Your family tree doesn't fork. Your daddy walked you to school because he was in the same grade. You refer to fifth grade as "my senior year." When the photographer says "cheese" you form a line. Your truck has nicer curtains than your trailer. Your two-year-old has more teeth than you. Your favorite car color is primer red. A trip to the bathroom in the middle of the night involves shoes and a flashlight.

Personally I don't think these jokes, most of them versions of the old hillbilly stereotypes, are all that funny. I ask myself, is it just me? Has aging cost me my sense of humor? I don't think so. Some things still make me roll on the floor with laughter (though it is increasingly difficult to get up afterward). But I keep finding myself in rooms with people who are cracking up at lines like, "How to tell you're a redneck: Your wife wears an orange vest to work. Directions to your house include, Turn off the paved road." We're not laughing at you, the jokesters reassure me. We're laughing with you. But I'm not laughing.

I live in a rural community where three of the recurring elements of redneck jokes—trucks, trailers, and toilets—are not uncommon. But I've never heard a redneck joke here. I hear them when I go other places, at lunch with lawyers and business people in the county seat, at meetings with arts administrators in Lexington and Louisville. Several collections of redneck jokes in Xerox folklore form have come into my hands, fifth- and sixth-generation copies dotted and streaked with toner. With comedian Jeff Foxworthy, redneck jokes made the crossover from small-town folklore to popular culture. You can find redneck jokes in books, on video and audiotapes and on the Internet.

Beneath the surface of something as seemingly inexplicable as the popularity of these jokes, there must be several explanations. I'd like to suggest the following, which I call Okay to Be a Redneck, Used to Be a Redneck, It Ain't Us, It's Them, Nobody to Kick Around Anymore, and If It Wasn't So Funny It'd Be Scary as Hell.

## Okay to Be a Redneck

When Jeff Foxworthy performs his "redneck" routine at a nightclub in Texas, he prefaces it by saying that he's from Georgia and that people in California, where he lives now, make fun of the way he talks. "Life in L.A.," he says, "has gotten too sophisticated." The mostly southern crowd howls with delight at lines like "You might be a redneck if . . . someone asks for your I.D. and you show them your belt buckle . . . if your checks feature pictures of hunting dogs . . . if you've ever been too drunk to fish." In certain groups and contexts these jokes can allow both the teller and the listener to identify with the group being defined. The jokes can say, Yeah, that's us. Funny but lovable. It's okay to be a redneck.

But the other side of this coin is considerably darker. Foxworthy's incest jokes draw audible moans and objections from the audience. Here what we recognize is not a reflection of ourselves but an old stereotype, and a vicious and inaccurate one at that. Where I live, almost everybody is kin to each other, one way or another. Some of the same families have lived here for two hundred years, up Bullskin, Crane, and Buffalo Creek, down Road Run, Teges, and Newfound. The older people know, and can tell you, who their great-great-grandparents were, the names of all their second cousins, how the Combses are related to the Barretts, the Bishops to the Gabbards, the Abners to the Gays. This information is important not just because it tells us who we are, though it does do that. It is also important because it guards against incest, which is strictly taboo. In a small community, you have to keep careful track.

## Used to Be a Redneck

Some of the people who seem to enjoy redneck jokes the most are those who, when called on it, defend themselves by producing their own "redneck credentials." They grew up on a farm. Their parents still live there. They love the mountains. But this isn't information they'd shared before or that you would necessarily have figured out on your own. For this group, the redneck joke works both ways. That's why they like it so much. It establishes a tenuous connection to the culture that is the subject of the joke, a connection that they, like Jeff Foxworthy, feel gives them a right to tell it. But more important the joke functions to put distance between the teller and the subject. For this group the joke says, Look at me, how far I've come, what good taste I have. I used to be a redneck. But I'm not anymore.

Trailer jokes are popular with this group as well as with the writers of television sitcoms. The jokes are based on the premise that people who live in trailers are somehow deserving of ridicule, that their choice of housing is the result of innate poor taste rather than dull economics. Selling, repossessing, and reselling trailers is a big business in my county, as it is in other economically depressed areas. Financing a house on a low income can be nearly impossible, but your local mobile home salesman can put you in a fully furnished double-wide in a matter of days. The price tag and the interest rates will be high, of course, as will the chance your home will be repossessed if you can't keep up the payments.

## It Ain't Us, It's Them

While identified with comedian Jeff Foxworthy, redneck jokes can be heard on other television programs as well, and they don't always use "the R word." On *Blossom* a young male character is being visited by his attractive fairy godmother. "Is it okay to marry your fairy godmother?" he asks. "Only in Kentucky," she replies. On *Friends* an assignation between a man and woman who don't know they're related is referred to as "an Appalachian cocktail." When her son D.J. doesn't want to kiss a girl in the school play, Roseanne assumes it's because the girl is black. "We're not some barefoot banjo-picking poor white trash," she tells him.

The latest cycle in the continuous recycling of Appalachian stereotypes features Appalachia as the homeland of racists and practitioners of incest. While talk shows and television newsmagazines provide disturbing evidence of sexual abuse in families of every region, race, and class, watching sitcoms would make you think that incest occurs only in Appalachia. While news programs report racial tensions in cities and corporations across the country, watching sitcoms would lead one to believe that racism exists only among "rednecks," "hillbillies," and "poor white trash." Unhappily, those problems do exist in Appalachia, as they do elsewhere. It hardly seems fair or helpful to pretend they belong to only one class or region. For the larger society, redneck jokes and other forms of Appalachian stereotypes serve the important function of providing a scapegoat for racism and incest. We aren't racists. We aren't perverts, the jokes say. There they are, over there. It ain't us. It's them.

## Nobody to Kick Around Anymore

When you're standing at the end of a long line, it's a relief when somebody comes up and stands behind you. Now you're not at the end of the line anymore. Individually and in groups, we seem to need to define ourselves positively by defining other people negatively. We need somebody to laugh at, to feel superior to, someone beside whom we feel smart, attractive, successful, and cool. Sometimes neighbors are good for this, or certain relatives, or the idiots at work.

As a country, we used to have numerous groups who served this important function: Jews, blacks, women, drunks, gays, the Irish, and the Polish, to name a few. But those days are gone, and many people seem to resent what they perceive as pressure to be "politically correct." "There's nobody to make fun of anymore", they complain. "Now we have to remember: Alcoholism is a disease. Being gay is not. Tell a joke to a woman and you could get slapped—with a sexual harassment suit. There's nobody to make fun of anymore. Everybody takes themselves so seriously. Hey guys! Lighten up! We were just kidding!" But we weren't just kidding. And we're not kidding now.

Some people know, of course, that what we unfortunately call "political correctness" isn't just about manners; it's human dignity. Acknowledging the dignity, the full humanity, of another person or group means not telling belittling stories about them. It means calling them by their right names, the names they choose for themselves.

But even people who seem to understand this, who would never make bad jokes about Polish people and lightbulbs, for example, feel perfectly free to stereotype rural southerners—farmers, Baptists, Holy Rollers, hillbillies, rednecks, poor white trash. To stereotype is to dehumanize; to make ridiculous; to ignore history, politics, economics, and culture. To deny full humanity. It's the same trick, no matter who it's played on. It's the same joke, no matter who's the butt. Maybe people who do this have only so much compassion, so much sensitivity, so much political consciousness to go around. Maybe they think they have to draw the line somewhere and that's where they draw it—somewhere around the Mason-Dixon, or below ten thousand dollars a year.

But there's more to it than that. Jokes about blacks and women and Jews, about immigrants and gays, did more than provide a good laugh at somebody else's expense. They did more, even, than put distance between the teller and the subject so the teller could feel superior. By dehumanizing and reducing their subjects, they also served to dismiss legitimate complaints about discrimination and to deflect potentially disturbing questions about who has money and power, who doesn't, and why.

Jokes about rednecks work the same way. It is not a coincidence that redneck jokes, like hillbilly stereotypes, take as their subject some of the poorest people in America. The jokes effectively dismiss poverty as a function of politics and economics. Redneck jokes define poverty as a matter of inferior taste. If these people are poor, they probably deserve it, and it's probably their own fault. If they live in trailers, have bad teeth, and only go to the fifth grade, it's because they choose it, because they are ignorant and stupid, ridiculous somehow. They are, in any case, not to be taken seriously. If we had to take them seriously, what might we have to do? What guilt would we have to deal with? What inconvenient changes would we have to make? And what threat would they pose? Poor white people who live in the country seem not to raise these questions. If they did, they might be less amusing.

## If It Wasn't So Funny, It'd Be Scary as Hell

If movies are a nation's dreams, *Cape Fear* is one of its nightmares. It shows what might happen if hillbilly rednecks ever get educated, politicized, and majorly pissed off. This movie is supposed to be very scary. And it is if you identify with lawyer Sam Bowden, who is being stalked by his former client, Max Cady, who just got out of prison. Early on, Bowden describes Cady as "from the hills . . . a Pentecostal cracker." The detective Bowden hires calls Cady "poor white trash." But the threat Cady poses isn't just his demonstrated propensity to rape and murder. Cady sees through Bowden's hypocrisy and deceit, through the thin veneer of his family's stability, through the pretense and injustice of the society Bowden represents.

Martin Scorsese's remake of *Cape Fear* explores the political and social implications inherent but repressed in the original version made in the 1950s. It's still a thriller, but a thriller that knows about gender, race, and class in America. Red, white, and blue are everywhere. Cady sits threateningly on the stone fence outside Bowden's house, Fourth of July fireworks exploding in the sky behind him. We watch the Fourth of July parade—flags, balloons, and scenes from American history—reflected in his sunglasses. He drives a red Mustang and wears red, white, and blue shirts. He's identified with women, blacks, and Hispanics. Sodomized in prison, Cady tells Bowden he knows what it's like to be a woman. He tells Bowden's wife that they have a connection: Bowden has betrayed them both. To gain entrance to the Bowden's kitchen, Cady puts on clothes of the Hispanic maid. Black from his hiding place under the Bowden's car, he exchanges glances with a black woman, who does not turn him in.

Scorsese's Cady is a monster, but an interesting, perceptive, and sometimes charming one, dangerous because he embodies the long-repressed anger of "poor white trash." In prison, he taught himself to read ("law books mostly"); developed seemingly superhuman strength and resistance to pain ("Mommie handled snakes. Granddaddy drank strychnine. You might say I had a leg up, genetically speaking"); saved his money; decorated himself with tattoos of Bible verses about the vengeance of the Lord and a torso-sized scale with justice on one side, truth on the other. "You judged me and condemned me," he tells Bowden. "You thought you were better than me." Bowden, of course, denies this. "Well if you're no better than I am," Cady says, "then I can have what you have."

The fear in *Cape Fear* is that one crazy guy will cut your throat with a piano wire and rape your wife and daughter. But that fear rests on another fear: the frightening possibility that "poor white trash" might stop taking their anger out on each other and turn it on the middle and upper classes. They might, if given time to think about it, come up with a dangerous synthesis of religion, politics, and violence. At the end of the movie, Bowden tries to kill Cady, but fails. Cady goes down, but on his own terms—speaking in tongues and singing "I Am Bound for the Promised Land." Sam Bowden has finally "learned about loss," has become more human. I don't think he'll be so condescending to "Pentecostal crackers" anymore.

I know how I feel when I hear yet another redneck joke or see yet another tired hillbilly stereotype on a popular television show. I do not know the effect these have on the millions of children in the region who are seeing and hearing the same things, but I worry about it. The stereotypes seem designed to produce confusion, self-doubt, passivity, frustration, anger. This is probably not deliberate. It is probably only thoughtless. Either way, stereotypes are attacks upon the human spirit. They find their mark, and no good comes of it.

# Appalachian Images

## A Personal History

### *Denise Giardina*

In 1934, English historian Arnold Toynbee wrote in his *Study of History,*

> The Scotch-Irish immigrants who forced their way into these natural fast-
> nesses have come to be isolated from the rest of the World. They have re-
> lapsed into illiteracy and witchcraft. The Appalachian "Mountain People" at
> this day are no better than barbarians. . . . It is possible . . . that barbarism
> will disappear in Appalachia likewise. Indeed, the process of assimilation is
> already at work among a considerable number of Appalachians who have
> descended from their mountains and changed their way of life in order to
> earn wages in the North Carolinian cotton mills.[1]

My mother's people came to the mountains from a variety of places. Some,
Honakers and Whitts and Pauleys, followed the early westward migration
through Virginia to Kentucky after the Revolutionary War. Others came later,
Quakers escaping Confederate North Carolina to the Union stronghold of eastern Kentucky.

They were mostly farmers, with at least one rascal, great-grandfather Fred
Alexander Smiley, thrown in for fun. One family legend has Papaw Smiley run-
ning off to Oklahoma where he obtained and then gambled away a fortune in
oil wells. Another has him losing an entire coal-rich hollow near Elkhorn City,
Kentucky, in a similar fashion. Whether his exploits are true or not, Papaw
Smiley seems to me a mythic figure, fitting for a region of fabulous lost wealth.

There were at least two writers among my mother's people. Great-great-
uncle James Thornbury joined the Union army and was captured by Confederates near the Big Sandy River in eastern Kentucky. He was sent to Libby prison
in Richmond, Virginia, then to Macon, Georgia, and after the fall of Atlanta, to
Charleston, then Columbia, in South Carolina. There he managed to escape
and headed to the mountains of East Tennessee, Union territory and home to

the first abolitionist newspaper in the United States (the *Emancipator*, published when William Lloyd Garrison was still a child). He composed an incompetent but heartfelt poem about his experiences:

> My troubles there were great and not very much to eat
> In the sun we were kept and nearly died with heat . . .
> The Southern Confederacy, Oh it I left behind
> And started up the river a better land to find.
> And when I arrived at Knoxville, Tennessee
> I was treated like a brother and set at liberty.
> And now I have met my friends in communion
> Where the Stars and the Stripes are waving for the Union.[2]

The Thornburys had been Quakers from Ulster, but converted to Methodism in the Kentucky mountains. Upon his return from the war, James Thornbury became a minister in the Methodist Episcopal Church in Pikeville. His daughter, Kizzie, wrote poetry and hymn lyrics. Her poems were mostly of children dying young, religious paeans, or comments on community affairs, composed in the sentimental language common to the Victorian age and apparently familiar to the poet:

> Don't brighten room or casket
> With roses when I'm gone,
> The time to scatter flowers
> Will be forever flown.
> Life is the time for roses,
> A smile or kindly deed;
> Life is the time for flowers,
> The time to sow the seed.[3]

A family friend, the Reverend Thomas Ashley, sent Kizzie Thornbury's poems to The Abingdon Press. The published volume opens with the lyrics of a hymn, "When the Battle Is Over," written to the tune—appropriate for a rock-ribbed Unionist—of "Marching Through Georgia."

My Reynolds ancestors, like the early Thornburys, were Quakers. It is easy to trace them in meeting records and in *The Quaker Genealogies*. One ancestor, Richard Browne, was involved in radical affairs in Northamptonshire during the ferment of the English seventeenth century, became a Baptist, and "was convinced a Quaker by William Dewsbury," sometime before his death in 1662. Another, William Clayton of Chichester, England, traveled to America on the *Kent*, a ship carrying men responsible for establishing William Penn's colony. And Henry Reynolds, whose patriarchal last name remains constant through the generations, ran a tavern near the present Chester, Pennsylvania. The family moved to a Quaker stronghold in North Carolina in 1751, then fled the persecution of southern Quakers during the Civil War, probably following the route of the Underground Railroad into the mountains.[4]

In Kentucky my great-grandfather, Orlendo Reynolds, lost his Quaker religion and turned to moonshining. He was good at it, produced a popular brew, and proved adept at hiding his stock from federal officials beneath the potatoes in the root cellar and behind jars of preserves. He fathered eight children by Mary Smiley and, after her death, ten more by his second wife.

I examine old photographs of these kin, looking for signs of encroaching barbarism. Orlendo Reynolds and his first family posed for a formal photograph on Grapevine Creek in Pike County, Kentucky, at the turn of the century. Orlendo is seated beside his wife, Mary. They are surrounded by their six oldest children, and they hold the two youngest, an infant and a toddler, in their laps. One daughter, my grandmother Flora, stands in the back beside ghost-like William Harrison, the oldest brother, destined to die in a logging accident soon after the photograph was taken.

The images are soft and faded. Orlendo has high cheekbones and a sloping mustache. His wife's head is a blur of motion. She must have ducked her head just as the shutter was snapped, glanced down at the baby in her lap, Andy, who wears a long gown with lace at the collar and white petticoat at the hem. Alec and Miles, around six or seven years old, flank their parents. Their hair is neatly combed, they wear homemade suits, and they are barefoot. Jesse, his hand on Miles's shoulder, is shod, as is his father. The mother wears a long dark skirt and a tailored jacket with full shoulders and dark piping on the lapels and the collar of her blouse. Tabitha, the oldest girl, has a large, lacy collar and a brooch at the throat. Her face is broad, and she wears her hair pulled severely back like her mother's. My grandmother Flora looks eleven or twelve years old. Her hair is also combed back on top but is swept out in wings framing both sides of her face. She wears a jacket and what appears to be a scarf about her neck. No one is smiling, nor are they scowling. They are intent, dignified, aware of their own presence and the record they are making.

I search the photograph for clues. It seems my great-grandmother was an accomplished seamstress. Some small children in the mountains went without shoes some of the time, but perhaps not from necessity. My grandmother was a dainty and stylish child. My great-grandfather was comfortable holding his three-year-old daughter—who is reaching for something off-camera—on his knee. It seems mountain people in 1900 knew what a camera was. It seems mountain people looked normal.

There are other things the camera doesn't show. The Reynolds family did not go to the mills of North Carolina to be civilized, as Toynbee suggested, where people were dying at the looms and presses, were being shot or discharged for trying to bring in a union. My ancestors lived out their lives in the Kentucky mountains, in a large log house with a massive fireplace in the common room. They had a steady stream of boarders, including most of the young school-teachers who came to Grapevine. Orlendo lived to be ninety-six years old. Mary died young, probably of a ruptured appendix. William Harrison was killed at eighteen when a tree he was felling toppled over on him. (I am not surprised as I study his face. He does not have the aspect of an outdoorsman. He has the lightly bearded face of a college freshman, the musing eyes of a computer sci-entist or poet. Perhaps he was daydreaming when the tree buckled.)

Tabitha is remembered by the family as strong and feisty. In the photograph she has the strong body and broad shoulders of a basketball player. She married a real estate man from Ashland, Kentucky. Jesse opened a mercantile store in the mountains. Andy, the baby and wildest of the children, fatally hit a man during a drunken poker game and served two years for manslaughter in the state peni-tentiary. Miles farmed and made liquor like his father before him, honorably if illegally. Alec became a school principal, and Lilly, the mother of a principal.

Flora married my grandfather, Lee Franklin Whitt, a farmer who lost his land during the depression, a storekeeper who gave away the merchandise through loose credit, the manager of a coal company store in West Virginia. They raised a mining engineer, a coal miner, several schoolteachers, a son crippled by polio who lived at home all his life, another son who tried to orga-nize atomic workers at Oak Ridge during World War II and died twenty years later of a virulent form of leukemia, studied by doctors at Johns Hopkins. They raised my mother, a nurse.

It is true my grandmother would not allow her menstruating daughters to help put up pickles for fear the cucumbers and corn and beans would go "off." Was this a sign of incipient barbarism?

Arnold Toynbee never visited the place he called "Appalachia." If he had come to the mountains and ended up on Orlendo Reynolds's doorstep, he would have been taken in. He would have had a seat beside the hearth on a cold night or a rocker on the porch in the summer, a cup of fiery potion from the still, a plate full of pork and pickled corn and beans and corn bread, and a feather bed when he grew sleepy.

It is hard to say who came to the mountains first, the mine owners or the mis-sionaries. As in Africa and Asia, they seem to have arrived simultaneously, the twin harbingers of empire. They were gentlemen from London and Philadel-phia, self-made capitalists from the eastern Pennsylvania coalfields, Pittsburgh robber barons, alongside high-minded New England ladies with impeccable credentials who were veterans of progressive movements for temperance, women's rights, and poor relief. I would also include a third group to form a trinity: a generation of yellow journalists and adventure writers who ventured into the wilds of the southern Appalachians to discover the natives and hold them up to view for the edification and entertainment of the rest of the country.

All those who came—entrepreneur, missionary, and journalist—carried with them the knowledge of the riches that lay beneath the mountains.

By the end of the nineteenth century, the industrial nations of the world had a great need for natural resources—coal, iron, magnesium, tin, rubber, sugar, coffee, tea, fruit, silver, gold, diamonds, platinum. It was the age of imperialism, when these same nations, led by Britain, France, Germany, and the United States, colonized vast territories to obtain these items for themselves and to sell them to their own advantage. Never mind that these resources were found in populated lands. Wealth belonged to the exploiter, not the inhabitant. Never mind that many people were unsettled by colonization, that traditional family and community structures were disrupted, that millions were forced into backbreaking, dangerous work producing these items for their European and American masters. After all, they had been given the benefits of "civilization." The people in the colonies were supposedly childlike, incapable of producing anything of value themselves, and so must be looked after by decent, educated, cultivated, energetic white men.

Mountain people were well aware that coal could be found beneath their land. As early as 1742, settlers had called a West Virginia stream the Coal River, after the deposits visible along its banks. In many other places, outcroppings of the mineral broke the surface, and large black chunks were broken up with picks and carted off to fuel iron stoves and hearth fires. But no one knew how vast the coal deposits were.

Contrary to popular mythology, mountaineers were not totally isolated from the outside world. Through newspapers, visitors, and the U.S. postal service, they kept up with current affairs. Boats traveled up the deep channels of the Tug Fork and Levisa and Guyandotte Rivers, bringing trade. Most people knew someone who had traveled outside the mountains, to visit far-flung relatives, to seek work, to join the army and fight in some conflict or other.

They were a hospitable people. In a land largely bereft of hotels, they took in travelers. Among those in the 1880s who slept in their beds and ate their food were agents scouting out mineral deposits, sometimes posing as traveling salesmen, and the journalists who later dispatched lurid reports of the violence and depravity of mountain people.

The coal men came early to the New River Gorge of West Virginia. A wild tract of river rapids and steep cliffs, the northern reaches of the New River were part of an ancient route from Virginia to the Ohio River blazed by generations of Indians, then explorers and settlers. George Washington passed this way, as did Chief Justice John Marshall, who proposed building a canal through the most rugged stretch of mountains. Civil War regiments also frequently traveled the road.

Some of the outsiders who passed through the New River Gorge came from old, established families on the eastern seaboard, families with wealth and political connections. These men didn't forget the mineral-rich area, and passed their knowledge on to sons and grandsons. Even as they sent surveyors to locate mineral deposits, they studied ways to gain ownership of the land. They had little difficulty. Early land surveys had claimed much of the region for absentee owners in eastern Virginia who had no intention of living in the mountains. Many early settlers were squatters who claimed land by living on it and working it for several generations. Others had purchased land from land agents and speculators who misrepresented their own ability to sell. Most farmers had deeds to the land in their county courthouses.

The mineral speculators who descended on West Virginia in the 1880s claimed to be descended from Revolutionary War soldiers from the northeast who had been granted absentee lands in the mountains in return for service to their new country. Or they claimed to have purchased the land from families who were so descended. They called their claims "senior patents," as opposed to the "junior patents" of mountain farmers. One New Yorker, Henry C. King, claimed five hundred thousand acres of southern West Virginia through Revolutionary War financial wizard Robert Morris of Philadelphia. (Morris himself, who never set foot in western Virginia, ended his days in debtor's prison. But his grandson, Samuel Fisher Morris, turned up at the turn of the century as a contributor to the building of an Episcopal Church for coal operators on Elkhorn Creek in West Virginia.)

Many of the speculators claimed that mineral deposits should be considered separately from surface land and that their ownership of the coal gave them the right to the entire tract of land, even though a farmer might prove ownership of the surface.

Or they claimed they would take advantage of the above situation unless farmers signed over mineral rights for a few cents an acre and that such a signature would allow the farmer to remain on the land; and later they evicted him anyway.

Or they burned out those who refused to sign.

Or they forged Xs on deeds wholesale, claiming extensive mountain illiteracy.

Or courthouses burned down mysteriously, and new deeds showed up a few months later, proving new ownership.

Or men were jailed on trumped-up charges and ordered to put up their mineral rights as bond.

Or residents who spoke out against signing mineral rights turned up dead.

Local farmers could appeal the seizure of their land. Because those claiming ownership were from out of state, the cases were heard in federal court in northern cities such as Parkersburg and Clarksburg. Most farmers were unable to make the arduous journey to court or afford lawyers. If they did wage a legal battle, they faced federal judges like John J. Jackson. Jackson always ruled in favor of the companies.

The coal men. They praised themselves, and their self-made hagiographies are something between the *Lives of the Saints* and a high school yearbook.

Captain F.L. Paddock of Pennsylvania: "He has the confidence, esteem and respect of the officers of his company . . . as well as with all of whom he is brought in contact almost daily in business relations. He resides in Bramwell and is recognized as one of its most influential citizens, having been prominently identified with every movement for the improvement and beautifying of the town. He is a member of the Episcopal Church, and was largely instrumental in having erected the beautiful church which adorns the city."[5]

John Freeman, native of England, lately of Pennsylvania: "One of the little band of pioneers who, with but little in the way of capital, but with an abundant supply of energy and determination, proceeded to transpose the mountain wilderness which they found into a hive of human industry, and mark the way for the world-wide fame which the products of the Field have attained, largely through their efforts."[6]

Richard Mellon turned down workers' demands for better housing and wages, but spent fifteen thousand dollars on a Christian missionary effort to his coal camps. Of the machine guns he also installed, he said, "It is necessary. You could not run without them."[7]

Then there were the overachievers:

John Cooper, English Horatio Alger, child miner in Lancashire, who after great suffering, study, and frugality became a West Virginia entrepreneur and Republican Party leader.

Jenkin Jones, Welsh Horatio Alger, likewise suffering and diligent and frugal, not to mention talented: "He inherits, in a large degree, the characteristic love of the Welsh people for melody, and is the author of a number of poems which show decided merit, though as yet, the general public has had little opportunity to judge of his talents in this direction, his personal friends being the only ones to whom his productions have thus far been accessible."[8]

John C.C. Mayo, Kentucky Horatio Alger, who helped the coal men grab up several counties of his home state, was noted for refusing to lace his shoes. He built a railroad spur beside his Kentucky mansion to accommodate private train cars. Mayo visited Argentina and came back aglow at the prospects of buying mineral rights there. Fortunately, he immediately dropped dead.

Justin Collins claimed mine explosions were caused by outside agitators and timed to coincide with West Virginia's legislative sessions.

Robert Stearns wrote sentimental books such as *The Ass and the Barnacles* and *Ossawald Crum*. On Christmas Day 1908, he burned down his own Kentucky hotel so union organizers hiding inside could be flushed out and shot.

Others, including Pratts, Guggenheims, Roosevelts, Morgans, and Mellons, employed minions for less pleasant tasks, and stayed away.

The coal men moved from the New River through southern West Virginia to Kentucky and Tennessee. They made a clean sweep. Within a few years, 60 to 80 percent of the surface land and virtually all the minerals were owned by absentee corporations. As of this writing, that has not changed.

> The wealth of this State is immense; the development of this wealth will earn vast private fortunes far beyond the dreams even of a modern Croesus; the question is, whether this vast wealth shall belong to persons who live here and who are permanently identified with the future of West Virginia, or whether it shall pass into the hands of persons who do not live here and who care nothing for our State except to pocket the treasures which lie buried in our hills?
>
> If the people of West Virginia can be roused to an appreciation of the situation we ourselves will gather this harvest now ripe on the lands inherited from our ancestors; on the other hand if the people are not roused to an understanding of the situation in less than ten years this vast wealth will have passed from our present population into the hands of non-residents, and West Virginia will be almost like Ireland and her history will be like that of Poland.[9]

The initial probings of mineral agents were accompanied by missionaries and journalists set on reproducing the exploits of their colleagues in "darkest" Africa a little closer to home. Like their peers who took their imperial and racist attitudes to the sub-Sahara, most came with a sublime faith in their own values, and attitudes toward those they encountered ranging from pity and condescension to outright contempt. There is little evidence they considered that they could learn anything from mountain people or that they were themselves not wholly worthy of admiration. According to Loyal Jones, "No group in the country . . . has aroused more suspicion and alarm among mainstream Christians than have Appalachian Christians, and never have so many Christian missionaries been sent to save so many Christians than is the case in this region."

The missionaries left the most ambiguous legacy. Some of them did genuine good, especially in eastern Kentucky. West Virginia had the good fortune to separate itself from the neglectful authorities in Richmond during the Civil War and to create its own institutions. West Virginia was thus spared the worst missionary onslaught.

But the Kentucky mountains were ignored by the state government in Frankfort, and tax money from local residents went for schools and hospitals outside the region. The missionaries who chose Kentucky found a need for medical facilities and secondary schools. So they founded boarding schools and colleges and clinics. One group of independent and refreshingly down-to-earth feminists from Boston started the Frontier Nursing Service, which sent midwife nurses on horses and mules to distant hollow farms for home deliveries and postnatal care. The nursing service continues to this day, with jeeps replacing animals as transportation, a valuable asset in a rural community still underserved by physicians.

Institutions like the Hindman and Pine Mountain Settlement Schools later passed into the hands of mountain people instead of outsiders bent on charity. These institutions continue today as vibrant and innovative community centers that supplement the offerings of local schools and host grassroots political gatherings, writing workshops, and festivals for music, folklore, and other arts.

But even the best-intentioned early missionaries came laden with prejudices. The founders of settlement schools raised money back east by touting Appalachia as a repository of "old English" language and culture untouched by American civilization. They lovingly cherished the dulcimers and seventeenth-century ballads they encountered but scorned indigenous banjo and fiddle music, and in some cases, forbade their students to play it. And their fundraising efforts were more successful if predicated upon making the objects of their charity seem as pathetic as possible.

Typical of the missionaries was Alice Spencer Geddes Lloyd, Bostonian, graduate of Radcliffe, founder of the Caney Creek School, now Alice Lloyd College in Kentucky. For decades, Alice Lloyd ruled her domain with an iron hand. Strict dress code: coat and tie for boys, long white(!) skirts for girls, no makeup or jewelry or heeled shoes. No tobacco, alcohol, dancing, or playing cards, no contact with the opposite sex, separate seating by sex in the classroom and dining hall, separate hours by sex in the library.

Mrs. Lloyd told a Lexington newspaperman, "No more than 25 percent of the local people have the mental capacity for more than the most elementary education. Intermarriage—oh, terrible intermarriage—has resulted in the development of racial weaknesses—low intelligence, bad eyes, epilepsy, and so on."

She continued, "The mountaineer is suspicious, independent, and uncooperative. . . . I had a man fixing one of the porches. I looked it over and said, 'That board there isn't straight. Don't you think you'd better take it up and straighten it?' He glared at me, dropped his hammer, and said, 'Do it yourself if you don't like it.'"

Her conclusion? "The mountain people are not good workmen to hire. They have to be circumvented like children."[10]

Here I begin to apply what I call the Mamaw and Papaw Test. I recall my own people. I compare them with the judgments of Alice Lloyd. Alice Lloyd fails the Mamaw and Papaw Test.

What motivated the frenzy of missionary activity in the turn-of-the-century mountains? Many Appalachian scholars think the region offered an outlet after the closing of the western frontier. Others believe the nation needed to justify its imminent rape of the mountains by seeking to denigrate and transform that which it would soon destroy. In any case, the journalists who interpreted this newly "discovered" place approached it with the same prejudices as the missionaries.

One of the best known and most sympathetic journalists was Horace Kephart, whose *Our Southern Highlanders* is still read today. Even Kephart, more balanced and less sensational than most, helped foist ridiculous stereotypes of Appalachia on the larger public that have persisted to the present day. "The mountain farmer's wife is not only a household drudge, but a field-hand as well. She helps to plant, hoes corn, gathers fodder, sometimes even plows or splits rails. It is the commonest of sights for a woman to be awkwardly hacking up firewood. . . . [Such treatment shows] an indifference to woman's weakness, a disregard for her finer nature, a denial of her proper rank."[11]

Kephart's observations about women led him to the logical conclusion that women must be forced into such work because mountain men were "shiftless" and "afflicted with that malady which Barrie calls 'acute disinclination to work.'" Thus the twin stereotypes of the lazy mountaineer and his hag of a wife, grown out of an ignorance of the physical labor required by all parties to maintain a mountain farm, and sexist assumptions of his time and place about the "nature" of women and the work that suited them.

Another caricature, with a direct lineage from Victorian journalists through Jethro Bodine to *Deliverance*, is the mountaineer as mentally and physically defective. Again Kephart is more illuminating than he knows:

> Every stranger in Appalachia is quick to note the high percentage of defectives among the people. However, we should bear in mind that in the mountains proper there are few, if any, public refuges for this class, and that home ties are so powerful the mountaineers never send their "fitified folks" or "half-wits," or other unfortunates, to any institution in the lowlands, so long as it is bearable to have them around. Such poor creatures as would be segregated in more advanced communities, far from the public eye, here go at large and reproduce their kind.[12]

Modern readers are more likely to approve of mountain behavior here than that of Kephart's "more advanced communities."

Other writers were not so gentle as Kephart: "The buying up of the mountain lands has unsettled a large part of these strange people. . . . [They may move] at the approach of civilization to remoter regions, where they may live without criticism or observation of their hereditary, squalid, unambitious, stationary life.[13]

The earliest white settlers of my native McDowell County, West Virginia, were Harmons, Cartwrights, Milams, Dillons, Murphys. In the late 1700s they fought a battle against the Shawnee led by a chief named Black Wolf. Black Wolf and his family were forced to flee. The Dillons and Murphys and Harmons farmed the land and raised sheep for wool. Their descendants encountered Col. I.A. Welch, who had been hired to survey a half-million-acre expanse, the "Wilson-Cary-Nicholas grant," which supposedly had been given to his clients by the Commonwealth of Virginia in 1795. The area covered most of southeastern and south-central West Virginia, including part of McDowell County and stretching to the New River, and was now claimed by the Flat-Top and Crozer Land Associations.

Colonel Welch wrote an account of his exploration. He called the area a "jungle." Ignoring all previous habitation and settlement, he claimed, "The Grahams of Philadelphia were the first to penetrate the wilds of McDowell, Mercer and Wyoming [Counties] and after a critical examination of the field determined to construct a narrow gauge railway." A map of the "grant" accompanying Welch's account shows this vast territory cut into rectangular sections. The legend says, "All Lands Not Marked 'Crozer Land Association' are the Property of the Flat-Top Land Association." Publications trumpet the valuable nature of the land "consolidated" by these intrepid land companies. The previous owners are never mentioned.

When Welch arrived in McDowell County, the hamlet of English served as county seat. In 1885 he engineered the purchase of land for a new town. He spent forty dollars. The new county seat bore his name, and the new courthouse held new deeds. Farther north, the first coal had already been mined and shipped from the New River coal camp of Quinnimont.

Advertisement:
Castner and Curran are the general agents for the sale of Pocahontas Flat-Top Smokeless Semi-Bituminous Coal. Their Main Office is located at No. 328 Chestnut Street, Philadelphia, Pa. [with agents in New York, Boston, Chicago, Cincinnati, London, and Bluefield, West Virginia] The only coal in the world that has been officially endorsed by the Governments of Great Britain and the United States. It is always used in testing the speed of Government cruisers built on the Atlantic Seaboard, the Secretary of the Navy having

issued an order to this effect several years ago. The Cunard and White Star Steamship Companies use it exclusively.

Endorsement of Pocahontas Coal by the United States War Department: Quartermaster General's Office, War Department, February 4th, 1896 . . . the tests made by this Department show the Pocahontas to have an equivalence superior to any other coal tested by this office since 1880.[14]

With the coming of the coal industry, the population of the Appalachian Mountains changed. Native mountain families were joined by immigrants from southern and eastern Europe, especially Italy, Poland, Hungary, and Slavic nations. Large numbers of African Americans also sought to escape the southern backlash against Reconstruction by moving to the coalfields. All these groups were victims of prejudices and stereotypes. When they joined other miners throughout the region in rebellion, they were met with violence by the coal industry, which employed armed guards and secret police. Miners fought back. A U.S. government commission, which sought to explain the violence to the American people in 1922, reported: "Local traditions still exert a dominating influence and account very largely for the outbreaks of violence. Much of the violence had nothing to do with the coal industry but had to do with the nature and racial characteristics of the people."[15]

The misunderstandings continue to this day. "There is another America hidden in Appalachia's hills—a disturbing journey to a separate world. Back in the hills of Floyd County, Kentucky, you'll find some of the poorest places in America. This is where Washington waged a war on poverty and lost. But that's not tonight's story. The people here know they are poor, they know there's almost no work, but most of them say they want to stay here, get married here, grow old here. What is it that keeps them tied to a place that seems like something out of another century?"[16]

## Notes

1. Arnold Toynbee, *A Study of History* (London: Oxford Univ. Press, 1934).

2. James Thornbury, poem, author's collection.

3. Kizzie Thornbury, *Scattering Flowers* (Cincinnati, Ohio: The Abingdon Press, 1919).

4. Willard C. Heiss, *The Quaker Genealogies: A Preliminary List* (Thomson, Ill.: Heritage House, 1974).

5. Public relations documents, author's collection.

6. Ibid.

7. Ibid.

8. Ibid.

9. J.M. Mason, E.A. Bennett, and Joseph Bell, report to West Virginia Tax Commission, Nov. 22, 1884.

10. Alice Lloyd, quoted in John Day, *Bloody Ground* (Lexington: Univ. Press of Kentucky, 1941).

11. Horace Kephart, *Our Southern Highlanders* (Univ. of Tennessee Press, 1913).

12. Kephart, *Our Southern Highlanders.*

13. *New York Times,* 2 Sept. 1890, quoted in Altina Waller, *Feud* (Univ. of North Carolina Press, 1988).

14. Castner and Curran advertisement, author's collection.

15. David Corbin, *Life, Work, and Rebellion in the Coal Fields* (Urbana: Univ. of Illinois Press, 1981).

16. *48 Hours,* CBS-TV, 1991.

# Up in the Country

## *Fred Hobson*

It is a strange destiny, Thomas Wolfe begins *Look Homeward, Angel*, that leads from England to Pennsylvania and down into the Carolinas. Or, in my case, a strange destiny (although, in fact, no stranger than any other, for all destinies are equally improbable) that in 1756 brought a Pennsylvania Quaker down the Valley of Virginia into the western Piedmont of North Carolina; and some forty years later brought a restless young Connecticut Yankee, a son of the Puritans, down from New Haven to Burke County (that part of it that later became Caldwell County), North Carolina, within sight of the Blue Ridge.

The Quaker was my father's remote ancestor, who moved into the hills northwest of the Moravian settlement of Salem (Winston was still more than a half-century away) and began a line of farmers and teachers, many of whom never left the Yadkin Valley. The Puritan was my mother's great-great-grandfather, Andrew Hull Tuttle, who in his travels through the Carolina hills met and married a farmer's daughter, Elizabeth McCall, and settled down on her father's fertile acres in a broad, green valley not far from Grandfather Mountain. He began a line of Methodist preachers and missionaries who, over the next century and a half, would venture as far away as China, usually (the preachers, that is, after 1890) after playing football and running track while absorbing Wesleyan theology at little Trinity College and its successor, Duke University. (Sturdy, red-headed, indomitable, the earlier Tuttles, more than any mortals I have known, embodied that Victorian ideal, "muscular Christianity.") These Tuttles went out from Caldwell County, but they always came back to the place "up in the country," as they called it, for summer vacations, family reunions, and long hikes up Grandfather Mountain. In a number of cases, they came home to grow old and die and to be buried in the old cemetery on a high hill above Littlejohn Church.

It is these families and the places they came to that I want to consider—for after nearly two centuries, the families and the places became essentially one. The two places, Yadkin County and Caldwell—neither particularly remarkable in the larger scheme of things—are some fifty miles apart, and neither is truly *in* the mountains but rather just at the place the mountains begin, each with a defining peak—Pilot Mountain for Yadkin, Grandfather Mountain for Caldwell—just across the county line. Yadkin, south and west of the river called Yadkin (meaning "valley of peace" in Cherokee, I was told—probably mistakenly—as a child, but because nothing ever happened there, that seemed reasonable enough), is the last county in North Carolina's northwestern Piedmont, just before rip-roaring and mountainous Wilkes, legendary home of moonshiners and stock car racers, including the man, Junior Johnson, whom Tom Wolfe—in a famous *Esquire* piece in 1965—designated "The Last American Hero." Caldwell County is farther south and west, some thirty miles south of Boone, eighty miles northeast of Asheville, and in somewhat higher hills. The counties, as I remember them, were as different as any two places so close could be. Or, rather, of course, they probably were not different at all. It just seemed that way to me when I was a boy, living most of my life in Yadkin County, but going up in the country for a week or two in the summer.

Those summer interludes in Caldwell County are among the best memories I have. We stayed in the old Tuttle homestead, a large two-story frame house built in 1870, shortly after Benedict Marcus Tuttle came back from the war, and, in my childhood, presided over by Great-Uncle George—a wiry, toothy octogenarian who almost alone among the Tuttles of his generation had not taken to the pulpit—and his wife, Aunt Jess, stern, patrician, bearing a strong facial resemblance, I thought, to the pictures of Franklin D. Roosevelt I had seen. In fact, the whole contingent of great-aunts and great-uncles up at Tuttlefields seemed—as I look back—something of a gerontocracy: Uncle John, a retired preacher in his eighties, always genial, always playing jokes and telling stories; Cuddin Rob, another retired preacher, even more a jokester; and Aunt Luley, unlike all the others because she was an outlander, from Cleveland, brought south by Cuddin Rob after he ventured north and married her.

But most remarkable by far was Aunt Lelia, retired to Tuttlefields after forty years in China and another ten or fifteen traveling around the Southeast speaking in Methodist churches about her China experiences. She had gone out as a missionary shortly after 1900, after taking an M.A. in English at Columbia, had taught the future Madame Sun Yat-sen and Madame Chiang Kai-shek at the McTyeire School in Shanghai (and kept in touch with Madame Chiang for years following), and later became dean of women at Soochow University, before being sent home in 1942, well after the Japanese invasion. She had plenty of stories to tell: after her death I came across the letters she had written from China, including one that described having tea with Madame Chiang and another remarking favorably on the insurgence of communism in the countryside.

But the stories she was most famous for had nothing to do with China. She had gained a reputation in Methodist churches across the South as a superb teller of Uncle Remus stories. In fact, she had come to be *called*, in some circles, Br'er Rabbit, and now—gray, shriveled, but always with a sparkle in her eye and a general feistiness—to me she even looked like Br'er Rabbit. She was my favorite of those great-aunts and great-uncles up in the country. She embodied even more than the other Tuttles that quality of high thinking and plain living the Tuttles always held to. Now back in America, she preferred to live in something approaching genteel poverty. When she died ten years later, she left to the State of North Carolina her share of Tuttle woodlands, out of which was created Tuttle State Forest.

At the time I thought Aunt Lelia must have learned the Br'er Rabbit stories from those few freed slaves who had stayed on at Tuttlefields after the war. But I'm not sure that was the case at all. She may have just read Joel Chandler Harris. In the mid-1950s there were only two blacks left on the farm, and the one I remember best, the ageless Lily, private and dignified, did not look like she had ever been a candidate for Br'er Rabbit tale-telling. This, of course, was the highland South, not the greater South, the plantation land which Thomas Wolfe from the vantage point of Asheville called "the hot, rich South." It was— both my counties were, in fact—overwhelmingly white, with just enough of a black presence to make me feel a small part of that larger South.

Most of the talk at Tuttlefields, as I recall, revolved around Littlejohn Church, the annual hike up Grandfather Mountain, and adventures and misadventures of Tuttles past and present: Cuddin Lee Tuttle, who had gained fame at Duke in the 1920s by once, in the face of an oncoming rush, punting backward, over his head, but who had recovered to ascend rapidly in the Methodist church on his way to becoming secretary of the World Methodist Council; Uncle Bob Tuttle, my mother's brother, who had set Southern Conference cross-country records at Duke, had now written a couple of books, and was himself achieving a lofty eminence in the Methodist Church; Aunt Emily Tuttle, my mother's sister, beautiful, ethereal (more a Gregory—the other family line—than a Tuttle, seeming little kin to spunky Aunt Lelia), an old maid college English professor; and Cuddin Magruder Tuttle, who had played football at the U.S. Naval Academy and had later commanded—he told me years afterward—the ship on which young Paul Bryant, not yet famed as the Bear, had served in World War II.

We talked about the Tuttles, but preparation for Grandfather Mountain was the primary topic of discussion. The Tuttles had been climbing "the Grandfather," as they always called it, for a century, had so appropriated the mountain that in those earliest days I thought the mountain had been named for *my* grandfather, Robert Gamewell Tuttle, another Methodist preacher who had played football at Trinity and then, for good measure, at Vanderbilt. As a child, of course, one accepts as important whatever one's family thinks is important, and that's why I saw the Grandfather as the greatest of all mountains. It was not, of course. But I must confess that in later years I have been delighted when I have seen someone else, in print, offer up superlatives about the Grandfather and have—like Mark Twain on the Mississippi and Herman Melville on the whale—proceeded to copy them down. Such as—I quote from the *Journal* of Andre Michaux those entries dated August 26 and 30, 1794—"Started for Grandfather Mountain, the most elevated of all those which form the chain of the Alleghanies and the Appalachians. . . . Climbed to the summit of the highest mountain of all North America, and, with my companion and guide, sang the Marseillaise Hymn, and cried, 'Long live America and the French Republic! long live Liberty. . . .'"[1]

The Grandfather was hardly the highest mountain in North America. It was hardly the highest in the United States, hardly the highest east of the Rockies, not even the highest in North Carolina. Mount Mitchell and Clingman's Dome, among others in the southern Appalachians, rose higher. But it nonetheless was exciting to read that someone else thought—and said so in French (*"la plus haute montagne de toute l'Am"*)—that it was such a spectacle. I have since read other things about the Grandfather, and not all of them are in accord with what I earlier learned. I have read, for example, that it takes its name from a particular great stone face, looking like an old man's, on one side of the mountain. I had been *told*, rather, that the mountain took its name from its resemblance, seen from afar, to the profile of the entire upper body of an old man, lying down, with chest and beard and nose and forehead displayed. In fact, one of the great tests to which a young Tuttle was subjected was to determine whether he could *see* the "grandfather" in the mountain (not unlike one of those pictures in which, as proof of one's salvation, one is supposed to see the face of Jesus Christ in an otherwise unremarkable photograph). I could not identify the Grandfather until I was eight or nine.

Because I had always thought the mountain was somehow ours, or at least anyone's who climbed it, you can understand how upset I was when at an early age I discovered that it was in fact owned by the MacRaes and the Mortons—who, of course, in subsequent years erected a mile-high swinging bridge, imported Mildred the Bear, and made millions off the mountain. But none of that had happened during my earliest Grandfather excursions. The night before the hike we always drove up to a rocky plateau, then brought out World War II surplus "sleeping bags" (nothing but blankets sewn together), and camped under the stars, looking across at Brown Mountain whose eerily flickering lights remain one of the great mysteries of the Carolina highlands. The next morning we would set out on an all-day hike, experiencing what passed in the East in those days as rugged passage. We would scramble up boulders, climb ladders over deep chasms, hug the sides of ledges—little real danger but the illusion of danger—and in midafternoon we would reach the far peaks of the Grandfather.

Sometimes we took lowlanders with us. I can still remember the wails of a Tidewater mother, a friend of ours from the Albemarle Sound, certain that her son, my age, was about to pitch out into nothingness and be dashed onto the rocks below. My mother, the kindest soul who ever lived, nonetheless, I believe, took a kind of perverse delight—at the least, felt a great superiority—at having bested a Coastal Plainer. It was her family's mountain, her mountain, and she would continue to climb it until she was in her sixties.

I felt Grandfather was my mountain too, but, to repeat, I did not fully belong to the mountains. Neither, in all respects, did the Tuttles, who had lived in the broad valleys below for a century and a half. They were never fully a part of that rich culture of the hemmed-in inhabitants of the hollow, that culture of the dulcimer and the fiddle and the jug that I later came to read about and then, if still at some distance, to see firsthand. The Tuttles, for all their love of the mountains, tended to view them more aesthetically and spiritually than otherwise, looking upon the Grandfather as the Japanese look upon Mount Fuji. At other times, they viewed the mountains around them as Thoreau approached Walden woods, every spring identifying each new plant and flower as it made its appearance on the slopes, each fall marveling at the colorful majesty of maples and hickories and poplars.

And—as I was about to say—Caldwell County and Tuttlefields were not *my* home after all. I lived most of my days in my father's home county, Yadkin, and though I liked it, I can't say I liked everything about it. One reason was that Yadkin, unlike Caldwell, was Republican (more truly hill country in that respect), and early on I came to abhor Republicans because, it seemed, every two or three years they voted down a bond election that my school superintendent father tried to pass. Or I should say I abhorred Republicanism, not Republicans—the sin, not the sinners. For these Republicans were our neighbors, and I liked most of them a great deal, and their children were my friends. Our fights came only in occasional Mays, when the bond elections were held, and every fourth November. I still recall taking on a gang of young Eisenhower toughs who tried to tear off my Adlai Stevenson badge.

Yadkin County, even more than Caldwell, was plain folks, devoid of class structure and unpretentious with a vengeance, as egalitarian as any place could be. The eastern part of the county, especially down by the Yadkin River, was relatively prosperous, but the western half of the county, culminating in the Brushy Mountains, was rugged and hardscrabble. Nearly everyone in those western regions was Republican. The county seat, Yadkinville, where I lived, was in the middle. The entire county would have been deemed benighted by those indexes of culture emanating from departments of sociology. Yadkinville— the very name suggested benightedness, an Atlanta friend later told me—was considered by outsiders to be truly rube-infested, and not only by the country clubbers in Winston-Salem, but even by the lint-heads in a series of textile and furniture manufacturing towns scattered across the western Piedmont. Its reputation for backwardness was at least partly deserved. Yadkin was—and still is—said to be the only one of North Carolina's one hundred counties that has not, at some point in its history, had so much as a foot of railroad track. It was relentlessly unprogressive, then, something I took at that time to be a flaw. Its passion for business, for industry and boosterism, came only after I left for college in the 1960s. Now it is, in its modest way, thoroughly modern, boasting a textile mill or two, a population approaching three thousand, and a country club. The road I would take today coming into town to my childhood home—the house my parents lived in for fifty-five years—is now called Progress Lane.

When I was a child my feelings about the place I was born and raised (though I could hardly have expressed them then) might best be described in terms of layers of approval and disapproval—or better, circles within circles, with me, blithely and happily caught up in whatever sport happened to be in season, firmly at the center. The inner circle would have been my immediate family, of which I approved altogether and in which I felt altogether comfortable: my father, the oldest of eleven children of a tobacco and dairy farmer, *of* Yadkin County and completely devoted to it, but who had gone off to Chapel Hill, sat at the feet of the sainted Frank Porter Graham, absorbed Graham's gospel of service and reform, and returned to the county determined to make its schools better and to "improve" it in general; my mother, who, despite her roots in Caldwell County, had grown up in a series of Methodist parsonages in Greensboro and other small Piedmont cities and thus must have, at first, viewed Yadkinville with curiosity at best; and my two older sisters, one perhaps more of Yadkin County than the other. That was the first circle, the inner one, and it would have included my street, a classic tree-lined thoroughfare with old houses and broad front porches with swings. I loved that street and the people on it, and (despite their politics) I still do.

But beyond the street, unqualified affection came harder. It was not that I lacked friends: I played baseball all summer with them, and basketball all winter, and climbed trees and explored woods and traded baseball cards and occasionally went to stock car races with them and their fathers, just as they went to Carolina football games with me and my father. After a while I even fell into the habit of going with them up to Mackie's funeral home to view, in open caskets, the bodies of those who, it seemed every week or so, wrapped their cars around trees and were hauled in, made presentable, and put on display.

Speed was everything in Yadkin County, speed and cars. The proximity to Wilkes County meant everything in that respect. I must have been the only boy in town who could not identify every car on the road, who did not have a favorite car and a favorite stock car driver, who did not know how to drive by age twelve or thirteen, who could not diagnose what ailed a disabled car and fix it. Although accepted on most other fronts—because I had a good jump shot— I was accepted on the automotive front only when, ten days after getting my license at sixteen, I turned my father's car over, rolled it magnificently, while speeding on a dirt road.

These were my friends, all of Celtic and Scotch-Irish stock, though I certainly wouldn't have known that at the time, just as I had no idea that there were in northern cities people called Poles and Czechs and Lithuanians. We knew only white and black. I had a casual black friend or two, but none of those classic interracial boyhood friendships celebrated by Deep Southerners, simply because there were few blacks around. As for Catholics, there was not a single such family in the county until I was sixteen, and then only one; and Jews were as remote and unknown as Zoroastrians. I thought of all this when, during college in the '60s, I saw a *Newsweek* map of religious inclinations in the United States; the color red was for Protestant, and the only completely red area in the entire country was northwest North Carolina.

The fact that there were few black families in town hardly meant that racial consciousness was absent. The town's prejudices, generally speaking, were about as firm as Alabama's. I still remember that day in May 1954 when I was roaming around the woods looking for arrowheads with Red Royall and Jackie Goss, and Red, not usually a student of Supreme Court decisions, suddenly turned on me and charged; "Your daddy is gonna make us go to school with niggers." The next week another school bond election was defeated.

So the second circle, Yadkinville and Yadkin County beyond family and street, was not altogether comfortable. *Part* of it was, though—my grandmother's farm, eight miles away, down near the Yadkin River, looking across at Surry County and Pilot Mountain. We went there every Sunday afternoon and always saw a good number of Hobson uncles and aunts and cousins, large, and hearty, optimistic souls.

The circles extended beyond the county as well. I felt good—very good— about living in North Carolina, and I felt good about living at, though not quite in, the mountains. But I did not always feel so good about inhabiting the next circle, the *South*. For some reason I thoroughly disliked the anthem "Dixie" and the Confederate flag, and I remember, in the books I read about the Civil War, I was always glad the Yankees had won. I'm still not altogether sure why. The Hobsons and the Tuttles had been in the South almost two centuries, and other branches of the family—Gregorys, Moores, Mullinses, and Martins— had been in the South longer than that. My brand of southern apostasy was hardly the usual southern Appalachian kind, that is, of a descendant of Union sympathizers during the Civil War. (If that had been the case, we probably would have been Republicans.) All Hobsons and Tuttles and Gregorys and so on had fought for the Confederacy, and there was no American living or dead (except possibly Frank Graham and Franklin D. Roosevelt) I was taught to revere more than Robert E. Lee.

But there it was: I did not like "Dixie" and the Stars and Bars, and I don't think it was because of anything in particular my parents had *said*. But perhaps, as I look back, it was something that went unsaid, something they embodied. They were hardly the southerners of legend, given to strong drink and fast horses and hunting and general excess. In spirit, I think, they remained in most respects, even after two centuries, precisely what their first American forebears had been, Quakers and Puritans only with better senses of humor.

It was partly that and partly, I believe, the hills themselves that made them different from the lowlanders, both the Virginians and the Deep Southerners. Half my mother's family, in fact, had originally come from Tidewater Virginia and North Carolina (it was the only side that had any real claim to social prominence), but that side—with its love of excess and style and its broad A's—simply had not taken. The Tuttles' muscular Christianity had overwhelmed it. Thus both my parents, as I suggested about the earlier Tuttles, were creatures of plain living and high thinking, finding nothing so offensive—so *tasteless*—as conspicuous consumption and waste.

My northern friends in college, and even some of my Deep South friends, could never quite place my parents: Adlai Stevenson Democrats—and, in latter days, abominators of Jesse Helms—who knew something of the world and had traveled in Europe several times, but who nonetheless never touched a drop of alcohol and voted dry in every county referendum on package stores, not to mention liquor by the drink. From my western Piedmont point of view, it was not at all hard to understand. They were *moralists* in every sense of the word. My mother's jut-jawed brand of moralism, inherited from those New England Tuttles (Jonathan Edwards's grandmother was a Tuttle, after all, in the same line), had been reinforced by a century and a half in the hills. It perhaps *seemed* more rigid than my father's gentler Quaker brand, but in fact it was pretty much all the same. I can name any number of other North Carolinians of my parents' generation and before who represented that same apparent combination of enlightenment and provincialism. What else was their hero Frank Graham, that Tar Heel Calvinist who fought off the forces of southern evil until, in that infamous North Carolina senate race of 1950, those forces finally defeated him and left him a martyr. It was no accident that one of the stories my mother most enjoyed telling was about the time she and my father ran into Graham at a reception of some sort and she learned that *her* father had been Graham's childhood football hero. It was the merging of two heroes, my father's (Graham) and hers (her own father).

I left Yadkin County at age eighteen and never really came back except for brief visits. Despite my occasional quarrels with the place, I felt about my town something of what Sherwood Anderson describes in *Winesburg, Ohio*: "One shudders at the thought of the meaninglessness of life while at the same instant, and if the people of the town are his people, one loves life so intensely that tears come into the eyes."[2] There was, whatever else might be said, an unpretentious, uncalculating friendliness in that place that I will never find anywhere else.

I left the hills, then, eventually to wander to teaching jobs in Alabama and Louisiana, and it was there in the Deep South that I came to think about the hills as never before. Every summer I came back for two or three weeks to a cabin my parents had built in the North Carolina mountains, on a ridge in Ashe County overlooking the New River. Every October I scheduled exams for two days so I could return to see the changing leaves that had inspired my Aunt Emily to quote Wordsworth and William Cullen Bryant—and every Christmas I returned to see the mountains wearing their stern, gray winter face.

The New River came to assume in the family lore that same position Grandfather Mountain had occupied in my childhood, and this time most of the superlatives were justified. The New River—heading up just south of us near Boone and, contrary to most rivers, flowing north, into Virginia and West Virginia, into the Kanawha and the Ohio—*is* one of the oldest rivers in the world. This time we had it on good authority; *Science Monthly* and various geologists—in articles posted on the walls of the cabin—said so, asserted that the ironically named New River formed the headwaters of the ancient Teays River system one million years ago. According to such sources, the New River is much older than the Mississippi, Missouri, and Ohio Rivers. It is, in fact, probably the oldest river in North America and, as such, has all varieties of flora and fauna unique to it.

About fifteen years ago I began to canoe the New River, just as long before I had climbed the Grandfather—annually, almost ritualistically. Over several summers I paddled its South Fork for some sixty miles, from near its tranquil beginnings down to its confluence with the North Fork and its rocky entry into Virginia. In doing so, I learned to read that stretch of the river, learned its shoals and rapids and occasional sinkholes like—I told myself—Samuel Clemens learned to read the Mississippi. I paddled, and still paddle, through stretches of dense forest, by open meadows and pastures, under cliffs rising from the river, never in really treacherous waters (like climbing the Grandfather, the danger is mostly illusory) but always aware of the fact that two hundred miles downstream, in West Virginia's New River Gorge, the waters are the wildest in the eastern half of the country. And even in these humbler Ashe County reaches, I see the wildness when the New River floods, as it does two or three times a year, taking out low-water bridges, uprooting trees, and reconstructing channels along the way.

But the New River is no more my river than the Grandfather was the Tuttles' mountain. To a certain extent I have gotten to know the people along its banks and in its hills, have commiserated about its floods with them, have rejoiced with them when they beat the Appalachian Power Company and kept off the river a dam that would have flooded farmland and cemeteries and changed the valley forever. But I haven't *lived* along the river as they have, I don't really know it in all seasons, and I don't truly know the people either. Mining, with all its attendant horrors, has been the curse of the mountains, the ultimate exploitation, and I sometimes feel myself a sort of cultural miner, taking resources as valuable as coal, as I marvel at the language of the people (I categorize it: Elizabethan?) and listen to their stories (equally classified: frontier humor?) and then go back to the cabin and write them down.

I am of the hills, but I am not truly of the mountains, even less so than the earlier Tuttles, in sight of the Grandfather, were. Nonetheless, in most ways, I feel more at home here at thirty-four hundred feet, looking down on the New River, than any other place on earth, and I can well imagine inhabiting these precincts for much of the rest of my life. I walk down the back trail and see the wildflowers that my mother, who died four years ago, loved and knew by heart; cut through the brush of the overgrown front trail to the huge boulder under which, my mother told her young grandchildren, an Indian princess was buried; walk past the birches and the dogwoods and the sourwoods that my father transplanted over the past thirty years. I look north into Virginia, west into Tennessee; in all directions I see the peaks—what Thomas Wolfe called the hills beyond. In a world in which faith of any sort is hard to come by, I will indeed lift up my eyes.

## Notes

1. Andre Michaux, *Journal,* quoted in Shepherd M. Dugger, *The Balsam Groves of the Grandfather Mountain* (1934; reprint ed., Banner Elk, N.C.: Puddingstone Press, 1974), 262.

2. Sherwood Anderson, *Winesburg, Ohio* (1919; reprint ed., New York: Viking Press, 1960), 240–41.

# On Being "Country"

## One Affrilachian Woman's Return Home

### Crystal E. Wilkinson

"Country-rural areas," "wide-open spaces," "backwoods," are used in the African American vernacular to mean "from or acting as though from the boondocks, socially inept, backwards."

One thing I vividly recall about growing up in Indian Creek, Kentucky, with my grandparents is the square-offs between my city cousins and me, the country cousin, during June family reunions. They laughed at the way I spoke and called me country. Country? I had never thought of myself as anything else. I lived on a farm, nestled in a holler in Casey County. We had a house with no plumbing that sat on sixty-four acres of land, a gravel road and a creek only a few hundred feet from the edge of our yard. How much more country could anybody be? But still, the way they giggled when I talked and the way "country" rolled off their tongues like a cuss word planted a hurtful seed. Being and talking country, having a twang in my voice, became something to be kept to myself.

Whenever I traveled, the question I feared most was "Where are you from?" I was already a quiet kid, but outside Indian Creek, I became even more hushed, afraid someone would question my accent.

At sixteen when I graduated from Casey County High School, I spent a good deal of my summer preparing for college. Part of that preparation was standing in front of the mirror attached to my granny's "shift-and-robe" (chifforobe) watching and listening to myself speak. I tried to mimic the people I had seen on television, trying to repel the "country" from my voice.

In the fall of 1979 when I stepped foot on Eastern Kentucky University's campus, I considered my "country" life behind me. I had practiced all summer long on my new voice. Now seventeen, I was extremely careful to tiptoe around everything that could possibly be identified as country. I had tried to copy fashions from popular black magazines like *Right On* and *Essence*. That was a success. My new college friends were impressed with my trendy wardrobe. But when I spoke, "Where are you from?" was the question asked. "Oh, about an hour and a half away from here," became my pat answer. As a freshman, other black students came up to me saying, "There she is. Hey Crystal, say something. Say 'night.'" Almost always the conversation would end with me saying a few words and one of the other people saying, "See, I told you she was country."

The teasing was for the most part short-lived, but I kept it close. Most people got over the fact that I was a black woman from a mostly white rural area with an accent that carried a map from the boonies. I was never a social outcast, though. I had quite a few friends and did a decent job of keeping my grades up. I became a little sister to Omega Psi Phi, a black fraternity, went to parties, had a boyfriend, and did all the things that young women in college do. My place of origin became less and less important, and looking back, I think that I was probably the only one who really agonized over it—constantly trying to disprove that I was a black version of Ellie Mae Clampett or Daisy Duke.

I majored in journalism and took speech classes. I made every effort to remove all that was country. Soon my i's were curved in all the right places and I blended into homogeneity.

After college nobody ever questioned my accent. I didn't have one. The people I came in contact with seemed surprised that I was from Kentucky, period, and certainly not rural Kentucky. I, a black professional woman with a trained, homogenized tongue, not staking claim to any particular region, at the brink of my self-proclaimed sophistication, had finally done it—erased it all.

Words sprinkled off my tongue like water—somewhat refined, smooth. Only when I returned to Indian Creek did I allow my jaw to loosen, my tongue to rest in its normal state. Only then did I dare let my toes dance in the grass or allow myself to be seen breaking Blue Lake beans on my lap. On my trips back to Casey County I would wallow in the things I had always done—wade in creek waters, shoot the breeze with the farmers at the corner store, shuck corn in a big white tub in the backyard. My vacations were spent gathering hickory nuts or picking blackberries.

It was there at my homeplace, as I approached thirty, that I truly returned. Over the past few years, much had changed. I had begun to write poetry and short fiction again. I found myself keeping company more and more with Frank X. Walker, Daundra Scisney-Givens, Nikky Finney, Kelli Ellis, and others, who were all a part of the Affrilachian Poets. We shut ourselves away on a weekly basis in the back room of a local coffee house, sharing "poetry moments." Most of us were Affrilachian or at least country, and we gathered to embrace everything that made us who we were. With them I felt free to allow my tongue and pen to slip back home.

Stories of home poured out of me like a spring, recapturing my life growing up on the farm and all the richness of the language and people there. Story after story worked its way free, while I tried to continue the guise of my pretend self when away from my new friends.

It was returning home more often that brought it all into focus. I would walk across the bottoms of the farm surrounded by the vastness of green land and blue sky as far as I could see. This land had been in our family since the time of slavery. The health of my grandparents was faltering. It became important to me to sit for hours and hours and listen to them telling our history in their beautiful country voices. The true grandness of my heritage became more and more clear. I would visit friends and cousins and talk nonstop using as many "reckons" and drawing out my i's as long as I pleased. Over the course of time, I realized that being country was as much a part of me as being black or being a woman. Creeks, one-room churches, outhouses, gravel roads, old men whittling at Hill's Grocery down in Needmore, daisies, Big Boy tomatoes, and buttercups. It was all mine. It is the makeup of my spirit. Country is as much a part of me as my full lips, my wide hips, my dreadlocks, my high cheekbones.

The way the words roll off my tongue is the voice of my people—the country Affrilachian folks. The voice of my grandparents' parents and all those who came before. Of Daddy Joe and Ma Lillie, Pa Jim and Aunt Francis. A country twang—a melodic use of language that is distinctively woodburning stove, come in and sit a spell, patchwork quilt, summer swimming hole, sweet iced tea, you are always welcome here. . . . warm.

# Appalachian Stepchild

## Stephen L. Fisher

I was born and raised in Charleston, West Virginia. My working-class father, ashamed of his lack of education and my mother's coal camp background, was determined to "make it." He worked two jobs, and as his income rose, we moved to "better" neighborhoods and adopted middle-class values and attitudes. As we ascended the urban class scale, I acquired very few of the traits commonly attributed to rural Appalachians.[1] I was exposed to liberal Presbyterianism, not religious fundamentalism. I didn't develop a love of the land (I quit the Boy Scouts after my first overnight hike) or a sense of individualism (I wanted only to be accepted by my new suburban classmates). What I did learn was the importance of money and status and a fear of "hillbillies."

My family moved from a working-class neighborhood to the suburbs just as I was starting junior high school. There was little interaction in the school between the middle-class whites from the suburbs, inner-city blacks, and the "hillbillies" or "creekers" from the surrounding hollows. I didn't fit. The suburban kids knew from my dress, accent, and mannerisms that I wasn't one of them, the blacks knew I was white, and the "creekers" knew only that I was from the suburbs. I tried to become a part of the suburban in-crowd, but to no avail. One of my most vivid memories is sitting teary-eyed in the back of Latin class after learning that, despite better grades than many of the members, I had not been elected to the school's honor society by my suburban peers. I grew to despise them as I tried harder and harder to join them. In the process, I came to despise myself.

My contact with the "creekers" was restricted to the times they would hustle me for small change or my homework assignment. This extortion usually occurred in gym class, and if I refused, they would either inflict immediate punishment during a dodgeball game or wait until after school on a street corner. At the time, I couldn't understand their hostility toward me.[2] Where was the challenge? I was a skinny kid, usually alone, such an easy mark. Years later, when I visited Cincinnati's Over-the-Rhine, a low-income Appalachian neighborhood, my immediate response was fear. There was no ostensible basis for that fear because I was with friends from the neighborhood, but I could not suppress memories of those beatings I took during my junior high years. Hatred and envy of those "above" me, fear of those "below" me, personal feelings of powerlessness and self-hatred—I was well on my way to becoming a typical American middle-class citizen.

I continued my education at Wake Forest University, where I learned to be ashamed of where I was from. I became so sensitive to the response I received when I told other students I was from West Virginia that I began saying only that I was from Charleston, hoping they might think it was Charleston, South Carolina. Soon I began to join in the fun. At fraternity parties I would wear a hillbilly hat and drunkenly sing "The West Virginia Hills," and I would win the prize for best-dressed hillbilly at the fraternity's annual hillbilly party. I was being stereotyped as the "hillbilly" I feared, but I used that stereotype to gain acceptance by my peers.[3]

When I entered graduate school in political science at Tulane University in 1966, I was what was called in those days a "good liberal." I knew that poverty and discrimination existed and that I should feel guilty about it. I knew that President Johnson was a southerner and was therefore to be distrusted. I knew that something was wrong with the war in Vietnam, but I also knew that I would serve my country if called.

A year of dissertation research in Germany profoundly shook my faith in the American way. Pressured by West German students to defend the war and American racism, I started to read and think seriously about both for the first time in my life. The realization that I had been lied to about these issues sent me into a rage from which I've yet to recover.[4] Arriving back in the United States angry and self-righteous, I became involved in the civil rights and antiwar movements. But my anger took me only so far. I knew there were many problems, but I didn't know why. I focused my anger on LBJ, on Nixon, on the police, on southern bigots, on my father, on myself. I had moved from "good liberal" to "angry liberal."

In 1971 I accepted a teaching job at Emory & Henry College, a small liberal arts, church-related school in the hills of southwestern Virginia. It was more coincidence than desire that brought me back to Appalachia—it was the best job offer I had. My arrival in Emory, a town of three hundred, left me in shock. There was no hint of an antiwar movement or of a political community of any sort; and there were few black students, something that shouldn't have surprised me given the school's nickname (the WASPS). Near the end of my first year on campus I attended a symposium on Appalachia at which Helen Lewis, Harry Caudill, Jim Branscome, and others held forth on the problems of the region. This was the first time I had ever heard anyone speak of West Virginia with a sense of pride. I latched onto the implications of their analysis for myself almost immediately. I was searching for a personal and a political identity;

oppressed mountaineer seemed perfect. After all, I had been born and raised in West Virginia; and hadn't people been calling me a hillbilly? I was making real progress—I had moved from good liberal to angry liberal to oppressed minority.

It, of course, was not that easy. In what sense could I call myself an Appalachian? Although I grew up in Appalachia, I am largely a product of urban "mainstream" American culture. A trip to the old homeplace took me not to coal camps, farms, or the mountains but to the city. No matter how great the desire, no matter how many gardens I planted, no matter how many times I stood in solidarity with mine workers on a union picket line, I felt like an imposter whenever I bragged about my "Appalachian" roots.

And then there was the business about being oppressed. I could point to my working-class origins, could describe how I had been ridiculed for being from Appalachia, and using the jargon of the day, could talk about the common oppression of us all. But the bottom line was that I was a white, male, middle-class college professor specializing in German politics. It just didn't wash.

So, by what right could I call myself an Appalachian? Eventually, I decided that it just didn't matter. As Mike Maloney put it, if your parents, grandparents, or great-grandparents were from Appalachia, then you, too, are an Appalachian, if you want to be. And I wanted to be. Reading and learning about the region was empowering—it was like discovering a missing part of myself. Claiming Appalachia has given me a place, a people, a sense of who I am and who I want to become. It has helped me better understand and accept my parents and the decisions they made. And it has brought focus and commitment to my work and politics.

I still don't have a pat answer when I'm asked what I mean when I say I am an Appalachian. But I often say that I see myself as one of the region's stepchildren: the product of a divorce from working-class, rural life and a remarriage with urban, middle-class culture. As a stepchild, I have a right to the label "Appalachian." But in asserting my identity as an Appalachian, I have had to rethink and reinterpret my relationship with my kin from both sides of the family. My newly defined relationships may not be completely fulfilling or all that I desire. But they are certainly healthier than relationships based on ignorance, shame, or fear.

## Notes

1. Growing up in urban Appalachia can be a vastly different experience from coming of age in rural Appalachia. Many in Appalachian cities are trying to lose traditional rural traits. Their primary concern is to become a part of the American middle class or, if they can't achieve this status during their lifetime, to ensure that their children do.

2. I don't remember any mention of the concept "social class" throughout my twenty years of formal education. Surely I'm wrong about that, but I do know that I emerged, Ph.D. in hand, with no idea of the concept's meaning or significance. As I struggled in the 1970s to make sense of Appalachia and its problems, I began to appreciate the value of class as an analytical tool and to come to grips with how important my own class background has been in determining my relationships with others and in shaping who I am.

3. This happened in other contexts. For example, on a ship full of Fulbright scholars headed for Germany, I was asked to dance by Ivy League coeds who had "never danced with a hillbilly before."

4. This rage is a primary difference between me and the students I now teach. Growing up after Vietnam and Watergate and during the Reagan-Bush years, they are very cynical about American politics and life. But there is often no anger, no motivating force to act. My anger, the anger growing out of believing we were a country of equality and justice and then discovering we weren't, is what makes and keeps me politically active.

# If There's One Thing You Can Tell Them, It's that You're Free

*Eula Hall*

I'll tell you, to get to where I am today has not been easy. I was born an Appalachian child in poverty. I was reared in poverty, deprived of an education. But you know, I held onto one dream. I wanted to be somebody. I wanted to do things for other people, and I wanted to change lives for people in the same position I was in.

I didn't get along with my parents because I felt like I was a slave. I felt like I was a servant. I had no freedom as a child. I don't have one happy memory of my life as a child. All we did was work. We worked. We worked. We worked. We worked to survive because fifty or sixty years ago, things weren't like they are now. Things were very, very hard. The children had to help support the family. Because I was the oldest girl of seven children, education was out of the question. You stayed home. You helped raise your brothers and sisters, you cooked, you milked cows, and you worked in the cornfield. You did it all. But I always wanted to learn. And I knew if I never got an education, I'd be stuck where I was. I got through the eighth grade in five years. But that was it, no more education.

I became a hired girl. A hired girl was nothing more than a slave for people with money—people with money who had sickness or needed someone to live in and cook and clean, cook for borders, wash on the washboard and all that. That's what you did. I got a dollar and a half to two dollars a week to buy clothes. Well, I didn't like that. That wasn't what I wanted to be. That was still deeper in.

So I met and married this big handsome prince. I thought, this will solve my problem. Thought I'd landed good. Well, you know what you see ain't always what is. What I got was a wolf in lamb's clothes. He always said I was a tiger. And you know wolves and tigers don't get along so well. Believe me, I was trapped. First thing after my marriage, I became pregnant with my first child. I don't think that you could have been in any deeper trouble than I was in. But I didn't know how to get out. My father had died. My mother still had three small children to raise, and I could not go back home. I didn't want to go back home. My husband was very threatening, very abusive. And here I was, stuck. So I tried to make plans to get out.

When you see women in horrible situations like this, you ask, "Why does she stay? Why doesn't she leave? Why does she do this and why does she do that?" I've been there. I know why you stay. I know why you don't leave. You can't leave. You have nowhere to go. Now we have some shelters, but they aren't permanent solutions. So here I was, pregnant, having a child, but the abuse was still going on. But I never gave up. I had one dream. Someday I would be free and I'd be somebody. I'd live my life the way I wanted to live it and how I wanted to live it. I'd do as I pleased. And I'd help other people do the same. That kept me going. When I looked at my husband, I thought, you may be the devil in disguise, but you know you ain't going to conquer me. You may beat better and you may abuse better, but if you don't kill me, I'll outlive you and I'll be somebody. So I hung on to that and it looked—well, sometimes it looked very grim and gray.

I raised four children with this man before I saw an opportunity to break away. In spite of all the trials and tribulations and all the trouble I went through with him, I had sneaked and learned to drive a vehicle. He had a car but rode to work with another man, and he'd leave his car parked in the driveway. And I'd hire somebody to turn it over, to start it, and I'd run it all day. I'd take the odometer loose and draw me some lines and I'd park it back where he'd had it. He never knew until I hit a big stack of rocks one day. And then the story was told.

But I always planned how I could get ahead of him and how I could prepare myself to live someday when he was gone, when I got away. And one thing that I gave my children that I never had—I made this vow when I started having my children and raising a family—one thing my children would have regardless of how bad things were: they'd have my love and they'd have me. Those things I didn't have. So I stuck by it and stuck with them and sent them to school. I educated them as best I could. I worked for them. I supported them. They never went hungry.

When my last two were seven years old I saw an opportunity to get away. During the War on Poverty in the 1960s, there were the Appalachian Volunteers and the VISTA workers. And I decided that I could be one or the other. Regardless of what *he* does or what *he* says, I vowed, I'll be a VISTA or an Appalachian Volunteer. So I started to act. I signed up to be a VISTA and I went down to Atlanta to train. I wanted so much for the VISTAs to continue to do what they'd been doing in our area. They let me train for the national group that would be coming back to Floyd County, Kentucky.

But when we got back to Floyd County, the fiscal court had ousted VISTA. But they forgot to oust the Appalachian Volunteers, so I just transferred over from being a VISTA worker to being an Appalachian Volunteer. That gave me a vehicle and fifty dollars a week. Well, it wasn't enough money to pay rent and leave, but it was enough money to make plans. It was enough money to prepare myself for a new adventure.

During this time, we Appalachian Volunteers were working on problems of all people in Appalachia: roads and schools and school lunches and health care and education. I was still a long way from working only on health care. I'd seen so much suffering as a child from the lack of health care. It would really haunt you at night to see a mother with five or six children suffer and die from a nail puncture and tetanus when one shot could have saved this woman and those babies. When we were growing up, we didn't go to the doctor. I never knew what a doctor's office looked like. The closest thing to health care I ever got as a child—really until I was probably thirty-five or forty years old—was an immunization at school. I've seen so much suffering out of women, suffering like I was going through. It's too easy to criticize: Why won't they do something? Why won't they at least stand up and be somebody?

If you can't ever be yourself, who are you? Who can you be? I was never a person to let others dictate to me; I didn't yield and say "Amen" or "Yes, sir" to things I didn't believe in. And, for having that attitude, boy, I paid the price. I really paid the price for being the person that I was. But I hung on to one theory and one dream: One day I'll be free. One day I'll be who I want to be. I'll do what I want to do and I'll help people. I'll bring services here that nobody's ever thought possible

The first local community thing I got into came about because of the new school building. Now when I went to school, we went to one- or two-room schoolhouses and we had no electricity, no windows. Finally we got electricity and they consolidated the small schools and built a big fancy elementary school in Mud Creek, Kentucky. In that school there was a lunchroom, a beautiful modern lunchroom. I had three children going to school. They come home and they said, "We don't get to eat in the lunchroom." I asked why. And they said, "If you can't pay full price, you can't eat." Only the ones who could afford to eat got to, and the ones who couldn't afford it had to sit up on the stage and watch the others eat. You know that just didn't go over well with me.

I knew from training to become a VISTA and Appalachian Volunteer that the federal government provided most of this food and that there should be free or reduced price lunches for the school kids who didn't have money to pay full price. I got up a group of people from a local welfare rights organization, and we tried to find out the process for the free or the reduced price school lunches. We were told there wasn't any process. But we knew better and decided one day that we might have to show the board of education just what we knew.

So we went, about sixty of us together, and marched on the board of education. And of course, somebody had let them know we were coming. They had the city police from Prestonsburg. If you've ever been there, you know there's just not that many police. So we marched. The police couldn't do a thing with us. A big brawl broke out and some people went to jail. I didn't go that time. Anyway, we'd played our cards right. The news media was there and the march made big headlines. Now we have the best lunch program in Floyd County. And we have a breakfast program there, too. Sometimes you have to fight for what you get. You have to stand up for what's right. Things just don't always happen the way they should. You've got to make them happen. And I wasn't a bit sorry about making things happen if I could make sure that every child in that school had a meal.

I feel the same way about all the abuse and problems of women in our area. Many are going through the very same problems I had. At first I couldn't get some women to even try to drive a car. I offered to teach them to drive and finally some did learn. Finally, we have some women going to GED classes and now we got women who have come a long way in that area.

And we've got the Mud Creek clinic. I started the clinic with fourteen hundred dollars and volunteers. I got the fourteen hundred dollars because the Appalachian Volunteers went under and there was fourteen hundred dollars left in their account. They gave it to the clinic. We had already health-screened people with med students from the University of Kentucky and local people trained by the students. We screened hundreds and hundreds and hundreds of patients in the Mud Creek area. And we found out that most had no family physician and that they had severe medical problems: hypertension, some had had strokes, black lung disease, and we found too many heart problems. They had nothing, nowhere to go, no money, no medical insurance. I'd think, if the government's going to spend money on anything worthwhile, why can't they spend it on health care? But the really big money for such problems just ended up in the politicians' hands and pockets.

So I took the fourteen hundred dollars and the volunteers and started the Mud Creek clinic. I said, well, if we can't get federal money to do it, we'll do it ourselves. And then we'll know it's done right. We'll take care of everybody. So we got some volunteers to get started and we still get volunteers. We got students from the University of Kentucky, and we still get students from different medical schools. They do a great job to help us. But we have our own doctors now. We've had the clinic now for twenty-three years. We've got full-time doctors; we have a pharmacy, X-ray, dental, transportation, and health education. We've got it all under one roof. And that's because the need was so great and somebody had to take the bull by the horns. People tell me today they never thought that there would be a clinic in Mud Creek. You see, you just don't know, you really don't know, how far you can go or how much you can do until you try.

I moved the clinic into my house. When we started up, it was in a little bitty, run-down house up in the hollow. You couldn't even drive through the gate to get in. At night when I'd go home, I'd think, I only have two kids living at home and I really don't need this whole house. I'd just sit and look at the place and figure out what and how I could do it. I could take my living room and make it a waiting room and so on.

I thought, first thing I have to do, I've got to get rid of my old man. You all might think this is awful, but I did it. If you could get him stoned out of his mind, you could get him to do anything. He was always out of the house drinking anyway, so it wasn't that hard to do. I set him up with some drinking buddies in order to get him to sign the papers. That's how I got my divorce. I got him out of the house and I put the clinic in it. And we kept the clinic in my house until 1982 when the clinic burned. On June 15, 1982, our clinic burned to the ground. It was as if we were back at day one. First we thought we would become a part of Big Sandy development district health care, send everyone to Magoffin County. I called, but that office wasn't enthusiastic. They told me to tell the rest of the staff to come in and accept their lay-off slips, and then *they* would figure out what we could do.

But if we had done that, we would have lost hundreds of patients in the meantime. They couldn't have seen the doctor. They couldn't have the things they needed. So the next morning we went out to talk to the staff and see what they wanted to do. We met a lot of the patients there, and everybody was really sad. It was worse than any funeral that I've ever attended. The patients asked, "What are we going to do? We'll die without the medicine and we'll die without the care." So I talked to the staff and said, "Let's not give up. If we give up, we'll never be able to come back again. It was hard to get started. And it will be even harder now to get it back if we give up."

We had a picnic table in the back under the weeping willow tree where we had had a birthday party for one of the staff people. I asked our doctor if he would care to go over to the picnic table and stay in the shade and talk to the patients as they came. I told him to just give people some hope and tell them we're not going to give up, that we're going to try, that I'm going to try to do something. The doctor agreed.

Well now, I thought, we've got to stay in touch with the world, too. We can't just be out here like this, silent. So I called the telephone company and asked them to put a telephone on the tree so the nurses could stay in touch with the patients, and I could use the phone to get things done. The telephone company thought I had lost my mind. So, I said, "Well, look"—I always had an argument prepared—"you all don't care to go to the big coal companies and hang telephones on their poles at the top of the hill. What's the difference? As long as you get your money for the telephone bill, don't ask any questions. Just give us a telephone." And they did.

We also went to the school and started a temporary clinic in that building. Our old wounds had kind of healed between the community group and the board of education. Our relationship with the superintendent had healed to an extent. When we first had it out with him, he had gotten restraining orders against us and we weren't allowed to go back on the school ground. But in my area, the rural area, it takes a while to get the police. You can get away and they are not going to hunt for you. So I didn't let it bother me too much about the restraining order. So, immediately after the fire, we got the clinic going in the school. But school started in August and we knew we had to get out by then. We thought about a tent and some people offered us one. People were trying to help us as much as they could. But we couldn't stay in a tent through the winter. We couldn't do much real help in a tent. So we got hold of an old, used, double-wide trailer and brought it up to the lot next to the burned clinic. I let that burnt stuff lay there for two or three years. I was so hurt over the loss of my home and what we had in there. We had had one of the best black lung treatment centers in Floyd County when the clinic burned. All the equipment burned.

But anyway, we moved into that trailer and I started fund-raising. I thought that it was time to go bigger and better. I got in touch with the Appalachian Commission and they indicated that we could get funded to build a primary care center if we had the local matching funds. They don't give you a 100 percent grant outright. We had to raise eighty thousand dollars in ninety days in order to get the grant by the end of September. Even my family said it was impossible. They said, "You'll never do it, raise eighty thousand dollars in a poverty area like this." And I said, "Well, I'll have to try. You never know how far you can go, you don't know what you can do, until you try." I said, "Let me try since I don't have anything to lose except my hard work and time." I didn't mind that. So I started fund-raising, and the news media was my biggest source of help. Local people really came through. At the end of the ninety days I had about $102,000, more than even I had bargained for. I knew just what to do with this extra money. I bought X-ray equipment. Since then, we've put in new services and we've built a twenty-five-thousand-dollar addition to the clinic.

The clinic shows what you can do if you just try and you've got the willpower. But as far as having the education, I didn't have it. Sometimes I think, is it common sense or am I just crazy to take the chances I've taken and do the things I've done? Like trying to stop the strip mining. A lot of times it was just women. We'd get out there and try to stop those strip miners. They'd get the police, but we'd get into areas the police couldn't get to. You know they don't like to wade in mud and climb hills. So we could do what we'd set out to do before they could do much of anything to stop us, and we stopped the strip mining on Mud Creek. It was the women who did it.

But to organize the women, to get them together, to get them to do anything, you have to get them away from their husbands. I'd go out and I'd try to talk to the women about problems we had, and they were interested. But if their husbands were there at home, they were different. They are different. They don't talk much. He doesn't talk much, but he would be the one to tell you what she could or could not do.

I got away from that, but the price that I paid for my freedom and the price I paid to be here today was high. My husband was one of the most violent people that you could ever meet. I don't know how I survived a few times. But the way I hurt *him* most was making sure he couldn't be like those other men, his friends and his buddies. He couldn't control me. There was no way he could control me. Most men can control their wives. After so much torture and so much pain, they can control them. Mine, he never could. I mean he was rough with me. He was mean to me. But as far as keeping me from doing the things I wanted to do, I'd do it if I thought it was right and I thought that it was something I wanted to do. But I really paid the price to be here today, to stand up for what I believe in, to do things I've done and help the people I've helped. I've had several fractures, I've been stabbed, and I've been shot. And I praise God that I'm here. But I can still see why there aren't many women in Appalachia in the same abusive situation who manage to get out. They really can't. They're destroyed physically by men.

Things that happened to me as a child, before I got away, were not pretty. I've got scars. These scars will never heal and they leave memories that will never die. Truly, my suffering and my witness to the suffering and other bad things happening in our area made me what I am. I had one dream and one hope, and I followed it and it came true. I could get away and I could get myself free and I could help other people. And I never ceased to try.

I drive a four-wheel drive and transport patients. I represent patients in need of help. I represent people at disability hearings. I do whatever is necessary to help somebody who can't help themselves. I get as many people back in school as I can, because I still wish I could have gone. But I don't want to go to school now. I can do what I want to do without it. I've done a lot of things I've wanted to do without trying to further my education, and I just want to keep doing what I've been doing. But if I were twenty years old, I would go to school and get my degree.

Things just don't happen, especially for women. You have to make them happen. You can't give up over the first little thing that goes wrong. Many nights, I'd think, "Am I ever going to get out of here? How am I going to make a break?" Sometimes I really thought of doing something bad. The only thing that kept me from it was my love for my children. I could have done away with him. But I love my children and I knew that if I messed up, then they would have to live with a scandal that I had done something that I shouldn't have, that I had broken the law. Most of all they would have done without my love and my care. So I stuck it out and hung on for that reason, for my children. If it hadn't been for them, I don't know what I would have done. But I'm sure I would have eliminated him.

But we've come a long way as women. There are a lot of opportunities for women that I didn't have. I was trapped, stuck as deep as you could be in something bad. But now there are opportunities that women can pursue. There are shelters and there are programs for education and there's more police protection. But we still don't have enough. I was never able to keep him in jail more than overnight, which just makes them really mad and ready to kill you. It just aggravated him. So you have to just figure out what is the best route, which way to go, and what to do when the time for escape happens. But, in the meantime, you never know at night if you'll be around when daylight comes. After you live with it so long, the memories never die. The experience can make you or it can break you.

I guess I just hung tough and hung on. I don't think that anything more could happen to me than has already happened without my just dying. But my children are now grown and I don't have to worry about leaving any children for that man to abuse. I am truly proud to say that I have done more than I thought I could do by hanging on and being tough and taking abuse and hanging with it to try to do things for people, mainly women and children.

Our clinic is first a place for women with children, but anybody can come. We have a minimum payment, but if you don't have the money, then I'll manage some way to pay it. Federal regulations require a minimum payment of five dollars a visit and five dollars a prescription, but nobody leaves that clinic because they don't have five dollars. People often don't have it, but I manage to make sure the money's there for them. That's something I took upon myself to do. And I've done it. I'm on a lot of boards and a lot of committees because I want to know what's going on, where the money goes, how it is spent, and who gets it. That's the only way I can do that—as a member of boards and committees. I keep my eyes open and my ears open.

And I'm real proud to be here. When I was invited to come here and speak to this conference, I said, "Why me?" I don't have the education that everybody's going to have. I'm not a good speaker. I'm not a speaker at all. Why me? The organizers told me to talk about freedom. "If there's one thing that you can tell them, it's that you're free. You can tell people at this conference that you're free." Well, I earned it. I paid the price and I got it. And that's something to be proud of.

## Notes

This chapter was adapted from an oral presentation given by the author at the November 1994 conference "Women in Appalachia," sponsored by the Appalachian Center at the University of Kentucky.

# IV

# Sometimes Actions Speak
# Louder than Words

## Activism in Appalachia

# The Grass Roots Speak Back

*Stephen L. Fisher*

Contrary to popular images of Appalachians as passive victims, there exists throughout the Appalachian Mountains a tradition of individual and organized citizen efforts to establish community services and preserve community values. This essay describes the variety and extent of local and regional efforts for change in Appalachia since 1960 and examines the lessons to be learned from these efforts.[1]

The Appalachian region has never lacked a politics of change and alternative development. But what stands out in the literature describing life in Appalachia before 1960 is not the extent of change efforts but rather the obstacles to change, the conditions leading to quiescence.[2] The industrialization of Appalachia was characterized by single-industry economies, the control of land and resources by large absentee companies, high levels of poverty and unemployment, the frequent use of red baiting, intimidation, and physical force to squelch dissent, political corruption, and a highly stratified and oppressive class system. Collective struggles for change were further undermined by cultural traditions that stressed individualism, by the strength of capitalist ideology, by racism and sexism, by the lack of strong local organizations, by high illiteracy rates, and by poor transportation and communication systems.

During this period, one could find throughout Appalachia examples of the starkest political and economic oppression in American society. In recent years, anthropologists and social and feminist historians have taught us that, when faced with such repressive conditions, people find ways to resist. This was certainly true in Appalachia. The organized efforts of workers in the coal, textile, and steel industries to improve their working and living conditions are well documented. But in other parts of the Appalachian Mountains, responses to these conditions often assumed forms far less visible than picket lines and organized movements and included such individual acts of behavior as gossip, back talk, holding on to one's dialect, refusal to cooperate with outside authority figures, and migration. This type of protest is part of what James Scott refers to as the "hidden transcript" of the oppressed.[3]

Increasingly, Appalachian scholars are coming to recognize the existence and importance of such protest in Appalachia's history and to understand that it has most frequently occurred in struggles to preserve traditional values and ways of life against the forces of modernization. For example, Helen Lewis, Sue Kobak, and Linda Johnson describe the various ways in which mountain families and churches became defensive and inward in order to protect their members from some of the harmful impacts of industrialization and the actions of outside change agents.[4] Kathleen Blee and Dwight Billings reinterpret early ethnographic studies of the region to show that work attitudes and other practices previously viewed as traits of a culture of poverty could better be understood as forms of resistance to the capitalist separation of work and control.[5] Altina Waller argues that the legendary Hatfield-McCoy feud can be seen as a battle between local defenders of community autonomy and outside industrial interests.[6] These and similar studies broaden our understanding of the nature and extent of resistance by rural working-class and poor people in Appalachia 1960.

Many of the obstacles that made collective struggles so difficult throughout Appalachia's history are still present today, and individual protests continue on a number of fronts. But new conditions after 1960 provided impetus and support to organized resistance efforts throughout Appalachia. The civil rights movement helped legitimize the notion of dissent in general and the strategy of nonviolent civil disobedience in particular throughout the region and the nation. The environmental and women's movements offered models and resources for local groups in the mountains. Moreover, these movements provided the impetus for national legislation that created opportunities for local organizations fighting to save their land and communities from environmental destruction or working to create alternative economic opportunities for women. The antiwar and student movements called into question the notions of progress, modernization, and national interest that had been used for so long to justify the destruction of traditional ways of life in Appalachia.

The War on Poverty spawned the Appalachian Volunteers and community action agencies throughout the mountains. While these programs had many weaknesses, they did bring young organizers into the region and provided opportunities for local leadership development. Mainstream churches, reflecting a new social consciousness, sent to Appalachia clergy and other church workers who were committed to working for social and economic justice. The construction of more and better roads, the availability of video recording equipment, open meeting and record laws, and increased church and foundation funding of Appalachian citizen groups also contributed to local organizing efforts.

These and other factors led to an outburst of grassroots community organizing across Appalachia in the late 1960s and early 1970s. Local residents fought to prevent the destruction of their land and homes by strip miners, dam and highway builders, the U.S. Forest Service, toxic waste dumpers, and recreation and second-home developers. People organized to secure welfare benefits, to enact tax reform, to build rural community centers and health clinics, to fight for better schools for their children, and to establish programs in literacy and child care. Community groups pursued a wide variety of alternative economic development strategies that resulted in agricultural and craft cooperatives, worker-owned factories, and new job opportunities for women. Efforts to preserve and celebrate local culture flourished in the mountains, as people began to develop a consciousness of and pride in being Appalachian.

In the 1990s people across Appalachia are still fighting back, often around similar issues.[7] The battle over strip mining continues as local groups challenge the Office of Surface Mining's nonenforcement of the federal strip mining law and join with other groups to lobby Washington for better water protection laws. Communities throughout rural Appalachia struggle to prevent their landfills from becoming the dumping grounds for the nation's trash, sludge, and toxic waste. The Yellow Creek Concerned Citizens and the Dayhoit Concerned Citizens in east Kentucky, the Dead Pigeon River Council and the Oak Ridge Environmental Peace Alliance in East Tennessee, and the Dickenson County Citizens Committee in Southwest Virginia are just a few of the groups across the region fighting the poisoning of their land, air, and water. The Ohio Valley Environmental Coalition organizes around industrial pollution where Ohio, Kentucky, and West Virginia meet. The Ivanhoe Civic League and the Dungannon Development Commission in Southwest Virginia and the Appalachian Center for Economic Networks in Athens, Ohio, pursue innovative grassroots alternative economic development plans. The Mountain Women's Exchange in East Tennessee and Women and Employment in West Virginia work to improve the economic position of women in the region.

In sum, since the 1960s, hundreds of new citizen groups have been organized throughout Appalachia. Most arose in response to a particular issue. These single-issue groups have worked together from time to time, helped create local leadership, and won important victories. But because they have focused on a single issue, many of these groups have been short-lived, disappearing once their issue has been resolved. Thus, one of the most exciting and hopeful developments in community organizing in Appalachia in recent years has been the establishment and success of thriving and influential multi-issue, membership-driven organizations such as Save Our Cumberland Mountains (SOCM), Kentuckians for the Commonwealth (KFTC), and the Community Farm Alliance (CFA).

SOCM, organized in 1972 to fight strip mining in a five-county area in the northern coalfields of Tennessee, changed from a single-issue, staff-run group to a multi-issue, grassroots organization able to exercise power and influence at the state and national levels.[8] KFTC, started in mid-1981 by a small group of eastern Kentucky residents who wanted to address community problems that crossed county lines, has grown into a statewide, multi-issue, social justice organization of more than twenty-three hundred members in ninety counties.[9] CFA was transformed from a handful of people who were replicating the mistakes of the national farm movement of the 1980s to a growing and successful membership-based organization with over a dozen chapters across Kentucky.[10]

These organizations stress the significance of local indigenous leadership recruitment and training, shared and long-term consciousness raising, the development of internal democratic social relations, ideological patience, and the willingness to connect with people as they are. Their success illustrates the importance of using county chapters to build statewide organizations and of connecting local issues to state, national, and global patterns and concerns.

Since the 1960s, activists have attempted to organize citizen organizations in the Appalachian Mountains into a regionwide grassroots social movement. The most important attempts were by the Council of the Southern Mountains, the Peoples Appalachia Research Collective, the Congress for Appalachian Development, the Highlander Research and Education Center, and the Appalachian Alliance.[11] These attempts to build a unified movement failed for a variety of reasons, but primarily because, unlike class, race, and gender, region in the United States does not provide an adequate political and economic focus for social movements.

This failure to create a social movement in Appalachia similar to the civil rights or women's movements does not mean that change efforts in the region have occurred in isolation. While many of these struggles have been local and concerned with a single issue, they have often been assisted by and associated with other groups and individuals within a loose alliance or network of Appalachian organizations. At times the network has had a name; at other times, it has been little more than an informal chain of individuals and groups. Organizations and activists come and go and financial support is rarely stable; but the network persists, and there may be no other like it in the United States.[12] Key players in this network today include the Highlander Research and Education Center, an adult education center in eastern Tennessee that has served as a meeting place, training center, and catalyst for social action throughout Appalachia and the South; the Southern Empowerment Project, an organizer training program established and controlled by grassroots community groups; and the Appalachian Community Fund, a community-controlled foundation that provides seed money and small grants to groups in the Appalachian region.

As Bill Horton points out, this loose, informal network "is the form that the Appalachian social movement has taken—slowly winning victories, working together, laying the groundwork, building or trying to build democratic organizations. Perhaps this is the way the movement will be built, piece by piece like a patchwork quilt until it comes together to rid the region of oppressive structures and practices, in turn becoming a piece of a much larger quilt that must be created to rid the nation of those same structures and practices."[13]

Over the past three decades, activists and academics have learned a number of important lessons about the politics of change in Appalachia. Successful change efforts in the Appalachian mountains have centered more often around the concept of community than around the centralized workplace of the mine, mill, or factory. In addition, historical memory and a reliance on and defense of traditional values—a strong commitment to land, kin, and religious beliefs, an emphasis on self-rule and social equality, and patriotism—have fueled many of the popular struggles in the region. Indeed, the fact that so many of the protests in Appalachia have been the result of defensive behavior—action to prevent the destruction of a way of life and a set of values that could be labeled traditional or conservative—has led one observer to refer to Appalachians as "reactionary rebels."[14]

While it is important to understand that grassroots resistance in Appalachian history has most frequently occurred in single-issue battles to preserve traditional values and ways of life, it is also necessary to recognize that there are limits to community-based organizing strategies that focus on single issues and rely heavily on localism and traditional values and institutions.[15] Community in our history entails exclusion as well as inclusion. Tradition and local values include racism, sexism, homophobia, and isolationism. In addition, while localism offers a number of advantages, few significant problems can be solved at the local level. Local resources have been depleted and local economies gutted by national and global market forces and the actions of the federal government and multinational corporations. Those organizing in Appalachia must find ways to make clear the connections that exist between local work and national and international institutions if local citizens are to understand the importance of national and international forces as determinants of what happens locally and to see themselves as actors at the national level.

Without attention to the larger questions of power in society, local community groups are often not prepared for the legal, political, and cultural forces that established powers bring against them. This results in a politics of gradualism—a strategy of adaptation and retrenchment—and a suspicion of outsiders and their programs. Further, it does not create the conditions necessary for coalition work with potential allies—be they health professionals, church workers, or environmentalists. Many local revolts throughout Appalachia turn out to be "flashes of independent anger" rather than sustained efforts at effective movement building precisely because they lack an analysis and understanding of power beyond the local level.[16]

In sum, single-issue, defensive, localized work, which has characterized much of the organizing in Appalachia, can win occasional victories but cannot by itself lead to substantive change at an individual or structural level.[17] Tackling issues as complex as poverty, strip mining, or inadequate health care requires ongoing, multi-issue, reflective, democratic organizations, the type of organizing being conducted by SOCM, KFTC, and CFA—the multi-issue, membership-run organizations described above. These groups pursue an organizing approach that is flexible, pragmatic, and grounded in the past and present of members' lives. But unlike the narrow single-issue organizing of the past, these groups' primary concern is to empower their members for the long haul— to provide a schooling in politics and personal empowerment. They do so by offering a self-conscious leadership training program designed to develop democratic skills and build a sense of ownership and community. These organizations provide the space where participants can begin to see the connection between their concerns and those of other exploited people, where members can come to confront issues of racism and sexism, and where people can start to envision new alternatives to the world in which they live. As Connie White, a past SOCM president, puts it, "We don't care just about winning issues; we care more about helping people get stronger. In the long run, that is how you win issues and make real changes."[18]

In the past, many organizers have arrived in Appalachia with pejorative, romanticized, or contrived notions of the cultural forces and values present in the Appalachian mountains. Appalachian culture is "a web of both resistance and complicity,"[19] and it is important for those organizing in the region to develop an understanding of the ways in which regional culture informs the construction of class consciousness, race and gender relations, regional identity, and community life.

Several points need to be emphasized in this regard. First, regional identity and cultural pride are not naturally part of community life. Regional identity is not a geographical or cultural given in Appalachia, but must be understood as an outgrowth of political dynamics and social change. Similarly, local cultural traditions are selective and fluid in nature; they are "historically formed, situated, and altered by people interacting with each other and with social and economic forces."[20] These cultural traditions are at the heart of the community networks necessary to sustain people during protracted struggles and enable them to foster change on their own terms. But cultural expression does not always arise spontaneously in struggles to challenge oppression and inequality. The seeds for such expression exist; but these seeds must often be deliberately cultivated and nourished by organizers and institutions that recognize the value of cultural forms to resistance efforts.[21]

Second, neither class nor culture alone is a sufficient tool for understanding political action in Appalachia. Although classes are shaped by economic concerns, they are cultural configurations. Indeed, the United States is one of the few places where class and culture are thought of separately. Lived experience is different—our lives are a messy amalgam of identities out of which social relations are conducted.[22] The difficult but crucial task is not to decide between culture and class, but to discover how class, race, and gender conflicts express themselves today in cultural and political formations in Appalachia.

In Appalachian research, some of the most important work in this regard is being done by Mary Anglin and Sally Maggard. Using different approaches and studying protest in different locales and industries, Anglin and Maggard probe the ways in which gender, kinship, and social class interact to specify women's political experience, action, and consciousness. They demonstrate convincingly how and why change efforts, to be successful, must be situated in a web of work, family, and community needs and histories.[23] Other significant contributions include Michael Yarrow's investigation of the ways in which Appalachian coal miners' gender consciousness affects their class consciousness;[24] Richard Couto's discussion of community-based approaches to environmental risks;[25] and Dwight Billings's use of Antonio Gramsci's approach to religion to explain activism and quiescence among textile workers and coal miners.[26]

Third, racism is a major barrier to successful grassroots organizing and coalition-building in Appalachia, as it is throughout the nation. Don Manning-Miller charges that many of the community organizations in Appalachia, while committed either explicitly or implicitly to combating racism and to building a multiracial people's coalition for progressive social change, in practice pursue a process of organizing and struggle that fails to challenge the cultural conservatism and racism of their constituency. Manning-Miller urges organizers and activists to use all available media and organizational forms to confront people's racism and offers a number of valuable tactical measures and suggestions for developing a systematic program to confront racism in Appalachia.[27]

Finally, to be successful over the long haul, those engaged in cultural, educational, and political work must search through the regional culture to locate its most humane, progressive, and transformative elements and then look for ways to link these transformative elements to a larger human agenda for change.[28]

This brief consideration of organized grassroots change efforts in Appalachia should dispel the stereotypical notion of Appalachians as apathetic and dependent. Activists and scholars have made major advances since the 1960s in terms of building effective community organizations and in intellectual efforts to grapple with some of the tough issues involved in mounting effective resistance.

What is currently needed in the region is a critical discourse and practice "rooted in an awareness of popular traditions and resistance, but not blind to the wider contours of power within national and international capital." This requires a knowledge of a "people's" history and a history of capitalism.[29] It involves the creation of resistance organizations that take culture and community seriously as places for political action while encouraging their members to discover the ways their grievances are a result of "structural processes occurring at an economic, geographic, and political level far beyond the particular locale where the grievance is experienced."[30] It requires creating an alternative radicalism that chooses to complicate rather than simplify by incorporating themes from the many movements and traditions present in Appalachia and the United States.[31]

This critical discourse and practice require courage, commitment, struggle, and patience, and at times it is difficult to imagine that they are even possible. But occasionally an event occurs that helps us focus, that provides us with a glimpse of what could be. The United Mine Workers of America's occupation of the Moss 3 coal preparation plant during the 1989–90 Pittston strike was one such occasion.

The resistance leading up to the takeover was fueled by family, community, and union loyalties that had instilled in generation after generation a deeply felt class awareness and anger. Camp Solidarity, local community centers, and weekly rallies provided free spaces where striking miners, relatives, and supporters from all over the country shared life stories and experiences that reinforced bonds of community and class solidarity. Old labor and gospel songs rang out along the picket lines. American flags and yellow ribbons became the symbols of resistance to uncaring corporate and governmental leaders and structures. The miners and their supporters drew upon their religious beliefs to strengthen their resolve and justify their dissent. Strike leaders worked hard to educate the miners about the issues of the strike, to forge links with other social movements nationally and abroad, and to involve African Americans and women in a wide variety of strike activities. Mistakes were made, and much still remains unresolved. But for those few days those who were there were able to "feel the possibilities that reside within us, and in the groups of which we are or can be a part."[32]

## Notes

1. This discussion draws heavily from the introduction and conclusion in Stephen L. Fisher, ed., *Fighting Back in Appalachia: Traditions of Resistance and Change* (Phila-

delphia: Temple Univ. Press, 1993); and Stephen L. Fisher, "Lessons from Change Efforts in Appalachia," in *Sowing Seeds in the Mountains: Community-Based Coalitions for Cancer Prevention and Control,* eds. Richard A. Couto, Nancy K. Simpson, and Gale Harris, (Washington, D.C.: National Institutes of Health, 1994), 81–95.

2. Ronald D Eller, *Miners, Millhands, and Mountaineers: Industrialization of the Appalachian South, 1880–1930* (Knoxville: Univ. of Tennessee Press, 1982); John Gaventa, *Power and Powerlessness: Quiescence and Rebelliion in an Appalachian Valley* (Urbana: Univ. of Illinois Press, 1980).

3. James C. Scott, *Domination and the Arts of Resistance: Hidden Transcripts* (New Haven, Conn.: Yale Univ. Press, 1990).

4. Helen Lewis, Sue Kobak, and Linda Johnson, "Family, Religion, and Colonialism in Central Appalachia or Bury My Rigle in Big Stone Gap," in *Colonialism in Modern America: The Appalachin Case,* eds. Helen Lewis, Linda Johnson, and Don Askins (Boone, N.C.: Appalachian Consortium Press 1978), 113–39.

5. Kathleen Blee and Dwight Billings, "Reconstructing Daily Life in the Past: An Hermeneutical Approach to Ethnographic Data," *Sociological Quarterly* 27 (winter 1986): 443–62.

6. Altina L. Waller, *Feud: Hatfields, McCoys, and Social Change in Appalachia, 1860–1900* (Chapel Hill: Univ. of North Carolina Press, 1988).

7. See "Dissent in Appalachia: A Bibliography," in *Fighting Back in Appalachia: Traditions of Resistance and Change,* ed. Stephen L. Fisher (Philadelphia: Temple Univ. Press, 1993), 339–60.

8. Bill Allen, "Save Our Cumberland Mountains: Growth and Change within a Grassroots Organization," in *Fighting Back in Appalachia,* Fisher, 85–99.

9. Melanie Zuercher, ed., *Making History: The First Ten Years of KFTC* (Prestonsburg, Ky.: Kentuckians for the Commonwealth, 1991).

10. Hal Hamilton and Ellen Ryan, "The Community Farm Alliance in Kentucky: The Growth, Mistakes, and Lessons of the Farm Movement of the 1980s," in *Fighting Back in Appalachia,* Fisher, 123–47.

11. David E. Wisnant, *Modernizing the Mountaineer: People, Power, and Planning in Appalachia* (Boone, N.C.: Appalachian Consortium Press, 1981). Pierre Clavel, *Opposition and Planning in Wales and Appalachia* (Philadelphia: Temple Univ. Press, 1983); John M. Glen, "Like a Flower Slowly Blooming: Highlander and the Nurturing of an Appalachian Movement," in *Fighting Back in Appalachia,* Fisher, 31–55.

12. Bill Horton, review of *Highlander: No Ordinary School, 1932–1962,* by John Glen, *Appalachian Journal* 16 (summer 1989): 370; Glen, "Like a Flower Slowly Blooming."

13. Horton, review of *Highlander.*

14. Helen Lewis, "Backwoods Rebels: Resistance in the Appalachian Mountains," in *Conflict and Peacemaking in Appalachia,* Coalition for Appalachian Ministry (Amesville, Ohio: Coalition for Appalachian Ministry, 1987), 22.

15. The following discussion draws from a variety of sources that are part of a vigorous debate in community organizing circles during the past decade over what organizational instruments and strategies are best suited for building progressive citizen groups and political movements. Stephen L. Fisher, "Conclusion: New Populist

Theory and the Study of Dissent in Appalachia," in *Fighting Back in Appalachia*, Fisher, 317–36.

16.Jim Green, "Culture, Politics, and Workers' Response to Industrialization in the U.S.," *Radical America* 16 (Jan.-Feb. 1982): 114, 117.

17. Mary Beth Bingman, "Stopping the Bulldozers: What Difference Did It Make?" in *Fighting Back in Appalachia*, Fisher, 17–30.

18. Allen, "Save Our Cumberland Mountains," 96.

19. David E. Wisnant, "Brief Notes toward a Reconsideration of Appalachian Values," *Appalachian Journal* 4 (autumn 1976): 46.

20. Laura A. Schwartz, "Immigrant Voices from Home, Work, and Community: Women and Family in the Migration Process, 1890–1938" (Ph.D. diss., State Univ. of New York at Stony Brook, 1983), 78.

21. Guy Carawan and Candie Carawan "Sowing on the Mountain: Nurturing Cultural Roots and Creativity for Community Change," in *Fighting Back in Appalachia*, Fisher, 245–61.

22. James C. Scott, *Weapons of the Weak: Everyday Forms of Resistance* (New Haven, Conn.: Yale Univ. Press, 1985), 45.

23. Mary Anglin, "'A Lost and Dying World': Women's Labor in the Mica Industry of Southern Appalachia" (Ph.D. diss., New School for Social Research, 1990); Sally M. Maggard, "Gender Contested: Women's Participation in the Brookside Coal Strike," in *Women and Social Protest*, eds. Guida West and Rhoda Blumberg (New York: Oxford Univ. Press, 1990), 75–98.

24. Michael Yarrow, "The Gender-Specific Class Consciousness of Appalachian Coal Miners: Structure and Change," in *Bringing Class Back In: Historical and Contemporary Perspectives*, eds., Scott G. McNall, Rhonda F. Levine, and Rick Fantasia (Boulder, Colo.: Westview Press, 1991), 285–310.

25.Richard A. Couto, "Failing Health and New Prescriptions: Community-Based Approaches to Environmental Risks," in *Current Health Policy Issues and Alternatives: An Applied Social Science Perspective*, ed. Carole E. Hill (Athens: Univ. of Georgia Press, 1986), 53–70.

26. Dwight Billings, "Religion as Opposition: A Gramscian Analysis," *American Journal of Sociology* 96 (July 1990): 1–31.

27. Don Manning-Miller, "Racism and Organizing in Appalachia," in *Fighting Back in Appalachia*, Fisher, 57–68.

28. D.E. Wisnant, "Farther Along: The Next Phase of Cultural Work in the South," *Southern Change* 13 (May 1991): 7–8.

29. Barry Goldberg, "A New Look at Labor History," *Social Policy* 12 (winter 1982): 61.

30. Prudence S. Posner, introduction to *Dilemmas of Activism: Class, Community, and the Politics of Local Mobilization*, eds. Joseph M. King and Prudence S. Posner (Philadelphia: Temple Univ. Press, 1990), 5.

31. Green, "Culture, Politics, and Workers' Response."

32. Jim Sessions and Fran Ansley, "Singing across Dark Spaces: The Union/Community Takeover of Pittston's Moss 3 Plant," in *Fighting Back in Appalachia*, Fisher, 217.

# Bibliography

Allen, Bill. "Save Our Cumberland Mountains: Growth and Change within a Grassroots Organization." In *Fighting Back in Appalachia: Traditions of Resistance and Change,* ed. S.L. Fisher. Philadelphia: Temple Univ. Press, 1993, 85–99.

Anglin, Mary. K. "'A Lost and Dying World': Women's Labor in the Mica Industry of Southern Appalachia." Ph.D. diss., New School for Social Research, 1990.

Billings, Dwight. "Religion as Opposition: A Gramscian Analysis." *American Journal of Sociology* 96 (July 1990): 1–31.

Bingman, Mary Beth. "Stopping the Bulldozers: What Difference Did It Make?" In *Fighting Back in Appalachia: Traditions of Resistance and Change,* ed. S.L. Fisher, 17–30. Philadelphia: Temple Univ. Press, 1993.

Blee, Kathleen, and Dwight Billings. "Reconstructing Daily Life in the Past: An Hermeneutical Approach to Ethnographic Data." *Sociological Quarterly* 27 (winter 1986): 443–62.

Carawan, Guy, and Candie Carawan. "Sowing on the Mountain: Nurturing Cultural Roots and Creativity for Community Change." In *Fighting Back in Appalachia: Traditions of Resistance and Change,* ed. S.L. Fisher, 245–61. Philadelphia: Temple Univ. Press, 1993.

Clavel, Pierre. *Opposition and Planning in Wales and Appalachia.* Philadelphia: Temple Univ. Press, 1983.

Couto, Richard A. "Failing Health and New Prescriptions: Community-Based Approaches to Environmental Risks." In *Current Health Policy Issues and Alternatives: An Applied Social Science Perspective,* ed., C.E. Hill, 53–70. Athens: Univ. of Georgia Press. 1986.

Eller, Ronald D. *Miners, Millhands, and Mountaineers: Industrialization of the Appalachian South, 1880–1930.* Knoxville: Univ. of Tennessee Press, 1982.

Gaventa, John. *Power and Powerlessness: Quiescence and Rebellion in an Appalachian Valley.* Urbana: Univ. of Illinois Press, 1980.

Glen, John M. "Like a Flower Slowly Blooming: Highlander and the Nurturing of an Appalachian Movement." In *Fighting Back in Appalachia: Traditions of Resistance and Change,* ed. S.L. Fisher, 31–55. Philadelphia: Temple Univ. Press, 1993.

Goldberg, Barry. "A New Look at Labor History." *Social Policy* 12 (winter 1982): 61.

Green, Jim. "Culture, Politics and Workers' Response to Industrialization in the U. S." *Radical America* 16 (Jan.-Feb. 1982): 114, 117.

Hamilton, Hal, and Ellen Ryan. "The Community Farm Alliance in Kentucky: The Growth, Mistakes, and Lessons of the Farm Movement of the 1980s." In *Fighting Back in Appalachia:Traditions of Resistance and Change,* ed. S.L. Fisher, 123–47. Philadelphia: Temple Univ. Press, 1993.

Horton, Bill. Review of *Highlander: No Ordinary School, 1932–1962,* by John Glen. *Appalachian Journal* 16 (summer 1989): 370.

Lewis, Helen. "Backwoods Rebels: Resistance in the Appalachian Mountains." In *Conflict and Peacemaking in Appalachia,* Coalition for Appalachian Ministry, Amesville, Ohio: Coalition for Appalachian Ministry, 1987.

Lewis, Helen, Sue Kobak, and Linda Johnson. "Family, Religion, and Colonialism in Central Appalachia or Bury My Rifle in Big Stone Gap." In *Colonialism in Modern America: The Appalachian Case,* eds. H. Lewis, L. Johnson, and D. Askins, 113–39. Boone, N.C.: Appalachian Consortium Press, 1978.

Maggard, Sally M. "Gender Contested: Women's Participation in the Brookside Coal Strike." In *Women and Social Protest,* eds. G. West and R.L. Blumberg, 75–98. New York: Oxford Univ. Press, 1990.

Manning-Miller, Don. "Racism and Organizing in Appalachia." In *Fighting Back in Appalachia: Traditions of Resistance and Change,* ed., S.L. Fisher, 57–68. Philadelphia: Temple Univ. Press, 1993.

Posner, Prudence S. Introduction to *Dilemmas of Activism: Class, Community, and the Politics of Local Mobilization,* eds. J.M. Kling and P.S. Posner, 5. Philadelphia: Temple Univ. Press, 1990.

Schwartz, Laura A. "Immigrant Voices from Home, Work, and Community: Women and Family in the Migration Process, 1890–1938." Ph.D. diss., State Univ. of New York at Stony Brook, 1983.

Scott, James C. *Domination and the Arts of Resistance: Hidden Transcripts.* New Haven: Yale Univ. Press, 1990.

———. *Weapons of the Weak: Everyday Forms of Resistance.* New Haven: Yale Univ. Press, 1985.

Sessions, Jim and Fran Ansley. "Singing across Dark Spaces: The Union/Community Takeover of Pittston's Moss 3 Plant." In *Fighting Back in Appalachia: Traditions of Resistance and Change,* eds. S.L. Fisher, 195–223. Philadelphia: Temple Univ. Press, 1993.

Waller, Altina L. *Feud: Hatfields, McCoys, and Social Change in Appalachia, 1860–1900.* Chapel Hill: Univ. of North Carolina Press, 1988.

Whisnant, David E. "Brief Notes toward a Reconsideration of Appalachian Values." *Appalachian Journal* 4 (autumn 1976): 46.

———. "Farther Along: The Next Phase of Cultural Work in the South." *Southern Changes* 13 (May 1991): 7–8.

———. *Modernizing the Mountaineer: People, Power, and Planning in Appalachia.* Boone, N.C.: Appalachian Consortium Press, 1981.

Yarrow, Michael. "The Gender-Specific Class Consciousness of Appalachian Coal Miners: Structure and Change." In *Bringing Class Back In: Historical and Contemporary Perspectives,* eds., S.G. McNall, R.F. Levine, and R. Fantasia, 285–310. Boulder, Colo.: Westview Press, 1991.

Zuercher, Melanie, ed. *Making History: The First Ten Years of KFTC.* Prestonsburg, Ky.: Kentuckians for the Commonwealth, 1991.

# Miners Talk Back

## Labor Activism in Southeastern Kentucky in 1922

### *Alan Banks*

Many writers have worked to overcome stereotypical images of southern Appalachia in recent years. Some of the more stubborn characterizations of the place include Appalachia as a dysfunctional culture, a quaint and unindustrialized wilderness, an internal colony, a hotbed of labor militancy, and/or a deficient gene pool. Critics have discounted these one-sided and often pejorative views of the region and its people; they argue that these views rely on broad generalizations that overstate the uniqueness of the region and its supposed uniformity. In the case of Appalachian coal miners, popular images tend to vary between two competing and contradictory extremes. Miners are sometimes portrayed as militant, class-conscious workers willing to risk all in their pursuit of class solidarity, unionization, and/or socialist ideals. A brief look at some of the more strident resolutions passed at United Mine Workers of America (UMWA) conventions during this century or discussions about the National Miners Union in Harlan County during the 1930s provides examples to bolster this view. At the other extreme, Appalachian coal miners are depicted as diffident unionists (docile diggers) or as fiercely independent Appalachian mountaineers uninterested in their own collective self-improvement. These stereotypes have been reinforced by the very popular books of Jack Weller and Harry Caudill, by movies such as *Next of Kin*, and by the recent Pulitzer Prize–winning play *The Kentucky Cycle*.[1] Each of these contradictory views of miners' human nature might fit with some carefully selected evidence, but they must not be accepted as a totally neutral response to some objective reality. Instead, these images must be understood in the economic, social, and cultural context in which they were constructed, recognizing that the transformation of perception into conception is mediated through the ideas of real people with material interests of their own.

What follows is a look at popular representations of southeastern Kentucky miners in the 1922 coal strike. I have chosen this example because it illustrates how stereotyping can shape public opinion as well as the writings of social scientists and government officials. The 1922 coal strike in southeastern Kentucky also demonstrates how miners' actions frequently speak louder than their words.

The assumption in 1922 was that southeastern Kentucky miners were not part of the national strike. In the writings of government officials, labor historians, and union officials, Kentucky coal miners emerge as fiercely independent mountaineers uninterested in their own collective self-improvement. The implication is that a *real* strike never took place in southeastern Kentucky and that the area was scarcely touched by the industrial turmoil rocking the rest of the nation. The problem with this view is that it is not in accord with the evidence. It generalizes unjustifiably and is misleading. It directs our attention away from other aspects of coalfield struggles and thereby becomes an obstacle to better understanding. The view is also depreciating. The image of contented nonunion men and women deliberately defying a national strike order reinforces destructive stereotypes of Kentuckians as docile, selfish, and/or lazy individuals uninterested in their own collective struggles or those of other workers across the nation.

The nation's coal miners struck on April 1, 1922, to oppose operators' continued attempts to dismantle the practice of negotiating interstate collective bargaining agreements to determine wage levels. Many of these operators felt that district-by-district negotiations would provide the added flexibility needed for survival in a marketplace increasingly influenced by price competition from southern nonunion coal operations. The strike was also about union gains made during the World War I period. Union membership had almost doubled during the war years to reach more than 415,000 members. Hourly wage rates had increased from 37 cents to 94 cents.[2] After failing to break the union in 1919, the coal industry was clearly out to finish the job in 1922. The atmosphere was tense as miners across the nation dug in to defend their hard-earned gains. In their annual review of coal production for 1922, government researchers commented with undisguised amazement on the effectiveness of the UMWA's organizational efforts. The popular belief that miners were extremely vulnerable against a prolonged operator offensive made it difficult for them to understand the strength of the strike.

> Prior to April there had been many operators and many consumers who were of the opinion that the union could not hold out against a demand for a reduction in wages. This opinion had been encouraged by the rumors of dis-

sension within the union ranks and the factional fights waged against the international officers. When April 1 came, however, every organized field not working under an expired contract—*and that included every important organized district except Kentucky and Tennessee*—went out in response to the strike call. Moreover, the union took operators by surprise by making successful invasions of the non-union strongholds in the Connellsville, Westmoreland, and Somerset [western Pennsylvania] fields. (Emphasis added.)[3]

For these industry watchers, it seemed commonplace to think of District 19 miners (southeastern Kentucky and East Tennessee) as diffident unionists. Commenting on the extraordinary length and strength of the 122–day coal strike, these researchers wrote: "*[A]ll members of the union outside Kentucky and many thousands of non-union miners as well . . .* shut the industry down." (Emphasis added.)[4] Little is offered in the way of explanation as to why Kentucky and a few other miners were alone in their reluctance to strike.

Scholarly accounts of southeastern Kentucky miners' role in the 1922 national strike tend to follow this same line of argument. In his excellent study of labor troubles in Harlan County, for instance, John Hevener claims that southeastern Kentucky miners "dissipated" their strength before the 1922 coal strike by making two unfortunate decisions. First, they elected a relatively inexperienced man, S.A. Keller, as UMWA District 19 president. Second, in 1920, Kentucky miners rejected a contract negotiated by Van Bittner, an organizer sent in from the Pittsburgh area by John L. Lewis. Hevener suggested that the failure to submit to Van Bittner's authority and elect a president more in tune with national leadership reflected a lack of discipline that eventually led to a 1922 strike that was "failed and feeble."[5] Hevener's account is an insightful one. Indeed, his is one of the few studies that attempts to carefully examine the role that Keller and Van Bittner played in the 1922 labor troubles. Yet, in defense of southeastern Kentucky miners, it should be pointed out that local miners' objections to Van Bittner's plans were justified. The Van Bittner agreement did not recognize the union and did not cover many miners working in some of the largest mines in the areas. Local miners claimed that continued union recognition was their primary demand and that an open-shop agreement was unacceptable.[6]

Two similar accounts of the 1922 coal strike in southeastern Kentucky can be found in Melvyn Dubofsky and Warren Van Tine's outstanding biography of UMWA leader John L. Lewis and Shaunna Scott's recent excellent book on class consciousness in Harlan County. In a discussion of Lewis's critics, who argued that he had mismanaged the national coal strike of 1922, Dubofsky and Van Tine fall back on an argument that relies on the dangers of docility among southern Appalachian miners. "The solidarity and militancy exhibited by coal miners during the strike of 1922 was indeed remarkable. But so was the resistance of the largest mine owners." Dubofsky and Van Tine add that operators' strength was due, in part at least, to the fact that "the 1922 coal strike scarcely touched the nonunion fields of West Virginia, Kentucky and Alabama."[7] In this way, Kentucky miners became a central component in the explanation of the failure of the national union's organizational policies. They were depicted as a powerful wedge against national union solidarity. From their view, eastern Kentucky miners failed the union; the union did not fail eastern Kentucky miners. Shaunna Scott describes the situation in Harlan this way:

> All things considered, Harlan coal production and work relations proceeded rather smoothly in the 1910's and 1920's. The Harlan field had been opened during a time of high coal demand, when industrial growth and World War I were in full swing. Harlan had high-quality coal, ideal for use in steel manufacturing. . . . Operators were able to grant wage concessions to workers during this boom period; wages rose to nearly forty cents per ton.
>
> [Unionization] . . . did not occur in Harlan County. . . . Perhaps because they were new to the industry, Harlan miners lacked the experience, resources and collective identity for such activity. Their counterparts in Pennsylvania, Ohio, and Illinois, after all, had been working underground for two or three generations, some of them having migrated from established coalfields in Europe, including Wales, England, and Germany. They had started their own fraternal organizations and benevolent societies, some of which had developed into quasi unions in their own right. Harlan miners had not. Indeed, coal operators had expanded into the Harlan field in part to escape the power of organized labor elsewhere. Initially, this maneuver was quite successful. Harlan miners withdrew quickly from their first strike attempt in 1922, although this national coal strike dragged on for several months in the northern fields.[8]

How these writers came to the conclusion that Kentucky miners, along with their nonunion associates elsewhere, were alone in their refusal to strike in 1922 is difficult to comprehend. One possible explanation is that internal dissension led national union leaders to give up on eastern Kentucky as a hopeless case or that it was necessary to consolidate their organizational gains elsewhere. It may have become convenient for UMWA leaders to let stand prominent stereotypes of Kentucky miners to justify their own lack of progress in District 19. A cursory glance at the *UMW Journal* during the weeks of the strike, for example, would lead one to think that unionization activities in southeastern Kentucky were nonexistent, a fact that must have been disconcerting to those District 19 miners risking their jobs and lives to win their right to union representation.[9] For coal operators, it was undoubtedly convenient to blame southern coal operators and cutthroat competition for union losses nationwide despite the fact that the dominant firms in southeastern Kentucky were in large measure the very same firms who were dominant in the Central Competitive Fields in northern more unionized states.

Still another explanation for the popularity of the docile-digger image might be found in production and employment statistics. For the four largest coal-producing counties in southeastern Kentucky (Bell, Harlan, Letcher, and Perry), coal production increased from 15,226,754 tons in 1921 to 15,686,776 tons in 1922. Similarly, the number of underground miners in these four counties increased from 11,504 in 1921 to 12,500 in 1922. These data may have led some to conclude that production and employment in southeastern Kentucky were unaffected by the nationwide strike.[10] A closer look at these figures, however, should caution writers about the plausibility of such a conclusion. While coal production and employment of underground miners remained rather stable in this four-county area, the average number of days worked per year fell dramatically from 170 in 1921 to 124 in 1922, a decrease of over 25 percent. If, as many argue, southeastern Kentucky miners were scabbing during the strike, the average number of days worked during the year would likely have been larger than it was in 1921; increased demand eventually would have created lucrative opportunities and stimulated production. The fact that average days worked per year declined so dramatically suggests that something else was going on. Maybe the docile-digger assumption is off the mark.[11]

The coal strike of 1922 began with a great deal of posturing by business, government, and labor leaders. When John L. Lewis, UMWA president, called an initial meeting to negotiate wage scales in January 1922, even long-unionized Central Competitive Field operators refused to attend.[12] Operators were contractually obligated to enter wage talks with the union as a part of the previous agreement worked out to resolve the 1919 national coal strike. Nonetheless, as late as mid-March, operators' reluctance to talk remained unchanged. They insisted that the new agreement would be one worked out with individual miners independent of any national agreement.[13]

Members of the Harding administration made it clear that their sympathies rested with coal operators, not miners. As long as operators appeared to have an upper hand relative to miners, administration officials felt that the coal strike could best be dealt with through a policy of government inaction. The conditions on the labor market that favored operators would produce a desirable outcome.[14] When asked by reporters whether the government would compel operators to negotiate with the union, as was required by the government-mediated 1919 agreement, Secretary of Labor Davis remarked that such actions would "do no possible good." They would lead to "a talk fest barren of real solution."[15] Market forces and the changing balance of power in favor of operators would, Harding officials hoped, bring miners in line. Similarly, President

Harding announced that the problem with the coal industry lay with the rise of labor and transportation costs that have "put the United States out of the class of exporting countries."[16] While the export situation is of debatable significance, the message to labor was clear. Miners (and rail workers) should expect no help from government.

In southeastern Kentucky, the lack of sympathy from administration officials and national coal leaders was coupled with determined local resistance to miners' unionization goals. Local coal operators refused to meet with miners and even went so far as to claim that a legitimate union contract had never been signed in either 1917 or 1919. As far as they were concerned, workers and operators would negotiate on an individual basis; the union contract had no binding force in District 19. By simply stating that a union never existed in the strict legal sense, local operators hoped to create an atmosphere of confusion to reinforce their effort to roll back more than five years of UMWA organizational gains. They tried to use their power to influence the local inhabitants' sense of self-understanding to achieve their open-shop goals. A spokesman for the Southern Appalachian Coal Operators' Association put the operators' position this way: "An agreement was made between three operators in the Southern Appalachian field and three miners relative to wages. . . . On behalf of the miners, it was signed by S. Keller, Frank Walters and Van Bittner. This agreement will expire simultaneously with the wage agreement of the UMW. . . . but the agreement here is unlike the others in that it is not an agreement that recognizes the union, but is signed on both sides by parties as individuals."[17] Clearly on the offensive, these operators wanted to roll back the significant union gains of the World War I period. They wanted to operate outside the context of any union agreement. Miners' wages, they felt, should be cut. They should "share in the general deflation that has been going on in other industries."[18]

As the first of April strike date neared, various federal officials expressed concern and confusion over the prospects and causes of another nationwide coal strike. Some took a hard line against miners. The attorney general, for instance, issued stern warnings that violence to prevent coal production would not be tolerated. Coal, he said, "is an indispensable part of transportation," and therefore, government has the same authority to "act as it would in the event of an interruption of the nation's transportation system." He added that the "government would not wait until there was an actual shortage of coal before taking action."[19] Others were confused over the general causes of the second nationwide coal strike in less than three years. John Noan, chairman of the House Committee on Labor, urged the creation of a federal commission to investigate labor conditions in the coalfields. Noan's pleas were reinforced by a similar request from Federal Trade Commission chairman Gaskill. Oscar Bland, an Indiana legislator, went on record as saying that coal operators, not miners, ought to be the target of any federal investigation. Bland argued that operators were manipulating the crisis for their own ends. "In refusing to meet with the miners," he said, "operators . . . want to have an unsettled condition of affairs in order to boost the price of coal, and they are boosting it." Increasingly, many Washingtonians suspected that there was something seriously amiss with the nation's coal industry.[20]

On April 1, about five hundred miners from three mines in the Middlesboro, Kentucky, area walked off the job.[21] Within two days, only one major concern, the Southern Mining Company, was still operating. Reports out of Harlan, Letcher, Perry, and Bell Counties were confusing, but not hard to read. Operators sought to give the impression that all was well in the area and that they were unaffected by the strike. One reporter said that "the UMW order has not affected coal production as it remained at ninety percent." E.E. Clayton, secretary of the Harlan Coal Operators' Association, told reporters that "all mines in Harlan county, except those closed before the strike, were operating." When a reporter asked why coal production figures appeared to be at a standstill, Clayton explained that some of the mines would be shut down for repairs for the next few weeks and that substantial reductions in output could be expected. He added that such developments were not out of the ordinary and had little to do with the miners' strike. Despite operators' attempts to hide the extent of the strike, reporters in the area informed their readers that the strike was on in southeastern Kentucky. On April 3, reporters' estimates of the number of District 19 miners on strike were in excess of twelve thousand. One reporter put it simply: the strike in the area "is complete."[22]

As the strike set in, operators' plans to defeat miners' attempts to retain their union status took shape. These efforts provide one piece of evidence that miners in the area were not as docile as some would have us believe. Legal attempts to hinder union activities were quickly initiated. Two news dispatches revealed that eastern Kentucky coal operators were filing an injunction against the UMWA in federal court in Lexington to prevent strike activities in general and picketing in particular.[23] This effort to curtail unionization activities was combined with reliance upon the recently passed Kentucky Sedition Bill to limit the physical movement and the freedom of speech of those sympathetic with the unionization campaign.[24] The stakes were high. With coal prices on the rise, coal interests were simply obliged to use any instrumentality available to get the coal to the marketplace.

Forcible eviction of miners from company housing provides another indication of miners' resistance and their willingness to join with their UMWA peers in other states. As early as April, many miners were being evicted from company housing for refusing to work and/or for having sympathies with the union. Most operators denied charges of wholesale evictions, claiming that the evictions were selective. One operator, however, openly admitted turning more than sixty miners and their families out of company housing. The company, he remarked, had provided "houses with light, water and coal," but "generosity had its limits." Evictions came about when "these miners not only refused to work in the owner's mines but refused to let anyone else work there and shot at workers who tried to." "There would be no thought of evictions," he continued, "if the men would pay rental or work for the company that furnished them with houses."[25] Stories about evictions and abusive foremen and mine guards were common in the spring and summer of 1922 in southeastern Kentucky. Still, Kentucky miners struggled to retain the UMWA status.

Further evidence of strike activity can be found in an effort by coal operators to negotiate an acceptable labor agreement with local labor leaders. These negotiations involved attempts to negotiate a nonunion, or open-shop, agreement in some of the mines in the district. Union leaders S.A. Keller and E.L. Reed met with representatives from seven local mines owned by the Logan-Pocahontas Fuel Company and with the agents from the Federal Coal Company, which operated fourteen mines in the area. By late April, an agreement was signed to immediately end the strike in these mines. Whether Keller and Reed saw this as the only way to get something good out of a bad situation or as a means of improving their personal conditions by winning the favor of selected local employers is unclear. What is certain is that miners were left leaderless and confused. In an attempt to win miners' acceptance of the agreement, a representative of the Kentucky-Tennessee Coal Operators' Association announced that the goal of the accord was "to harmonize to the fullest extent a close relationship between miners and operators, feeling that through the existence of a cordial relationship the public will at all times be taken care of."[26] Despite the order to return to work and the conciliatory rhetoric of operators, local miners continued their walkout. For good reasons, they were deeply suspicious of the Keller-Reed agreement.[27] While Keller and Reed negotiated, local coal miners rejected the settlement and renewed the strike.

Confronted with a union leadership out of touch with local rank-and-file miners and considerable opposition from coal operators, the strike stretched into the summer. The concerns of political and industry leaders for a quick resolution of the strike were mounting. Prices for coal were increasing rapidly. Lucrative profit opportunities were being lost. Calls for a federal investigation of the coal industry and possible government involvement in labor relations were on the increase. In this situation, bitterness between miners and operators, and between miners and union officials, intensified and occasionally led to sporadic outbreaks of violence. At operators' urging, authorities called the militia into several southeastern Kentucky communities to "protect lives and restore public order." These troops were called in response to the continued militancy, not docility, of southeastern Kentucky miners and their determination to win union recognition for District 19.

Three and a half months after the beginning of the strike, Kentucky miners were still on the picket line. Their refusal to return to work was increasingly becoming an issue in the area. In Whitley County, Sheriff H.M. Young requested troops from then Governor Morrow. "The non-union workers have been threatened and intimidated. . . . [U]nless soldiers are sent to the mines loss of life and destruction of property would probably result." Morrow sent twenty-five guardsmen and two machine-gun crews to the Mahan-Jellico Coal Company, at Packard, where several hundred striking miners were trying to prevent sixty nonunion workers from entering the mines. No major clashes had developed, but trouble was anticipated. As one reporter put it, "the suit of the Mahan-Jellico Coal Company to oust the striking union miners from the company's houses has been threatened here. . . . It is believed that fear of what might result in the event the operators should decide to oust the strikers in large measure prompted the call for troops."[28]

Several detachments of troops were also sent into Bell County, along the Tennessee border. At the Yellow Creek Mine, near Middlesboro, a platoon of guardsmen and some machine-gun crews were sent to maintain public order. The mine was located near an old tavern, the site of a government raid that left seven dead and many wounded in 1901, and the citizens of Yellow Creek were less than friendly toward the troops. In addition, shooting in this area had been difficult to stop. Miners dug coal on the Tennessee side of the border, but lived and loaded coal in Bell County on the Kentucky side. Kentucky soldiers had jurisdictional limitations that miners refused to recognize. And there was little help from the authorities on the Tennessee side of the border. In the midst of an election campaign, Governor "Alf" Taylor of Tennessee decided not to send troops to the area.[29]

Other nearby communities were also in turmoil. In Middlesboro, several hundred miners, their wives, and sympathetic citizens assembled to protest military rule. Near the community of Fonde, three miners were seized by a group of striking miners. With cowbells attached to their necks and hands tied behind their backs, these miners were "ordered to run to the accompaniment of shots being fired." They were then told to start down the railroad track and not return to work in the mines until a settlement was reached. Outside Middlesboro, one miner was wounded and about a dozen others escaped serious injury while on their way to work at the Bryson Mountain mines along the Tennessee border. The attack was seen by reporters as the "climax to a series of minor disturbances that have been occurring in the . . . district for several weeks." The same reporter described over two hundred "heavily armed" men marching through mining camps along the border with one simple message: "If State troops enter to protect the property and allow the non-union workers to mine coal, a war will be the inevitable result. . . . If we [miners and their families] don't get our rights now we will never get justice." Another reporter wrote about a group of Kentucky miners who crossed the border and captured the Claiborne County (Tennessee) judge, sheriff, and twenty-five other officials. "Festooned with cowbells," they were placed aboard a train bound for Knoxville. Upon return, the local judge denied the reports of how they were humiliated but added that the situation is "absolutely beyond control and we must have [more] troops."[30]

The militancy of southeastern Kentucky miners during the national coal strike of 1922 was strong and widespread. Out of Frankfort, the state capital, came a report declaring the disturbance along the border a "mine war." Governor Morrow deployed and hurriedly redeployed troops in response to miners' activities designed to win them union recognition and civil respect. One reporter, on July 8, put it this way: "[A] clash in this mining district is believed imminent. . . . The situation is regarded as critical despite the coming of troops, as many sympathizers have decided that a battle is almost certain. . . . Disorderly elements are reported to have practically terrorized the district by parading with a display of arms." Another reporter, on July 28, wrote, "The entire territory is reported as terrorized as a result of armed miners parading through the mine region last night and today."[31]

Looking back, it is clear that the coal strike of 1922 was not a victory for southeastern Kentucky soft-coal miners. Though wages held firm for a time, union recognition was not achieved. National union leaders failed to include eastern Kentucky miners in wage scale agreements. Whether the idea of Kentucky miners as fiercely independent nonunionists was a convenient defense to justify the exclusionary decisions of national union leaders is open to debate, but one uncomfortable fact remains: southeast Kentucky miners did strike. They thought of themselves as union miners and acted in a manner consistent with the highest union ideals. By taking up arms and confronting local authorities, many miners and their families faced awesome obstacles. Whole families confronted eviction and abusive treatment from company officials. Speaking their own minds, many faced arbitrary incarceration under the recently passed Kentucky Sedition Bill. Still others faced the added quandary of whether to continue the strike when ordered to go back to work by local union officials Keller and Reed. That these men and women were able to confront and survive these obstacles is a significant accomplishment.

Words and ideas are powerful. And the assumption that Kentucky miners refused to participate in the national coal strike of 1922 is dangerous and misleading. It is dangerous because it serves to reinforce negative stereotypes of southern workers as either docile or fiercely independent mountaineers lacking the good sense to organize in their own self-interest. It is misleading because it tends to gloss over regional events that deserve thoughtful consideration. What, for instance, was the role of the UMWA and Lewis's man on the scene, Van Bittner, in the southeastern Kentucky strike of 1922? How might coal operators have benefited from the belief that southeastern Kentucky miners were diffident unionists? How and why did miners in southeastern Kentucky and East Tennessee maintain a strike in the face of hostile operators and uncertain local union leadership? Why has the cultural stereotype of the diffident unionist persisted in the face of counterevidence? Answers to these sorts of questions are important. They can help achieve a more comprehensive and sympathetic understanding of the role that Kentucky miners played in the 1922 coal strike, overcome superficial stereotypes of southern mountaineers and workers in general, and lay a foundation for better informed and more reasonable strategies for improvement of citizens' lives and for community hopes in the region.

## Notes

1. The problem with each of these views is that they generalize unjustifiably and thus rob Appalachian culture of its richness/diversity and Appalachians of their history-making potential. See Alan Banks, Dwight Billings, and Karen Tice, "Appalachian Studies, Resistance and Postmodernism," in *Fighting Back in Appalachia: Traditions of Resistance and Change,* ed. Steve Fisher (Philadelphia: Temple Univ. Press, 1993); also, Shaunna L. Scott, *Two Sides to Everything: The Cultural Construction of Class Consciousness in Harlan County, Kentucky* (Albany: State Univ. of New York Press, 1995); and, Mary Beth Pudup, Dwight Billings, and Altina Waller, *The Making of Appalachia* (Chapel Hill: Univ. of North Carolina Press, 1995).

2. Data on UMWA membership can be found in *Proceedings of the Twenty-Sixth Consecutive Convention of the United Mine Workers of America* (Indianapolis: Bookwalter-Ball, 1918). Also note that the gains in union membership occurred during World War I when the U.S. Fuel Administration, directed by Harry Garfield, encouraged coal operators to accept union arrangements in exchange for government guarantees of labor stability and fixed prices. Information about miners' wages can be found in U.S. Bureau of the Census, *Historical Statistics of the United States: From Colonial Times to 1970* (Washington, D.C.: Government Printing Office, 1975), pt. 1, series D, 811–17.

3. U.S. Department of the Interior, *Mineral Resources of the United States* (Washington, D.C.: Government Printing Office, 1922) pt. 2, 447.

4. U.S. Department of the Interior, *Mineral Resources,* 514.

5. John Hevener, *Which Side Are You On?* (Urbana: Univ. of Illinois Press, 1978) 1–11.

6. An added factor was mistrust of Van Bittner and S.A. Keller by many local miners. This mistrust was partially based on their performance during the 1919 strike. In

the midst of the strike, Keller left the district for Indianapolis where he sought to negotiate an open-shop district agreement with nonunion operators. When Keller's orders
to call off the strike arrived, local miners refused, claiming that the orders did not bear
the official seal of the UMWA.

7. Melvyn Dubofsky and Warren Van Tine, *John L. Lewis: A Biography* (New York:
Quadrangle, 1977) 89; Shaunna Scott, *Two Sides to Everything.*

8. Scott, *Two Sides to Everything,* 23–24.

9. A cursory look at the journal during the 1916–19 period, when significant
organizational gains were achieved, reveals extensive coverage of organizing activities
in District 19.

10. U.S. Department of the Interior, *Mineral Resources,* 598–99.

11. It should be pointed out that there was a national rail workers' strike at the
same time as the coal miners' strike and that there were many complaints coming out
of eastern Kentucky about a shortage of rail cars. While this may account for some of
the decline in days worked per miner, it is, at best, only a partial explanation.

12. *Middlesboro Daily News,* Jan. 16, 1922, 1.

13. One journalist described the situation this way: "[N]otwithstanding representations made to them by the Secretary of Labor who holds that existing contracts require them [operators] to at least enter negotiations, mine operators continue to refuse
to enter a conference with the UMW looking to the creation of a new wage contract."
*Louisville Courier-Journal,* March 14, 1922; March 28, 1922.

14. The prestrike conditions alluded to here involved stagnant demand for coal,
excess capacity, and an oversupplied labor market. These conditions combined to jeopardize miners' standard of living and hence make them more likely to accept concessions.

15. *Louisville Courier-Journal,* March 25, 1922, 1.

16. *Louisville Courier-Journal,* March 18, 1922, 1. The reference to transportation
costs is connected with the nationwide railroad workers' strike that helped complicate
matters for politicians and the captains of industry in the spring of 1922.

17. *Middlesboro Daily News,* Jan. 21, 1922, 1.

18. *Louisville Courier-Journal,* March 14, 1922, 1. Note that the issue of unreason-
able cost of labor as the primary source of trouble in the coal industry was repeated
over and over again in industry publications. For example, see *Coal Age* and *Manufacturers Record.*

19. *Middlesboro Daily News,* March 26, 1922, 1.

20. *Middlesboro Daily News,* March 26, 1922; April 1, 1922; April 3, 1922; April 10,
1922; *Louisville Courier-Journal,* March 26, 1922; March 18, 1922.

21. *Louisville Courier-Journal,* April 2, 1922.

22. Ibid.; *Lexington Leader,* April 3, 1922; *Middlesboro Daily News,* April 3, 1922;
April 4, 1922; April 10, 1922.

23. *Middlesboro Daily News,* April 20, 1922; April 23, 1922.

24. For operators, the effectiveness of the bill rested upon the loose way that sedition was defined. Sedition was broadly defined as "the advocacy or suggestion by word,
act, deed, writing of public disorder or resistance to the Government of the United
States or the Commonwealth of Kentucky." This included public statements and writ-

ing, but was also extended to cover posters, placards, bumper stickers, and certain magazines (such as the *Daily Worker*). Possession of any of these was deemed sedition, unlawful and subject to severe penalties on the basis that such materials/ideas might "incite or fix enmity, discord or strife or ill feeling between classes of people." See *Acts of the General Assembly of the Commonwealth of Kentucky*, 1920, 520. The penalty for being found guilty of sedition could include ten years imprisonment, a ten-thousand-dollar fine, or both.

25. *Middlesboro Daily News,* April 14, 1922, 1.

26. *Lexington Leader,* April 20, 1922.

27. The suspicions about the credibility of the Keller-Reed agreement were not new. Two days after the 1919 strike began, Keller, as president of District 19, left eastern Kentucky for Indianapolis where he sought to negotiate similar nonunion agreements with coal operators. Left without leadership in 1919, District 19 miners maintained the strike in an impressive display of solidarity. When Keller sent orders calling off the strike, miners, claiming that the order did not bear the official seal of the UMWA, stayed out of the mines.

28. "Morrow Sends Guardsmen to Whitley Mine," *Lexington Herald,* July 14, 1922, 1; *Louisville Courier-Journal,* July 14, 1922, 1. Commenting on the depressing effect the strikes (coal and rail) were having on local business, a reporter from Letcher County remarked that social conditions were tense and coal production was drastically curtailed in the Elkhorn district and several other sections of eastern Kentucky. "Elkhorn Field Hit," *Louisville Courier-Journal,* July 25, 1922, 1. For more on the rail strike, see "East Kentucky Mines Hard Hit by Rail Strike," *Lexington Herald,* July 1, 1922, 1.

29. "War Impending in Bell County," *Louisville Courier-Journal,* July 28, 1922, 1–3; "Troops Sent to Bell County Mine War," *Louisville Courier-Journal,* July 26, 1922, 1, 11.

30. "Mine War," *Lexington Herald,* July 27, 1922, 1; *Lexington Herald,* July 27, 1922; "Troops Sent to Bell Mine War," July 26, 1922, 1, 11; *Lexington Herald,* July 30, 1922, 1, 10.

31. "More Trouble Reported," *Lexington Herald,* July 28, 1922, 4; *Lexington Leader,* July 8, 1922, 1; "More Violence Feared," *Lexington Leader,* July 28, 1922, 1.

# Coalfield Women Making History

## Sally Ward Maggard

We made history! I mean, you know, what would Pikeville be without us strikers?

Mae Fields, Pike County, Kentucky

On the night of June 10, 1972, over two hundred people walked off their jobs at the end of the evening shift at a large eastern Kentucky hospital. Almost all of them were women. The rest of the night they milled around in a huge crowd gathered at the mouth of Harold's Branch where it runs into the Levisa Fork of the Kentucky River in Pike County. Across the parking lot behind them, administrators and members of the board of directors were gathered in the lobby of a shiny new concrete-and-glass, eight-story hospital. The face-off that began that night was over working conditions and union representation, and it lasted eleven years.

Eventually, after a bitter strike and years of court battles, these women and their allies outdistanced some of eastern Kentucky's most powerful economic, political, and social elites. While the strikers failed to win union representation, the back pay settlement they eventually won remains one of the largest in the history of strikes in this country. Most important, their strike changed the nation's labor relations laws. Amendments to the National Labor Relations Act that resulted from the strike extended coverage to employees of nonprofit health care institutions and greatly expanded the possibility of organizing unions among service workers in the health care industry.

About a year into the hospital strike in Pike County, another strike broke out in neighboring Harlan County, Kentucky. Again, women were heavily involved in this organizing drive, which brought more national attention to Appalachia. The United Mine Workers of America (UMWA) was trying to organize a coal mine owned by Duke Power Company at Brookside, Kentucky. In the fall of 1973, court action limited the number of strikers on picket lines and threatened to cripple the strike. Women from the Brookside coal camp got together, went to the mine, and shut it down. As word of their confrontation with strikebreakers got out, other women from Harlan County and nearby coal counties joined in the strike effort. They formed the now famous Brookside Women's Club featured in the academy award–winning documentary *Harlan*

*County, U.S.A.*, and remained at the forefront of the strike until it was resolved in August 1974. These women crossed an unofficial line in the sand that had historically relegated women to auxiliary roles in the mine workers' union. Their participation is widely recognized as pivotal in the resolution of the thirteen-month strike and successful negotiation of a union contract.

Stereotypes of Appalachian women would never lead anyone to predict women's participation and leadership in such events. According to popular images of Appalachia, these women simply could not exist. Two distinct kinds of stereotypes, one romantic and the other degrading, dominate common notions of Appalachian women. Romantic images portray mountain women as enigmatic but talented people who make beautiful quilts, spin wool into thread, weave it into coverlets, and play dulcimers in their spare time. Good at handicrafts, gardening, and cooking such delicacies as corn bread, spoon bread, and apple stack cake, Appalachian women are characterized as the quiet caretakers of an idealized rural mountain way of life.

In contrast, degrading stereotypes of Appalachian women are tied up with four popular caricatures in cartoons, television, and film: Daisy Mae, the star of the "Li'l Abner" cartoon strip; her latter-day Daisy counterpart in the television series *Dukes of Hazzard*; and Ellie Mae and Granny Clampett of *The Beverly Hillbillies* television series and its recent film adaptation. The two Daisys and Ellie Mae are voluptuous, vacuous, barefoot, and likely to be, if not already, pregnant. They tempt, confuse, and distract their menfolk, but they do not lead, instruct, or direct the events that shape their lives. Granny is wizened, wiry, and wrinkled, an older Appalachian woman with enough rural smarts to outwit city slicker bankers. But she tends to her goats and pigs in her urban Beverly Hills mansion, uninterested in achieving some upper-middle-class lifestyle her newfound riches would support.

In both kinds of images mountain women seem to be standing outside of or apart from the rest of America. They are counterpoints to the modern world, representing either a simpler rural life or a ridiculous fringe population of deficient, mysterious characters.[1] Neither set of images would suggest that Appalachian women are capable of the concerted, organized, public action that could defeat Duke Power Company and challenge Pike County's powerful political and economic leaders. Yet, here were these women in the mid-1970s in eastern Kentucky taking prominent roles in two nationally significant labor disputes.

How did a group of low-waged, nonprofessional Appalachian women at an eastern Kentucky hospital manage to change national laws that protect the rights of workers and shape labor-management relations? How could women emerge from their domestic duties in coal camps, walk away from the kitchen sink and laundry room, and assume a national voice in articulating the need for social and economic change in the coalfields?

In the pages that follow, the stories of the women involved in these two strikes dispel stereotypes of Appalachian women and of the region in general. The actions and achievements of these women expose as myth any thoughts of Appalachia as a region of defeated, passive, debased people prone either to violent action or to no action at all. There are no easy victims incapable of collective action in these stories. Nor are there ignorant, irrational, backward, barefoot-and-pregnant hillbillies. These women are hardworking, ordinary, everyday people who choose up sides, take a stand, and shape the course of history.

The Pikeville and Brookside strikes broke out in a period of political action and protest in the central Appalachian coalfields. Community groups and regional coalitions were raising demands for environmental protection and the regulation of strip mining, improved community and government services, direct relief for families living in poverty, and legislation to improve mine safety and provide relief for victims of black lung (coal miners' pneumoconiosis). There was a general sense that change was possible and that ordinary people could successfully alter conditions that led to poverty and a poor quality of life in the coalfields.[2] In all of these efforts, women were prominent participants and leaders. The odds they faced as they worked for change were stiff.

Local economies in central Appalachian counties are dominated by one industry: coal mining. While great fortunes have been made in the industry, most coalfield residents have not enjoyed such riches. Restricted economic opportunity, polarized class relations, high injury and death rates in mining, and volatile fluctuations in the demand for the "black gold" that undergirds the region's economy leave people vulnerable to deep and persistent poverty.

Corporate leaders exercise heavy influence over local politics, and one of the only avenues for questioning the political and economic structure is through organized labor. This helps to explain the long history of corporate and political opposition to unions in the coalfields. It was no surprise in the mid-1970s when powerful forces lined up in Pike and Harlan Counties to oppose these two drives for union representation.

The slogan developed by the Pike County hospital strikers, "We're Fighting Millionaires," captured the stark class divisions that characterize the coalfields. Membership on the board of directors of the Pikeville Methodist Hospital read like a "Who's Who in Pike County." Leaders of business, banking, insurance, the media, the medical establishment, the religious community, and the coal industry were all represented. Almost every one of the thirty people serving on the board was virulently anti-union.

Pikeville Methodist Hospital (PMH) was one of eastern Kentucky's largest hospitals in 1971 and was just reorganizing as a regional health care facility.

From the workers' point of view it was a hybrid, created by the merger of a Methodist missionary hospital built in the early 1920s and one of the Miners' Memorial Hospitals built in the 1950s by the UMWA. Consolidation under new ownership ushered in a new era of bureaucratic and impersonal management, the end of a paternalistic administration at the Methodist facility, and the loss of union representation at the Miners' Hospital.

Working conditions deteriorated as employees moved into the new single-hospital facility built around and engulfing the old Miners' Hospital. Patient load nearly doubled for the nursing staff. Kitchen, maintenance, housekeeping, and dietary departments had to service many more people in a much larger facility with little or no additional help. The average wage among nonprofessional employees was $1.68 an hour. Many women reported that they had worked at the hospital for over twenty years for almost the same low wage at which they had been hired. Ardena Wheeler, a nurse's aide with thirty-one years at the hospital, is an example. She was earning $1.87 an hour when she came out on strike.

The list of grievances was staggering and encompassed far more than wages. Above all, employees complained of excessive workloads, serious understaffing, having to do work for which they were not qualified, and the inability to provide quality care and do their jobs properly in the new hospital. One nurse's aide summed up her grievances when she said, "I did everything but firing the furnace."[3]

For nine months employees tried unsuccessfully to get the administration to acknowledge and address these problems, while hospital officials tried unsuccessfully to quell unrest and union activism. As frustration deepened, the hospital employees turned to the Communication Workers of America (CWA) for representation. (CWA members had installed the telephone system in the new building.) Over 90 percent of the employees signed union cards. When the hospital fired two union activists on June 9, 1972, the employees saw no alternative but a strike.

Of the 220 people on strike, five-sixths were women. For the next twenty-eight months they ran a twenty-four-hour picket line, worked the union office, did community and public relations, raised money, worked on legal and court actions, and organized and attended meetings, rallies, and marches. They argued with organizers about union strategy and picketed union coal mines and UMWA offices when promised support failed to materialize. The national media focused on the strike when the strikers picketed state, regional, and national offices of the Methodist church, turning its nominal connection to the anti-union hospital into a major embarrassment for a church with a "Social Gospel" commitment to the rights of workers.

The strike was fought for six years in the courts after the picket line was disbanded. A series of unfair labor practice rulings favored the strikers, but the hospital board invested hundreds of thousands of dollars to contest every ruling. Eventually in 1980, the United States Supreme Court refused to hear the hospital's final appeal. The hospital was forced to offer to reinstate workers and compensate them for economic losses. Many workers never got their jobs back. Checks for court-awarded back pay, totaling $697,000, were not in the hands of strikers until early in 1981, just shy of eleven years after the night of the walkout.

In July 1973, when the hospital strike had been going on for over a year, the UMWA strike in Harlan County broke out. Pike borders Harlan County, and there was a good deal of interest among both groups of strikers in the progress each union effort was making. At several points over the next year supporters and strikers from both disputes traveled to each other's picket lines, rallies, and demonstrations.

The coal strike pitted 180 miners against Duke Power Company, a fairly new actor on the corporate scene in the coal industry. Duke had bought the Brookside Mine in 1970, created Eastover Mining Company to manage its coal interests, and soon added other coal properties. At the time of the strike, Duke was the sixth-largest utility company in the nation and a major coal consumer.

When Eastover took over the mine, employees were told they were working under a contract with the Southern Labor Union (SLU), a "company union" known for its cozy relationship with management and lax efforts on mine safety and health. Miners worried about dangerous conditions at Brookside, particularly the mine's "bad top" (roof) and its tendency to flood. They began to sign UMWA cards when the contract with the SLU was about to expire. Enough miners signed that the National Labor Relations Board ordered an election, but when UMWA supporters won, the company refused to sign a union contract. The miners struck.

A reform-minded leadership had just been elected to lead the UMWA after campaigning on a platform promising an end to union corruption and a commitment to organize any unorganized mines. The Brookside strike was the first under the new leadership, and union officers defined it as the flagship strike of a new UMWA era. Their opponents at Eastover were determined to break this ominous new UMWA militance, and they were solidly supported by the Harlan County Coal Operators Association.

Two months into the strike Eastover managed to get a court injunction limiting the number of pickets so severely that strikebreakers were having no trouble crossing union picket lines and working the mine. Women living in the Brookside coal camp were aware that the company was trying to break the strike. They worried about a 1930s-style coalfields war, and they knew that if the UMWA lost the strike the miners would be blacklisted and permanently out of work in Harlan and surrounding counties. For Ruby Stacy and her friends, things had come to a head: "A few of us got together talking about how it was going with the men under a restraining order keeping them from picketing. About twenty of us decided to go down to the mine and try to talk to the scabs. None of us had any plans about what to do."[4] At shift change the women were met by a car caravan of strikebreakers. Betty Eldridge described what happened: "Here come these cars off the mountain. Car after car after car. Instead of stopping, they done their best to run over us. If I hadn't flattened against that store building, they would have killed me. . . . From that day on, I swore to God that I would do everything in my power to stop them from working."[5]

The women shut down the mine that day and organized a regular women's picket line. Soon they were joined by women from all over Harlan County. Most stayed actively involved in the strike despite the danger and hardships and criticisms they faced. They stood on picket lines, did public relations work, organized broad-based support, encouraged merchants to support the strike, boycotted those who refused support, and challenged biased press coverage. They spoke out about life in Harlan County at informational picket lines around the country and testified at hearings into conditions in the coalfields. When confrontations grew more and more violent, they risked their lives to keep the mine from running coal. Many were arrested and jailed for their strike involvement.

In the end, the UMWA won the strike. On August 31, 1974, the miners unanimously ratified a contract between the UMWA and Eastover Mining Company, and in early September the miners went back to work. According to Brookside miner Louie Stacy, "I'd say if them women hadn't done what they done, I'd say we'd a lost it."[6]

During most of the 1970s when these strikes and other social change efforts were under way in central Appalachia, I was employed by the Council of the Southern Mountains (CSM). First as director and then as a member of the CSM central leadership collective, I worked to support these efforts and to write about them for the organization's monthly newsmagazine, *Mountain Life and Work*.

My initial attraction to activist work was based on my shock at what strip mining had done to almost all the lands of my youth. On return to eastern Kentucky in 1970 after completing a master of science degree at Purdue University, I was appalled to find my homeland ravished. At first I blamed my parents. In one memorable explosion around our kitchen table in Hazard, I demanded of them, "How could you let this happen?" Because they were as opposed to strip mining as I was, they did not assume responsibility for the rapid development of this method of mining coal. Instead, they encouraged me to redirect my outrage, develop a more reasoned analysis of the region's economic and political structure, and work through education to change the situation. But in my new position as a college professor at Berea College, I was too distant from the kind of work needed to bring a halt to the devastation that was happening all around me, the college, and my students. So, I resigned from my first teaching job and went to work for the CSM.

The broad membership of the organization was anchored in a coalition of grassroots organizations and political and social activists who believed union representation was one avenue to improving the quality of life for ordinary citizens in Appalachia. The composition of the board of directors was the opposite of the Pikeville Hospital's board. It read like a "Who's Who of Working-Class and Community-Based Groups" working for social and economic justice in Central Appalachia. The board committed CSM to programs addressing the uneven playing field and imbalances of power that make social change so difficult in the region. It was through my work with the members of that board of directors—Mart Shepherd, Bessie Smith, Eula Hall, Helen Powell, Madeline James, Almetor King, Shelby Steele, and others—that my understanding of the forces that shaped the region's problems and history matured.

When the Pikeville and Brookside strikes broke open, representatives of both groups asked CSM for help. We answered yes and threw our energy into the efforts. During these years in the early 1970s, I found myself on picket lines, in union strategy meetings, in demonstrations, and traveling to strike-related events. I worked with union organizers, wrote news stories, and, above all, spent a lot of time in people's homes listening to them tell about their lives and discuss their strikes. As a result, many doors were open to me during these strikes that would not have been open to others. When I returned to Harlan and Pike Counties over a decade later, I found those doors still open.

During 1986 and 1987 I lived in Harlan and Pike Counties and conducted research on women's participation in the strikes. By this time I had left CSM and was working on a Ph.D. dissertation.[7] Twenty Harlan County women and twenty-four Pike County women served as my principal informants. Over many months I conducted lengthy, taped semistructured and open-ended interviews with them. Personal records, CSM records of the strikes, outtakes of *Harlan County, U.S.A.* provided by filmmaker Barbara Kopple,[8] county and state newspaper archives, and a host of auxiliary interviews with people involved in and knowledgeable about the strikes provided the data needed for checking and crosschecking facts and interpretations of events. The record of the research is housed in the Appalachian Special Collection at the University of Kentucky in a permanent archive the strikers and I named "Women and Collective Protest in Eastern Kentucky."

My knowledge of these strikes is based on the remarkable opportunity I had to participate in them and on the trust the strikers and their supporters placed in me. Far from compromising the quality and integrity of my research, familiarity with the area as a native of eastern Kentucky and personal involvement in the strikes made it possible to successfully carry out the research that is the basis of this chapter.

Fortunate to have witnessed these dramatic events, I am in debt to the generous women, their families, and their friends who understood that my research would record their history-making efforts. It is to the lives and actions of these remarkable people that I now turn.

In many ways the women in these strikes were just ordinary working-class people doing the routine, hard work that keeps households and businesses going. Their personal work histories began in childhood and reveal an understanding of work and the local economy that prepared the women to fight for a collective voice for labor and that contributed to the strength of character that saw them through the strikes.

In their interviews, the women talked at length about the work they did. Sometimes they got paid money for doing it, and sometimes they didn't. Sometimes their work was challenging and fun. Other times it was "brutish," as one woman described her job at the Pikeville Methodist Hospital. All of the time, "work" was under way.[9]

In hard-pressed families, child labor was a resource that kept households operating. That is, the paid and unpaid work these women did as children was understood as part of the economic landscape of the homes in which they were reared. They did the "women's work" of caring for the sick, tending young children, cleaning up after people, raising food, preparing food, and making and cleaning clothes. Sometimes they sacrificed their schooling. Eunice McCoy, who worked as a cook at the hospital, gave this account:

> After my mother died I didn't get to go [to school]. I was the only girl at home. I was working, but at home. I'd go places and help people out where there was a new born baby. Do their cooking and washing and ironing. If anybody was down sick, I went and helped. Most of the time I didn't get money because they didn't have the money to pay. I helped take care of my step-mother's sister until two weeks before she died. Then my grandmother, she was real bad off. Aunt Meg had arthritis so bad she had to walk around on crutches. They had a big family, and they run a saw mill. Aunt Meg could sit and peel potatoes, but I did the rest of it. I washed on the board for them. They was four of the boys at home. By the time I'd get through washing their overalls and work clothes plus all their other clothes, I'll tell you, that was a job![10]

Many of the women recalled a variety of strategies for earning money needed in desperate times. Sudie Crusenberry of Harlan County talked of crawling over slate dumps to find lumps of coal and picking wild berries to sell:

I picked up coal along the tram track. I've had the motormans to kick it off. I've went down on the slate fill and asked, "Do you care for me to [be] picking coal out of the slate and selling it?" "No," they'd say. And I went to selling it. I'd hit the tops of them mountains, the tip spurs of them yonder, with a half bushel tub and a water bucket and pick them full of berries. Take them down here where this filling station is. They'd say, "We don't need them, but to help you we will." They would give me fifty cents a gallon. So, I would take that. I'd get what we needed.[11]

When they could find paid work, their jobs were in the lowest wage sectors of the local economy. They recalled working as young girls in personal services (housekeeping, dry cleaning, laundry), food services (cooking, serving, dishwashing), farm work (tending gardens, harvesting), and retail (sales). Alpha Ratliff, one of the hospital kitchen helpers, described her first paying job. It was in a laundry: "In the dry cleaners over in Pikeville—I worked for $25 a week. Oh, my goodness! Pressed. I checked out. I started in as check out girl, and then I went to pressing."[12]

As adults the women had very few options for full-time, stable employment. They lived in an undiversified local economy dominated by mining. Coal mining jobs paid well when there was a demand for coal, but these jobs were restricted to men until late in the 1970s when legal challenges opened up mining to some women.[13] In Harlan and Pike Counties making an honest living was an extremely tough proposition for women.

Many of the women in the hospital strike were heads of households. All were major contributors to the financial base of their families. They had moved from job to job, pressing clothes in laundries, selling merchandise in discount stores, cooking in area restaurants, washing dishes, and cleaning motel rooms and middle-class homes. When they were hired on at the hospital, they got some of the best jobs open to women in the coalfields at that time. Still, wages were so low that many women held second and even third jobs. Edith Williams, a nurse's aide, reared four children this way: "I've did odds and ends work all my life. When I worked on the day shift, I used to work at a steak house in the evening three nights a week to make enough money for me and the kids. I have cleaned houses of an evening after I get off from work. I have worked at motels, cleaned rooms, worked in kitchens, washed dishes. Just anything to make an honest dollar."[14]

Most of the women described their hospital jobs as the hardest work they had ever done. Peggy Robinette, another nurse's aide, described the pressure she was under just before the strike: "You work like a dog. Work for 89 cents an hour for years trying to raise six kids. Then $1.05. Then $1.10. After we moved in that big hospital you couldn't get the [patients] all fed and bathed. The work load was too heavy. It just got till you couldn't handle it."[15] Alpha Ratliff, who worked in the kitchen, said, "I always loved to work. I was brought up to work. But I think that there is brutish work that hurts. We really had that there at the hospital."[16]

The Pike County women cleaned the hospital, fed its staff and patients, took care of sick people, and ran the hospital office. After hours, they looked around Pike County for second jobs to add to the low wages they earned at the hospital. Then they took their wages home, provided for other family members, and managed households. Despite having jobs that were considered prized jobs for women in that labor market, they believed that union representation would improve the conditions of their work and their ability to provide for their families.

In Harlan County, most of the women were hard at work managing households and families in the coal camps and towns that surrounded the industrial world of coal mining. They saw to the needs of large numbers of children, took care of household affairs in the midst of harsh living conditions in coal camps, and managed wages earned by coal-mining relatives.

When there were layoffs in the mines, families often moved to urban areas in search of work. In some cases, women went to work in light manufacturing, laundries, and domestic service. Ruby Stacy described her experiences working on assembly lines in Indianapolis. "We would put picture frames together," she said. "Fixed, made, put the pictures in, and sealed them. Shipped them out to K-Marts and Woolworth's. Some were even shipped all the way to Texas. Just made pictures for everywhere." In another job she packed doughnuts. "I worked on the conveyor packing doughnuts in boxes. You talk about fast work, now that was fast!" None of her jobs paid well, and she was quite aware that women were being exploited for cheap labor: "I don't think I ever had a job in a union place. Back then you didn't get nothing. Women didn't get nothing for their labor. We worked harder than men. That's the truth now. And we got less pay. I think I worked for a dollar and a quarter an hour."[17]

Conditions in coal camps created special problems for the work involved in housekeeping. The situation in the Brookside coal camp was deplorable. Duke Power Company owned the Brookside coal camp, and the giant utility did little to improve dilapidated camp houses and unsanitary conditions. Since the camp was located near mining operations, women faced a never-ending problem of cleaning away coal dust, grime, and soot.

Lack of adequate plumbing and running water made this work particularly arduous. A few camp residents had installed their own plumbing, but during the strike the company cut off the water supply. Even in normal times water service was irregular. According to Freda Armes, "The water has been so bad it has been black. I would take a cloth and strain it and they would be a scum, old mine dust, just like dirt. Coal dust on the cloth."[18] The camp was so unsanitary that in 1973 the county health department ruled it highly contaminated with fecal bacteria. A public inquiry held during the strike exposed the living conditions and the poor quality of life at Brookside: "Conditions there take one back a century or more in time. The houses are in rows, each with four rooms. There is no running water; an outdoor spigot serves each row of houses. The water comes from a well owned by the mining company. Apparently the pipes are rusty, as the quality of the water is very poor. Privies line what was once a beautiful creek, but which is now an open sewer."[19]

These women also lived with constant economic uncertainty. Every day they feared that miners would return from work injured or would not return at all. Further, they knew they were vulnerable to the sudden loss of income when downswings or mechanization in the industry caused mine layoffs.

All of the women from the coal strike spoke often in their interviews about the importance of a UMWA presence for their hopes for an improved quality of life and economic security. Betty Eldridge explained: "With the union you have a better life, that's for sure. You have more money for one thing. Some of their benefits are real good. All the benefits we have around here come through the union. They built these hospitals. The miners get their pensions."[20] The understanding that a strong UMWA translates into an improved standard of living for residents of the coalfields brought hundreds of supporters to the picket lines and rallies of the UMWA organizing drive at Brookside.[21]

Stepping away from the routines of daily life to participate in these strikes required a series of difficult and courageous decisions. Participation moved the women into new places in their homes, families, communities, and unions. They made hard personal choices, negotiated their way through tough domestic changes, and faced harsh public opposition, all while they were very much in the public eye.

In both strikes, the women struggled to explain why they were involved in the union organizing drives. Expectations in the coalfields were that women would be homemakers. If for some reason they were forced into waged work, then they were expected to get by with the help of family and what income they could earn in minimum wage jobs that rarely included benefits. The public roles the women assumed in the strikes shocked residents in both counties and shredded the gendered landscape to which people had long been accustomed.

In Pikeville, the women were up against hospital officials who not only opposed unions, but also believed that the wages and workloads for nonprofessionals at the hospital were fair. They simply did not understand what the women were going through holding down multiple jobs, trying to keep children in schools, and managing households. Louise Huffman, a nurse's aide, confronted the chairman of the board in a hallway of the hospital not long before the strike: "I told him that I'd like to see him buy his groceries and eat on what I made. I showed him my check. He said, 'Well, that's not really very much, is it?' I said, 'No, that's not enough to pay my grocery bill, and I have bills to pay out of this, too.' He walked on off. He didn't have nothing else to say about it."[22]

They were also up against the widespread sentiment that women who worked in a hospital and cared for the sick should not go on strike, no matter what their wages and working conditions were. Over and over the women told of people stopping cars by the picket line and yelling such comments as "Get back in there and work!" Nancy Lee Fields, who worked in dietary, said, "They'd say that we was keeping them from taking care of the people in the hospital. They didn't understand that we was out there trying to get more money and better conditions and things."[23]

The strikers expected solid support from other working people in the region served by the hospital. In particular, since this was UMWA country, they expected automatic backing from coal miners. They were bitterly disappointed when miners and members of coal mining families did not honor their picket line, in sharp contrast to the Harlan County strike. Lue Vicie Gibson described her encounter with a UMWA member: "Old man Holbrook took [his daughter] to work. I got him on the street over here. I said, 'You ready to haul them scabs back in? You're hauling one every day. You're supposed to be a UMW member.' He was! He was from Wheelwright mines. His daughter, he took her in. She's working over there yet."[24]

Louise Huffman expressed her anger over the situation. She said: "Any time you've got a strike going on if you're a union person I don't think you should cross any picket lines whatsoever. I think you should take your patients somewhere else. Some of the UMW people would take their wives in there . . . I told them they ought to be ashamed. If they was on strike at the mines would they like it if we went in and worked in their place? Or went across and helped? No they wouldn't have liked it."[25]

The major unions in the area and many national and international unions officially endorsed the strike. Donations poured into Pike County from labor organizations all over the country. But locally many working people who usually supported unions were outspoken in their opposition to the strike. Members of union families crossed the picket line for routine examinations and nonemergency treatment. Others took jobs as replacement workers. One nursing supervisor, married to a UMWA miner, even reported the names of employees suspected of union activity before the walkout. Ardena Wheeler recalled comments this supervisor made in the weeks before the strike: "She'd say, 'I wonder when them old strikers, when are they going to have their strike? I just don't see why they want to strike the hospital. The hospital ain't no place to have a union.' All the time her husband worked for a big union mines. He was UMWA, honey!"[26]

The women were criticized for crippling a health care institution. They struggled throughout the strike with the attitude that people who work in hospitals should not have the right to organize, negotiate the conditions of their work, or strike. Hazel Ratliff, one of the strike leaders, disagreed. She was passionate about the rights of the hospital workers. She had worked under a union contract at the Appalachian Regional Hospital, which had operated the former Miners' Hospital for a brief period between ownership by the UMWA and the Pikeville Methodist Hospital. She loved her job there and the opportunities she had to acquire skills and advance:

> I had belonged to a union before, and I knew the working conditions under a union. . . . It was real nice to work for the ARH, believe me! I started out as a dishwasher. It was union. I had chances to grow. Go on up and get out of the dish room. And I did. Went from the dish room to cashier in the cafeteria. . . . The reason we called it "our" hospital: it was the ARH hospital, and it was union. We called it our hospital, and at the time it was our hospital. I felt that we should have back what we'd lost. I was just dying for a union.[27]

Lue Vicie Gibson, a cook at the hospital, also disagreed with the idea that she should not be on strike. She made a quilt with the names of all the strikers appliqued on it while she sat peacefully on the picket line. She bore up under the criticism with this belief: "We had some smarties come along the picket line. Told us we shouldn't be out there. We should be at work. I said, 'Well, I'll go home in about four hours, but it's our duty here. If we don't stand up for our rights there's nobody going to stand up for us.'"[28]

The Pikeville women had the nerve and stamina to stand up to their critics, and their determination shocked Pike County. They organized, went out on strike, and held on for years. Striker Edith Williams said: "They thought that we would all quit. Give up. They thought a week or two would kill us. 'They're just women. They'll just give up and throw their signs down and quit.' But we didn't. We stuck it out."[29]

In Harlan County, strike participation generated different kinds of criticism. The women who initiated women's picketing felt compelled to take action. Jan Bargo was twenty-five with three young children when the strike broke out. For her there was no question but that she should participate: "The longer it [strikebreaking] went on, the less chance we had of getting a contract . . . There were rumors that they couldn't get a job anywhere in the county. With no other type of life, or type of job that they knew, it was like we didn't have a choice in the matter. We had to make a stand."[30] But many residents of Harlan County did not see things the same way. One woman recalled being yelled at by someone driving by the picket line: "'If you was my wife, you'd be home where you belong.' I just felt like I belonged there. It was my livelihood, really, his job. So, there I was."[31] Nannie Rainey had seven small children when her husband went out on strike. She said, "It takes a lot to feed and clothe kids, and I didn't know what we was going to do." What she did was take a very active role in the strike. She described one incident when the women stopped a truck trying to cross the picket line: "This guy . . . called us bitches. He said we should be home taking care of our kids instead of out on the picket line, that wasn't where women was supposed to be. We told him we was there to help our husbands keep their job. . . . We asked him to turn around and go back."[32]

While such attacks troubled many of the women, they were also amused by some critics. The company attorney in particular was the brunt of much sarcasm because he refused to call them "ladies": "According to Eastover's lawyer we wasn't ladies. We were women. He kept saying any woman that would be on a picket line is not a lady. His wife was a lady. . . . He said ladies didn't go out for stuff like that."[33]

Ambiguous responses from husbands and close relatives caused more serious problems than public censure. The men on strike knew the women were succeeding in shutting down the mine when the courts had tied their hands, but this was a hard situation for the men to swallow. The women were suddenly leading double lives, picketing in a miners' strike and running their households. To resolve tensions, the women worked out an unofficial scheme for running the picket line. Nannie Rainey described the way it worked: "Me and Tub [her husband] walked over every morning at five a.m. Then I'd go back home about seven to get [the children] ready. Then I went back to the picket line and stayed. We had that planned out. The ones that didn't have no children would stay over there while the ones that had children would go get them ready. That way there would always be somebody over there *all* the time. We stayed there all day. So we had it all planned."[34] Such strategizing integrated family roles with strike participation. The women kept up a dangerous, demanding campaign against strikebreakers at the same time that they did the laundry, prepared meals, cleaned houses, and took care of children.

Still, some men tried to prevent women in their families from participating. Daisy Perry often went to the picket line with her mother-in-law and other female members of her husband's family. When her husband opposed them, they all ignored him: "He tried to get me and his mom and all to stay home. I wouldn't. He said he was scared . . . we'd get hurt. When I told him I was going anyway, he wouldn't say much. He just let me go on, because he knew I'd go anyway. Even if I had to sneak off."[35]

Some women did drop out, especially after violence on the picket line escalated. Others were determined to continue despite opposition from home. As one woman said, "I don't think there could be anybody else stronger in the union. . . . But he could divorce me. If I wanted to go on that picket line I would. If it come right to that!"[36] One of her friends added, "That's exactly where I sit. . . . They tried to say in court that my husband had me go out on the picket line. . . . He don't tell me what to do. I go when I get ready."[37]

Once they were into the strike most of the women were determined to stay. As Betty Eldridge said: "After I got involved with it I couldn't quit. I would have liked to. It was hard. It was nerve-wracking. It was scary. I had a harder time sleeping. It was really hard . . . there was a few times that I was frightened to death. But I couldn't quit."[38] Like the women at Pikeville, the Brookside women stood up to their critics and held on.

In both strikes, the women found themselves at odds with the unions organizing the strikes. In Pikeville, they had to carve out a voice within CWA at the same time that they were dependent on the union for strike benefits, strike management, and negotiation with the hospital. At Brookside the women stood outside the union and enjoyed a good deal of autonomy, but often they were on uneasy ground collaborating with union organizers and the men on strike.

CWA officials had expected the hospital strikers to follow their lead, obey strict behavior codes, and accept rather than participate in decisions about strike direction. But there was considerable frustration among strikers over the way CWA ran the strike. They felt the union's strategies were misdirected, meek, poorly timed, and ineffective. Still, they were not in the position to demand changes.

The most serious disagreements centered around the union's insistence on lobbying the national offices of the Methodist church to put pressure on the hospital board and on running a peaceful, orderly picket line. CWA invested tremendous time and resources in urging the United Methodist Church to enforce its Social Gospel, a set of principles that endorsed collective bargaining. But the church had no direct way to influence hospital affairs. Methodist in name only after the merger and reorganization, the hospital was neither owned, run, nor financed by the church. It was simply "affiliated." This meant one third of the board members had to be either clergy or members of the church. Since many of Pike County's local elite belonged to the Pikeville congregation, this requirement was easily met.

CWA's district organizer, Lonnie Daniel, was a deeply religious man. He believed that church leaders should be taken at their word, that they would pressure local hospital officials into signing a contract. The strikers knew better. Mae Fields, one of the most active strikers, explained: "I know this local Methodist Church over here at Pikeville. . . . A lot of the members there was against us. I couldn't see as it helped any. The church leaders could never have done nothing with them board members, even if they'd wanted to."[39]

At Daniel's direction, strikers traveled all over the country to picket at meetings of the United Methodist Church. Lue Vicie Gibson described her feelings about a trip strikers made to Louisville, Kentucky, to picket the offices of Methodist Bishop Robertson: "I knew he wasn't going to help us. No! We all knew that! We knew before we went down there. Lonnie Daniel wanted us to go down there and picket the Methodist Church. We knew we wasn't going to get nothing from [Robertson] before we went."[40] And Phyllis Cummins, a nurse's aide who traveled to lobby church leaders, said, "I just went because I was told to . . . I really think that it was a lot of wasted money and effort."[41] In the end, she was right.

Strikers wanted CWA to focus on Pike County and target members of the hospital board and their allies, not Methodist ministers or bishops. As one striker said of their adversaries, "They was 50 millionaires in Pikeville. They don't believe in unions. . . . They all stick together. Too many millionaires in Pikeville."[42]

To put pressure directly on the people who controlled the outcome of the dispute, a number of militant strikers devised alternative, behind-the-scenes strike strategies. They worked with a coalition of supporters to form the People's Committee on Organized Labor (PCOL) as a vehicle for activities CWA was reluctant to pursue. For several weeks during the first winter of the strike, the PCOL ran a series of "informational" picket lines that functioned as secondary boycotts.

Picket lines were set up at area businesses connected to board members and maintained until each owner obtained court injunctions banning the pickets. Board members were worried as the picketing began to take its toll. A car dealership was threatened with loss of its franchise, and several retail stores reported substantial loss of sales.

The strategy was reluctantly and temporarily endorsed by the strike director, but he decided it was too controversial and insisted the strikers drop it. Essentially, Daniel wanted to present the image of a peaceful, "orderly" strike inside Pike County while he concentrated outside the county on strategies which might persuade the board to bargain with the union. Secondary boycotts threatened this image of the strike. So did efforts to stop patronage of the hospital.

Strikers were frustrated with their inability to shut down the hospital and with CWA's willingness to tolerate violations of the picket line. They expected area residents to respect their strike and use the hospital for emergencies only. But as the strike dragged on, people routinely crossed the picket line to use the hospital and to work as replacement labor. Strikers wanted more publicity and public forums to explain the strike and build local support. Phyllis Cummins said, "I really think that money could have been spent on our own people. Invite people that weren't union. Let everybody come and hear our cause. Just let the people come and let us explain why. I really think that people would have [boycotted the hospital more]."[43]

Routine use of the hospital increased as the strike continued, and strikers grew more and more angry about CWA's rules for picket line behavior. CWA's strategy hinged on strict codes for polite public strike behavior. The union wanted a nonviolent strike with well-mannered hospital employees peacefully requesting collective bargaining. But the strikers knew that this suited the hospital board fine. From the day of the first formal communication CWA issued informing the hospital administrator that over 90 percent of the employees had signed a petition for union representation, the administration never changed its position: "that union representation is not consistent with the purposes of the institution."[44] A polite strike was not going to change the hospital's mind. According to Peggy Robinette, "I think CWA has a rule that you're supposed to be extremely nice on the picket line. Let's face it. I wasn't out there for my health. I was out there for my job. I didn't want to be nice all the time."[45]

Women ignored strike schedules that locked them into daytime picket duty. CWA wanted people driving by the picket line to see women quilting, sewing, waving, reading Harlequin novels, cooking over barrels, and just passing the time. Ladylike behavior by women involved in "womanly" activities did help normalize the strike in Pike County, but it also allowed anyone to cross the picket line and keep the hospital operating.

Despite the union's policy, many women came to the picket line throughout the evening shifts and joined in militant late-night action on and off the picket line. One striker's shoulder was dislocated when a strikebreaker rammed her with a pickup truck. Several women were beaten by strikebreakers or people who came to the picket line intentionally to harass them. Many were shot at from passing cars. Women on all the shifts had to jump guardrails to get away from people driving at high speeds in and out of the hospital, but the danger was greatest after dark. Still, many women preferred to pull picket duty at these times.

These women had walked away from the routines of work in the hospital and home and become militant public antagonists of powerful hometown opponents. Yet they were dependent on a union that seemed to be making little progress on their behalf and that tried to minimize and control their roles in the strike. In the end, many women felt that with a different union representing them, they could have won the strike.

"My children go hungry while Carl Horn gets rich!" On May 14, 1974, Dorothy Johnson walked back and forth across the street in front of the Harlan County Courthouse carrying a large sign with these words attacking Duke Power

Company's president. She was waiting for her husband, six other strikers, and four women to be released from jail on bond. They had been sentenced to stiff jail terms for contempt of court. Dorothy had herself been jailed during the strike. On one occasion when there had been a large number of arrests, the women involved took their children to jail with them. Nan Rainey explained, "When they arrested me . . . I took three of the kids to jail . . . I didn't have nobody to stay with them. So I had to take them with me."[46]

Photographs of women and children locked up behind bars in the Harlan County Jail hit the wire services. Women stopping strikebreakers at a coal mine picket line and ending up with their children behind bars made the national news. The UMWA had not planned on a contingent of women in this strike, but it quickly seized the opportunity to exploit their participation for its symbolic value. The women proved to be a valuable asset to one of the union's most successful strike strategies, the "Dump Duke" campaign designed to discourage investors and hamper the company's ability to generate capital.

Aware of their important role in the strike, the women used their status to influence strike direction. They carried out their own strategies, sometimes with and sometimes without the collaboration of strikers and union officials. The news media made much play over the women's tactics, especially when they "switched" scabs. One woman recalled, "We had sticks. Broom handles. Just whatever we could find, shaking them at the miners—the ones that was trying to cross the picket line." She went on to brag, "It was quite a few miners whipped with switches up there. But there was only one that got up in court and testified that he was whipped with a switch!"[47]

There were many physical altercations. Mary Widner, who jumped on the back of and soundly whipped an armed scab, said, "I asked him nicely, 'How about not crossing the picket line in the morning?' He said, 'If you was a man, I'd show you what I'd do to you.' He tried to show me. He had a gun in his hand. But, when I was done, he ran."[48] According to her daughter, Oudia Rigney, "It really shamed them. Mom took a limb to quite a few of them. I think it upset them more having to fight a woman. They was quite a few of them left because of that."[49]

Women realized that police, strikebreakers, company personnel, and union organizers often did not know how to respond to militant women turning scabs away from a coal mine. Because these women had no formal organizational tie to the union, their participation in the strike was more free-floating and self-directed than that of the hospital strikers. It tended to be episodic, responding to the company's periodic efforts to run the mine. It was also in the context of a more violent situation and in the face of extreme physical danger.

Barbara Callahan described an early morning incident after the Kentucky governor had sent extra state police to escort strikebreakers across the picket line. "Everywhere you looked there was a blue light flashing! Big, tall troopers around. It was really . . . it was over-powering. I just thought,'They could shoot me!'"[50] And Betty Eldridge described her shock at facing armed opponents this way: "Seeing all those men . . . most of them had pistols sticking out of their pockets. It just scared me to death . . . afraid somebody was just absolutely going to get killed. I worried more about that than anything. It was really some dangerous times. . . . My life had always been fairly peaceful!"[51]

One of the most dramatic incidents on the picket line happened when women lay down in the road to stop strikebreakers from entering the mine. As Barbara Callahan recalled: "[I was] terrified! I was scared to death. We knew that if those cars started coming through we had to stop them. The only way that we could stop them was lay down in the road. I was such a coward. I knew if I saw a car coming for me I would probably get up. So I laid down with my back to them so I couldn't see them coming!"[52]

These activities shut down the mine. They also reaffirmed the importance of the women's involvement and built up their confidence in their role. There were times when the women and UMWA representatives got into fierce arguments. One woman who complained about the slow pace organizers set for the strike said, "I'd tell them I just figured the best way to do it, if they want to play rough, then you play rough. They'd tell me to shut up and go do my cooking."[53] Unlike the hospital strikers, these women were more or less free to ignore such instruction. Lois Scott, one of the most influential women, reflected on her relationship with the organizers: "Sometimes we'd all get together and go up there to that motel [UMWA strike headquarters] . . . and talk. But really, we listened more to what the men said than the organizers. Because, sometimes what the organizers said was right and made sense and other times it didn't."[54]

Crystal Ferguson publicly attacked Arnold Miller, the international president of the UMWA, at a rally of thirty-five-hundred people in Harlan. Gun thugs had shot into her home, narrowly missing her children. After failing to be recognized to speak at the rally, she walked onto the stage and told Miller, "You gotta fight fire with fire."[55] He had urged the miners to sit and whittle on the picket line.

The strong voice women at Brookside developed in the strike is in contrast to their statuses before the strike. They had been homemakers, dependent on wages earned in the mines by male coal miners in their families and living in communities where women's roles were very traditionally defined. From that dependent status, they earned authority and influence in one of the UMWA's most famous organizing drives. At a meeting after the contract was signed, UMWA lead organizer Houston Elmore acknowledged their contribution: "I want to thank you women again for all you've done for the strike. I think the men know now that the strike's over that several times you've saved the strike and you've also saved their skins on several occasions. I appreciate it personally and hope to be working with you again.[56]

There is no question that participating in these strikes changed these women's lives. Women in both strikes recall their strike involvement as "fun," "an exciting time," "a challenge." All but two said they would get involved again if they had the strikes to live over and that they would be even more militant. They miss the interaction with other women on the picket line, at meetings, and in strike events.

Women from the coal strike have gone on to new roles and identities while they continue to be homemakers. Five of them went back to school or learned new skills in vocational school. Two women completed undergraduate degrees at community colleges, and one went on to earn a master's degree and pursue a Ph.D. degree. Two are self-employed and own their own businesses, and one works full-time in a religious mission. Many women stayed active as UMWA supporters during national contract strikes and other organizing drives (although not as regular members of picket lines). Others have been active in black lung organizing and community service work. They emerged from the coal strike with a new sense of personal efficacy and political possibility.

In Pikeville, a few of the strikers returned to work at the hospital, but most lost their jobs there. Some found other jobs, working once again as dishwashers, short order cooks, grocery checkers, retail clerks, motel housekeepers, and the like. Two women got skilled jobs weighing coal shipments, and one striker works for a radio station where she occasionally dedicates late-night music to the strikers. Still key providers for their households, these women continue to work wherever they can find jobs in Pike County's local economy.

The strike left them with a personal identity they never had before: "Pikeville striker." Nurse's aide Edith Williams, said, "I think it's the best thing that we ever done when we came out on strike. I still say it's the best thing that ever happened to me."[57] Eunice McCoy, a hospital cook, spoke for many of the strikers when she said with some satisfaction, "They thought we was just a bunch of dumb women out there. We was a bunch of women out there, but I don't think we was quite as dumb as they thought we were. We may not have got the union, but we got them straightened out a little bit. The experience of this now is worth more than gold!"[58]

Stereotypes of passive Appalachian women would suggest that the women who participated in these strikes were the least likely people to be involved in collective action. Yet here they were, standing in the middle of the road, facing armed opponents, arguing with state police and strikebreakers, and explaining their strikes and their participation through the television cameras of national news media. They stood their ground in the face of harsh criticism and articulated the needs of Appalachia's workers, families, and communities. In sharp contrast to the myths of Daisy Mae and downtrodden Appalachia, these women continue to live their lives as people of commitment, courage, and vision.

## Notes

1. In this volume, several scholars link persistent images of the region to literary figures, filmmakers, explorers, educators, missionaries, social reformers, ballad collectors, industrialists, politicians, historians, and social scientists. While our scholarship on the origins and the staying power of notions about Appalachia has certainly matured in recent years, careful attention to gender, ethnicity, and race is needed to more fully understand the processes and consequences of stereotyped thinking. In his critique of hillbilly stereotypes in motion pictures, Jerry Williamson argues that the hillbilly "is, most frequently, male. Even as a she, the hillbilly is often a mock male." *Hillbillyland: What the Movies Did to the Mountains and What the Mountains Did to the Movies* (Chapel Hill, Univ. of North Carolina Press, 1995), ix. It is important to note that Williamson's hillbilly is also very white; yet gendered and racial images fold together in the history of caricatures of rural and urban Appalachian people. As this chapter shows, gendered hillbilly stereotypes filter perceptions of Appalachian resistance in different ways and have very real consequences for political action.

2. For regular reporting on these groups and issues see *Mountain Life and Work,* the monthly newsmagazine published by the Council of the Southern Mountains from 1925 until the mid-1980s.

3. Author's interview with Ruby Prater, July 1, 1987, Shelbiana, Kentucky.

4. Author's interview with Ruby Stacy, November 12, 1986, Ages, Kentucky.

5. Author's interview with Betty Eldridge, July 23, 1986, Dartmont, Kentucky.

6. Author's interview with Louie Stacy, November 12, 1986, Ages, Kentucky.

7. See Sally Ward Maggard, "Eastern Kentucky Women on Strike: A Study of Gender, Class, and Political Action in the 1970s," (Ph.D. diss., Univ. of Kentucky, 1988). For additional related publications see Sally Ward Maggard, "Gender Contested: Women's Participation in the Brookside Coal Strike," *Women and Social Protest,* eds. Guida West and Rhoda Blumberg (New York: Oxford Univ. Press, 1990), 75–98; Sally Ward Maggard, "Gender and Schooling in Appalachia: Lessons for an Era of Economic Restructuring," *Journal of the Appalachian Studies Association* 7 (1995): 140–51; Sally Ward Maggard, "'We're Fighting Millionaires!' The Clash of Gender and Class in Appalachian Women's Union Organizing," in *No Middle Ground: Women and Radical Protest,* ed. Kathleen M. Blee (New York: New York Univ. Press, 1998), 289–306.

8. *Harlan County, U.S.A.* outtakes are housed in the Appalachian Special Collection, Margaret I. King Library, Univ. of Kentucky, Lexington. I am in debt to Barbara Kopple for her permission to use this valuable archive in my research.

9. Author's interview with Alpha Ratliff, May 31, 1987, Zebulon, Kentucky.

10. Author's interview with Eunice McCoy, July 2, 1987, Pikeville, Kentucky.

11. Author's interview with Sudie Crusenberry, July 15–16, 1986, Ages, Kentucky.

12. Author's interview with Alpha Ratliff.

13. See Betty Jean Hall, "Women Miners Can Dig It Too!" in *Communities in Economic Crisis: Appalachia and the South*, eds. John Gaventa, Barbara Ellen Smith, and Alex Willingham (Philadelphia: Temple Univ. Press, 1990), 53–60.

14. Author's interview with Edith Williams, June 16, 1987, Pikeville, Kentucky.

15. Author's interview with Peggy Robinette, June 13, 1987, Varney, Kentucky.

16. Author's interview with Alpha Ratliff.

17. Author's interview with Ruby Stacy.

18. Freda Armes, quoted in Paul H. Sherry, ed., "Harlan County Revisited," Special Issue, *Journal of Current Social Issues* 11(6): 48 (spring 1974).

19. Sherry, "Harlan County Revisited," 11.

20. Author's interview with Betty Eldridge.

21. Similar dramatic community support mobilized thousands of residents of southwestern Virginia and eastern Kentucky during the UMWA strike against the Pittston Coal Company in the late 1980s. This strike also involved many women. See Dwayne Yancey, "Thunder in the Coalfields," *Southern Exposure* 18:(4): 36–41 (winter 1990); Jim Sessions and Fran Ansley, "Singing across Dark Spaces: The Union/Community Takeover of Pittston's Moss 3 Plant," in *Fighting Back in Appalachia: Traditions of Resistance and Change*, ed., Stephen L. Fisher (Philadelphia: Temple Univ. Press, 1993), 195–223.

22. Author's interview with Louise Huffman, June 15, 1987, Pikeville, Kentucky.

23. Author's interview with Nancy Lee Fields, June 10, 1987, Robinson Creek, Kentucky.

24. Author's interview with Lue Vicie Gibson, June 1, 1987, Pikeville, Kentucky.

25. Author's interview with Louise Huffman.

26. Author's interview with Ardena Wheeler, June 1, 1987, Pikeville, Kentucky.

27. Author's interview with Hazel Ratliff, June 2, 1987, Chloe Creek, Kentucky.

28. Author's interview with Lue Vicie Gibson.

29. Author's interview with Edith Williams.

30. Author's interview with Jan Bargo, September 23, 1986, Keith, Kentucky.

31. Author's interview with Ruby Stacy.

32. Author's interview with Nannie Rainey, September 23, 1986, Ages, Kentucky.

33. Author's interview with Mary Widner, October 9, 1986, Colts, Kentucky.

34. Author's interview with Nannie Rainey.

35. Author's interview with Daisy Perry, October 24, 1986, Verda, Kentucky.

36. Mary Phillips, *Harlan County U.S.A.*, outtakes, Box 142, CR 813, Appalachia Special Collection.

37. Dorothy Johnson, *Harlan County, U.S.A.*, outtakes, Box 142, CR 813, Appalachia Special Collection.

38. Author's interview with Betty Eldridge.

39. Author's interview with Mae Fields, May 30, 1987, Pikeville, Kentucky.

40. Author's interview with Lue Vicie Gibson.

41. Author's interview with Phyllis Cummins, June 2, 1987, Pikeville, Kentucky.

42. Author's interview with Mae Fields.

43. Author's interview with Phyllis Cummins.

44. Lee Keene, quoted in Gene E. Layne, president, CWA Local 10317, CWA letter to Members, Board of Directors, Methodist Hospital, July 8, 1972. Document in possession of the author.

45. Author's interview with Peggy Robinette, June 13, 1987, Varney, Kentucky.

46. Author's interview with Nannie Rainey.

47. Author's interview with Sue Noe, October 16, 1986, Harlan, Kentucky.

48. Author's interview with Mary Widner.

49. Author's interview with Oudia Rigney, September 29, 1986, Ages, Kentucky.

50. Author's interview with Barbara Callahan, November 28, 1986, Harlan, Kentucky.

51. Author's interview with Betty Eldridge.

52. Author's interview with Barbara Callahan.

53. Author's interview with Mary Widner.

54. Author's interview with Lois Scott.

55. Author's interview with Crystal Ferguson, November 13, 1986, Kildav, Kentucky.

56. *Harlan County, U.S.A.* outtakes, Box 204, CR 941, 943, Appalachian Special Collection.

57. Author's interview with Edith Williams.

58. Author's interview with Eunice McCoy, July 2, 1987, Zebulon, Kentucky.

# Paving the Way

## Urban Organizations and the Image of Appalachians

*Phillip J. Obermiller*

> I'd heard the city streets were paved with gold. But when I got here I discovered three things—that the streets weren't paved with gold . . . that some of them weren't paved at all . . . and that I was supposed to help pave them.
>
> American immigrant saying

For the millions of Appalachians who left the mountains and migrated to urban centers outside the region, the first priority was to find a job and a place to live. Appalachians were—and still are—generally quite competent in finding employment and housing in the host cities. In a few places, such as Chicago and Cincinnati, the migrants set up social service organizations to assist with the fundamentals of relocation. But more often, urban Appalachian organizations formed in response to the widespread denigration they experienced in their new—and largely unwelcoming—social and cultural settings. These organizations, which emerged in Akron, Detroit, Dayton, Hamilton, and Cincinnati, to name a few, were established to celebrate and communicate Appalachian culture and heritage. Service and cultural organizations have attempted to replace negative stereotypes with a more accurate and positive image of Appalachians in cities. This essay examines and evaluates the progress of urban Appalachian organizations in "paving the way" for migrants not only to persist in the urban setting, but also to become a visible and valued part of urban life and culture.

To define the framework for this discussion, the first section briefly presents some stereotypes of urban Appalachians, stereotypes that are familiar because they are ubiquitous in American popular culture. The next section describes four urban Appalachian organizations in Cincinnati, a city with the greatest number and diversity of Appalachian organizations of any metropolis outside the Appalachian region.[1] The four organizations have different primary missions—social, cultural, political, and educational—although specific goals and membership frequently overlap. With individual lifespans ranging from nine to twenty-six years, the organizations have been in existence for an average of twenty-one years—a reasonable opportunity for influencing the image of Appalachians in the city.

The last section examines outcomes. Have these Appalachian organizations improved the image and life chances of urban Appalachians? If so, what positive achievements can be documented? The chapter concludes with an assessment of the progress these Appalachian organizations collectively have made toward a more positive image for urban Appalachians.

The same negative labels are applied to Appalachians whether they live in Appalachia or away from it. Urban Appalachians, however, encounter a different degree of stereotyping. As a minority group living in densely populated neighborhoods in cities and suburbs, urban Appalachians experience stereotyping and its effects in their daily lives more often and more pervasively than do their rural kin. Appalachians living in the region experience stereotypes most frequently as the work of outsiders, whereas urban Appalachians often encounter negative labeling from their neighbors, their coworkers, and the public institutions in their own community.

Albert Votaw's infamous "Hillbillies Invade Chicago," published in *Harper's Magazine* early in 1958,[2] remains the most widely cited example of Appalachian migrant stereotyping. Votaw's notoriety, however, derives primarily from *Harper's* national readership; he was a relative latecomer to urban Appalachian bashing, and his essay seems mild compared with a 1957 *Chicago Tribune* article. Published at the height of the Appalachian migration, "Girl Reporter Visits Jungles of Hillbillies" gave front-page prominence to a detailed, local, and vitriolic attack.

According to the article's introduction, Norma Lee Browning, the "girl reporter" of the headline, set out to explore the "junglelands of the strange breed of people pouring into Chicago by the truckloads." The tone of the article is unambiguous from the opening paragraph: "Skid row dives, opium parlors, and assorted other dens of iniquity collectively are as safe as a Sunday school picnic compared with the joints taken over by clans of fightin', feudin' southern hillbillies and their shootin' cousins, who today constitute one of the most dangerous and lawless elements of Chicago's fast growing migrant population. Most authorities rate them at the bottom of the heap, socially, morally, [and] mentally." Browning cites a police lieutenant and the chief investigator for the Chicago Crime Commission as authorities for the following "facts": "the southern hillbilly migrants, who have descended on Chicago like a plague of locusts in the last few years, have the lowest standard of living and moral code, if any, . . . the biggest capacity for liquor, and the most savage and vicious tactics when drunk, which is most of the time." Continuing in this vein on the back pages, the article deplores the "hillbillies'" proclivity for marrying thirteen-year-old girls, skipping out on the rent, making raucous music, and murdering strangers.[3]

These nearly forty-year-old examples of stereotyping, rather than being historically interesting but unthinkable today, are very much alive in the 1990s. In a recent issue of *Newsweek,* U.S. Congressman Mark Souder from Indiana, commenting on his belief that the only law David Koresh broke was having sex with minors, was quoted as saying, "Do you send tanks and government troops into . . . Kentucky and Tennessee and other places where such things occur?"[4] (Perhaps the realization that he had urban Appalachian constituents in Fort Wayne led to Souder's subsequent apology.) The front page of the *New York Times* quoted an Emory University student who was dismayed by racial conflict on the Atlanta campus: "This is a college campus; it's not a bunch of ignorant hillbillies. But you feel as if someone turned the clock back 30 years."[5]

On the streets of Cincinnati, "hillbilly" jokes and imagery are part and parcel of the urban social environment.[6] More insidious because it is institutionally tolerated is the pattern of Appalachian stereotyping that emerges in the Cincinnati media. The *Cincinnati Enquirer,* with a regional circulation of about five hundred thousand, casually scapegoats "rednecks" as a source of the city's problems in its editorials. The *Enquirer* carried the *Snuffy Smith* comic strip until early 1995. WLW, a 50,000-watt Cincinnati radio station, broadcasts a traffic reporter announcing from his helicopter, "Somebody ought to tell those dumb hillbillies to get that car off the viaduct." On a WLW call-in talk show, a deputy sheriff from nearby Butler County, Ohio, matter-of-factly refers to an arrested suspect as a "drunken hillbilly." Cincinnati television stations offer viewers daily reruns of *The Beverly Hillbillies* and *Dukes of Hazzard.*[7]

The assumptions underlying the continuing tolerance for stereotyping Appalachians seem to have the following logic: The cause of society's problems cannot be us, because we are, by definition, the good guys; but if we point to the usual suspects (often people of African, Asian, or Hispanic ancestry), we will be fired or fined under some federal antidiscrimination regulation or state ethnic intimidation law; so we might as well blame "rednecks" and "hillbillies," because we can say whatever we want about them with impunity. In fact, reprimands for such behavior are usually mild, unspecific, and infrequent.[8]

Southwestern Ohio has long been a destination area for Appalachian migrants. In the mid-1930s, sociologist Grace Leybourne documented the presence of a sizable Appalachian community in Cincinnati.[9] The migration streams continued to ebb and flow over the subsequent decades until about one in every four

Cincinnatians had Appalachian roots.[10] Appalachian organizations, however, did not begin to affect the urban milieu in Cincinnati until the 1970s and 1980s.

This discussion focuses on four organizations, each of which carries out its mission in the Cincinnati metropolitan area. The urban Appalachian street academy, the Lower Price Hill Community School, was organized in 1972. The Appalachian Community Development Association, dedicated to promoting Appalachian culture, was founded in late 1973; the Urban Appalachian Council, an advocacy and social welfare organization, was incorporated in 1974. In 1989 the Appalachian political action group, Appal-PAC, was formed.

Today there are community schools in seven Cincinnati neighborhoods—Lower Price Hill, Northside, East End, East Price Hill, Camp Washington, South Fairmount, and Over-the-Rhine. These community schools serve Appalachians and other low-income and minority students who have been pushed out of the public school system. The largest, the Lower Price Hill Community School, enrolls about 250 students a year; of these, approximately 30 students receive their General Education Diploma (GED) and another 60 are working toward a college-level associate degree.[11]

The Appalachian Community Development Association (ACDA) organizes the annual Appalachian Festival, which celebrated its twenty-fifth anniversary in 1994. The ACDA, in cooperation with the Urban Appalachian Council, also sponsors "Home to the Hills," an annual Appalachian arts celebration that features works by Appalachian photographers and painters, quilts and textiles by mountain craftspersons, Appalachian folk art, plays "in the grand Appalachian tradition," and concerts by leading bluegrass bands. These festivals and celebrations generate revenues that are returned to Appalachian neighborhoods and groups in the form of grants for local activities. In a recent year, the ACDA awarded seventeen thousand dollars to local cultural and social service projects.

The Urban Appalachian Council is a multipurpose agency working in eight predominantly Appalachian neighborhoods across the city. In a typical year, the council assists over 1,400 clients in community-based human service programs, helps some 550 individuals with job placement and training, provides training on Appalachian issues to nearly 900 individuals, and consults on about twenty-five research projects. The Urban Appalachian Council mission also includes creating cultural awareness. The council staff interacts with over 1,600 students in the local schools during Appalachian Month, arranges cultural events attended by some 1,500 people, and provides technical assistance for artist residencies that result in exhibits attended by 750 patrons.[12]

Appal-PAC is a membership organization dedicated to placing Appalachian issues, concerns, and candidates on the political agendas of the city and the county. Appal-PAC also conducts voter registration drives in Appalachian neighborhoods. In recent local elections, Appal-PAC distributed five thousand sample ballots to publicize its endorsements. Six of the nine city council candidates endorsed by Appal-PAC were elected, as were two of the three endorsed Cincinnati Public School Board candidates. A county mental health levy supported by Appal-PAC was also passed.

These Appalachian organizations provide a sense of identity, not just among individuals, but among neighborhoods and cities as well. Phyllis Shelton, an Urban Appalachian Council human services coordinator, said, "There is a strong sense of community among Appalachian groups, not just across neighborhood lines, but across the [Ohio] river in Northern Kentucky and even in whole other cities. It is important for us to know there are others like us out there."[13]

Has all this organizational activity had an effect on Appalachian identity in the Cincinnati metropolitan area? Assessment of the outcomes of nearly twenty years of aggregate organizational effort is arranged in this analysis into discrete areas of influence: religion, politics, the arts and humanities, education, the media, human relations, medical and social services, and philanthropy.

Over the years, Cincinnati Appalachian organizations have established and maintained contact with the dominant Catholic, Protestant, and Jewish bodies in the city. These relationships have a certain reciprocity: Appalachians have benefited from the level of support that major denominations provide, and the religious groups have gained a greater appreciation of Appalachian people and their organizations.

In 1964 the Roman Catholic Archdiocese of Cincinnati set up a ministry to low-income blacks and Appalachians through its Main Street Bible Center in Over-the-Rhine, a port-of-entry neighborhood for Appalachian migrants.[14] At that time the Appalachian leadership in Cincinnati was organized into United Appalachian Cincinnati (later to become the Appalachian Committee, and finally incorporated as the Urban Appalachian Council). Encouraged by Appalachian leaders like Ernie Mynatt, the Bible Center, which was initially organized to address spiritual concerns, evolved into a neighborhood human services provider. By the late 1960s the same Appalachian leaders led by Mynatt cooperated in founding Hub Services, Inc., one of the fourteen Pilot Cities social service demonstration projects instituted nationwide. Following the Hub experiment, an Appalachian Identity Center was established in Over-the-Rhine, and the Bible Center subsequently closed.[15] The resources dedicated to the Bible Center were redirected eventually to the Appalachian Area Office of Catholic Social Services. A small staff with a modest budget now serves the central city and the rural Appalachian counties east of Cincinnati within the archdiocese.

The Episcopal Diocese of Southern Ohio took a different tack and created an urban arm of its clerically led Appalachian Peoples Service Organization.

This administrative unit eventually metamorphosed into the Episcopal Appalachian Ministries, with a governing board led by an Appalachian layman. In addition to funding various urban Appalachian projects, the Episcopal diocese supports independent programs run by neighborhood people. For example, the Northside Community School is housed in buildings provided by an Episcopal parish.

The Wise Temple congregation lends substantial help to the Lower Price Hill Community School. Through its Wise Up group, the congregation has produced a video and a brochure describing the school. These materials have been used to raise the school's annual operating budget and to build a small endowment. Most recently, they were successfully used in a capital campaign to fund school renovations.

In the early 1970s, a candidate for Cincinnati City Council was asked in a public forum about an Appalachian constituency. His flippant response was, "Appalachians? Screw 'em, they don't vote." The urban political arena has changed significantly since then. Ten years after this cavalier remark, a careful look at patterns of Appalachian political participation in Hamilton County documented a very different story: 60 percent of the Appalachians contacted in a random, countywide survey reported voting in the 1980 presidential election.[16]

The candidate questionnaires collected by Appal-PAC in advance of recent Cincinnati City Council elections show that candidates now take the Appalachian electorate more seriously, at least during the campaign season. For example, most of the school board candidates indicated support for the inclusion of Appalachians in the board's equal opportunity policies. City council candidates generally favored intensifying economic development, human services delivery, and the enforcement of environmental regulations in Appalachian neighborhoods.[17]

The clearest indication of the political effectiveness of urban Appalachian organizations is on the books in Cincinnati. As a direct result of organizing and testimony by members of Appal-PAC and the Urban Appalachian Council, Cincinnati is the only metropolis in the country with a human rights ordinance explicitly protecting the civil rights of Appalachian people. Although the ordinance was contested in the courts for its protection of gay and lesbian citizens, no opposition has been voiced to its provision concerning Appalachians. Moreover, the city also has adopted explicit regulations prohibiting discrimination against Appalachians in the hiring and employment practices of the city and of agencies using city funds.

The community schools, the Urban Appalachian Council, and the Appalachian Community Development Association have developed a good working relationship with the Ohio Arts Council. The arts council has urban Appalachian representatives on its Ethnic Arts Panel, which consistently recognizes and funds Appalachian projects. For example, the arts council has backed two independent film projects that made videos in Appalachian neighborhoods. These films have subsequently been broadcast on the public-access cable network in Cincinnati and by the local Public Broadcasting System (PBS) affiliate. Most recently the arts council has sponsored an Ohio Appalachian Arts Initiative for promoting rural and urban arts programs. The initiative has been singled out for praise and additional funding by the National Endowment for the Arts.

A volunteer member of the Urban Appalachian Council's research committee also serves as a paid consultant to the Ohio Historical Society and to the Cincinnati Historical Society. To date, the consultant has participated in the production of an Appalachian component for a permanent museum display on migration to Ohio and in organizing a workshop for high school history teachers on immigration to Cincinnati.

Decisions about the artistic presentation of Appalachian culture are carefully considered within the organizations. Don Corathers has served on the Appalachian Community Development Association's board, including a term as its president. He believes that his organization must showcase the best of traditional Appalachian arts and crafts for the residents of Cincinnati. He points out, however, the tension his organization deals with in preserving the traditional aspects of the culture while simultaneously "pointing out what happens when Appalachian traditions meet other cultural traditions or trends in contemporary mass culture." For example, recent Appalachian festivals have featured traditional bluegrass groups along with Appalachian and African American musicians playing a fusion of gospel, bluegrass, rock-and-roll, and blues. "These are tough decisions to make," Corathers notes, "but we have to make them because Appalachian culture is a living thing. It would be boring if there weren't hard choices to make . . . it wouldn't be worth doing."[18]

Each of the four Appalachian organizations has an ongoing involvement in public education in its broadest sense, but certain specific activities stand out. The research committee of the Urban Appalachian Council has successfully recruited Cincinnati-area college and university faculty to develop and teach Appalachian studies courses at their respective institutions. The committee has also initiated and coordinated student and faculty research projects that have resulted in the publication of books and articles dealing with urban Appalachian issues.[19]

Beginning in 1973 with the first issues of its Working Papers series, the council's research committee has responded to numerous requests for information, speakers, consultants, and workshops. It has also organized several academic conferences; the most recent, organized around the theme "Down Home, Downtown: Urban Appalachians Today" drew nearly two hundred participants from eight states and Canada. The proceedings of two of these conferences have been published as books.[20]

The four organizations have been distinctly less successful in their efforts with the Cincinnati Public Schools. The Urban Appalachian Council and the Appalachian Community Development Association provide cultural programs, curriculum components, and workshops for public school teachers and students. Appal-PAC endorses school board candidates who appear to have a commitment to policies that take into consideration the needs of Appalachian students and parents. But two decades of trying to influence the local educational bureaucracy have not produced many tangible results. Appalachian awareness and appreciation have taken root in some individual schools and classrooms throughout the system but receive little if any attention from the Cincinnati Public Schools' administrative staff or from the overwhelming majority of its teachers.

In the absence of a systemic awareness and effort on the part of the public schools, the community schools have assumed responsibility for remediating some of the educational problems faced by urban Appalachians and other minorities. Larry Holcomb, coordinator of the Northside Community School, notes: "What we have consciously tried to do, and have had some success in doing, is to help people feel and know it is OK to be who they are. We've had Appalachian and African-American students say that they just like to be treated 'right' not 'differently.'"[21]

Beyond the concrete academic benefits they provide, the community schools counter the "dumb hillbilly" stereotype. The network of community schools is a powerful refutation of the myth that Appalachian people disdain educational opportunities. Most students, all of whom are sixteen or older, attend the community schools voluntarily, and the neighborhoods housing the schools are vigorous supporters of their community schools. The Lower Price Hill Community School recently enrolled a record number of students in the satellite program it operates in cooperation with Chatfield College, a small liberal arts college located in an Appalachian county east of Cincinnati.

This kind of image building comes at a price. Jake Kroger, director of the Lower Price Hill Community School, comments: "What we're doing is very hard . . . providing tuition-free education in an inner-city neighborhood is a very difficult situation. The schools are on the [financial] edge all the time."[22] But the price seems worthwhile to Kroger because of the positive outcomes seen in the lives of many of the community schools' students. A number of students who initially came to the Lower Price Hill Community School seeking a GED are now board members or instructors. Sandra "Sam" Kraft is a former student who became an instructor at the school in 1992. She describes the role of the schools in raising the Appalachian image among students as a process of building self-confidence: "Before we can believe in our culture, we've got to learn to believe in ourselves."[23]

Organized efforts to change the media's perceptions of urban Appalachians in Cincinnati have met with mixed results. Among communications professionals, there is a dramatic range of attitudes toward mountaineers. Some are wedded to the powerful, albeit negative, imagery of "hillbillies" and "rednecks"; others are able to produce respectful and, at times, even insightful commentaries about Appalachian people and culture.[24]

Members of the Urban Appalachian Council often take public action to counter the more blatant stereotypes of Appalachian people, for instance, picketing the opening of the movie *The Beverly Hillbillies*. Members of the Council and the ACDA also protested a derogatory on-air statement by a radio talk show host. After reading a public service announcement about the Appalachian Festival, the talk show host commented that people from the mountains have no culture and therefore have no reason to celebrate it with a festival. The resulting letters of concern to the Federal Communications Commission were placed in the station's files for consideration when the station applies to renew its license.

For a variety of reasons, including their southern roots, urban Appalachians are frequently considered to be quintessential racists. This myth conveniently ignores two facts: first, a sizable portion of the urban Appalachian community is African American, and second, there is no evidence that Appalachians are more or less racist that any other urban group.[25] Survey research has found, however, that white Appalachians in the city often have social characteristics that more closely resemble the African American population than the non-Appalachian white population; members of both groups all too often experience the effects of poverty in common.[26] Moreover, some of the Cincinnati neighborhoods with the longest history of racial integration—East End and Northside, for example—predominantly comprise African American and white Appalachian residents.

The Urban Appalachian Council gained tremendous momentum in its initial years from the support of black leaders such as Virginia Coffee, former director of the Cincinnati Human Relations Commission. Since its founding, the council has had African American staff and board members, many of whom have Appalachian roots. Members of the four Appalachian organizations also maintain memberships or participate in other associations such as the Anti-Klan Network, the National Association for the Advancement of Colored People

(NAACP), and the Urban League. While Appalachians and African Americans in Cincinnati do not always hold the same social or political views, more often than not they do share some common ground that the Appalachian organizations are careful to acknowledge. Because of this effort, a number of black leaders in Cincinnati recognize the common cause they have with Appalachians and encourage their own organizations to cooperate with the city's "invisible minority."

The "redneck" stereotype also carries connotations of intolerance for women and minorities. This myth is debunked by the profile of the Appalachian organizations' leadership and workforce. The Appalachian Community Development Association, the Urban Appalachian Council, and the community schools all have long had women in volunteer leadership and decision-making positions as well as in paid staff positions. Significantly, Appal-PAC worked closely and visibly with gay and lesbian rights groups in formulating and passing the city's human rights ordinance. 

In short, these four organizations consistently project a public image of Appalachians that is distinctly different from the false perceptions perpetrated by the "redneck" myth. Working on a daily basis with other ethnic and minority organizations across the city, they make clear to their colleagues in word and action that bigotry is not a part of the urban Appalachian agenda.

The Urban Appalachian Council makes workshops and training sessions available to social service personnel working in over 130 Community Chest agencies in the Greater Cincinnati area. Human service workers, particularly in the medical fields, often have a professional and programmatic view of the world that is not shared by their clients. The council staff is adept at bringing a culture-specific perspective to resolving problems of medical and social service delivery. Training in Appalachian cultural awareness has enabled human service personnel to get beyond complaints about Appalachian nonparticipation or noncompliance and to realize that the programs and the providers can adapt to fit the needs of their Appalachian clients.

The council also encourages medical and social service organizations to include Appalachians in their data collection and analysis, even though they are not legally required to do so. By establishing and carefully interpreting an empirical base of information about their Appalachian clients, the agencies themselves dispel many misconceptions about the Appalachians they serve.

Another effect of the Urban Appalachian Council's organizational presence is the legitimation of Appalachian culture within the professional milieu. Often after a presentation by council staff, Appalachian educators, mental health workers, nurses, or social workers emerge from the audience to thank the speakers for giving them a sense of their heritage. Longtime Appalachian leader and

Appal-PAC member Michael Maloney calls this "giving voice to Appalachians who are 'already there.' We make it okay for professionals to be Appalachian—to claim their identity—to speak out when they see injustice."[27]

Countering the stereotype that all Appalachians are beset by poverty, this process of identification demonstrates that the Appalachian community is similar to other urban groups: it includes middle-class and professional cohorts along with working-class and poor members. The self-identity process for professionals also changes being Appalachian from a career handicap to an occupational advantage; some agencies with large Appalachian clienteles now seek out culturally competent employees.

When the cooperative approach does not work, the Appalachian organizations sometimes act to embarrass social and governmental agencies into doing their jobs. When the Cincinnati Health Department refused to respond to an Appalachian neighborhood's complaints about heavy industrial pollution, the Urban Appalachian Council organized a task force to investigate the problem. The results of the task force's yearlong study were provided to neighborhood leaders, the board of health, the board of education, and the city council. The research findings were also reported on the front pages of newspapers and in local radio and television newscasts.[28] The evidence presented in the task force report and the political pressure brought to bear subsequently forced the health department to accept environmental pollution as a serious health risk for the neighborhood's children.

Although of only modest benefit to the children already affected by the pollution, this was an important victory for two reasons. First, it refuted the stereotypical thinking of some public health officials who intimated that the children's health problems were likely due to the defective behavior of Appalachian parents—for example, cigarette smoking and incest—assumptions without any scientific basis.[29] Second, the victory demonstrated to the wider urban community that Appalachians had the intellectual and organizational resources to examine and discredit biased assumptions promoted by "experts."

Bringing attention to Appalachian social concerns while at the same time praising Appalachian values is like walking a log bridge—a misstep to one side or the other can be perilous. Satisfying the public and professional "need to know" without replacing old stereotypes with new ones is a constant concern for the Appalachian organizations. Pauletta Hansel, a former board president and currently an associate director of the Urban Appalachian Council, describes the dilemma: "When we are asked, 'What are Appalachian needs and what should be done about them?' it is almost necessary to fall into stereotypes to respond. . . . How do you raise the banner of need and at the same time raise the banner of strength and value? People are into problem-solving and have low tolerance for the ambiguity of a regional culture. . . . We're not a race, not a gender, so what are Appalachians? . . . One of the hardest things about working in an Appalachian organization is resisting peoples' need to have a list of 'Appalachian' characteristics."[30]

Each of the four Appalachian organizations operates with funding from individuals, churches, foundations, and special events, as well as from local, state, and federal contracts such as substance abuse prevention, job training, summer youth programs, and environmental health education. Government contracts are important not only for the improved life chances they provide urban Appalachians, but because these jurisdictions have been brought to recognize Appalachians as a legitimate constituency. Similarly, foundation funding produces a degree of Appalachian awareness within the power structures that control philanthropic activity in the city. For example, the Greater Cincinnati Foundation oversees assets of some $125 million on behalf of 750 individual funds. After a portion of the Herbert and Ruth McGurk Faber Appalachian Fund was moved from independent management in Berea, Kentucky, to become a part of the Greater Cincinnati Foundation in 1986, local grant applicants reported a greater openness on the part of the foundation to funding requests from Appalachian groups.

While these anecdotal examples are only intimations of the respect Appalachians have in the philanthropic community, they signal an important outcome for the Appalachian organizations. To be refused funding by a governmental or philanthropic agency threatens the very legitimacy of the applicant group. The fact that Appalachian proposals are being more favorably received by grant-making bodies indicates that the groundwork laid by the Appalachian organizations has successfully established an Appalachian awareness among key government leaders and philanthropic personnel.

In accepting funding for Appalachian programs, the four organizations are aware of the danger of being co-opted by the funding organizations' social perspectives and agendas. As one Appalachian observer puts it, "Sometimes you have to work the stereotype to get the funding." Willing to compromise for the sake of addressing real concerns in the local community, some of the Appalachian organizations nevertheless have had to reject funding opportunities because of the potential damage that requirements ancillary to the funding would do to successful programs. The organizations are also concerned about tokenism. They are sometimes asked to lend their names to promote specific issues without having "a place at the table" when decisions are made. It is a measure of the organizations' success that an Appalachian constituency is usually recruited to lend legitimacy to new coalitions in the city. At the same time, it is a measure of the work that remains to be done when such invitations prove to be mere window dressing that simply exploits the Appalachian community.

Like the migrants to the city who found that the paved streets had no gold and that other streets were simply unpaved, the four Cincinnati Appalachian organizations have functioned in an environment in which the image of Appalachians is either absent or in need of serious refurbishing. What progress have they realized in their collective efforts?

Perhaps their most important contribution has been to dignify what it means to be Appalachian in the eyes of Appalachians themselves. Through these organizations, Appalachian people have reclaimed their own identity and are no longer subject solely to the negative imagery of mountaineers others impose on them. Just as feminists have insisted that "woman" replace "gal" or "girl," just as blacks and African Americans have made "colored" and worse terms taboo, the Appalachian migrants have substituted "Appalachian" for "hillbilly" or "redneck" in the urban lexicon. This substitution is not about dictating political correctness or establishing linguistic orthodoxy; it is, rather, a point of pride.

From a sociological viewpoint, the four organizations raise questions about the process of cultural assimilation. For Appalachian migrants, the process appears to be slower than many anticipated. Second- and third-generation migrants in Cincinnati are active participants in these organizations and their educational and cultural activities. The process of assimilation is certainly less than inevitable; the persistence of these Appalachian organizations and the involvement of their constituency belies the predictions of many that, within a generation, migrant Appalachians blend into the general urban population and have no need or desire for Appalachian-identified activities. Intriguingly, cultural assimilation also appears to be reversible, as in the case of the professionals who reclaim their Appalachian identity.

When asked how the Appalachian organizations in Cincinnati would evaluate their own success in improving the image of urban Appalachians, the leaders consistently combined the need for "changing the system" with the need to enable individuals to change their own lives. Maureen Sullivan, executive director of the Urban Appalachian Council, summarizes this point of view: "Public recognition is important, but I am inclined to believe that in the long term the measure of our work is how individual lives are changed. Appalachians must know for themselves that they are a part of a people of worth . . . [a people] who have strong ties to both a past and a future."[31]

Another accomplishment cited by the leaders is the hard-won respect for Appalachians that has emerged in many sectors of the urban community. Discussing the Cincinnati Public Schools, West Virginia native Jake Kroger remembers: "When I first came here [in 1978] they would hardly give us the time of day. Now we're meeting with Virginia Griffin [Board of Education member] and Michael Brandt [superintendent of schools]."[32]

The degree of respect for Appalachians in the city varies and is obviously not ubiquitous. In fact, it is the inability to institutionalize their reforms in the urban milieu that most troubles the Appalachian organizations. Much of their success with urban institutions comes from the persistence of a few overworked leaders; when this pressure is absent, urban leaders and their institutions tend to revert to old behaviors and uninformed attitudes. The urban Appalachian organizations have adopted an effective watchdog mode but have yet to instill an awareness of and sensitivity to Appalachian concerns at the very core of the city's institutional processes. As a consequence, Appalachian representatives must frequently reopen their negotiations with other urban institutions whose staffs are in constant flux, often leaving behind little or no institutional memory of the gains Appalachians have made with their predecessors.

The price of Appalachian dignity may, in fact, be constant vigilance. The Appalachian organizations in Cincinnati provide a sense of permanence and continuity within the Appalachian community. New generations of leadership are identified and nurtured within the organizations, either as paid staff members or as volunteers working on boards and committees. Appalachian poets, writers, artists, and scholars find in the organizations a critical touchstone and a supportive community for their work. To this extent, the urban organizations are nurturing future generations of leaders who will continue to shape the public perception of Appalachian people.

Twenty-one years is not much time to change patterns of thinking, speaking, and acting that are well over one hundred years old.[33] Within this constraint, the Appalachian organizations in Cincinnati are engaging in a successful process of advocacy for their constituents. Given that such an effort requires a great deal of ingenuity and tenacity, the Appalachian organizations considered here have by all accounts done quite well.

## Notes

1. As part of a self-evaluation in 1992, the Urban Appalachian Council surveyed public officials and media representatives in Toledo, Ohio, Detroit, Michigan, Chicago, Illinois, Hamilton, Ohio, Middletown, Ohio, Indianapolis, Indiana, Columbus, Ohio, and Dayton, Ohio, regarding perceptions of Appalachian people and culture, community knowledge and interest in Appalachian issues, and the extent to which the Appalachian community had a voice in local decision making. The report of the survey results concluded that, primarily because of the activities of the council, "No other city had a degree of recognition, representation, and services designed to meet the needs of Appalachians that even approached that of Cincinnati."

2. Albert N. Votaw, "Hillbillies Invade Chicago," *Harper's Magazine* (Feb. 1958): 64–67.

3. Norma Lee Browning, "Girl Reporter Visits Jungles of Hillbillies," *Chicago Tribune,* March 3, 1957, 1.

4. *Newsweek,* "Perspectives" (Aug. 14, 1995), 19.

5. Peter Applebome, "On Once Liberal Campuses, Racial Divide Grows Wider," *New York Times,* Oct. 25, 1995, 1.

6. See also Phillip J. Obermiller, "Labeling Urban Appalachians," in *Too Few Tomorrows: Urban Appalachians in the 1980's,* eds. Phillip J. Obermiller and William W. Philliber (Boone, N.C.: Appalachian Consortium Press, 1987), 35–42; Clyde B. McCoy and Virginia M. Watkins, "Stereotypes of Appalachians in Urban Areas," in *The Invisible Minority: Urban Appalachians,* eds. William W. Philliber and Clyde B. McCoy (Lexington: Univ. Press of Kentucky, 1981), 20–31.

7. The *Appalachian Journal,* a regional studies review published quarterly in Boone, N.C., does a particularly good job of documenting stereotypes in a regular feature, "Signs of the Times."

8. See also Lloyd Van Brunt, "Whites without Money," *New York Times Magazine* (March 27, 1994), 38; Rebecca Thomas Kirkendall, "Who's a Hillbilly?" *Newsweek* (Nov. 27, 1995), 22; James Webb, "In Defense of Joe Six-Pack," *Wall Street Journal,* June 5, 1995, A14.

9. Grace G. Leybourne, "Urban Adjustments of Migrants from the Southern Appalachian Plateaus," *Social Forces* 16 (1937): 238–46.

10. Phillip J. Obermiller and Robert W. Oldendick, "Moving On: Recent Patterns of Appalachian Migration," in *Too Few Tomorrows,* Obermiller and Philliber, 51–62.

11. "Lower Price Hill Community School News," winter 1995. Lower Price Hill Community School, Cincinnati, Ohio, mimeo.

12. *Urban Appalachian Council Annual Report,* Cincinnati Urban Appalachian Council, Cincinnati, Ohio, 1994.

13. Interview with Phyllis Shelton, Feb. 9, 1996, Cincinnati, Ohio. This quote and those that follow are taken from interviews conducted by the author in Cincinnati between November 1995 and February 1996. All quotations are used with the permission of the interviewees. The author gratefully acknowledges the insights these interviews provided in the preparation and writing of this essay.

14. See also Bruce Tucker, "An Interview with Mike Maloney," *Appalachian Journal* 17 (1989): 34–48.

15. The Appalachian Identity Center continues today as an active site under the Urban Appalachian Council umbrella. Located in Over-the-Rhine, the Center provides GED and nutrition classes, drop-in services, and parenting and job readiness instruction for youth, as well as other seasonal and cultural activities.

16. Obermiller and Oldendick, "Two Studies of Appalachian Civic Involvement," in *Too Few Tomorrows,* Obermiller and Philliber, eds., 69–80.

17. Appal-PAC, *1995 Candidate Responses,* Cincinnati, Ohio, mimeo.

18. Interview with Don Corathers, Jan. 17, 1996, Cincinnati, Ohio.

19. See also William W. Philliber, *Appalachian Migrants in Urban America: Cultural Conflict or Ethnic Group Formation?* (New York: Praeger, 1981).

20. Phillip J. Obermiller, ed., *Down Home, Downtown: Urban Appalachians Today* (Dubuque, Iowa: Kendall/Hunt, 1996); William W. Philliber and Clyde B. McCoy, eds., *The Invisible Minority: Urban Appalachians* (Lexington: Univ. Press of Kentucky, 1981).

21. Interview with Larry Holcomb, Dec. 12, 1995, Cincinnati, Ohio.

22. Interview with Jane Kroger, Dec. 13, 1995, Cincinnati, Ohio.

23. Interview with Sam Kraft, Dec. 13, 1995, Cincinnati, Ohio.

24. Cf. Judy Pasternak, "Bias Blights Life Outside of Appalachia," *Los Angeles Times,* March 29, 1994, 1; Jonathan Tilove, "The White Underclass: 'Last Acceptable Ethnic Fools' Struggle for Respect," *Fort Worth Star-Telegram,* Sept. 18, 1994, C1; Barbara Zigli, "The Urban Appalachians," a special booklet reprint of a series of articles published by the *Cincinnati Enquirer,* 1981; James Adams, "A Series on Appalachians in Cincinnati," a special booklet reprint of a series of articles published by the *Cincinnati Post and Times Star,* 1971.

25. John Hartigan Jr., "'Disgrace to the Race': 'Hillbillies' and the Color-Line in Detroit," in *Down Home, Downtown,* ed. Phillip J. Obermiller, 55–72.

26. Phillip J. Obermiller and Michael E. Maloney, "Living City and Feeling Country: The Current Status and Future Prospects of Urban Appalachians," in *From Mountain to Metropolis: Appalachian Migrants in American Cities,* eds. Kathryn M. Borman and Phillip J. Obermiller (Westport, Conn.: Bergin and Garvey, 1994), 3–12.

27. Interview with Michael Maloney, Jan. 23, 1996, Cincinnati, Ohio.

28. Lower Price Hill Task Force, "Report on Health, Education, and Pollution in Lower Price Hill," Cincinnati Urban Appalachian Council, 1990, mimeo.

29. Smoking is a serious health risk, and survey research in Cincinnati shows that Appalachian adults are more likely to be smokers than are non-Appalachians. However, the Task Force controlled for smoking by comparing the Lower Price Hill neighborhood with another predominantly Appalachian neighborhood of equivalent socioeconomic status. Given similar exposures to the passive inhalation of cigarette smoke, the children in the polluted neighborhood had significantly higher rates of hospital admissions and far more serious conditions than those in the control neighborhood.

The Health Department provided no scientific evidence of elevated rates of incest in Lower Price Hill.

30. Interview with Pauletta Hansel, Jan. 9, 1996, Cincinnati, Ohio.

31. Interview with Maureen Sullivan, Jan. 18, 1996, Cincinnati, Ohio.

32. Interview with Jane Kroger, Dec. 13, 1995, Cincinnati, Ohio.

33. "Redneck" first appeared in the American lexicon in the 1830s, according to the *Oxford English Dictionary,* just about the time of the first migrations out of the Appalachias to the rural West. "Hillbilly" came into common use at the beginning of the twentieth century, just as these migration flows were turning from the West into the urban North.

# Stories of AIDS in Appalachia

## Mary K. Anglin

History is memory's skin, under which pulses the blood and guts of our real lives. Our stories are our way of fashioning a surface with which we can live, that we may present to our neighbors, our friends, our family, our children (especially these last). The truth lies not in the facts of the stories but in the longings that set them in motion.

Fenton Johnson, *Scissors, Paper, Rock*

There are many stories about human immunodeficiency virus (HIV) and acquired immune deficiency syndrome (AIDS). Some of these are the "official" accounts offered by journalists and experts on AIDS, and some, the literary imaginings of writers such as Fenton Johnson. Others are stories of ordinary people living, and dying, with HIV disease. This essay explores each of these kinds of stories for what they tell us about Appalachia, and the motivating forces behind these accounts.

However, the purpose of this inquiry is more sharply fixed. It is to show that in the 1990s, stories of HIV and AIDS have been presented in a manner that portrays Appalachia as backward and inhumane. While these stories are told in lively and even compassionate ways, they have no more truth to them than accounts that show how families and communities have cared for men and women, often all too young, who are dying from AIDS. In part, what makes the negative tales so compelling is that they resonate with centuries-old imagery of Appalachia as "broken" and in need of fixing by those with greater knowledge and resources.

*My Own Country,* by Abraham Verghese, is a good example of these issues. Subtitled *A Doctor's Story of a Town and Its People in the Age of AIDS*, the book chronicled the difficult circumstances experienced by people living with AIDS in the southern mountains. Presenting himself as a "foreign physician" and "Western shaman," Verghese described how he tried to make a difference in the lives of his patients during the mid- to late eighties, when he was an infectious disease doctor in East Tennessee.[1]

To explain what these experiences meant, Verghese offered a portrait of the mountains he called his own: "I know how the road rises, sheer rock on one side, how in places the kudzu takes over and seems to hold up a hillside, and how, in the early afternoon, the sun glares directly into the windshield . . . [I can see] hay rolled into tidy bundles, lined up on the edges of fields. And to-bacco plants and sagging sheds with their rusted, corrugated-tin roofs and shut-terless side-openings."[2] In this rustic setting were an "earthy and appreciative" people who sought care in the regional hospitals where Verghese worked, first as a physician just out of medical school, and later as a specialist.[3] The residents, as much as the beauty of the place, were what enticed Verghese back to southern Appalachia after he had completed his training elsewhere.

There were, according to Verghese, two kinds of people in East Tennessee: "rednecks" and "good ole boys." The former term applied to people whom he characterized as living in "little hollows," in trailers "with no underpinning and dogs all around . . . and children playing under[neath]. . . . *That* world was food stamps and ignorance and rotted teeth and rheumatic fever and a suspi-cion of all strangers." (Italics Verghese's.)[4] "Rednecks," from this perspective, lived in poverty and ill health, conditions they were apparently unable or un-willing to change.

"Good ole boys," however, "had evolved from fighting with the Indians and feuding with each other to become folk who, as they told you themselves, would give you the shirt off their back—if you were their friend."[5] They lived in an increasingly gentrified world of shopping malls and high-tech medical cen-ters, and wore their flannel shirts tucked in their jeans. These were the people who drew Verghese back to the mountains of East Tennessee and to the mis-sion of a rural doctor.

What marks this account is its mixture of sympathy and stereotype. Yet even the sympathetic dimensions of Verghese's characterizations reveal the dis-tance that separated him from the east Tennesseans he came to know during his five-year stay. Negotiating that gap was certainly not easy for the young physician whose foreign accent and appearance distinguished him from many residents of the region and whose work with people living with AIDS often served to alienate him from other health care providers in the early years.

While mindful of the complex position occupied by Verghese, we must be equally sensitive to elements of prejudice in his version of a story, as well as in our responses to it. The representation of colorful dialogue and customs em-blematic of cultural difference is not a neutral activity, particularly in light of century-old stories about the quaint but unenlightened folk of Appalachia.

To call people ignorant and suspicious, to invoke old myths about feuding, or to talk about people "mak[ing] do with Choctaw and Cherokee squaws" when left without "women of their own kind" is to recreate a form of bigotry.[6]

When this kind of narrative is provided by a physician employing clinical experience and professional judgment as justification—or, for that matter, journalists or social scientists drawing upon their presumed expertise—it carries an aura of respectability that is difficult to counter.

To the categories of "redneck" and "good ole boy," Verghese added a third: "gay man" at risk for HIV disease. They were anomalies. Gay men, "without the confounding influence of women," invented their own versions of femininity and became "Southern queens" or were aggressively masculine, adopting the clothes and mannerisms of "the Castro clone." The latter was an especially problematic image for Verghese, who wrote that one of his patients fitting this description might have had contact with the infamous "Patient Zero" during his days in San Francisco.[7] Patient Zero was the code name given to a Canadian flight attendant, whom the journalist Randy Shilts (1987) blamed—without evidence—for the start of the AIDS epidemic in the United States.[8] The implications of this imagined meeting should be obvious: responsibility for Appalachia's AIDS epidemic rested with those who defied the boundaries of "normal" masculinity.

Verghese likened himself to the gay men of East Tennessee in being "alien," but with a crucial distinction. As a recent immigrant from India, Verghese described his adaptation to the dominant culture of the United States as "voluntary, even joyful." By contrast, in the aftermath of AIDS, gay men experienced "shame and guilt" for a way of life at odds with regional and national mores.[9]

Verghese, however, "took delight" in learning about gay men's lives. He collected patient histories with the objective of better understanding how his patients might have been infected with HIV, and sometimes simply to document what fascinated him: "Occasionally I would hear a story so outrageous that I would dictate it to be included in the chart for the sake of posterity."[10] What boundaries might exist between clinical case histories of people living with AIDS (PWAs) and chronicles of so-called deviant subcultures, we are not told.

But, if the most prestigious, this is not the only description of AIDS in Appalachia. There are other narratives, some of which echo observations made by Verghese and some of which present other interpretations. Inasmuch as the purpose of this essay is to suggest that there is a variety of stories to be related about Appalachia and about AIDS, it is useful to examine these different points of view in conjunction with one another.

My own reading of AIDS in southern Appalachia is based on previous anthropological research on women's work in the mica factories of western Carolina, as well as on an ongoing research project about people living with AIDS in the southern mountains. At the factory where I conducted the first research in 1987, women talked about AIDS with some enthusiasm. AIDS was an issue that had received considerable attention in the media, particularly around the question of disease transmission. Women in the factory referred to the *National Enquirer* as a major source of information on this topic and professed great curiosity about how AIDS might be communicated.

The most detailed conversation about AIDS as a local phenomenon took place outside the factory walls during the afternoon break. June Robbins asked me to take a walk with her, and she started the discussion by reminding me about her routine of going to the beauty parlor on Friday afternoons.[11] In addition to having her hair done, she told me, it was an opportunity to hear about events and issues in the county. Through these means, she had heard about "a boy in [the town nearby] who died of AIDS last week." His mother had been working at a factory within commuting distance from the mountains, but she had to quit a good-paying job to be able to care for her son. She was left alone to tend to him, before and after his death. The funeral home refused to deal with the young man's body, and the family's church had rejected them all on learning that one family member had AIDS. June Robbins told me this with evident sympathy for the mother, who had done all she could to look after her own, and with frustration expressed toward the funeral home for its callousness. She made no further comment about the church.

Robbins added that she thought the whole family should be tested for AIDS, as was the public health procedure for venereal disease.[12] This was something she knew about, because she had been subjected to these procedures as a young woman after her brother-in-law had been diagnosed with syphilis. She noted, "[t]he county should take some of its money and put it into AIDS tests for everyone." "[I]f they have AIDS," it would then be the county's responsibility to "keep them up" and not have "them" work.[13]

It is easy to see these remarks as simply an indication of Robbins's fear about contact with PWAs. I contend that there were other issues involved as well: Robbins's own past experience of county health interventions, in addition to her ideas about the obligation of local governments to protect the public and to provide economic support for working-class households when someone was disabled.

However, June Robbins's story raised more questions than answers for me. While she was openly critical about the funeral home, she said nothing about a church that had abandoned its own members in a time of great need. What did she know that she was not telling me? Where did her own loyalties lie? Given the context in which the remarks occurred—the rarity of a private conversation, made possible only by leaving the factory—my initial reaction was, "Why is she telling me this?" To paraphrase the quote that began this essay, we would do well to contemplate the longings that set this particular narrative into motion.

It is instructive to compare Robbins's commentary on AIDS in southern Appalachia to an article written in 1994 by a journalist for the *Philadelphia Inquirer*. Fleishman declared:

> In Appalachia there is no meaner and lonelier way to die than by AIDS.
>
> Much of the nation has put away its fear and prejudice of the disease, but in these rugged mountains, people like Rick [a PWA whom Fleishman characterized as "once the busiest hairdresser in a gossipy little town"] are seen as a threat to a culture. AIDS is viewed as strictly a homosexual disease and an affront to the traditional roles this region has set for men and women. Hate has sprung from ignorance, and from Eastern Kentucky to SouthWestern Virginia, there is a belief that God has left a deadly virus in hollows once rich in coal.[14]

There is no room in this account for ambiguity, nor for the force of personal experience and local history to shape responses to HIV disease. According to the author, the problem of AIDS in Appalachia was that of discrimination attributable to a combination of factors. These included bigotry underwritten by traditional culture; social and economic problems, particularly in the coal mining region of central Appalachia; and neglect on the part of local institutions and area health care providers.

Other than quoting selected providers and PWAs from Kentucky, Fleishman offered his readers little indication as to how he came to these conclusions about AIDS or about Appalachia. The author simply stated, in a subtitle to the article, that "Appalachia shuns people with AIDS." From this perspective, while the nation had apparently transcended ignorance and prejudice toward people living with AIDS, Appalachia was bogged down in a culture of poverty such that it could only respond with hostility toward those diagnosed with the disease. In the words of Troy Townsend, another of Fleishman's informants, "This town is typical redneck country people and the presence of AIDS shatters that. Even if they wanted to feel compassion, they couldn't."[15]

If Fleishman's objective was to ensure that people with AIDS in rural Appalachia received the attention they deserved, he accomplished this by casting their predicament in extreme terms and depicting the region itself as violent, cruel, and without sympathy for those in need. The alternatives he envisioned for PWAs in eastern Kentucky were either to leave their homes in search of better treatment elsewhere or to hope that those outside the mountains—the director of an AIDS organization in a city nearby and the head of the Kentucky Medical Association named in the article, in addition to the readership of the northern newspaper—would somehow come to their assistance.

The portrait Verghese rendered in his book on AIDS in southern Appalachia (specifically, East Tennessee/Southwest Virginia) was more elaborate and certainly more sympathetic than Fleishman's brief account for the *Philadelphia Inquirer*. Although Verghese, like Fleishman, subscribed to the notion of the "typical redneck," he also acknowledged other inhabitants of the southern mountains—the aforementioned "good ole boys" and gay men. "Good ole boys," en route to middle-class life, were capable of transformations in outlook as well as vocation, and presumably this capacity for change included the scenario of AIDS in eastern Tennessee. Gay men, by his definition, were aliens, native sons who did not fit into the traditional culture of the mountains and became outsiders by default. Some went underground. Some left Appalachia altogether, returning only when they had become too ill to live on their own.

It is unclear where, in this typology, June Robbins and her coworkers at the factory might fit. Ironically, the persons who best illustrated the possibilities of personal growth and kindness characteristic of Verghese's (gender specific) "good ole boys" were two women whom Verghese came to know through his work in the hospitals of Tennessee and Virginia. One was Eleanor (no last name given), a nurse who willingly provided care to patients being treated for complications due to AIDS. In the first instance, she did so because "To me he was an old friend. I *had* to take care of him. There was no way I was going to walk away from him." (Italics in original.) It was only with reluctance that Eleanor told Verghese about problems with some of the nursing staff who refused outright to tend to AIDS patients or else gave them inadequate care. Her candor demolished the doctor's "elation" about the quality of treatment given AIDS patients in rural Tennessee, but confirmed his good opinion of her.[16]

The second example was Essie Vines, a lab technician, "natural storyteller," and sister to Gordon, Verghese's "first AIDS case in Tennessee." Gordon (Vines?) was a gay man who had left the mountains for a good job in Atlanta and disappeared from the view of his family. He returned years later, seriously ill with AIDS. For Essie Vines, "it was like a test God was giving us. 'Here,' He said, 'let's see what you all do now.' And there wasn't two ways about it—I *knew* what I was going to do." (Italics in original.) On taking her brother in to provide him the daily nursing care he required, Essie Vines told neighbors and the members of her church about Gordon's illness. She remarked to Verghese, "If there is a negative reaction, they sure better not come by and say anything to me."[17] And when Gordon died, Vines fought the funeral home director to secure the proper treatment for her brother's body and the burial he had requested.

Essie Vines had accepted her brother wholeheartedly. As she put it, "Gay may have been what he did, but it wasn't who he was." For Verghese, however, homosexuality, AIDS, and shame were inextricably linked—and he was "guilty" by association with his patients. When Verghese developed a paradigm to explain the route of HIV infection for his burgeoning practice, it hinged around these factors: "infection with HIV in rural Tennessee was largely an *imported* disease. Imported to the country from the city. Imported by native sons who had left long ago and were now returning because of HIV infection." (Italics in original.) AIDS, in other words, was a disease of the outside world. It had been brought into the mountains by (adult) male children who had moved to big cities like Atlanta, New York, and San Francisco to explore their sexual identities and pursue new lives. After they became sick and could no longer care for themselves, gay men returned "home" to families who understood little about them and the lives they had led away from Appalachia. Hobart Carter epitomized this paradigm: "At home, his opportunities to meet other gay men would be limited and there would have been his parents to deal with: their knowledge, their attitude. His greatest fear was that he might embarrass them, bring them shame. . . . He had to separate, despite the part of him that might have wanted to stay."[18]

Hobart Carter left East Tennessee for San Francisco when he was eighteen. Once there, he adopted the "look" and the life of the "Castro clone." Like Gordon, Hobart Carter's contact with his family was limited until he learned he had AIDS. Upon being hospitalized for an acute case of shingles, Carter was diagnosed simultaneously as being HIV-positive and having AIDS, the advanced stage of HIV disease. All of the sudden, Hobart Carter learned he had a terminal illness and that, during his hospital stay, he had lost both his apartment and his job.

> He called his parents to say he was sick, he had lost his job, and that he planned to come home. He told his parents over the phone that he had "the virus that causes AIDS."
>
> To his parents, this must have seemed terribly unfair: Mr. Carter had just had diverticulitis and bowel surgery. Mrs. Carter was not herself because of her own medical problems. Now, Hobart, who had never once invited them to San Francisco, was coming home with AIDS.

Verghese described at length the nightmare of Carter's homecoming to "the same town he had once felt imprisoned by." While Carter had had an apartment in San Francisco furnished with art works that conveyed his "vision of the world," there were "crucifixes in every room" and a "giant, somewhat gaudy rendering of Christ at Gethsemene" in his family's home.[19] It was not long after returning to his East Tennessee home that Hobart Carter died. The cycle, from Verghese's perspective, was completed.

There were, of course, exceptions to the paradigm of HIV as a disease "[i]mported by native sons" who had become outsiders. For the most part, these consisted of gay men who had made shorter voyages outside the region, partners of AIDS patients, hemophiliacs, and blood transfusion recipients. An exception that confirmed Verghese's paradigm was Will Johnson, an older heterosexual man who became infected with HIV through the blood transfusions that had accompanied his heart surgery. When Will Johnson referred to himself as an "innocent victim" of the epidemic, Verghese "said nothing because for the briefest moment [he] had accepted what [Johnson] said *as if he were stating a well known fact!*" (Italics in original.)[20]

What seemed to distinguish Will Johnson in the eyes of the doctor was that he was respectable, an elite man whose life and marriage Verghese "would shamelessly copy if [he] only knew its ingredients."[21] Moreover, as the head of a successful coal company, Johnson had once had plans for rebuilding mining communities in the heart of eastern Kentucky: "'Abraham, who knows to what heights people can rise if given the best living circumstances instead of a hellhole built on a slag heap? I believe that geography is destiny, and Chuck and I had in mind a new kind of geography, a different destiny for the people of our county.'"[22] Here was a man who broke through Verghese's typology. He was a "patrician," rather than a prodigal son whose promiscuity had brought him into contact with HIV.[23]

While Verghese was honest enough to acknowledge his own biases in the example of Will Johnson, he did so in a way that suggested that they could still be credible opinions about a man with "a different destiny for the people of our county."[24] A similar point might be made with respect to Verghese's approach to the gay men who were his patients, for whom he showed compassion even as he maintained stereotypes about them.

It is vital that we consider these commentaries on AIDS in Appalachia with respect to the history of the AIDS epidemic in North America and the progression of scientific and popular knowledge about HIV disease. If we do not do this, we deny the possibility of change to those who are the subjects of our research. "They" are presented as bogged down in limited worldviews, while "we" as authors and readers acquire increasingly sophisticated understandings of our world.

With respect to Appalachia, the choice is to maintain well-entrenched images of rugged scenery and rich lore filled with superstition, or to recognize the limits of our understanding of a part of North America characterized by complex local histories, people of diverse racial/ethnic/national origins, and heterogeneous cultural traditions. To pursue the latter course means, among other things, that we be attentive to the dates and origins of various notions about AIDS, rather than present them as yet more evidence of the backwardness of the region.

Thus, my conversation with June Robbins took place in January 1988, six and a half years after the "discovery" of AIDS, three years after the development of a test for HIV. It was a time when there was national speculation about routes of transmission and who might be infected with the virus. Knowing this casts a different light on the concerns expressed by factory workers, for their questions coincided with issues raised by health care providers and an American public astounded by a disease that was lethal and increasingly widespread.

Those most directly affected—people diagnosed with HIV disease, relatives of PWAs, and members of "high risk groups"—were finding ways to cope with a new disease about which relatively little was known in the mid- to late 1980s, when Verghese worked in Johnson City, Tennessee. Will Johnson came to see Verghese in 1987, two years after having had heart surgery. His blood transfusion had occurred just before blood supplies were routinely tested for HIV. Some time in the late 1980s, Hobart Carter came back to Tennessee and became one of Verghese's patients. Neither he nor his parents, nor the doctor himself, had the means to prepare for what lay in store. Indeed, Carter's last act was to offer his body to Verghese for clinical investigation: "In death he wanted to give me some clues as to what had gone on from an infectious disease point of view."[25]

It is easy to lose sight of the historical dimension of Verghese's narrative, despite the chronology he provided. This is at least partly due to the inclusion of contemporary (1994) observations about AIDS, along with episodes recounted from his five years in Appalachia, in the story Verghese had to tell. The end result is that the narrator appears to have learned from experience, while those about whom he spoke remain fixed in time.

One of the tragedies of AIDS in the first decade was that few PWAs or their friends or relations had the time to learn how to respond effectively to this rapidly progressive disease. Fortuitously, physicians such as Verghese and successive generations of people living with HIV disease have had the opportunity to benefit from the early history of the epidemic and from increasingly successful medical therapies. That the latter might hold true for Appalachia is less than evident in Verghese's account. It is flatly denied in Fleishman's 1994 article on eastern Kentucky. In that article, Fleishman contrasted the "ignorance" of central Appalachia, with its alleged belief that "God has left a deadly virus in [the] hollows," to the knowledge and sophistication about AIDS displayed by the nation at large.

This essay argues for an alternative version that blurs the boundaries between Appalachia and "the outside." Such an approach seeks to contextualize portraits of AIDS in Appalachia, such as those offered by Fleishman and Verghese, and to draw attention to the subjectivity and vested interests of all involved, be they journalists, social scientists, physicians, or persons living with AIDS. In this version, there is a middle ground between so-called authorities and the persons whose lives become sources of material for scholarly articles and popular accounts. Here, no one has an exclusive hold on the truth. Everyone's voice is needed as author, rather than simply as subject of research.

From that middle ground, Appalachia is not to be construed as an authentic, if otherworldly, culture inhabited by descendants of the "original mountain men." Neither should it be seen as a backwater of hostility and unenlightenment. Instead, Appalachia might be viewed as a place where people with disparate gender identities and ways of life have co-existed amidst contravailing forces of sexism, homophobia, and tolerance.

Certainly, AIDS has brought forth the opportunity for community hospitals and health care providers, funeral homes and churches, to express prejudice against people whose lives do not form part of the mainstream. Sadly enough, this does not make Appalachia unique, even in the 1990s. However, that is only one aspect of the history of AIDS in Appalachia and America. AIDS has likewise served as the occasion for people to oppose bigotry. Gay community organizations, families, and individuals fighting for compassionate treatment of people diagnosed with AIDS—whatever their "risk factors"—are also part of the history to be related.

Despite Verghese's remarks about having to serve as a "surrogate activist" due to the fear and passivity of his patients,[26] and Fleishman's call for outside intervention on the same grounds,[27] there are and have *been* AIDS organizations and activists in the mountains. That is not to suggest that such groups have resembled ACT-UP in form or degree of militancy, nor that they should. In western North Carolina, for example, some of the most active grassroots organizations have been organized through area churches and church networks.[28]

The community organization in Tennessee referred to by Verghese as a "support group" may well have provided information about new therapies and/ or the occasion to discuss problems with health and social service providers, along with the chance for people living with HIV disease to convene. We can only speculate, because Verghese was unable to attend the meetings.[29]

Furthermore, grassroots organizations have been only one, if an important, part of the response to the AIDS epidemic in Appalachia. That response has also included the work of physicians such as Abraham Verghese, nurses like Eleanor, and social services providers willing to confront racism, elitism, homophobia, sexism, and fear of infection in order to provide care for people with AIDS.

Equally important have been the local people who quietly contended with prejudice in order to care for their own kin. These experiences have often received little notice, such as the story of an eastern Kentucky family who took their son, previously diagnosed with AIDS, to a major medical facility out of the mountains.[30] The hospital staff handled the family as if they were, of course, hostile and intolerant of PWAs. In fact, all the family wanted was for the son to receive medical treatment for an AIDS-related condition so that they could take him back home to care for him. The hospital staff did not know how to deal with a loving, attentive, and knowledgeable family who stayed (en masse) to tend to the young man until he was well enough to return to eastern Kentucky.

Accounts from the middle ground would also acknowledge the changing face of AIDS in Appalachia. In contrast to the predominantly gay male population Verghese treated in East Tennessee in the mid- to late 1980s, for example, reports by the HIV/STD Branch of the North Carolina Department of Environment, Health, and Natural Resources indicate that the demography of HIV disease has been undergoing transformation in western North Carolina in the 1990s. As elsewhere in the United States, increases have been observed in rates of HIV infection among women, minorities, heterosexuals, children, and substance users. While gay men currently comprise the largest percentage of AIDS cases in western Carolina—51 percent of the cases diagnosed in 1992—the increase in rates of new infections among other populations signals a shift in the AIDS epidemic and a new calculation of "risk factors" for HIV disease.[31]

Changes in the demography of the epidemic, in conjunction with further stories about homosexuality and AIDS in Appalachia, have the effect of destabilizing Verghese's "metaphor of shame and guilt," not to mention Fleishman's portrait of fear and isolation. In the story that Black related of the family from eastern Kentucky, the failing health of the son concerned them, not the fact of his diagnosis with AIDS nor his homosexuality. To the contrary, despite his early identification as a gay man, their son had always been well regarded by the local community, and his male partner was incorporated as a member of their extended family. These issues were not flaunted, because there was always the possibility for someone in authority, such as an employer or a health care provider, to express her/his own forms of intolerance in ways that could hurt the family.[32]

Johnson presented observations of a similar tenor in his novel about a rural Kentucky family. Although Raphael Hardin in many respects resembled Verghese's notion of the native son, his interactions with other members of the Hardin family inspire the reader to a more complex interpretation. Just as Raphael Hardin had come to know himself in different ways over the course of his life, so too, had his family. That recognition and acceptance were not easily achieved did not belie the possibility of people learning to see things in a new light—or of older family members and friends having something yet to offer adult male sons. For example, Rose Ella Hardin, Raphael's mother, had this to say to him: "That's the problem with you Californians—you think everything has to be tackled head-on. Like everything under the sun that people do has got an explanation and if you talk long enough you'll find out what it is, when the only thing you can really do is give things a little nudge and hope for the best."[33]

And when Raphael Hardin grew angry at his mother's indirectness and her inability to acknowledge his homosexuality twenty years earlier, she responded, "I'm no fool, even if I do watch TV. I know what's going on out there. What are the words for all that? What words do you use?"[34] With that, Raphael and Rose Ella Harding discussed what it meant for him to have HIV disease and what might happen to him in the future. Their conversation had no obvious impact; it was just part of that family's history.

There are no easy explanations in the stories Black and Johnson provided of AIDS in rural Kentucky, nor can there be. Rather than a way to analyze the significance of AIDS in Appalachia, we as the audience are presented with an assortment of motivations and perspectives that have inspired these various narratives into being.

We are also left with the recognition that there are more stories to be told from the middle ground. Through differences in social class, religion, race, ethnicity, sexuality, gender, and urbanity/ruralness written large by the AIDS epidemic, these stories will help us to revise understandings of identity and culture in Appalachia. Perhaps then we may be able to leave the old stereotypes behind.

## Notes

I would like to thank Dwight Billings, Kate Black, Steve Fisher, Jane Hatcher, Ann Kingsolver, and the anonymous reviewers for their valuable comments. I also want to thank Elizabeth A. Williams for her help as research assistant and the College of Arts and Sciences, the University of Kentucky, for funding in support of my research. Finally and most importantly, thanks to all those who shared their stories with me. An earlier version of this essay was published as "AIDS in Appalachia: Medical Pathologies and the Problem of Identity," *Journal of Appalachian Studies* 3: 171–87.

1. Abraham Verghese, *My Own Country: A Doctor's Story of a Town and Its People in the Age of AIDS* (New York: Simon and Schuster, 1994), 19–20, 343.

2. Ibid., 9–10.

3. Ibid., 21.

4. Ibid., 38.

5. Ibid., 37.

6. Ibid.

7. Ibid., 52, 57, 117, 230.

8. Randy Shilts, *And the Band Played On* (New York: Penguin Books, 1987).

9. Verghese, *My Own Country*, 51.

10. Ibid., 103, 104.

11. The name "June Robbins" is a pseudonym, as are all proper names used in reference to my research. Pseudonyms are used to protect the confidentiality of those who have participated in my research.

12. The distinction to be made here is between the human immune deficiency virus (HIV), with which someone can be infected, and AIDS as a later stage of HIV infection. One is tested for the presence or absence of HIV. One is diagnosed with AIDS through various means. These include but are not limited to (1) being diagnosed with an AIDS-defining condition, such as Kaposi's sarcoma (KS) or pneumocystis carinii pneumonia (PCP), and (2) having a T-4 lymphocyte count of under 200. In the mid- to late 1980s, there was much confusion among physicians and researchers as well as the public concerning what the various tests indicated and how AIDS was to be defined.

13. Mary K. Anglin, "Questions of Care: Resources and Responsibilities towards People Living with HIV in the Rural U.S.," 88 (Paper presented at the annual meeting of the Society for Applied Anthropology, Seattle, Wash., 1997).

14. Jeffrey Fleishman, "In Appalachia, AIDS Patients Live in Fear, Isolation: They've Been Turned Away Even by Doctors and Ministers," *Philadelphia Inquirer*, July 21, 1994, A1, A16.

15. Ibid., A16.

16. Verghese, *My Own Country*, 88, 87–88.

17. Ibid., 64, 75, 75, 113.

18. Ibid., 78, 137, 204, 261–62, 320, 321.

19. Ibid., 321–22, 323, 324.

20. Ibid., 202.

21. Ibid., 232.

22. Will Johnson, quoted in Verghese, *My Own Country*, 195.

23. Verghese, *My Own Country*, 70, 194, 203.

24. Ibid., 195, 202–4.

25. Ibid., 325.

26. Ibid., 222.

27. Fleishman, "In Appalachia, AIDS Patients Live in Fear."

28. Anglin, "Questions of Care."

29. Verghese, *My Own Country*, 149 ff., 226.

30. Kate Black, "Rethinking Region: The Call of Stories," (panel presentation, annual meeting of the Appalachian Studies Conference, Morgantown, W. Va.), 1995.

31. HIV/STD Branch, North Carolina Department of Environment, Health, and Natural Resources, 1993. AIDS statistics by DEHNR Region, Raleigh, N.C., 1994.

32. Black, "Rethinking Region."

33. Fenton Johnson, *Scissors, Paper, Rock* (New York: Washington Square Press, 1993), 167.

34. Ibid., 168.

## Bibliography

Anglin, Mary K. "Questions of Care: Resources and Responsibilities towards People Living with HIV in the Rural U.S." Paper presented at the annual meeting of the Society for Applied Anthropology, Seattle, Wash., March 1997.

Black, Kate. "Rethinking Region: The Call of Stories." Panel presentation at the annual meeting of the Appalachian Studies Conference. Morgantown, W.Va., March 1995.

Fleishman, Jeffrey. "In Appalachia, AIDS Patients Live in Fear, Isolation: They've Been Turned Away Even by Doctors and Ministers." *Philadelphia Inquirer,* July 21, 1994, A1, A16.

HIV/STD Branch, North Carolina Department of Environment, Health, and Natural Resources. 1993. AIDS Statistics by DEHNR Region. Raleigh, N.C. 1994.

Johnson, Fenton. *Scissors, Paper, Rock.* New York: Washington Square Press, 1993.

Shilts, Randy. *And the Band Played On.* New York: Penguin Books, 1987.

Verghese, Abraham. *My Own Country: A Doctor's Story of a Town and Its People in the Age of AIDS.* New York: Simon and Schuster, 1994.

# V

# Recycling Old Stereotypes

## Critical Responses to *The Kentucky Cycle*

# America Needs Hillbillies

## The Case of *The Kentucky Cycle*

*Finlay Donesky*

Anyone familiar with *The Kentucky Cycle* has likely heard a variation on the following story, the essential details of which appear in most articles and reviews about the play. On a wet spring day in 1981, a twenty-eight-year-old actor by the name of Robert Schenkkan traveled across central Kentucky from Louisville to Hazard, a town set deep in the mountains of Perry County. A local physician had asked him if he wanted to accompany him as he made house calls in the area around Hazard. In the ten hours he spent in the region, Schenkkan witnessed environmental abuse from strip mining and disparities between wealth and poverty that left him feeling shocked, outraged, and puzzled.

In the author's note to the play, Schenkkan describes the poverty of a family living in a "holler" that he found especially memorable:

> Their house was a single-room "shotgun shack" with a tin roof, a dirt floor, and a coal-burning stove. It was situated on what looked like a combination garbage dump and gravel pit. The mother, who couldn't have been more than sixteen or seventeen, had two children below the age of two, one of whom was crippled. The father, not much older than his wife, was unemployed, with little training and few prospects. The smell in that house was what my friend with grim humor referred to as "the smell of poverty in the mountains"—as though you had taken a corn-chuck mattress, soaked it in piss, covered it with garbage and coal, and set it on fire.[1]

Schenkkan also visited a successful coal operator living in a palatial home on top of a mountain who, when asked about the plight of his poor neighbors, said, "these people are lazy—stupid—and that's why they suffer."[2]

At this point in his story in the Bobbie Ann Mason interview, Schenkkan says, "I just knew I was mad. And I was upset. I didn't understand how this could be—it was just so incongruous. This guy who was so blasé, to put it politely, about the extreme want of his neighbors."[3] Schenkkan was also astounded by corresponding incongruities in the landscape. Lush mountain forests full of flaming dogwood and azalea would suddenly give way to vast heaps of crushed rock and mine tailings left by strip miners. In Schenkkan's words, "It just looks like the fucking moon."[4] He returned to his home in southern California with feelings of rage and the desire to find out how and why such poverty and environmental ruin had come about.

He began his research by reading Harry Caudill's *Night Comes to the Cumberlands* (1963), a pioneering study that drew the attention of the country to the devastating impact of the coal industry on the land and people of eastern Kentucky. Schenkkan also credits the writings of Joseph Campbell for helping him realize that what he saw in eastern Kentucky was the consequence of dangerous myths at the heart of American society. He calls them the "Myth of Abundance" and the "Myth of Escape," which together form the "Myth of the Frontier."[5] He believes America is headed for "ruin on a grand scale" if it continues to pretend it can forever escape the consequences of plundering its natural resources as if they were inexhaustible. He believes such ruin can be averted if Americans face up to the destructive dark side of the American Dream. "One of our big problems," he says, "is how much we're in denial about our past, and how unwilling we are to examine our past and to come to terms with it. There's a river of loss that runs through the bedrock of this country—as deep as any seam of anthracite in Eastern Kentucky."[6]

*The Kentucky Cycle* thus appears to be a cautionary tale with eastern Kentucky as a paradigm of the American experience. In the two-hundred-year saga of three related families—the Rowens, the Biggs, and the Talberts—the play traces cycles of violence, greed, revenge, and betrayal that epitomize the mistakes Americans must acknowledge before they can move on and embrace myths that encourage responsibility and preservation.

Schenkkan's visit to eastern Kentucky followed up by his gift of concern— a cautionary tale in the form of a play—enacts a pattern of response Appalachians have seen repeated innumerable times during the past one hundred years. Ever since Will Wallace Harney visited the Cumberland mountain region and published his impressions in 1873 under the title "A Strange Land and Peculiar People," Appalachia has been visited by local colorists, then missionaries, then educators, northern industrialists, representatives of national benevolent institutions and charities, journalists, officials from federal agencies and commissions—all of whom have drawn lessons from and formulated remedies for the plight of its people.[7]

Appalachians have a history of not responding to the concern and help of outsiders with the expected level of gratitude. Their response to *The Kentucky Cycle* reminds me of an episode Harry Caudill describes near the beginning of *Watches of the Night* (1976), one of several updates to *Night Comes to the*

*Cumberlands.* In the fall of 1963, Homer Bigart, a reporter from the *New York Times,* visited eastern Kentucky, and by late October a series of front-page articles appeared about the poverty of coal mining communities. These articles caught the attention of John F. Kennedy, who revived the dormant President's Appalachian Regional Commission and promised to set aside $45 million for immediate relief efforts—thus began the famous War on Poverty of the mid-sixties. In response to the spirit of the times, *Life* magazine devoted its January 1964 issue to poverty in Appalachia. Soon food and clothing from the rest of the country began pouring in. Harry Caudill describes several contributions as follows: "An overwhelmed wholesaler sent 12,000 pairs of shoes to Letcher County—'Two pairs for every child,' he specified—and the town of Harlan was blessed with an entire carload of cabbages for several days on a side track while the cargo rotted, and the Louisville and Nashville—which touts itself as 'Old Reliable'—promptly discarded it on a riverbank. The ten tons of decaying vegetables sent an odoriferous pall to plague the county seat and raise serious doubts about the whole idea of Christian charity."[8]

I think it is safe to say that many Kentuckians feel that they need *The Kentucky Cycle* about as much as they need ten tons of rotting cabbages. John Ed Pearce, a columnist for the *Courier-Journal* of Louisville, calls the play "the literary equivalent of a drive-by-shooting."[9] Gurney Norman, a native of Hazard and a professor in the English Department at the University of Kentucky, says, "For many readers, especially those familiar with the 19th century 'local color' school of Appalachian literature, *The Kentucky Cycle* will be seen as only the latest narrative in the century-long stream of narratives that have portrayed the people of this region as mean, quaint, violent, brutish and generally low-down and sorry."[10] George Ella Lyon, an author and native of Harlan County, responded to the news that *The Kentucky Cycle* had won the Pulitzer Prize with the same questions Schenkkan asked upon seeing the poverty near Hazard: "What had happened here? How could this be?" "How could another dumbshow of stereotypes be lauded and certified and, worse still, guaranteed productions and audiences all over the country?"[11] When *The Kentucky Cycle* closed December 12, 1993, at a loss of $2.5 million after only three and a half weeks on Broadway, Loyal Jones, the former director of the Appalachian Center at Berea College, spoke for Kentuckians who had been following with dismay the play's progress across the country with his response, "Good news at last."[12]

The most persistent criticism Kentuckians level at *The Kentucky Cycle* is that it runs roughshod over the history of Appalachia. Dialogue with sentences such as "It don't make me no nevermind" and "Look like he done bust up your lip good" sound like hillbilly talk derived from television shows such as *The Beverly Hillbillies* and *Hee Haw.* But more important, they believe Schenkkan's portrait of the mountaineer is far too dark and mean-spirited.

The ongoing battle between Schenkkan and his Kentucky critics, conducted in many articles and reviews that appeared throughout 1993, sparked my interest in giving *The Kentucky Cycle* an historical analysis. The controversy intrigued me for it was marked by certainty and conviction on both sides with neither conceding anything to the other. According to Andrew Adler of the *Courier-Journal*, Schenkkan reacted with astonishment and sympathy to his critics: "Pop culture has created a whole slew of rather horrific stereotypes so I understand their sensitivity. I came out of this experience as an advocate for these people. Maybe it's a question of what is a genuine advocacy? Is it being a cheerleader? A chamber of commerce saying everything is right?"[13]

While Schenkkan remains invincibly confident of his good intentions, he is somewhat less sure about how to counter criticism regarding historicity. He alternates between saying that the play is historically accurate and that it has nothing to do with history. To Bobbie Ann Mason he said, "My mandate as a playwright is to tell the truth as I see it. It was important that I be as historically accurate as I could be: And I tried to do that. But, beyond that, if what I have to say is dark, or perhaps not the best advertising one would wish for oneself—well, that's just the way it is. And I'm sorry about, but not going to change what I see, what is for me truth, just to make someone feel better. The fact is there are a lot of problems there."[14]

Several weeks later he changed his tack in the Adler interview: "If you approach the play as history, you'll be disappointed. That's not what I am. I would say to virtually all of my audiences and to all of the press, that this is a larger epic, and we are in the realm of mythology, not history."[15]

These statements, of course, need not be read as contradictory: a play can be historically accurate and mythic at the same time. However, a play or novel fails to become mythic if it does violence to generally accepted notions of what is historically true. How can Kentuckians be expected to see the mythic resonances of *The Kentucky Cycle* if gross historical misrepresentations fill their vision? Their appeal to history has been and continues to be the recourse of ethnic and religious groups that feel robbed of complexity and humanity in the stories others tell of them.

As a northerner without a strong background in Appalachian history, my puzzlement took the form of these questions: How could someone so well-meaning, who intended to be an advocate of eastern Kentuckians and had spent several years researching their history, manage to offend so many Kentuckians? What is it precisely that offends them and do they have a good reason to be offended? Several Kentuckians have said that *The Kentucky Cycle* confirms once again that Appalachians remain the last group the rest of America feels it is all right to portray with demeaning stereotypes. If this is true, why is it true? What convergence of social and historical forces has made Appalachia the last dumping ground for psychosocial projections in America?

I emerged from my study of Appalachian history and culture with the position that Schenkkan recycles the most damaging stereotypes ever foisted upon Appalachia. In the past hundred years nearly all those who have been moved by the plight of Appalachians and felt compelled to do something for them have justified their efforts with two often mutually reinforcing explanations. Appalachians are poor and backward because of their regressive attitudes and degenerate character traits—this is the "culture of poverty," or pathological model. Or, Appalachians are considered poor and backward because of substandard health, educational, political, social, and economic facilities—this is the structural model. Both models are offensive to many Appalachians because they have been used for decades to justify doing things for them without respect for their opinions. Of the two, the "culture of poverty" model has been the most destructive for it perpetuates stereotypes that help to justify the exploitation of the natural resources of Appalachia.

As he sums up his impressions of eastern Kentucky in the author's note, Schenkkan mentions both models and endorses the culture-of-poverty one: "The poverty and the environmental abuse I witnessed there were not simply a failure of economics. It went much deeper than that; hence our continual failure to 'social engineer' meaningful change there. It was a poverty of the spirit; a poverty of the soul."[16]

For the past thirty years Appalachian artists, writers, and historians have been working hard to discredit the culture-of-poverty model. So naturally it was with considerable dismay and anger that they responded to a Pulitzer Prize–winning play whose animating principle is that the real root of the problems in eastern Kentucky is a "poverty of the soul."

Harry Caudill in three of his books—*Night Comes to the Cumberlands, Watches of the Night,* and *Darkness at Dawn* (1976)—and Jack Weller in his book *Yesterday's People* (1965) together have arguably done more than all other writers combined to popularize the notion that the real obstacle to change in Appalachia is the degenerate genetic quality of the people. What we see worked out in *The Kentucky Cycle* is a distillation of Harry Caudill's so-called gene theory.

In the first chapter of *Night Comes to the Cumberlands,* Caudill argues that the New England states were settled by hardworking, prosperous, educated, "hymn-singing pilgrims" from the farms and villages of England who were ideally equipped to rapidly establish cohesive, well-organized, and disciplined societies in the new world. In contrast, the Appalachian region was settled, he says, primarily by cynical, penniless, resentful, angry, uneducated street orphans, debtors, and criminals from the slums and prisons of English cities who came over as indentured servants to work for farmers in Georgia, Virginia, and the Carolinas before escaping into the mountains to avoid the discipline of civilized life. At the end of the first chapter of his book *Darkness at Dawn,* in which he reworks and amplifies his gene theory, Caudill quotes approvingly the following eugenics program jokingly suggested by a certain unidentified wag: "The best thing the Federal Government could do for the mountains is to move a big army camp in. The soldiers would get the local girls pregnant and the fresh genes would do more good than all the free grub they're giving away."[17] "The observation," says Caudill, "evoked laughter seasoned with the realization that it contained more truth than wit."[18]

No credible historian would agree with Caudill's unsubstantiated theory that the Appalachian region was settled by, in his words, the "human refuse" from English slums. Most historians agree that the region was settled by a mixture of Scotch, Irish, English, Welsh, and Germans who came primarily from Virginia and the Carolinas with smaller migrations from Georgia and Pennsylvania.[19]

Kentuckians manage to tolerate Caudill's gene theory nonsense as the perverse eccentricity of a favorite son. Warm regard for Caudill exists throughout Kentucky, for he was the first to effectively draw attention to the abuses of the coal industry; whereas *The Kentucky Cycle* contains very little to offset or qualify the poverty-of-spirit approach. That is, Schenkkan fully imbibed Caudill's essentialist gene theory without his keen awareness of how social, historical, and economic forces pauperized Appalachians.

In the first two of the nine sections—"Masters of the Trade" and "The Courtship of Morning Star"—Schenkkan applies Caudill's gene theory with a vengeance. They are set in 1775 and 1776, respectively, and focus primarily on Michael Rowen, the first settler in the region and the founder of one of the three families. He is portrayed as a treacherous, rapacious animal consumed with greed for land. His list of accomplishments is that of a vicious psychopath. He had killed the farmer he was indentured to in Georgia before escaping to the mountains of Kentucky. When a group of Indians asks him to pay a blood debt for a Scottish trader he helped kill, he instantly stabs to death his traveling companion Sam, a young farmer from Virginia. He then gives the same group of Indians smallpox-infected blankets to revenge the death of his family. After the disease destroys nearly the entire tribe, he drags back to his cabin a kicking and screaming young female survivor by the name of Morning Star to be his wife. After her second attempt to kill him and escape, he severs one of her tendons. Their first child is a girl, so he kills it and buries it in the forest nearby. As soon as he has enough cash he purchases a female slave with whom he promptly begins to breed to produce new field hands.

Violence and rapaciousness also characterize the next generation in the third section—"The Homecoming." Michael's sixteen-year-old son Patrick stabs him to death in his bath after his return from an extended trip to Louisville because he fears Michael will disinherit him. Patrick banishes his mother, Morning Star, for life and kills the neighbor, Joe Talbert, out of fear that their romantic liaison will jeopardize his claim to his father's land. He then marries Joe's daughter Rebecca, thus securing more valuable bottomland. These actions are the source of a feud between the Talberts and the Rowens that reaches a destructive climax on the eve of the Civil War sixty-nine years later.

In his *Time* magazine review, William Henry III says, "Many audience members will be tempted to say that *The Kentucky Cycle* is an imbalanced portrait of America. But historically it is real."[20] (Henry was the chair of the five-member nominating committee for the Pulitzer Prize in drama in 1992, the year *The Kentucky Cycle* won the award.) In a narrow sense, Henry is correct. Schenkkan's portrayal of Michael and Patrick Rowen is historically real. The early settlers committed many acts of murder and treachery as they drove the Indians off the land. Yet Schenkkan's portrayal of Michael and Patrick is historically unreal to the degree it is unrepresentative and reductive. The vast majority of settlers were not violent former indentured servants who could say, as Michael does to Morning Star in the brutal courtship scene, "I been killin' as long as I can remember."[21] Also, as Appalachians who are part Indian will tell you, Indian women often married the early trappers and hunters and did so willingly. There were slaves in the twenty-eight mountain counties of Kentucky, yet they were few, compared with the number in the Bluegrass and western regions. At the beginning of the Civil War in 1860, 5 percent of white males owned slaves, who comprised just under 5 percent of the population.[22]

One could no doubt find historical precedents for everything that happens in *The Kentucky Cycle;* the problem is that Schenkkan consistently presents mountain people in the worst possible light. The result is a portrait of a people without complexity or humanity. According to the well-known pronouncement of the English historian Arnold Toynbee, "Appalachians are the American counterparts of the latter day barbarians of the Old World—Rifis, Albanians, Kurd, Pathan, Hairy Ainus; but, whereas these latter are belated survivals of an ancient barbarism, the Appalachians present the melancholy spectacle of a people who have acquired civilization and then lost it."[23] In *The Kentucky Cycle* Schenkkan presents the even more melancholy spectacle of a people who never had civilization to lose.

Two general observations arise from my analysis of how Schenkkan represents Appalachians. First, nothing good or admirable comes from Appalachians. They are portrayed as passive, fatalistic, ignorant, gullible, easily flattered, greedy, violent, treacherous, and revengeful. On the few occasions they demonstrate courage, intelligence, creativity, and the strength to stand up for themselves in a productive way, it is the result of experience gained outside the mountains or the result of an outsider coming in to provide them the knowledge and inspiration to do so. It is difficult to see how Appalachia can function as a metaphor or paradigm for America, as Schenkkan seizes every opportunity to claim, if Appalachians are consistently portrayed as essentially different from other Americans.

Second, genetics nearly always eclipses historical, social, and economic causes for the behavior of Appalachians, thus the paradox of a play with all the trappings of an epic history play—the grand sweep of action covering two hundred years, the Brechtian production methods, and a wealth of detail that roots the action to a specific region—in which the characters remain untouched by history. Their genetically determined fate is to endlessly repeat the self-defeating behavior of their degenerate ancestor, Michael Rowen. Despite his good intentions, Schenkkan remains frozen in the attitudes of the literary tourist who, early in the century, described Appalachians as people "preserved as a mammoth in ice."[24]

In 1792, when Patrick Rowen kills his father and Joe Talbert and banishes his mother, he begins a feud between the Rowens and the Talberts that simmers until 1861 when Patrick's grandson Jed slaughters the entire Talbert family except for two daughters. The stereotype of the violent gun-toting hillbilly first lodged itself in the national consciousness because of the notorious feuding and high incidence of murder and political assassination that plagued many mountain regions for thirty-five years after the Civil War. The historical and social reasons for such violence have been well documented by numerous historians during the past fifty years, so it is remarkable how Schenkkan manages to radically distort historical realities that had a direct bearing on how and why feuding occurred. He foregrounds instead generational and genetic causes rooted in Patrick's murder of Joe Talbert in 1792, which was motivated by his greed for land inherited in turn from Michael.

In the fourth section, "Ties that Bind," set twenty-seven years later in 1819, Jeremiah Talbert revenges the murder of his father by reducing the Rowens to sharecroppers on their land. He purchases the Rowen debt from a bank about to go bankrupt and then forces them to pay him off with everything they own. After forty-two years of patiently waiting for the perfect opportunity, the Rowens exact terrible revenge during the first year of the Civil War in the next section, "God's Great Supper." Two-thirds of this section is devoted to showing how the Rowens trick their landlord, Richard Talbert, into thinking that twenty-eight-year-old Jed is eager to join his Confederate forces. He joins so as to kill Talbert at an opportune time in some battle. While crossing a river on a raft, Jed shoves Richard into the water and drowns him. Jed then deserts the Confederate army and joins a dissolute guerrilla force led by William Clarke Quantrill that plunders its way across the country as far as Lawrence, Kansas. After being routed by the army, Jed gathers the six remaining men, returns home, and proceeds to slaughter the remaining male Talberts, destroy all their possessions, and plow salt into their best bottomland.

Although this is rousing theater, there are several problems with the story from a historical standpoint. Schenkkan uses the Civil War merely as the opportunity for the Rowens to settle a long-standing grudge against the Talberts, whereas, in fact, the war was the major cause of feuding. As mountainous border regions, West Virginia and eastern Kentucky were uniquely positioned to suffer from long-term effects of the war. Both armies plundered the region for food and in the process often inflamed local communities divided in their sympathies. Add to this volatile mixture numerous deserters and draft evaders who found the mountains a good place to lose themselves, and you have all the ingredients for explosive violence. As one historian said, "As bad as the presence of regular armies was, the mountain population suffered even more from guerilla warfare. The mountain region provided a haven for draft evaders and deserters, and groups of these men preyed upon the local population."[25]

Against this norm of outside deserters causing mayhem in the mountains, contrast Schenkkan's portrayal of Jed deserting the Confederate army to pillage places as far away as Kansas with Quantrill. In the midst of these and other gross historical misrepresentations, it appears to be a case of the pot calling the kettle black when Schenkkan has a smooth-talking visitor by the name of J.T. Wells criticize the Rowens for creating a heroic myth out of Jed's bandit days with Quantrill.[26]

Although there are four or five contenders, the section "Tall Tales" takes the prize for presenting the most false and damaging portrait of Appalachians, for it suggests that they lost control of their vast mineral wealth strictly through their own greed and treachery. Set at the Rowen farm in 1885, the section begins with an encounter between Jed Rowen's fourteen-year-old daughter, Mary Anne, and J.T. Wells, who introduces himself as a storyteller who grew up in nearby Breathitt County[27] J.T. Wells charms his way into the Rowen home as well as into Mary Anne's heart, and after an evening of storytelling, eating, and drinking, he offers to do something for them in return for their hospitality. That something turns out to be an offer to purchase their mineral rights for fifty cents an acre. After explaining the terms of the contract that gives the owner of the mineral rights "all the usual and ordinary mining rights," such as the right to excavate, build access roads, and use local water, J.T. Wells agrees to a dollar an acre. And Jed, feeling proud of his shrewd bargaining ability, signs with an X.

After this plausible beginning the section ends by violating history in several particularly offensive ways. At the end of the evening, Mary Anne escorts

J.T. to the road. As their good-byes evolve into a passionate embrace on the ground, Mary Anne's boyfriend, Tommy Jackson, enters and tries to kill J.T. Mary Anne intervenes, and, out of a mixture of gratitude, affection, and guilt, J.T. confesses that he had lied to her father about everything. The minerals Jed sold—thinking he was as "slick as goose shit"—are actually worth millions. And furthermore, the mining companies, he says, "cut down all your trees. Then they cut into the land, deep—start huntin' those deep veins diggin em out in their deep mines, dumpin' the crap they can't use in your streams, your wells, your fields, whatever! And when they're finished, after they've squeezed out every nickel, they just move on. Leaving your land colder and deader'n that moon up there."[28] In a brief epilogue to the section, an adult Mary Anne recollects that the companies arrived several years later and did just what J.T. had said they would. When they cut down her favorite oak, her sky fell in "moon'n stars'n all."[29]

Contrast J.T. Wells's confession in this last section with historical accounts of mining practices in the 1880s and the process by which coal companies and northern financiers acquired mineral rights. Most of the speculators and surveyors who visited the homes of mountaineers on behalf of people like John D. Rockefeller, were outsiders, often ex-military officers who had seen the vast timber and coal resources of the region during the war. The pioneer prospector in eastern Kentucky was Richard Broas, an engineer and former captain in the Union army, from New York City.[30] According to Ronald D Eller, in his study *Miners, Millhands, and Mountaineers* (1982), local speculators became almost as important after the mountaineers developed a hostility toward outsiders who often resorted to violence and shady legal tactics if they refused to sell their land or mineral rights. "By 1900," Eller says, "the land agent was as likely to be met with a rifle as a 'halloo,' and he would seldom be invited inside the cabin."[31] As speculators, local merchants and lawyers were effective because they truly believed that developing the resources of the region was the key to progress and prosperity.

In contrast, J.T. Wells is a local boy who knowingly betrays his own mountain people on behalf of outsiders and does so five years before locals had started to replace outside speculators. And instead of believing in what he does, he knows, for reasons not historically available to him, that mining will devastate the land. He tells Mary Anne that mining leaves "your land colder and deader'n that moon up there," yet this is a description of the consequences of strip mining of the 1950s and 1960s, not of deep shaft mining of the 1880s. Electric tools were not introduced until the late 1890s, and it wasn't until the 1950s that strip mining caused the devastation Schenkkan clearly had in mind when J.T. says "deader'n that moon up there." In the author's note, Schenkkan concludes his description of the strip mining he saw during his ten-hour tour with the sentence "It looked like the moon."[32] He uses the moon image again in the Bobbie

Ann Mason interview when he says, "It just looks like the fucking moon."[33] Why this portrait of a local boy whose inexplicable betrayal appears considerably more villainous because of this historical anachronism? Once again, Harry Caudill's gene theory appears to come into play. J.T. Wells betrays his fellow mountaineers because that is the sort of thing mountaineers are destined to do with their degenerate genetic inheritance.

The seventh section, "Fire in the Hole," set in a coal company camp in 1920, focuses chiefly on Mary Anne, her ten-year-old son Joshua, her husband Tommy Jackson, and Abe Steinman, a union organizer recently from West Virginia who boards with them. To Schenkkan's credit, this section gives a fairly clear sense of the brutal power the coal companies used in their attempt to control every aspect of the miner's life; however, it offends by portraying Appalachians as too ignorant to realize that their lives could be better and too acquiescent and fatalistic to resist without the inspiration and organizational skills of outsiders. For example, Mary Anne's ignorance of the cause of her son's fever is the necessary precondition of self-loathing and fatalism rather than anger and protest. She thinks she is a bad mother for allowing four previous children to die of fever and refuses to believe Abe Steinman when he blames the coal company and tells her the solution is to strike for better living conditions as the miners did in Paint Creek, West Virginia. With words that echo her epilogue of the previous scene, Mary Anne explains that she can't believe in such things because "they tore my stars down a long time ago. Stars and moon and all."[34] These phrases indicate that her fatalism is less a function of oppressive coal camp conditions than of her father's foolhardy decision to sell his mineral rights, the loss of which brought about the destruction of her favorite oak that held her sky and world in place as a child. Family and genetics again eclipse social and historical explanations for behavior.

A mine explosion that kills twenty-three finally gives Abe Steinman the opportunity to convince reluctant miners to form a union. His role is absolutely central to the entire process. Even after the explosion he has to persuade them that a union would help, and then he has to show them how to organize each step of the way. The section ends with Abe dying a hero's death in a plot arranged by Tommy Jackson. When Tommy's betrayal is discovered, he is banished, and the women, under the leadership of Mary Anne, resume the struggle, inspired by Abe's stories of Mother Jones.

This story of courageous outsiders instructing and inspiring ignorant and passive miners has so little bearing on what happened in the coal fields in the 1920s that I am puzzled about what Schenkkan read during the two to three years he did research. Numerous books and articles, written in the past thirty years, document the militancy of miners from the 1890s to the present. The period after World War I until 1933 (when Congress passed the National Industrial

Recovery Act, which gave unions legal protection) was particularly violent with guerrilla warfare and minibattles occurring frequently throughout the entire mining region.[35] Miners accepted the help of outsiders such as Mother Jones, who was more a cheerleader than an organizer and educator; yet on the whole, they didn't depend on anybody to tell them that they were oppressed and what to do about it.[36] In 1920, only forty or fifty miles from Schenkkan's vision of ignorant quiescence, all of Mingo County, West Virginia, was at one point under the control of miners who had exploded in numerous wildcat strikes. The governor was forced to call in federal troops to help subdue them.[37]

Mary Anne's son, Joshua, grows up with union as family and becomes president of the United Mine Workers District 16. Section eight, as the title "Which Side Are You On" suggests, focuses on Joshua's complicity with mine owners on issues of safety. Schenkkan may have used UMWA presidents John L. Lewis and Tony Boyle, who were more interested in maintaining their power than in protecting the rights and safety of their miners, for his portrayal of the well-meaning but corrupt Joshua, whose betrayals and compromises are all the more disturbing coming from a local who proudly calls his mother the "Mother Jones of Howsen county."[38] The central conflict is between Joshua and his son Scotty, a recently appointed field rep for the union whose job is to collect grievances from the miners and report them to the president. While fighting in Korea, Scotty had vowed never to blindly follow orders again. His father tests this resolution when he orders Scotty not to pull men from an unsafe mine. Scotty decides to do so anyway and is killed in a massive mine explosion that leaves Joshua consumed with guilt. Joshua loses his son through an act of betrayal. It is significant that Scotty invokes his experience outside the mountains as the source of his moral strength to depart from the pattern.

The play effectively ends in 1954 with the death of Scotty. The last section, "The War on Poverty," is a brief coda that offers signs of hope and regeneration. It takes place in 1975 on the original Rowen homestead near Shilling Creek. The stage directions describe the setting as follows:

> The Schilling Creek is now full of silt and garbage and abandoned cars, and only occasionally rouses itself in memory of its former glory during one of those torrential thunderstorms that sometimes batter the plateau. The surrounding fields, heavily timbered and mined and then abandoned, have also accumulated their share of refuse over the years; but if you look closely, you can see that the land is slowly regenerating itself. Now it is mostly broom sedge and hard-rock, but here and there a young pine asserts itself. It is spring, after all, and the land, although bruised and battered, still remembers.[39]

The scene opens with Joshua describing a recurring dream. As a broken-down and unkempt man of sixty-five, he is "bruised and battered" like the land, yet his dream indicates that he is on the verge of experiencing a corresponding regeneration through sensitivity to the accumulated guilt of many generations. In his dream he crosses a desert and comes to a wide, deep river. On the other side a large group of people, including his father, mother, and son, stand yelling at him, telling him to do something, but he can't hear them. Although Joshua never consciously understands what his family and ancestors try to tell him in the dream, it's clear from the ensuing action that they want him to stop damaging the land and that in various mysterious ways he responds to their message and does the right thing.

The scene follows with two treasure hunters unearthing a small object covered with buckskin. A gunshot drives them off, and soon Joshua appears with a rifle, followed by the black businessman Franklin Biggs and the former mine owner James Talbert Winston. They have gathered to decide whether to sell the property to a coal company that intends to strip mine and level the surrounding mountains. With the nearby town of Morgan turned into a ghost town, the plan to build a hospital on the property had to be abandoned. James supports the sale and says, "Mountain top removal mining is fantastic—Gonna be the wave of the future," while Joshua, much to James's surprise and anger, is skeptical. Even though Joshua has spent his entire life living off coal, as James reminds him, he suddenly doesn't think strip mining is progress. Sensing a fight, Franklin leads James away as he yells, "To hell with him! Where does he get off with this holier'-n-thou attitude?"[40] Joshua then explains to Franklin that for several months he has been thinking about certain moments in the past: the inspirational union meeting they attended together as boys of eleven or twelve and the explosion that killed Scotty.

The pivotal confrontation occurs when James unearths a dead baby wrapped in buckskin covered with beautiful beadwork. James wants to sell the buckskin, while Joshua insists that they rebury the baby and forces James to comply at gunpoint. The voices in his dream have clearly been heard and appeased when Joshua convinces Franklin to consider blocking the sale of the land and then reburies the child. With these acts of atonement and respect for the land, the play concludes with a resurrection scene. The ground erupts and the figures of parents and children from the previous eight sections emerge and join Joshua. A wolf howls and he yells in "sheer joy and exultation."[41]

Ever since the 1980s, Americans have oscillated between viewing Appalachians as ignoble or noble savages, as backward and vicious barbarians or as the remnant of all that was pure and innocent about America in its early stages. It is far from coincidental that Appalachia was "discovered" as a frontier at about the time the real frontier disappeared, when the last Indian resistance was eliminated at Wounded Knee in 1890.[42] The Appalachian replaced the Indian as the savage needed to justify and define the imperatives of civilization.

Likewise, it is far from coincidental that Appalachia was discovered as the repository of wholesome American values and pure Anglo-Saxon blood at about the time immigrants from eastern Europe and from Mediterranean countries began pouring into America in the late 1890s.

One of the most famous articles ever written about Appalachia, "Our Contemporary Ancestors in the Southern Mountains," was written by William Goodell Frost, who was the president of Berea College in Berea, Kentucky. The article was published in the *Atlantic Monthly* in June 1899. By employing both images, Frost reveals more about his faith in progress and anxiety about immigration than the images do about Appalachia. Having noted the ignorance and backwardness of the mountaineer, he says, "Appalachian America may be useful as furnishing a fixed point which enables us to measure the progress of the moving world."[43] However, in the next paragraph he praises their pure strain of revolutionary patriotism that has persisted by virtue of having been protected from non-Saxon immigration: "As Appalachian America has received no foreign immigration, it now contains a larger proportion of 'Sons' and 'Daughters' of the Revolution than any other part of our country."[44] As Frost's phrase "fixed point" indicates, the demonized and romanticized images of Appalachia that emerged at the turn of the century share a common assumption: Appalachians never developed into fully mature adults. They are either bad children or good children.

In his analysis of how Appalachians appear on television, Horace Newcomb says "the real viciousness" of shows such as *The Andy Griffith Show*, *The Beverly Hillbillies*, and *Hee Haw* "is not that Hillbillies and Southerners are made fun of. It is that mountain people and Southerners are not considered part of the adult population of the country or of the culture."[45]

Schenkkan clearly intended the last section to suggest hope for change in the mountains, yet it is remarkable how once again he reinforces well-worn stereotypes: this time the Appalachian as noble savage or innocent child. He presents Appalachians as bad children in the first eight sections; therefore, it seems inevitable that he would switch to Appalachians as good children for his positive conclusion, the assumption throughout being that Appalachians are incapable of rational constructive behavior that arises from understanding and learning from their experience in the mountains.

What prompts Joshua's decision to block the sale of the land and thereby save it from being strip mined? Like the land that (as the stage directions say) "regenerates itself" and "still remembers," Joshua's change of heart is involuntary, natural, and mysterious. He becomes an agent of good only insofar as he becomes childlike and innocent and listens to the voices in his dreams and responds with delight to the appearance of a wolf. The Appalachian as actively and rationally engaged in preserving the environment is absent. And this is insulting to Kentuckians, especially in light of the past thirty years.

Since the mid-1960s Appalachians have undergone a renaissance of self-awareness and self-determination manifest in filmmaking, creative writing, folk festivals, and intensified political activism. One of their most notable successes on the environmental front occurred three years before *The Kentucky Cycle* was awarded the Pulitzer Prize. In 1989 the Kentucky state constitution was amended to prevent the owners of mineral rights from strip mining without the permission of the surface owner. Before that, if the mineral owners wanted to bulldoze someone's house, rip up graves, and remove the mountain in their backyard, there was nothing to stop them except angry, powerless citizens. The courts, at local and state levels, had consistently interpreted the provisions of the "broad form" deeds in the broadest possible way so that "the usual and ordinary mining rights" of the 1890s came to mean the right to strip mine, a practice introduced in the early 1950s. The image of a broken-down man in the middle of a field inspired by voices in a dream and the sight of a wolf has no relevance to the long struggle of Appalachians to control strip mining and preserve their environment.

Much could be said about why Schenkkan rediscovered the childish savagery and innocence of Appalachians in the 1980s. He did so for the same reasons many before him did. *The Kentucky Cycle* is a classic case of psychosocial projection. For the past one hundred years the rest of America has projected unwanted parts of itself, as well as a yearning for innocence, onto Appalachia. By scapegoating Appalachians as greedy, savage children wantonly destroying their environment, the rest of America can feel grown-up, responsible, and civilized. America's need to feel good about itself was particularly urgent in the 1980s—a decade notorious for spectacular acts of greed and regressive federal environmental policies. The grotesque irony of a southern Californian portraying Appalachians as greedy, destructive savages in the decade when California suffered the most acute social and environmental crises in the country, while eastern Kentucky achieved its greatest environmental successes, will be lost on America until it is prepared to recognize violence and greed in its own self-image. Until then, America will continue to need hillbillies.

## Notes

1. Robert Schenkkan, author's note in *The Kentucky Cycle* (New York: Penguin, 1993), 333, 334.
2. Bobbie Ann Mason, "Recycling Kentucky," *New Yorker*, Oct. 16, 1993, 54.
3. Ibid.
4. Ibid.
5. Schenkkan, author's note, 336, 337.

6. Mason, "Recycling Kentucky," 65.

7. Henry D. Shapiro, *Appalachia on Our Mind* (Chapel Hill: Univ. of North Carolina Press, 1978), 3.

8. Harry M. Caudill, *Watches of the Night* (Boston: Little, Brown, 1976), 8.

9. John Ed Pearce, "A Prize-Winning Slander," *Louisville Courier-Journal,* Oct. 5, 1993.

10. Gurney Norman, "*The Kentucky Cycle* Still Perplexes," *Lexington Herald-Leader,* June 6, 1993, D6.

11. George Ella Lyon, "Another Vicious Cycle," *Ace Magazine,* July 10, 1992.

12. Loyal Jones, *Lexington Herald-Leader,* Dec. 1993, T3.

13. Andrew Adler, "The Controversy," *Louisville Courier-Journal,* Nov. 14, 1993.

14. Mason, "Recycling Kentucky," 56.

15. Adler, "The Controversy."

16. Schenkkan, author's note, 337.

17. Harry M. Caudill, *Darkness at Dawn* (Lexington: Univ. Press of Kentucky, 1976), 36, 37.

18. Ibid., 37.

19. See Robert D. Mitchell, ed., *Appalachian Frontier: Settlement, Society, and Development in the Preindustrial Era* (Lexington: Univ. Press of Kentucky, 1991), 11; Rodger Cunningham, *Apples on the Flood* (Knoxville: Univ. of Tennessee Press, 1987), xxvii, xxix.

20. William A. Henry III, "America's Dark History," *Time,* Nov. 22, 1993, 72.

21. Schenkkan, *The Kentucky Cycle,* 34.

22. Dwight B. Billings and Kathleen M. Blee, "Appalachian Inequality in the Nineteenth Century: The Case of Beech Creek, Kentucky," *Journal of the Appalachian Studies Association* 4 (1992): 117; see also Marion B. Lucas, *A History of Blacks in Kentucky, vol. 1, From Slavery to Segregation, 1760–1891* (Frankfort: Kentucky Historical Society, 1992), xx, for the 1860 census figures that indicate that the average black population of the twenty-eight mountain counties was 4.6 percent; in *Slavery Times in Kentucky* (Chapel Hill: Univ. of North Carolina Press, 1940), 45, J. Winston Coleman Jr. says, "Agricultural pursuits were not so favorable in the eastern or mountainous sections of Kentucky, and the farmers were proportionately poor—many not able to own a single slave. What little work there was to be done, the mountaineers did themselves, or swapped work with their neighbors. Slavery among this class of mountain whites was almost unknown, and many of them rarely, if ever, saw a Negro, or had any contact with the slaveholders of the 'flat country' or cities, and were, therefore, little influenced by the institution."; Lowell H. Harrison, *The Antislavery Movement in Kentucky* (Lexington: Univ. Press of Kentucky, 1978), 4; John E. Kleber, ed., *The Kentucky Encyclopedia* (Lexington: Univ. Press of Kentucky, 1992), 827.

23. Arnold Toynbee, *A Study of History* (New York: Oxford Univ. Press, 1947), 311.

24. Ronald D Eller, *Miners, Millhands, and Mountaineers* (Knoxville: Univ. of Tennessee Press, 1982), xvi.

25. Gordon B. McKinnery, "Industrialization and Violence in Appalachia in the 1890s," in *An Appalachian Symposium,* ed. J.W. Williamson (Boone, N.C.: Appalachian State Univ. Press, 1997), 133.

26. Schenkkan, *The Kentucky Cycle*, 203.

27. Ibid., 175.

28. Ibid., 202–3.

29. Ibid., 206.

30. Eller, *Miners, Millhands*, 53.

31. Ibid., 57.

32. Schenkkan, author's note, 335.

33. Mason, "Recycling Kentucky," 54.

34. Schenkkan, *The Kentucky Cycle*, 231.

35. John Gaventa, *Power and Powerlessness: Quiescence and Rebellion in an Appalachian Valley* (Urbana: Univ. of Chicago Press, 1980), 117.

36. Mary Harris Jones, *The Autobiography of Mother Jones* (Chicago: Charles Kerr, 1990).

37. David Alan Corbin, *Life, Work, and Rebellion in the Coal Fields* (Urbana: Univ. of Illinois Press, 1987), 196.

38. Schenkkan, *The Kentucky Cycle*, 274.

39. Ibid., 315.

40. Ibid., 324.

41. Ibid., 332.

42. Michael Paul Rogin, *Fathers and Children: Andrew Jackson and the Subjugation of the American Indian* (New York: Alfred A. Knopf, 1975), 312.

43. William Goodell Frost, "Our Contemporary Ancestors in the Southern Mountains," *Atlantic Monthly* (June 1899): 313.

44. Ibid.

45. Horace Newcomb, "Appalachia on Television: Region as Symbol in American Popular Culture," *Appalachian Journal* 7, (autumn/winter 1979–80): 160.

# The View from the Castle

## Reflections on the
## *Kentucky Cycle* Phenomenon

### *Rodger Cunningham*

Just when Appalachian scholars, writers, and activists have begun to think that perhaps a quarter-century of their efforts had started to make some dent in public perception of their region, along comes *The Kentucky Cycle*. Robert Schenkkan's lengthy play cycle, inspired by a weekend visit to eastern Kentucky in 1981, won the Pulitzer Prize for 1992—the first play ever to do so without having yet opened in New York[1]—and though the play's reviews were mixed, it appears that little of the negative reaction on the part of non-Appalachians centered on the play's portrayal of mountain people. If anything, negative reviewers tended to regard Schenkkan as too far left for their tastes. Paradoxically, Schenkkan is a loudly self-proclaimed political progressive who says he intended his play as, among other things, an indictment of the industrial exploitation of the region. Nevertheless, as Appalachian commentators have noted, his work in fact adds to that exploitation.

This essay will not deal extensively with the defects of *The Kentucky Cycle* itself. These have been more than adequately dealt with by others[2]—its inept dialect, its historical and cultural inaccuracies,[3] and above all, its brutalizing and victim-blaming portrayal of mountain people (in spite of which Schenkkan says, "I reject so strenuously the idea of stereotype. . . . I feel quite bluntly that there is nothing in the play to bear that out. Nothing."[4] Rather, it is a study of the *Kentucky Cycle* phenomenon. It asks how such evidently sincere sympathy for the plight of Appalachia on Schenkkan's part could eventuate in such a damaging and disempowering portrait of its people. And it asks the related question of how such a picture can be taken at its own word as "progressive" by both the play's defenders and most of its critics in a liberal media culture which professes multiculturalism and universal sensitivity.

The *Kentucky Cycle* phenomenon is a particular case of a matter that has exercised Appalachians ad nauseam since at least the sixties: Why does sensitivity include everyone but mountain people? The answer has much to do with Schenkkan's chief ways of attempting to justify his work. Repeatedly and aggrievedly, as if it answered all objections, he claims that he is not writing about eastern Kentucky or Appalachia in particular at all, but rather, he is using Appalachia as "a metaphor for America." In the first place, however, this would not eliminate the objections regardless of what group or region he were writing about. "Metaphorical" is not the opposite of "accurate," as Schenkkan seems to think, judging from his use of the word as an excuse for all his work's failures of specificity. In his naive opposition between the "metaphorical" and the "documentary,"[5] Schenkkan's metaphorization becomes derealization. He paints Appalachians with a brush as broad as that road that is paved with good intentions. Of course Appalachia illuminates America, but Schenkkan's confused approach achieves the opposite of illuminating either America or Appalachia.[6]

In the second place, of course, there are special pitfalls involved in treating Appalachia in particular as a metaphor of America. All stereotypes are already unconscious metaphors for aspects of their perpetrators, and "America" has long used Appalachia as a projection-screen for the unacceptable[7] parts of itself. The identity of Appalachians as descendants (in large part) of the original settlers, as quintessentially "American" but somehow also peculiarly "other"—as "contemporary ancestors," in W.G. Frost's notorious phrase—only accentuates that projective tendency. It makes members of the dominant culture less able to see that they are in fact victimizing a particular group of people in the process, as much so as when they label any other group.[8] And it allows well-intentioned members of that dominant culture to feel free to "speak for" that presumably silent group—and hence to collaborate in its silencing—in a way that is now quite properly felt to be unacceptable for any other group. And this is what Schenkkan has done.

Appalachia is not a metaphor for America; Appalachia *is* America. Its relation to America is not one of metaphor to "reality," but of part to whole. However, it has long been treated as a land "apart" by those who fail to see oppression as "a part" of the U.S. and global systems. Schenkkan tries to engage this fact, but he does not do so on a level that seriously challenges it. Appalachia is not, in Schenkkan's tired sixties-developmentalist phrase, "'a failure of the American dream,'"[9] but a dialectical aspect of that dream. Schenkkan seems to flail around in the direction of this insight, but he never adequately grasps it. It takes a more developed political consciousness than Schenkkan's work has shown for one to keep one's metaphorizing from willy-nilly following the grooves created by flows of power. Schenkkan claims to be pointing the finger at America for what it has done to Appalachia, but his gaze is so misdirected that in fact he ends up simply pointing Appalachia to its place on the margins.

Thus, even if Schenkkan's concept of metaphor were not so inadequate to begin with, his use of it is fatally conditioned by his positioning with regard to flows and structures of power and his passivity with regard to these. Schenkkan is only a passive reflector of those flows and structures, a lucky exploiter, and a naive victim-turned-perpetrator. The case of his play, therefore, throws light on those wider flows and structures.

In exploring these matters, we may first look at Schenkkan's positioning within them as the child of upper-middle-class academic transients—members of the "New Class" of knowledge workers[10]—who slid west across the Sunbelt and fetched up in California (where, incidentally, this writer spent four years, not two days, and where he was in fact in the middle of writing the first draft of *Apples on the Flood* when Schenkkan made his fateful visit to that book's subjects). If anything is a metaphor for America, California is. Indeed, it is quite deliberately so on the part of many of its inhabitants. It is separated from most of the rest of the country by mountain and desert as America is separated from Europe by ocean, and its mystique of the Western Isle of Gold duplicates the early myth of America itself. It is full of immigrants from the East who moved there to solve their problems and only brought them along in denied form— people who wanted to escape "America" and ended up reproducing it twice over (just as Schenkkan is trying to escape American exploitation of Appalachia and only ends up joining in it). The resulting culture seems stuck to the landscape as if it might slide off and is prevented from doing so only by wishing it to be there. The hallmark of that culture is an individualism that identifies freedom with the right to act as if no other human beings existed.[11] In politics, this leads to an antistatist philosophy of "individual freedom" based on a sheer dichotomy between the state and the individual that veils the real control over people's lives exerted by corporate industry and media. In the society fostered by that culture and that politics, class is so obfuscated by racism that new-class Californians are always amazed to learn that other white people can "live that way," although in fact many do so right under their noses.

California, in short, is the America of America, a land where *everything* is metaphorical—unreal, penciled in, stuck on. Schenkkan says his themes are the myth of the Frontier and of Escape; these pervade California's mentality to the point of being *the* California myths. And they foster the derealization that corrupts Schenkkan's sense of metaphor. In a different way, Appalachia is also the America of America. Thus Appalachia and California are strange brothers, related to each other via two strong but divergent positionings with regard to America—strong but divergent in economic relationship and in imaginative relationship. As Appalachia is America's shadow, California is its narcissistic ego-ideal. Hence, Schenkkan's position induces him doubly to see Appalachia as "a metaphor of America," for America is a metaphor (of) itself. As Appalachia is middle-class America's shadow, it is doubly that of new-class California. And in *The Kentucky Cycle*, Schenkkan, longing for roots and at the same time fearing them, deals with these personal and collective shadows by projective identification, the fount of all stereotyping.[12]

As Schenkkan is positioned by region and class to have a certain relationship to Appalachia, so he is conditioned by his typical California new-class, new-age greenish beliefs. California is the most urbanized state in terms of population, but it is also among the "emptiest" in terms of proportion of area. This dichotomy of roaring cities and howling wilderness lays the groundwork for a great many of its residents' other attitudes. California-style environmentalists tend to look on human works as a blot on a pristine landscape made to be viewed only through the refined eyes of new-class appreciators. One senses more than a whiff of this attitude in Schenkkan. He dismisses his critics with talk of "the need to transcend our 'us-versus-them' attitudes. 'All of us are part of this gestalt, this living organism, this biosphere'"[13] This truth does not engage the criticism but rather attempts to evade it by invoking a level of discourse irrelevant to it. It does not engage Appalachian reality, or human reality at all, on any level pertinent to the matters of people's lives, with which Schenkkan attempts to deal. By invoking these truths in this context, he cloaks his writing in a spurious universalism to justify (to himself and others) its misappropriations. One recognizes in this attitude that of the new-class Californian described by Joel Kovel, who

> joins the Sierra Club, and protests against the desecration of her beautiful coast by offshore oil drilling. She might even join a campaign against the use of pesticides on her table grapes. What will likely elude her, however, is the sum set of the transformations of nature, mediated by crushing labor of billions of others, which puts food on her table and clothes on her back. . . . In sum, there is essentially no connection between life activity and the transformation of nature which is the material root of life. With no lived connection, consciousness cannot apprehend the humanity of nature, that is to say, the dominated labor which has in fact built the world. Nature remains wilderness, scenery: a surpassing Otherness toward which all spiritual ambitions are submerged into pseudo-universality without any recognition of the human form embedded within.[14]

Ward Churchill described a similar phenomenon in connection with new-age appropriations of the Native American heritage. Such people, he notes,

> would vehemently disavow the historical processes of physical genocide and expropriation. . . . In their own minds, they are typically steadfast opponents

of all such policies and the ideologies of violence which undergird them. . . . There can be no question that they've convinced themselves that they are divorced completely from the ugly flow of American history.

. . . While the New Age can hardly be accused rationally of performing the conquest of the Americas, and its adherents go to great lengths in expressing their dismay at the methods used therein, they have clearly inherited what their ancestors gained by conquest, both in terms of resources and in terms of relative power. Their task, then, is simultaneously to hang on to what has been stolen while separating themselves from the *way* in which it was stolen. . . . The project is essentially ideological.[15]

It is from this ideological perspective that Schenkkan approaches Appalachia. In his weekend trip to eastern Kentucky, he was taken deliberately on a "consciousness-raising" tour of contrasts, from the poorest to the richest, from quick drop-ins on various dirt-poor families to a substantial stay with a mine owner in his split-level, perched on a mountaintop like a castle. Though professing to be appalled by the mine owner's callousness toward the poverty around him,[16] he plainly only rejected the castle dweller's views while unconsciously sharing his viewpoint—the viewpoint of someone who is in denial about the sources of his own comfortable living. When Schenkkan returned to California, he started looking for explanations of what he had seen. The quest was plainly well-intentioned, but it was evidently purely bookish, entirely self-directed, and conducted at a two thousand–mile distance. With his view from such a distance, as filtered through the double castle window of ruling-class eastern Kentucky and new-class southern California, it is hardly surprising that he ended up relying heavily on a single informant: the late Harry Caudill.

Caudill was a great pioneer in bringing attention to the region's problems, but a pioneer is what he was, and in many ways he never moved beyond the terms of his own beginning. For all the good he did over three decades, his own sympathies were notoriously compromised by his own class position. And Caudill's most deeply compromised ideas are precisely those on which Schenkkan relies most heavily. Schenkkan's class position is resonant with Caudill's; the windows of Caudill's expansive house high above Whitesburg fit before Schenkkan's eyes as neatly as do those of the coal operator's he visited nearby.[17]

Caudill's contemptuous view of the bulk of his neighbors is part of the worldwide colonial phenomenon of the "nationalist bourgeoisie" that retains the idea of the "lazy native."[18] And his final despairing pessimism, besides stemming from his underestimation of mountain people in general, is also in a subtler way an ideological justification of his own class domination. His vision of the mountains as finally stripped of people inscribes the absence of the people's real existence from his consciousness in the first place.[19] And

Schenkkan's use of Caudill reinscribes all these deficiencies, largely in the absence of Caudill's compensating strengths.

By the time Schenkkan wrote, other views were available—especially to anyone as politically progressive as he claims to be—but he seems never to have encountered them. Indeed, Schenkkan hardly seems to realize that Appalachia has its own voices apart from Caudill's; that Appalachians are perfectly capable of telling their own story and have done so, repeatedly, to the nearly deaf ears of "America." This is related to another way Schenkkan resembles Caudill: his total inability to see the very point of his critics' objections. His statements in defense of his work are an exercise in missing the implications of his own discoveries. He supposes that anyone who criticizes his treatment of Appalachia's problems is denying the problems' existence; he cannot imagine that anyone could have a clearer, deeper view of them than he does. Anyone who can accuse Gurney Norman of being in cahoots with Peabody Coal and Standard Oil [*sic*][20] is plainly unaware of the very existence of most current Appalachian thought and writing. Hence he asks of his artistic purpose, with breathtaking naïveté: "'If I don't do that, who will? If writers don't begin that process, who will?'"[21] He utterly appropriates the representation of Appalachia in art—and "America" is all too ready to collude with him in that appropriation. As Joel Kovel says, the New Class is "the central industrial force of late capitalism, that devoted to information";[22] thus, though he would no doubt be appalled to realize it, Schenkkan's appropriation is an updated version of the industrial rape he decries. As Kovel also says, the New Class is "on the cutting edge of the New Age spiritual movements,"[23] and thus Schenkkan's work is another case of how, as Churchill notes, the New Age ideology is thoroughly implicated in the takeover by the colonizer of the production of "knowledge" of and about the colonized.[24] Schenkkan's appropriation of Appalachia as a "metaphor" of America is an exercise in justifying his own appropriation, as an American, of Appalachia's voice. That is, his claim that Appalachia "represents" America in this way implies a claim that he himself is able to "represent" Appalachia in the way he attempts.[25] If his concept of metaphor were more valid, so would be his personal claim; but it is not so. Schenkkan is trying to separate himself from being an "American" by projecting what he detests (quite properly, I think) about "America" on a safely powerless and voiceless, or effectively silenced, group—a group silenced by "America" itself in the person of Schenkkan's class. He is trying to have his cake and eat it too,[26] to reject the claim to power while keeping the power itself—especially the power of representation.

This deafness to the voice of Appalachia's thinkers and writers is, however, inevitable in someone who cannot attribute human consciousness to Appalachians in general except by a sort of freak occurrence. Speaking of the action of one of his characters at the very end of the play, in refusing to rob an Indian grave, Schenkkan says, "He does not understand why he takes a stand where he does. . . . He . . . couldn't understand and couldn't possibly explain [it] to anyone else."[27] This is all in the course of describing his theme as "the forces at work on these people . . . and through them."[28] Schenkkan, in short, sees mountain people entirely from the outside, and hence not as people at all. He thus unwittingly deprives them not only of voice but of all agency except insofar as they accept his terms. He takes toward them the typical colonial attitude that he understands the natives better than they understand themselves, and hence can represent them better than they can represent themselves. He denies that his work is stereotypical on the specific ground that it is not "sentimental" and that the characters are "much too complicated" to be stereotypes—complicated, that is, in terms of the "forces at work on" them. Indeed, by saying that the work "avoids sentimentality" he *means* specifically that the character in question "is unaware of" his own motivations.[29] All that this establishes, of course, is Schenkkan's own narrow, even eccentric, notion of the "stereotypical" (and of the "sentimental") and his utter lack of critical consciousness of the ideological presuppositions that complexly structure his own simpleminded, unaware use of stereotype.

For in fact it is Schenkkan himself who lacks a clear consciousness of what he is doing and of the forces acting on and through his own consciousness. He speaks of his character taking "personal responsibility"[30] at the end, but Schenkkan takes no responsibility himself for Appalachia's situation. It is his own quintessentially American denial that is, in his words, "'as deep as any vein of anthracite [*sic*] in Eastern Kentucky.'"[31] He seems entirely unaware of the system he is involved in, the "embroiled medium"[32] in which art is produced and accepted. His kind of sympathy and indignation, however sincere, is as inadequate to escape that system as his kind of knowledge is inadequate even to depict the situation. He decries industrial exploitation, but he says not a word about the media and literary exploitation that goes along with it—that follows the flows of semiosis that accompany the flows of power—for he is part of it and too far inside it to see it. He does not see that his approach is colonial because it assumes a difference in power, namely his own self-assumed power of representation ("If I don't do that, who will?").

*USA Today,* quoted on the back cover of *The Kentucky Cycle,* compares the play to *Dances with Wolves* in its "revisionist stance toward U.S. history"; and like *Dances with Wolves, The Kentucky Cycle* represents only a pseudocritical movement within the structure of dominance. Both works mythicize to cast a pall of inevitability over the destruction they deplore.[33] *The Kentucky Cycle* goes *Dances with Wolves* one worse, though, in centering that inevitability in the supposed defective characters of the victims themselves.

What gives the plainest lie to Schenkkan's claims that his play is not stereotypical is its treatment of Appalachian violence. Schenkkan's writing displays the same morbid fascination with that violence as has that of every local color writer from John Fox Jr. onward. Tongue-clucking attitudes toward violence have, of course, always been typical of the sort of people who do not have to use overt violence to get their way at the cost of other people's lives, and such attitudes are especially important for stereotyping in virtually all colonial situations. And though Schenkkan claims that his work demythologizes history, his work's treatment of violence is essentially mythical and ahistorical. To begin with, he evidently accepts Caudill's scum-of-London theory of Appalachian origins. In Schenkkan's hands this is plainly a projection of ruling-class fear and loathing of today's urban underclass. But at any rate, Appalachian violence (like inner-city violence) is the result of American violence—and more important, it is not only an example or metaphor of American violence, but a specific result of violent structures (both historical and present) set up by those who claim to despise violence.[34] Schenkkan is himself part of such a structure, but he is mystified by it into supposing that he can free himself from responsibility for it by simply proclaiming that he disapproves of its results. All this does is consolidate the position of his work as part of the problem.

Schenkkan, in short, does not understand the effect of unequal power relationships on his own perceptions—does not understand "how much the experience of the stronger party overlaps with, and, strangely, depends on the weaker."[35] But this relation is just what is reflected and reproduced in Schenkkan's confused notion of "metaphor." Once more, he does not understand that Appalachia's connection with America is not just metaphorical, or even exemplary, but causal. It is Schenkkan's failure to see this that degrades his well-meaning representation from true metaphor to projective identification. To be sure, he asserts that he is describing something "we" all share; but for all his good intentions, it still comes across only as a victim-blaming indictment of the weaker party. His play exemplifies the very "disassociation" he decries,[36] and thus he fails to see that the "poverty of the spirit . . . of the soul"[37] that he sees in Appalachia is a poverty of his art's own way of seeing, a function of its failure to make the right connections. It is Schenkkan himself, alas, who is the grave robber, using another people's history as a commodity for his own enrichment. The function of Appalachia in Schenkkan's artistic and professional ambitions is like the function of Appalachia in the U.S. and global economies—in fact it is an example, not just a parallel or metaphor, of the latter, in the "New World Information Order."[38] "Like everyone else," says Kovel, "members of the New Class have been thrown into history, and are free to transcend it or not";[39] but a characteristic of that class is its illusion(s) of transcendence, and Schenkkan shares those illusions to the full.

This thorough embeddedness in the national discourse of Appalachia explains how Schenkkan managed to get where he is today with a work characterized by such profound flaws, both political and aesthetic. If he had really succeeded in exposing "America" in the way he has attempted and claims to have succeeded at, his work would be so much more threatening to metropolitan audiences that it would hardly be greeted by horsey-set delicacies in the lobby,[40] let alone a Pulitzer. But in fact his work smoothly fits into the "frameworks of acceptance"[41] that reproduce the frameworks of power in the New World Information Order.

By whom, after all, is the Pulitzer awarded? By publishers and journalists. The interests of publishers are obvious enough. As for journalists, their interests are not only "material," but deeply involved in their own profoundly mystified sense of their identity and role.[42] There are individual exceptions, but the journalistic profession as a whole depends for its sense of its identity on a blindness to the forces acting on discourse in general and its own discourse in particular. Any admission that the framework of its utterances is imbricated with the framework of power would probably constitute such a breach of "objectivity" that someone whose awareness had reached that point would have trouble surviving journalism school.[43] At any rate, as Noam Chomsky repeatedly points out, the structural function of the so-called adversary culture of journalists is to define a pseudocritical line beyond which all criticism is deemed illegitimate. Schenkkan's pseudocritical attitude and his response to genuine criticism of it form such a perfect match for these journalistic attitudes that his success was virtually ensured.

Schenkkan is apparently not long for California. At last report he was moving up the coast to Seattle: "'I need more green in my life'" It was the green that particularly struck him on his visit to eastern Kentucky,[44] but he has no thought of moving there, of course; Appalachia is a land where no one actually lives, or should. One cannot live in a "metaphor." Besides, he has Harry Caudill's word for it that Appalachia's green is utterly doomed to be swallowed up by the lunar landscape of strip mining that also stunned his eyes. So he is relocating to a part of the country where the stripping is less obvious to the sensitive eye: where the salmon fisheries have closed for the year, where communities are filing for disaster-area status, and where the workers in the lumber industry (many of them of Appalachian origin) are finding their livelihoods squeezed out of existence between the depredations and manipulations of their employers and the contempt of a kind of "environmentalist" who is equally blinded by class interest. There will be plenty of green after the loggers and fishermen and even the stump farmers are starved out, of course. In the meantime, as they lift their eyes now and again to see the voluptuaries circling overhead, they may glimpse among them the hovering form of Robert Schenkkan, perhaps sniffing out a new metaphor.

# Notes

1. The *London Economist*, noting this fact, called the prize "a triumph for America's regional theatre," perhaps under the impression that the play was a Kentucky creation—certainly giving that impression.

2. Jim Wayne Miller, "The Kentucky (Re)Cycle," *Appalachia Heritage* 21 (spring 1993): 59–66; John Alexander Willians, "Appalachia Revisited," *Southern Theatre* 35(3): 12–14 (1994).

3. Williams has shown that Schenkkan's picture of eastern Kentucky rakes together events and situations from all over Appalachia and the upper South, especially West Virginia, and that Schenkkan's use of his sources sometimes displays what can be politely called a strong intertextuality.

4. Williams, "Appalachia Revisited," 13. Robert Schenkkan and John Filiatreau, "The Playwright's Side," *Louisville Magazine* 44 (Nov. 1993): 43.

5. Bobbie Anne Mason, "Recycling Kentucky," *New Yorker* 69 (Nov. 1, 1993): 50–62.

6. T.S. Eliot also chose a particular group to use as a "metaphor" of what he saw wrong with the entire twentieth century. When Schenkkan and I were in school, many of our teachers still thought that this "metaphorical" usage excused lines like "The rats are underneath the piles. / The jew [*sic*] is underneath the lot." What does Schenkkan think about that, I wonder?

7. Or idealized, of course—no basic improvement, in spite of Henry Shapiro; cf. Rodger Cunningham, *Apples on the Flood: Minority Discourse and Appalachia* (Knoxville: Univ. of Tennessee Press, 1987), 119–22).

8. I have discussed this matter in detail in *Apples on the Flood*, especially 113–16.

9. Schenkkan in Mason, "Recycling Kentucky," 56.

10. By the New Class I mean what Joel Kovel calls "the class defined by an allegiance to modernity made possible by control of technical means of power . . . the central industrial force of late capitalism, that devoted to information." *History and Spirit: An Inquiry into the Philosophy of Liberation* (Boston: Beacon, 1991), 204.

11. Philip Slater, *The Pursuit of Loneliness: American Culture at the Breaking Point* (Boston: Beacon, 1971), 131. This is Slater's characterization of all Americans, but Slater is a native Californian.

12. Robert Schenkkan, author's note in *The Kentucky Cycle* (New York: Plume, 1993), 336–37. This does not mean, of course, that Californians, or any other "outsiders," are automatically disqualified from writing sensibly about Appalachia. One need only think of Archie Green and Stephen W. Foster. The difference is that the latter have a conscious, rational, transferential relationship to the archetypes that California and Appalachia share in such different modes. Schenkkan's approach fails of this, and thus its dealings with those archetypes remain on the purely projective level. I owe to Dominick LaCapra the distinction between projective and transferential modes of personal engagement with history. *History and Criticism* (Ithaca, N.Y.: Cornell Univ. Press, 1985), 124.

13. Mason, "Recycling Kentucky," 56.

14. Kovel, *History and Spirit*, 206–7.

15. Ward Churchill, *Fantasies of the Master Race: Literature, Cinema, and the Colonization of the American Indian,* ed. M. Annette Jaimes (Monroe, Maine: Common Courage, 1992), 209–10.

16. Mason, "Recycling Kentucky," 52–54.

17. Steve Fisher's critique of Caudill could apply well to Schenkkan: "[H]is crusade must be judged in terms of how much it empowers people; does it tell us what we need to know to build the world we want to live in, or does it merely satiate our search for villains?" "As the World Turns: The Melodrama of Harry Caudell," *Appalachian Journal* 11 (1984): 268–73.

18. Edward W. Said, *Culture and Imperialism* (New York: Knopf, 1993), 249; cf. Ronald D Eller "Harry Caudill and the Burden of Mountain Liberalism," in *Critical Essays in Appalachian Life and Culture: Proceedings of the Fifth Annual Appalachian Studies Conference,* ed. Rick Simon (Boone, N.C.: Appalachian Consortium Press, 1982), 21–29.

19. I am indebted to Tal Stanley for pointing this out to me. Letter to the author, June 20, 1994.

20. Mason, "Recycling Kentucky," 62.

21. Schenkkan in Mason, "Recycling Kentucky," 56.

22. Kovel, *History and Spirit,* 204.

23. Ibid.

24. Churchill, *Fantasies of the Master Race,* 211.

25. It is impossible not to think of the quotation from Marx that Edward Said used as an epigraph to *Orientalism:* (New York: Random, 1979), xiii: "They cannot represent themselves; they must be represented."

26. A phrase used of Schenkkan's audience by John Alexander Williams, whose article I had not read when I wrote this passage. "Appalachia Revisited," 13.

27. Schenkkan and Filiatreau, "Playwright's Side," 43.

28. Ibid.

29. Ibid.

30. Ibid.

31. Mason, "Recycling Kentucky," 56.

32. George Eliot, quoted in Said, *Culture and Imperialism,* 194.

33. Cf. Churchill, *Fantasies of the Master Race,* 245.

34. As I have shown in *Apples on the Flood,* this pattern appears among the North British ancestors of many Appalachians as far back as the High Middle Ages, the very dawn of modernity. If Schenkkan really wanted to represent Appalachian settler history from the beginning, he would have begun not in 1775 but (at the latest) in 1717, when large numbers of North Britons began arriving in America at the invitation of their Ulster countryman James Logan, a convert to Quakerism and the provincial secretary of Pennsylvania. Logan's explicit purpose was to settle "Scotch-Irishmen" along the frontier—far from decent, civilized Quakers—to defend the latter against the Indians. In short, Quaker society encouraged North Britons to behave in ways Quakers officially disapproved of. (Quaker pacifism was not, incidentally, a part of the religion from the beginning. George Fox, in fact, had urged Cromwell to march on Rome. It was after the Restoration, when all dissenting sects were suspected of harboring plans for

violent subversion, that the Quaker leadership suddenly discovered that it disapproved of violence altogether.) In this case, as I have said elsewhere, the Quakers wanted "to commit violence against Native Americans without actually performing it—to have the violence done by agents who would at the same time be despised and expelled from the company of their betters [in] a literal, physical, socially externalized act of repression, projection, and denial toward a social group that stood for a [literally, historically] rejected part of the Quaker psyche [and ideology]." "Second and Third Thoughts on Albion's Seed," *Appalachian Journal* 19 (1991): 175.

This drama between dominant Quakers and marginal North Britons was played out on an individual scale in an incident in the writer's own family history, when my great-great-great-grandparents defended against Shawnee attack (or rather counterattack, pursuant to the assassination of Cornstalk) a Quaker who did nothing to help until his own daughter was wounded, so that "he was indebted for the preservation of his life, to the assistance of those whom he refused to aid in pressing need." Alexander Scott Withers, *Chronicles of Border Warfare*, ed., Reuben Gold Thwaites (Parsons, W.Va.: McClaim, 1989), 238–40, quote on 240. *Plus ça change . . .*

35. Said, *Culture and Imperialism,* 192.

36. Schenkkan, author's note, 337.

37. Ibid.

38. Said, *Culture and Imperialism,* 291.

39. Kovel, *History and Spirit,* 204.

40. Mason, "Recycling Kentucky," 56.

41. Kenneth Burke, quoted in Said, *Culture and Imperialism,* 303.

42. The first time I read the statement that journalists believed they were writing the first draft of history, I laughed; I thought it was a satirical remark, and a very on-target one, against journalistic pretensions. Only later did I discover with some horror that it is commonly said among journalists themselves in self-praise. In Appalachian studies, Altina Waller, writing of the Hatfield-McCoy feud, exposed in detail the deficiencies of the kind of history that takes journalists' accounts as its first draft. Most of us, at any rate, can think of our own examples. *Hatfield, McCoys, and Social Change in Appalachia, 1860–1900* (Chapel Hill: Univ. of North Carolina Press, 1988).

43. This explains the paradox that the so-called media-liberal "adversary culture" has joined with the right in a fierce assault on academe under the bugaboo banner of "political correctness." To be sure, some on the academic left do seem determined to illustrate Milton's rueful discovery that "*New Presbyter* is but *Old Priest* writ large." But what is really at stake here is the challenge posed by academics' critiques of knowledge and power to journalists' naive-realist copy theory (no pun intended) of representation and to the role for journalists that it implies.

44. Mason, "Recycling Kentucky," 51. Yes, and less brown too, one suspects.

## Bibliography

In addition to being indebted to the written works noted below, I have taken inspiration from various conversations with Archie Green, Jim Wayne Miller, Gurney Norman, and John Alexander Williams, as well as from the plenary session on *The Kentucky Cycle* that opened the 1994 Appalachian Studies Conference. All inaccuracies and defects are, of course, my own responsibility. Not cited directly but also present in my thinking were, among others, Allen Batteau's *The Invention of Appalachia* and Murray Bookchin's *The Ecology of Freedom, The Modern Crisis,* and *Toward an Ecological Society.*

Churchill, Ward. *Fantasies of the Master Race: Literature, Cinema, and the Colonization of the American Indian.* Edited by M. Annette Jaimes. Monroe, Maine: Common Courage, 1992.

Cunningham, Rodger. *Apples on the Flood: Minority Discourse and Appalachia.* Knoxville: Univ. of Tennessee Press, 1987.

———. "Second and Third Thoughts on *Albion's Seed.*" *Appalachian Journal* 19 (1991): 173–76.

Eller, Ronald D. "Harry Caudill and the Burden of Mountain Liberalism." In *Critical Essays in Appalachian Life and Culture: Proceedings of the Fifth Annual Appalachian Studies Conference.* Edited by Rick Simon, 21–29. Boone, N.C.: Appalachian Consortium Press, 1982.

Fisher, Steve. "As the World Turns: The Melodrama of Harry Caudill." *Appalachian Journal* 11 (1984): 268–73.

Frost, William Goodell. "Our Contemporary Ancestors in the Southern Mountains." *Atlantic Monthly* 83 (1899): 311–19.

"Grim but Good." *Economist,* Nov. 6, 1993, 117.

Kovel, Joel. *History and Spirit: An Inquiry into the Philosophy of Liberation.* Boston: Beacon, 1991.

LaCapra, Dominick. *History and Criticism.* Ithaca, N.Y.: Cornell Univ. Press, 1985.

Mason, Bobbie Ann. "Recycling Kentucky." *New Yorker* 69, Nov. 1, 1993, 50–62.

Miller, Jim Wayne. "The Kentucky (Re) Cycle." *Appalachian Heritage* 21 (spring 1993): 59–66.

———. "A Kentucky Travesty?" *Louisville Magazine* 44, Nov. 1993, 40–44.

Said, Edward W. *Culture and Imperialism.* New York: Knopf, 1993.

———. *Orientalism.* 1978. New York: Random, 1979.

Schenkkan, Robert. Author's note in *The Kentucky Cycle,* 333–38. New York: Plume, 1993.

———. *The Kentucky Cycle.* New York: Plume, 1993.

———, and John Filiatreau. "The Playwright's Side." *Louisville Magazine* 44 (Nov. 1993): 42–43.

Slater, Philip. *The Pursuit of Loneliness: American Culture at the Breaking Point.* 1970. Boston: Beacon, 1971.

Stanley, Tal. Letter to the author, June 20, 1994.

Waller, Altina L. *Feud: Hatfields, McCoys, and Social Change in Appalachia, 1860–1900.* Chapel Hill: Univ. of North Carolina Press, 1988.

Williams, John Alexander. "Appalachia Revisited." *Southern Theatre* 35(3): 12–14 (1994).

Withers, Alexander Scott. *Chronicles of Border Warfare.* 1831. Edited by Reuben Gold Thwaites, 1895. Parsons, W.Va.: McClain, 1989.

# Regional Consciousness and Political Imagination

## The Appalachian Connection in an Anxious Nation

### *Herbert Reid*

When I was about eighteen years old and a student in the Kansas University Library I discovered the history of racial lynching in the United States, especially in my native South. In 1956 my political education was accelerating in response to the Montgomery bus boycott led by Rosa Parks, E.D. Nixon, and Martin Luther King Jr., whose assassination twelve years later was to affect me more than that of either Kennedy. The next year I was stunned by the failure of national political leadership combined with the crass political opportunism of an Arkansas mountaineer governor that led to "Little Rock." But in 1956 I was beginning to formulate ideas of "democracy" and "justice" as my high school "cherry tree" story of America began to decompose in the history of labor struggles, lynchings, and so forth. While my family history as a WASP in the mountain South included a story of "Cherokee blood," I never feared being lynched. America does not hang its "hillbillies"—it laughs at them—although sometimes their alleged natural violence is an object of scornful concern.

I was an undergraduate in the 1950s when middle-class culture rattled with notions of "the American way of life." In the next couple of decades, one of the keywords of hegemonic discourse was the "American mainstream." It has become almost an academic commonplace to say that the forging of such an identity in our society is a process preoccupied with containing and controlling Otherness. When my small-town Kansas high school class graduated in 1955, we were sent out to become part of the great American "Success" story. The business manager addressing our commencement exercise employed the word "Progress" at least fifty times. Our capitalist society's narrative requirement of "Success" and "Progress" also generates stereotypes and stories of "failure" and "backwardness." The violence, real and sublimated, of this process of accumulation and redistribution would seem to require diversion through stereotypes that scapegoat by, for example, regionalizing and reifying public attention.

Our capitalist economy tends to generate constituencies that have no legitimate role or place. It would seem that such constituencies are culturally and politically marked for punishment. In such an economy the control of social violence might depend on sacrificial offerings that could reinforce order by containing and channeling the threat of contagion. After Foucault and Girard, we have begun to understand institutionally mandated corporeal disciplines for mediating and/or negotiating the social organization of desire. It is a myth to assume that a society mandates the same economy of desire for everyone or its various groups. Such economies are socially constituted and shaped in the process by historical and current patterns of violence and scapegoating.

"Marines Search Somalis' Homes for Arms but Find 'Hatfields and McCoys.'" This was the headline for a *New York Times* story on February 16, 1993.[1] It is a familiar American theme that depicts a matter of violence in terms of a ready-at-hand regional frame. Never mind that the "Harper's Index" for the February 1993 issue of *Harper's* also indicated, "Rank of the United States, among all countries, in arms sales to Somalia since 1985: 1."[2] Twenty years ago, Wilma Dykeman pointed out the pattern since the late nineteenth century:

> While robber barons were fleecing the people of public lands and treasured resource, while big city bosses and rural demagogues were subverting the essential democratic processes, while chain-gang labor enriched certain treasuries and lynching of blacks violated every sanction of law and order, national readers were invited to believe that moonshine stills and family feuds made Appalachia a unique example of lawlessness. Actually, violence was as American as apple pie—whether it was exemplified by a "splendid little war" in the Philippines, by John Dillinger, or by the Hatfields and McCoys. The variance in social acceptability seemed to be determined in part by the economic status of the participants and by the public enormity of the violence.[3]

As one of the regional critics of *The Kentucky Cycle,* Dykeman noted in her December 5, 1993, review for the *Knoxville News-Sentinel* the playwright's tendency to perpetuate the larger pattern by yielding to the darker regional romance while exchanging reality for melodrama.[4] What is involved is a regional stereotyping of American cycles of violence, the structural axes of which become even more difficult to focus, much less understand.

In "Anxious Nations, Nervous States," Homi K. Bhabha comments, "What if the 'big picture' of national culture has always dominated and silenced the anxious, split truths and double destinies of those who are minoritized and marginalized by the iniquities of modern society?"[5] Bhabha views his essay as an attempt to chart "the 'peripheric' path, where the anxiety of art and politics meets in the twisted borderlands of the nation's love and hate."[6] This has been the path of the Appalachian/"hillbilly" in the southern mountains, one of our society's "twisted borderlands." What I want to show in the following pages is that the Pulitzer Prize–winning play, *The Kentucky Cycle,* and the continuing controversy over it (at least in Kentucky) mirror this cultural pattern of inter-action between nation and region. The play's author, in other words, stumbled onto this path in an effort to illuminate the nation's love and hate, perhaps only to leave much of his audience with confused imagery of one of its "twisted borderlands." Those of us who have been engaged in the effort to advance a critical understanding of the play need to imagine this play from the future, long after the Home Box Office television version has been "rerun," as one more signpost on the postmodern mediascape affecting popular remembrance. When we imagine the state of regional identity we have to take into account how people have remembered (or forgotten) themselves.

In the 1950s, I discovered that for some Americans I was a southern "hill-billy." In the 1960s, I decided that I was and always would be in some sense a southern mountaineer. As you might expect, it is a long and complex story, so what I will offer here is a brief version. Right away, I should emphasize that this has been a dimension of identity (the regional) in a larger, growing spectrum of political consciousness. When I was a high school teenager, I was something of a southern mountain refugee in a small midwestern town. My family, like many others in the Korean War era, had moved from the Arkansas Ozarks to the Kansas City area in search of a more secure economic existence. Reflecting on the experiential dimension of this adventure now reveals a dynamic process of contradictory consciousness as teenagers negotiated issues of cultural dif-ference and conflict. There was always an interplay between recovery and re-pression or, put another way, memory (e.g., family history) was problematic in the youthful identity process. There was more "passing" in public than in pri-vate life. Most of us struggled to maintain a coherent identity across the two realms.

For a few, however, assimilationist pressures toward what was often called the "mainstream" of American life entailed repression to the point of denial. More of us were ready to aver that the label "hillbilly," under certain circum-stances, was a "fighting word." I still recall meeting a mountain youth I had known "down home" after his family had moved to Kansas by way of an eco-nomic interlude in Oregon. Buford told me Oregon wasn't "too bad" but that he had gotten into one terrific fight because a native had called him an "Arkan-sas son of a bitch." Buford allowed that it wouldn't have been so bad if he had just called him an "S.O.B." "But he wasn't going to call me an Arkansas S.O.B. and get away with it." We were alternately dubbed "Arkies" and "hillbillies." I remember well one of my initial encounters with the stereotype. It was a high school study hall situation, a conversation between myself and a new friend who pointed to a female student across the room, remarking that "she's a hill-billy, an Arkie." I looked at him with some astonishment and noted, "So am I." This sort of interaction was infrequent and, while it is important not to exaggerate this aspect of experience, neither should its significance be neglected. No doubt there was modest compensation for those of us who achieved a measure of local fame as athletes or promising scholars. But I also recall the embarrassment and ambivalence of the mountain-born among us when, on our "senior trip" to the highly commercialized Missouri Ozarks, we found ourselves in one of those tacky "Hillbillyland" recreational programs.

A comparable moment occurred later when, as a nineteen-year-old student working in the Kansas University library I came across the appalling February 1958 *Harper's Magazine* article by Albert Votaw, "Hillbillies Invade Chicago." It was a good many years later before I was to develop the historical concept of the "pejorative tradition" thanks, for example, to the July 1972 *People's Appalachia* article by Mike Maloney and Ben Huelsman. The Votaw article is just one of countless examples of this journalistic tradition, as suggested by, for example, the important Appalshop film *Strangers and Kin*. This film, the *Appalachian Journal* edited by Jerry Williamson, and a still-growing number of Appalachian studies have documented the pejorative tradition of journalistic, popular, and academic writing about the region's people, especially its least fortunate. The cultural deficiency perspective, in academic language, the "subculture of poverty" model, is part of this tradition. *The Kentucky Cycle* can't be understood apart from this tradition institutionalized by larger structures of authority and victimage. My reference to the evolving institutional context of this tradition is meant to indicate the view that cultural studies ultimately must account for the political economy and social relations within which culture is produced and consumed. To frame culture as a subjective process isolated from this context is no better than treating it as merely a "superstructural" effect of economic structures.

Bhabha defines "subaltern agency as the power to reinscribe and relocate the given symbols of authority and victimage."[7] This offers a valuable perspective for *The Kentucky Cycle*'s regional critics: it is fundamentally what our struggle with the play has been about. We have been forced to confront just how resistant these symbols are to reinscription and relocation in the larger cultural landscape beyond our academic subculture.

Monitoring the course of *The Kentucky Cycle* through the "cultural apparatus" or the "culture industry" (analyzed in critical social theory) is a daunting task for some regional critics. It has reminded us, to adapt J.G. Ballard's words, that "we live already in a world ruled by fictions of every kind. The fiction is already here and the role of the writer is to invent the reality."[8] The point is that the play, regardless of Schenkkan's intentions, is ensnared in powerful "symbols of authority and victimage" that it fails to transcend or rework. The cultural dialectic of nation/region once more feeds on the cadaverous stereotypes serving as so many mainstream signposts into the twisted borderland. Rather than rearticulating the popular, the *Cycle* is so caught up in some of its mythic roots that at the end of the play we're left with a mountain wolf symbolizing a resurgent Eden brought to us by the New Age inspiration of another American Adam. As politics this is not much more advanced than the television ads calling for President Reagan's re-election with the refrain, "Its morning again in America." As Bhabha argues, the cult of the national order requires a route bypassing "the differentiae of nation, people, culture."[9] The symbolism of national order must be understood for it cannot be escaped. The relationship between it and even the most eloquent of the Appalachian region's people is an ambiguous one. The late Harry Caudill's remarkable work and career is what I specifically have in mind.

The opening acts of *The Kentucky Cycle* reflect the influence of Caudill's *Night Comes to the Cumberlands*. The play seems to be dedicated to illustrating what the Whitesburg lawyer-writer called "the vital savagery which the mountaineer perpetuated so long."[10] While Schenkkan's portrait of the frontiersman of the mountains is drawn from Caudill's book of thirty years ago, his image of the Indian seems more reflective of *Dances with Wolves*, as several have observed. Caudill spoke of the Indian as a "simple savage" and emphasized the white man who "became, almost, a pale-faced Indian," while cherishing the freedom of a "primitive existence" and abhorring government according to his "lawless soul."[11]

Whatever "research" the playwright completed in the UCLA library, it does not seem to have introduced him to the field of Appalachian studies that emerged and matured over the past three decades. Schenkkan's interest in the political relevance of America's "myth of the frontier" is well taken, but he did not read Caudill's popular 1963 book in light of ongoing work on the frontier and its mythology in American and Appalachian studies. Some may be quick to excuse a playwright of such responsibilities, but surely someone must apply the corrective lens of scholarship to this Pulitzer Prize–winning drama. At least two traditions of mythical imagery have been put into critical, scholarly perspective since 1963.[12] I refer to the Progressive Frontier Myth and to the Myth of the Southern Mountaineer as Violent Primitive. Nevertheless, *The Kentucky Cycle* from 1792 to at least 1861 is ensnared in the assumptions and images of both. What I'm concerned to show is that this play is not just another instance of the region's submergence into a mainstream cultural process that is fundamentally ideological, i.e., having to do with the legitimation of relations of domination and subordination. The interpretive path it takes leads us into a therapeutic pseudopolitics prattling about how the Appalachian "poverty of the soul" Schenkkan saw in 1981 now has spread to every ward in the national asylum.

Of course, Schenkkan and some commentators see the *Cycle* forging a critical perspective on America's history that illuminates the deepest problems of our contemporary culture and polity. This response deserves serious scrutiny, for ours *is* a time when much of our national experience is marked by the "seemingly endless cycles of violence and loss"[13] referred to by Schenkkan in his afterword to the printed edition. The key question I've continued to ask is whether *The Kentucky Cycle* obscures and mystifies more than it clarifies regarding our historical forms of violence and loss. Capitalist development in the land of the free and the home of the brave has been at the center of our endless cycles of violence and loss. This play reinforces our mainstream culture's epistemological individualism that splits economics and violence in the popular imagination. This play's identity politics is based on a reified version of "difference" indebted to the "universal otherhood" that underpins our capitalist economy. This economic formula for violence, sublimated and overt, is not grasped. What I'd like to illuminate is how this play tends to foster one aspect of the cultural process of "disassociation" mentioned in the author's note.

"Ultimately, I realized that the play was about American mythology."[14] He tells us that as the play expanded it became apparent to him the topic was America, not merely or primarily eastern Kentucky or Appalachia. He identifies the myth of the frontier and two lesser myths of abundance and escape as comprising the chief ingredients for his stew. Reading on, we're impressed by his concern with the destruction of the environment and the denial of history: American problems with place and with past, we might say.

"The Myth of the Frontier is alive and well in America today and it is killing us."[15] Quoting Joseph Campbell with ambiguous results, Schenkkan contextualized his work amidst a people who feel "'disassociated' from each other and from their environment." It is an American problem but one he says he first recognized when he confronted "a poverty of the soul" among eastern Kentuckians in 1981. Caught in "seemingly endless cycles of violence and loss," Americans increasingly experience a "sense of helplessness [that] breeds a terrible anger."[16]

Schenkkan himself mentioned an experience of personal loss as having sensitized him politically in the period that led to his play. His author's note indeed closes with the playwright confronting the question, What are we to do? Family, class, and social movements are rejected. It would seem we live in a New Age (or "postmodern"?), postunion era of global relations requiring a cosmic perspective "big enough to embrace 'the whole of nature.'"[17] Now, I do not have any problems with Chef Schenkkan's hunger for a new worldview, but he tries to get by without some of the critical ingredients for a nourishing stew. He does not have the concepts of power and ideology to prevent his refreshing concern with American deficiencies of place and history from turning back on himself. I'm afraid this play reveals a deficient understanding of an American region, a shallow view of capitalist development in the nation's history, and the interaction of region/nation within that history. The historical, cultural, and political geography of *The Kentucky Cycle* is strip mined, and the Pulitzer reclamation job is another national Band-Aid for another regional hit-and-run case. While this sums up the critical response from the region in familiar terms, this play as a moment in capitalist development is a more challenging phenomenon.

One of Gramsci's key perspectives on hegemony was that it "always involves a struggle to rearticulate the popular." Grossberg's probe of "popular conservatism" as a hegemonic process leads us into the everyday life of disciplined mobilization that, since he wrote, can now be recognized as the world of *Forrest Gump*. This very popular movie and the Pulitzer *Cycle* can be read as episodes on the "postmodern frontier" that, as Grossberg says, is "inscribed by and on popular culture." I would explain the Appalachian critique of the *Cycle* as a regionalist scream protesting the *disappearance* of historicity, of the vestigially authentic, of those located outside the popular. The *Cycle*'s southern mountaineers have been relocated to the *postmodern frontier,* "a self-enclosing interiority with no exteriority." Those of us in the academic circuits of the globalizing corporate state must begin to confront better certain questions of political responsibility. If we do not, it seems likely more of us will acquiesce in an all too familiar postmodern sensibility of the authentically inauthentic, accepting a professional "good life" based on depoliticization (supposedly for the "masses" only) and "spaces without places." Some of the *Cycle*'s Appalachian critics already have been told, in so many words, that they should have less trouble "privileging mobility and space over stability and place."[18]

My argument is that the *Cycle* is another example of the deterritorialization that is so definitive of the new global capitalist regime of everyday life. This is not to promote a shallow, "populist" glorification of the local or regional that, after all, has been the stock in trade of romantic culturalists peddling "heritage" divorced from issues of political economy. We are doomed if our only options are tribal "homelands" or nomadic "homelessness." As Grossberg contends, we must move beyond "identity politics" to a politics of practice, of agency, of alliances transcending difference. To this I would add that different sites of affective investment must be reconfigured in social imagination and political rhetoric to provide globally relevant structures of feeling or affective commonalities that make collective action possible. This is precisely what Jesse Jackson did when he took his 1988 presidential nomination campaign to Hazard, Kentucky, in the Appalachian coalfields.

But let me return us to Grossberg's postmodern frontier and what we're up against today: what he calls "the disciplined mobilization of everyday life." "It restructures and transforms the very nature of people's affective relationship to the world so that such investments can no longer anchor them into something outside of everyday life." On campus we may also be up against an alienated academic left that uses a cynical image of politics merged with Disney World to justify its endless "theory" recycling of "popular culture." As Grossberg puts it, "Culture itself is articulated to capitalism's deconstruction of all fixities (places) and to its elimination of public spaces. It produces an endless flow of differences which make no difference but deny any stable moment of identity and commonality."[19] The corporate managers of our universities who administer campus life with such programs as "post-tenure review" know that academicians are not really above the struggle which, by any means, must be contained. The university in today's corporate state is chiefly about the production of symbolic analysts for service to global capital.

Increasingly, the denationalization of capital is encouraging new levels of public irresponsibility in a transnational class that confuses its levitation from place-based citizenship with a new doctrine of freedom. Elsewhere,[20] I've argued that this well-paid "Phoenix Self" rising above the stagnating places and provinces of a decaying society is a postmodern version of the American Adam. New Age subjectivism is one popular brand of fertilizer for this resurgent Edenic myth.

This postmodern frontier sensibility almost seems caricatured in the *Cycle*'s act called "Tall Tales" featuring "a storyteller," J.T. Wells.[21] The question must be raised whether this segment of the play constitutes a slander on Appalachia's storytelling traditions. Schenkkan takes a popular meaning of the word "story" (to tell a fib, a lie) and employs it in a singular or absolutist way that short-circuits some of our hermeneutical resources. Gurney Norman's use of the jack tale, his authorship and performance of "Ancient Creek" (initially on phonograph record) is an example of the hermeneutical resources I have in mind. "Ancient Creek" is definitely a story, but for some of us it is a populist utopia or folk opera as stirring as anything out of Brook Farm or the "city of quartz." Whatever research Schenkkan did, his play ignores the oral traditions and the appreciation of "a good story"—sometimes but not always including "tall stories" marked by exaggeration and embellishment.

J.T. Wells is a onetime boy off the creek who becomes a "storyteller" who is whoever he says he is. "I invent myself new every day." He sounds like the television commercials for milk of a few years ago: "There is a new you coming every day . . . drink milk." Is J.T. a version of the postmodern "protean self" or is he little more than a throwback to that now old American advertising ideology that truth is what sells? "I just tell people the stories they want to hear. I say what people want me to say and I am whatever they want me to be." Mary Anne Rowen's response is "I don't put no truck in stories no more."[22] It seems to me that Schenkkan's J.T. Wells turns back on his author who, by promoting a radical skepticism toward all stories, regional and national, unwittingly activates the myth of the American Adam.[23] At the end of *The Kentucky Cycle*, the American experiment is to be started over by an act of Cartesian resolution and one of reconciliation with Nature. From the 1960s to the 1990s, nothing has been learned: the mythic framework remains.

To use his own concept of "story" against him, Schenkkan has been suckered by Harry Caudill's story, failing to take into account its "mythistorical" framework. Merely turning Indians into "good guys" is no feat of ideology critique. Putting Mother Jones onstage doesn't guarantee an intelligent perspective on labor history and so on. When the mountaineer as violent primitive appears in fifty-seven varieties and mountain families seem little more than zones of guerrilla warfare, these truly dangerous people do indeed come off as "white savages." And that pattern of representation in *The Kentucky Cycle* is congruent with one of the managerial ideology's cultural paradigms, the Progressive Frontier Myth, which substituted the symbolism of "savage war" for that of "class war." From the 1870s onward, strikers were depicted as savages as the battle to advance a new paternalism of corporate capitalist relations proceeded. "To turn back the political initiatives of these underclass groups and to discredit the ideologies that sustained their popular support, the spokesmen for the new managerial order deployed the 'Indian metaphor,' which was intended to convince the uncommitted class of 'middling' proprietors that collective political action against the new order was a species of tribalism, a throwback to the savage past, a symptom of degeneracy."[24]

*The Kentucky Cycle* purports to be an attack on our frontier myth and hence on the problem of American violence. But the mythic frame adopted by Schenkkan was transformed in the late nineteenth century, as the southern mountains were beginning to be industrialized. The play's deployment of the old frontier myth poses the issue of violence in such a misleading way as to reinforce, however unwittingly, what Slotkin calls the Progressive Frontier Myth, which was especially attuned to legitimating an allegedly "modern" distribution of social power between managerial and laboring classes. The epistemological individualism of an earlier American liberalism, or what Gramsci would call "bad common sense," leads to a subjectivization and naturalization of characters and events, i.e., of history. In condemning one version of our frontier myth, the play tends to reinforce the latest on which our corporate state actually depends. The barbarism and "white savagery" that the play depicts in Kentucky's mountains not only individualizes (or deinstitutionalizes) historical problems of alienation and violence. This perspective (one-sided at best) trips a mechanism of cultural sacrifice that is in one aspect what Appalachian scholars have dubbed the "pejorative tradition." Later, I hope to show how the *Cycle*'s ideological categories sometimes have been eased into mainstream media frames as commentary on contemporary issues. But now the task is to elaborate on the failure of what I suspect is a sort of New Age libertarianism to come to grips with the managerial ideology of modernization at the core of the Progressive Frontier Myth.

It is precisely this mythicizing of Official Violence by the mainstream doctrine of "Progress" that is not overlooked in Appalshop's film *Strangers and Kin*. A *New York Times* editorial of 1912 titled "Education or Extermination" sternly argued that "the mountaineer, like the red Indian," must learn how to get on the bandwagon of modern industrial progress or be literally run over by it.[25] This was the same year that a book by Thomas Dawley found the answer to the nation's "mountain problem" in the cotton mills operated by child labor.[26] In whatever form, "education" has been the typical prescription of a touring American middle class shocked by poverty in the southern mountains. In 1961 I first read James Agee's *Let Us Now Praise Famous Men* and began to realize that the "education" prescribed by our liberal moralists of various stripes might well be in his haunting words "the very property of the world's misunderstanding."[27] Against all the Schenkkans then and since, it was clear that there is no getting around politics, around issues of power, conflict, class, social movements, and so on. One radical democratic project today, as yesterday, is helping cure the escapist tendencies of our middle-class reform liberals who, in some ways, depended on Cold War categories more than their mainstream alter egos, the reactionary liberals. There was indeed something splendid as well as dismaying about the way one of our most versatile liberal moralists shamed both moguls and victims. We may still have something to learn from the ideological ambivalence of Harry Caudill's work, for it is still manifested in cultural class relations in region and nation.

One of the major problems of historical explanation in Caudill's *Night Comes to the Cumberlands,* as I've read it, is never satisfactorily resolved. Caudill's interpretation of the mine worker's life before the Great Depression and the union drives of the 1930s rendered coal camp paternalism in totalistic terms. Relying too much on anecdotal evidence, Caudill's portrait emphasized the "pathetic helplessness of the workman . . . and his childish confidence in his employer." His negative portrait of the miner's deference to the big bosses left him hard put to explain their eager and vigorous embrace of unionism.[28] The reader gets two starkly contrasting frames in which evidence of hostility and resentment appears only in the later period. Unfortunately, this is much too mechanical and ahistorical because the struggle over unionization was continuous if uneven in the southern Appalachian region. Most miners were con-

Lewis, R.W.B. *The American Adam: Innocence, Tragedy, and Tradition in the Nineteenth Century.* Chicago: Univ. of Chicago Press, 1955.

Mason, Bobbie Ann. "Recycling Kentucky." *New Yorker,* Nov. 1, 1993, 50–62.

Nance, Kevin. "Does Kentucky Have Shot at *Cycle* Film Site?" *Lexington Herald-Leader,* Aug. 1, 1995.

*Nimrod Workman.* Whitesburg, Ky.: Appalshop, 1975. Film.

Pearce, John Ed. "A Prize-Winning Slander." *Louisville Courier-Journal,* Oct. 5, 1993.

Reid, Herbert G. *Up the Mainstream: A Critique of Ideology in American Politics and Everyday Life.* New York: McKay, 1974.

———. "Appalachian Studies: Class, Culture, and Politics—II," *Appalachian Journal* 9 (winter-spring 1982): 141–48.

———. "Appalachian Values, Social Policy, and Ideology Critique." In *Policy Analysis,* ed. William Dunn, 203–222. Greenwich: JAI Press, 1986.

———. "The Resurgence of the Market Machine-God and the Obsolescence of Liberal Democracy: On Metaphysical Rejections of the Public Realm and Their This-Worldly Complicities," Nov. 1994.

———. "Global Adjustments, Throwaway Regions, Appalachian Studies: Resituating *The Kentucky Cycle* on the Postmodern Frontier," *Journal of Appalachian Studies* 2, no. 2 (fall, 1996): 235–62.

Rich, Frank. "Two Hundred Years of a Nation's Sorrows, in Nine Chapters," *New York Times,* Nov. 15, 1993, B1, B4.

Schenkkan, Robert. *The Kentucky Cycle.* New York: Penguin Plume, 1993.

Shapiro, Henry David. *Appalachia On Our Mind.* Chapel Hill: Univ. of North Carolina Press, 1978.

Slotkin, Richard. *Regeneration through Violence: The Mythology of the American Frontier, 1600–1860.* Middletown, Conn.: Wesleyan Univ. Press, 1973.

———. *The Fatal Environment: The Myth of the Frontier in the Age of Industrialization, 1800–1890.* New York: Atheneum, 1985.

———. *Gunfighter Nation: The Myth of the Frontier in Twentieth-Century America.* New York: Atheneum, 1992.

*Strangers and Kin: A History of the Hillbilly Image.* Whitesburg, Ky.: Appalshop, 1984. Film.

versant on battles here and there in the coalfields (e.g., southern West Virginia in 1921), and very few lacked some sense of exploitation in the dangerous pursuit of their livelihood.

Schenkkan's play, reliant throughout on Caudill, reveals a related discontinuity as the author shifts from the first two centuries to our own. In fact, Schenkkan resorts to a sort of "PC" gimmick that slanders the brave rank-and-file miners and organizers involved in the union struggles of the depression era. One easily gets the impression that most are incapable of understanding their problems. Tommy Jackson says, for example, "I don't know how to fight the company." Scene 7 finds this miner paying the preacher to draw up a fake birth certificate so that his son can work in the mines a few years earlier. Schenkkan's Tommy Jackson even attacks his wife in insisting that their son go to the mines. A more representative picture is provided by the 1975 Appalshop film on a marvelous West Virginia miner and musician named Nimrod Workman. I think Nimrod's remarks to his son Tommy, when he followed his Dad to the mines one day, deserve quotation: "Go to school, so you don't have to work in the mines as I do."[29] And with the Bentsen-Quayle debate in mind, I might add that Nimrod "knew" Mother Jones, too, and that some of us were fortunate to get to know him during his long lifetime. But *The Kentucky Cycle* gives the heroic role to Mary Anne Rowen Jackson (and to some extent to Cassius Biggs) in the establishment of the union. The striking miners—halted by Tommy's treachery—give up. But Mary Anne proceeds to revive the strike and to lead all of them to "victory" over the mine owner. We hear Mary Anne saying, "I think if we always waited for the men to do somethin' we still be livin' in caves."[30]

Not surprisingly, the union in a few years seems to be a sort of primitive cave. When romantic stereotypes of identity politics lead to historical distortions of the labor traditions of an oppressed group, it is ludicrous to argue for public, historical memory. However, I must add that the labor history from this point on is credibly rendered, although the company's power and union corruption are myopically presented. Perhaps the overreliance on the family construct or theme is part of the problem. But ultimately the failure of historical imagination involved with this play shortchanges the audience of needed insights into the issues of power and violence that affect all of us today. Let me illustrate the problem by quoting *U.S. News and World Report*'s view of this "theatrical epic." "The violence in today's urban streets is not some aberration, Schenkkan insists, but a manifestation of an enduring American tradition," writes Miriam Horn.[31] Here is a classic example of the mass media's "penchant for *covering up* systemic violence in the 'real world,'" in Futrelle's words, for ignoring the "subtle and pervasive effects of economic violence in American slums and in the Third World."[32] The *U.S. News and World Report* frame or perspective is a "mythistorical" displacement or deflection of social conflict that reveals just how functional the play is for mainstream ideology.[33]

The "enduring American tradition" is projecting violence onto sacrificial groups that represent a potentially and politically troublesome Otherness. In the regional context, this stereotyping of national problems of violence and domination may be thought of as a corporate state politics of cultural downsizing that tends to deflect attention from the "economic violence" scored by Jesse Jackson in his last presidential campaign. *The Kentucky Cycle's* "Michael Rowen," like George Bush's Willie Horton, merges in the national symbolism carried partly by the pejorative traditions of the mainstream media. The historical interplay of such images and stereotypes in the cultural mainstream offers a number of unlearned lessons regarding an American cycle of public pity and official violence that continues today.

## Notes

1. "Marines Search Somalis' Homes for Arms but Find 'Hatfields and McCoys,'" *New York Times,* Feb. 16, 1993, A5.

2. "Harper's Index," *Harper's Magazine,* Feb. 1993.

3. Wilma Dykeman, "Appalachia in Context," in *An Appalachian Symposium,* ed. J.W. Williamson (Boone, N.C.: Appalachian State Univ. Press, 1977), 28–42.

4. Wilma Dykeman, review of *The Kentucky Cycle,* in the *Knoxville News-Sentinel,* Dec. 5, 1993.

5. Homi K. Bhabha, "Anxious Nations, Nervous States," in *Supposing the Subject,* ed. Joan Copjec (London: Verso, 1994), 201–17.

6. Ibid.

7. Ibid., 212–13.

8. J.G. Ballard, quoted in Timothy Druckery, introduction to *Culture on the Brink: Ideologies of Technology,* eds. Gretchen Bender and Timothy Druckery (Seattle: Bay Press, 1994), 2.

9. Babha, "Anxious Nations," 203.

10. Harry Caudill, *Night Comes to the Cumberlands* (Boston: Little, Brown, 1963), 79.

11. Ibid., 13–14.

12. Cf. Herbert G. Reid, "Global Adjustments, Throwaway Regions, Appalachian Studies: Resituating *The Kentucky Cycle* on the Postmodern Frontier," *Journal of Appalachian Studies* (fall 1996).

13. Robert Schenkkan, author's note to *The Kentucky Cycle* (New York: Penguin Plume, 1993), 338.

14. Schenkkan, author's note to *The Kentucky Cycle,* 336.

15. Joseph Campbell, quoted in Schenkkan, author's note to *The Kentucky Cycle,* 337.

16. Schenkkan, author's note, 337, 338.

17. Ibid., 338.

18. Lawrence Grossberg, *We Gotta Get Out of This Place: Popular Conservatis* *Postmodern Culture* (New York: Routledge, 1993), 247, 260, 262, 222–39, 295.

19. Ibid., 297, 356.

20. Herbert G. Reid, "The Resurgence of the Market Machine-God and the ( lescence of Liberal Democracy: On Metaphysical Rejections of the Public Realr Their This-Worldly Complicities," Nov. 1994.

21. Schenkkan, *The Kentucky Cycle,* 170 ff.

22. Ibid., 203, 204, 172.

23. R.W.B. Lewis, *The American Adam: Innocence, Tragedy, and Tradition Nineteenth Century* (Chicago: Univ. of Chicago Press, 1955).

24. Richard Slotkin, *Regeneration through Violence: The Mythology of the Am Frontier, 1600–1860* (Middletown, Conn.: Wesleyan Univ. Press, 1973), 316.

25. "Education or Extermination," *New York Times,* 1912, quoted in *Strangers an*

26. See *Strangers and Kin: A History of the Hillbilly Image* (Whitesburg Appalshop, 1984), film.

27. James Agee, *Let Us Now Praise Famous Men* (Boston: Houghton Mifflin, 1 290.

28. Caudill, *Night Comes to the Cumberlands,* 121, 176–77.

29. *Nimrod Workman: To Fit My Own Category* (Whitesburg, Ky.: Appelshop, 1 film

30. Schenkkan, *The Kentucky Cycle,* 261.

31. Miriam Horn, review of *The Kentucky Cycle,* in *U.S. News and World R* Sept. 20, 1993, 72, 74.

32. David Futrelle, "Van Damme Made Me Do It," *These Times,* Sept. 20, 199

33. Cf. Slotkin, *Regeneration through Violence.*

## Bibliography

Agee, James. *Let Us Now Praise Famous Men.* (Boston: Houghton Mifflin, 1960).

Bhabha, Homi K. "Anxious Nations, Nervous States." In *Supposing the Subject,* ed. Copjec, 201–17. London: Verso, 1994.

Caudill, Harry. *Night Comes to the Cumberlands.* Boston: Little, Brown, 1963.

Druckery, Timothy. Introduction in *Culture on the Brink: Ideologies of Technology* Gretchen Bender and Timothy Druckery, 1–12. Seattle: Bay Press, 1994.

Dykeman, Wilma. "Appalachia in Context." In *An Appalachian Symposium,* ed. Williamson, 28–42. Boone, N.C.: Appalachian State Univ. Press, 1977.

Eller, Ronald. "Harry Caudill and the Burden of Southern Mountain Liberalisn *Critical Essays in Appalachian Life and Culture,* 21–29. Boone, N.C.: Appala( Consortium Press, 1983.

Foucault, Michel. *The History of Sexuality. Vol. 1, An Introduction.* New York: Vii Books, 1990.

Girard, Rene. *Violence and the Sacred.* Baltimore: Johns Hopkins University Press,

Futrelle, David. "Van Damme Made Me Do It." *In These Times,* Sept. 20, 1993, 18.

Grossberg, Lawrence. *We Gotta Get Out of This Place: Popular Conservatism Postmodern Culture.* New York: Routledge, l993.

# Notes on *The Kentucky Cycle*

## *Gurney Norman*

The following notes represent a set of thoughts that have been accumulating since I first read *The Kentucky Cycle* in 1992.[1] At that time the play had already won approval by audiences and critics alike after performances in Seattle and Los Angeles. Within months the play would be awarded the Pulitzer Prize for Drama for 1992. I didn't like the play at all. Even though I consider myself to be a "Left Liberal Democrat," with a long history of identification with a range of liberal issues and causes, I resented the play's plodding recitation of "progressive" and "correct" positions. My chief complaint was that it was just not a good drama, even though many knowledgeable theater professionals reported that technically the staging of the play was innovative, even radical. It interested me greatly that, even as the play conquered the West Coast theater world in 1992, in Kentucky, where I have lived most of my life, there seemed to be no awareness of it at all. Clearly *The Kentucky Cycle* had created an interesting cultural, political, and artistic situation, one that continues long after the play folded in New York after a few performances. My purpose in publicly criticizing the play in 1993 was to try to generate awareness and discussion of *The Kentucky Cycle* in Kentucky. That remains my purpose in continuing to discuss it these years later.

When Robert Schenkkan's play *The Kentucky Cycle* opened at the Kennedy Center in Washington, D.C., in August 1993, ten or twelve Kentucky teachers, journalists, and writers went to see it. Most of us were friends and colleagues of various sorts who had been talking about *The Kentucky Cycle* since photocopies of the manuscript began circulating across Kentucky and down through the Appalachian mountain region in the summer of 1992. Our responses to the play had been mixed. Most of us had an appreciation of Schenkkan's earnestness, of his intellectual ambition. He is surely at work on serious ideas in *The Kentucky Cycle*.

But his use of Kentucky history, of the experience of my family and the families of most of the early critics of the play, was misplaced. I resented Schenkkan's basic view of our region's history. His gaze not only came from a position of presumed cultural superiority, it was a naive, unconscious practice of "Orientalism," as Edward Said has established that term. I resented Schenkkan's presumption of his right to appropriate the history of eastern Kentucky for his own "artistic" use and political agenda without any consideration of the effects of that use upon the people who live and struggle in the social matrix he viewed in such a limited way.

If Schenkkan had approached the Appalachian region with the clear intention to exploit its natural and human resources, it would have been another matter entirely. That approach is one of the oldest, most familiar stories in the mountains. People are quite used to it by now in the way urban people get used to smog. But Schenkkan wants to make a "progressive" statement in which the banners of environmentalism, feminism, antiracism, anticolonialism—no end of "isms" in *The Kentucky Cycle*—are waved above the lives and struggles of an indigenous local people who, in Schenkkan's eyes, are "disassociated" and who suffer "poverty of the soul."[2] There are many problems with *The Kentucky Cycle*, including the problem of the negative "hillbilly" stereotype, but to my mind, the problem of faux liberalism, abstract "elite" liberalism, is the basic weakness of the play and the reason it requires continued analysis.

The portrayal of Kentucky mountain people as passive victims of fate (indeed, in Schenkkan's view, as people so dumb, greedy, and shiftless that they have caused their fate) truly astounded me. For some reason, this representation was met with enthusiastic approval by the West Coast audiences. But anyone with one degree of real, local knowledge about eastern Kentucky would know how false that representation is. In the very years in which Schenkkan was writing his play, from about 1983 to 1990, eastern Kentucky and the southern Appalachian region were sites of some of the most dynamic examples of creative civic participation, in the spirit of true democratic liberalism, in North America at the time. In those years, several decades of grassroots political and cultural organizing efforts by ordinary local citizens, working people, came to fruition.

The most dramatic political victory by Schenkkan's "disassociated" Kentucky mountaineers suffering "poverty of the soul" came in 1988 when a civic group called Kentuckians for the Commonwealth, with headquarters in eastern Kentucky, mobilized voters statewide to amend the state constitution to outlaw the infamous broadform deed. This deed, by which coal companies gained control of minerals beneath the soil owned by private families, had oppressed small landowners and hillside farmers in the coalfields for nearly a century. The deed allowed coal operators to invade private lands to extract the coal by strip mining without protections or compensation to the owners. The owners were mostly families of modest means. Many were poor, the rough hillsides representing their only assets. (*The Kentucky Cycle*'s notion of landowning mountain families is one of the play's most egregious distortions of local social reality.)

In a technical sense, because the time frame of *The Kentucky Cycle* is 1775–1975, the civic life of the Kentucky mountains in the 1980s could be said to lie outside the time of Schenkkan's concern. But the point is, the brilliant, energetic, successful political efforts of citizens in the 1980s is rooted in an Appalachian tradition of resistance to oppressive forces. Resistance defines the very people Schenkkan portrays as being defeated. The roots of the 1980s efforts are decades deep. The civic work had to be sustained by effort over time. In other words, the work was expressive of Appalachian culture. The mountain people are leaders and teachers of civic virtue for the nation, not scabs upon the body politic as the negative hillbilly stereotype would have it.

Serious, organized citizen resistance to strip mining and the broadform deed began in July 1965 on Clear Creek in Knott County, Kentucky, when the Appalachian Group to Save the Land and People was organized. The members included teachers, farmers, miners, welfare recipients, educated and uneducated people, young and old, women and men, Republicans and Democrats. Working only with resources at hand (no grants, no foundations, no paid staff), the Appalachian Group marched on the state capital, persuaded the governor to tour the strip mines to see the destruction for himself, and within six months, caused the Kentucky legislature to pass the first strip mine control laws. From this beginning, it took twenty-three years of unremitting effort by local citizens to at last defeat the broadform deed when Kentucky voters amended the constitution by an 83 percent approval vote.

The Kentucky strip mine battle is only one instance of the vigor, the cultural strength, and the political courage of the American citizens who live in the Appalachian Mountains. Every mountain state has its own similar story. In Perry County, Kentucky, the Appalachian Committee for Full Employment fought hard in 1964 and 1965 for social and economic justice for poor people. In Southwest Virginia in the 1980s the efforts of the people of Brummley Gap to stop an electrical power company from flooding their valley inspired civic-minded citizens all over the region. In Magoffin County, Kentucky, in the late 1980s and early 1990s, local citizens successfully fought an attempt by a Florida waste disposal company to open a huge landfill for out-of-state waste in their county. To me, this level of participation in the democratic process, in which ordinary people cooperate to resist enormous forces that would control and oppress them, is the very definition of liberal democracy. The Appalachian region has for years been the center of shining examples of this spirit.

How could Robert Schenkkan have missed such a story?

One of the ironic issues of what has come to be called "*The Kentucky Cycle* controversy" is the debt both sides of the argument owe to Harry Caudill's great book *Night Comes to the Cumberlands*. (There are actually more than two sides to the argument.) Schenkkan has acknowledged his debt to the book several times. In a sense, *The Kentucky Cycle* is an attempt to dramatize aspects of *Night Comes to the Cumberlands*. I fully understand how Caudill's book affected Schenkkan so powerfully. It affected me and most of my generation of Appalachian writers and readers in life-changing ways. Harry Caudill's entire life and work are indispensable to all who would understand and work for the Appalachian region and for social justice everywhere.

But what Schenkkan did not understand was that, in addition to Caudill's work, there are books by a good hundred other writers that any person seeking to understand the Appalachian region must read. Many of these books have been written by younger members of the very generation of Appalachian thinkers that Caudill's work helped create. In addition to the works of fiction, poetry, drama, and scholarship by Appalachian writers that have poured from the presses since 1963, Appalachians have generated a stream of documentary films and television and radio programs that analyze a broad range of regional life and issues.

Some of the scholarship has been critical of Harry Caudill's work, particularly *Night Comes to the Cumberlands*, so as central as Caudill's work is, it has not spread a blanket of intellectual conformity over the community of writers and readers in the region. To the contrary, this regional community is as alive and dynamic and contentious with debate as any intellectual community anywhere. Schenkkan seems to have no inkling that all the premises of all writers on the Appalachian region are thoroughly studied and criticized by the mountain people themselves. He seems to not understand that life in the mountains is not static, that the region is not a museum. The Appalachian region is a vibrant place, always changing like any living organism or social situation. Millions of modern people live here. A good many of them have read the literature of postcolonialism. Quite a few Appalachian writers have contributed to it.

The new generation of thinkers and educators that has evolved in the Appalachian region since the early 1960s has developed a pedagogy which forms a basis for all citizens of this region who would participate in the progress of their communities. The writings of Paulo Freire have greatly influenced these thinkers and educators. In *Pedagogy of the Oppressed*, Freire writes, "The man who proclaims devotion to the cause of liberation yet is unable to enter into *communion* with the people, whom he continues to regard as totally ignorant, is grievously self-deceived."[3] Entering into communion with Kentucky mountain people is precisely what Robert Schenkkan was unable or unwilling to do as he researched and wrote *The Kentucky Cycle*. Schenkkan felt no need to become personally acquainted with people in the communities here. He wanted only to use the history of the Kentucky coalfields as a metaphor for his dire vision of American life. His attempt fails because it does not take into account the real lives of local people, their unruly resistance to being pigeonholed, categorized, essentialized, or consigned to the categories of "other" or "marginal."

Much of the controversy that surrounded *The Kentucky Cycle* after it opened in Washington and then in New York in the fall of 1993 had to do with the problem of the hillbilly stereotype. Most of the attention in this rather hot public discussion was on Schenkkan's representations of mountain people as violent, cruel, greedy, ignorant, etc. I was offended by this representation, but more bothersome to me was the willful omission of more positive images. The truth is, the segment of the American population that lives in the Appalachian region is good and bad, noble and ignoble, in about the same proportions as people anywhere else. So the question is why does the negative hillbilly image persist? Why are stereotypes against any racial, or ethnic, or regional group so intractable? Whose interest is served by the relentless reinscription on the national consciousness of any hateful images?

An interesting positive result of the kind of discourse *The Kentucky Cycle* has inspired is the reminder that the experience of being negatively stereotyped gives white Appalachian Americans, especially of the poorer classes, a way to comprehend the experience of African American, Native American, and other minority people. The shared experience of being socially despised is a powerful thing, opening the possibility of mutual recognition. There are very powerful interests in American society that would encourage animosity between poor whites and poor blacks. The notion of these groups figuring out how to make common cause, which was one of Martin Luther King's projects in the last years of his life, threatens many established orders. People are taught to hate. Yet there is something in the human spirit, often revealed in the works of artists, that longs to overcome division, that longs to cooperate, to reconcile.

It is significant that important African American leaders such as Jesse Jackson and Oprah Winfrey have indicated on a number of occasions their understanding of the struggles of poor Appalachian people, black and white. The response to this recognition in the mountains has been deeply felt. The Appalachian region is one site where better communication between the races is possible. Shared experience of negative stereotypes does not create a racial panacea by any means, but shared ground, shared place, creates a human bond.

In closing, let me say that the ideological broad brush strokes with which *The Kentucky Cycle* is painted is part of a profound national disease that afflicts the country in the 1990s. Public discourse in these times is so simplistic, so demagogic, so devoid of particular distinguishing details drawn from the real lives of real people, that little real thinking is going on and little real communication takes place. From the conservative right we have George Bush in 1988 trading on the image of Willie Horton, the "black thug" meant to represent all black males. From the liberal left we have Robert Schenkkan's character Michael Rowen, the "white male brute." Add "hillbilly" to white male brute and you have the vile image upon which to hang the liberals' worst fears and greatest blame. The national media, the national entertainment industry, and large segments of the national culture industry apparatus, including the universities, perpetuate these dread images by not deconstructing them. The culture industry is so myopic and partisan, it actually honored *The Kentucky Cycle* with the Pulitzer Prize.

Fortunately, there is in our multicultural nation a powerful surging impulse within every small, discrete, particular, local segment of society to supply the enriching details that give life and vibrancy and variety to the whole. A similar statement could be made about the world as a whole. In this era of devolution of old empires, the concept of "geographical region" is finding fresh currency and power. The geographical region of the Appalachian Mountains with its many varieties of people and local cultures is being seen in fresh ways. The Appalachian region is no longer merely a gleam in the gaze of an exploitive, culturally generic hegemony. It is a place that is learning to see itself and hear itself through the eyes and voices of its own citizens.

"You'd better listen to the voices from the mountains," says the song by Ruthie Gorton, "tryin' to tell you what you just might need to know."[4]

## Notes

1. These notes were prepared for a talk at the Center for American Studies at the University of Rome in December 1997.

2. Robert Schenkkan, author's note in *The Kentucky Cycle* (New York: Plume, 1993), 337.

3. Paulo Freire, *Pedagogy of the Oppressed* (New York: Herder and Herder, 1970), 47.

4. Ruthie Gorton, "Voices from the Mountains," in *Voices from the Mountains* (Athens: The University of Georgia Press, 1996), 206.

# Contributors

**Mary K. Anglin,** an assistant professor of anthropology at the University of Kentucky who has been involved in research on Southern Appalachia since the late 1970s, focuses on epidemiology and health.

**Alan Banks** is a professor of sociology at Eastern Kentucky University.

**Sandra L. Ballard** is an associate professor of English at Carson-Newman College.

**Dwight B. Billings,** professor of sociology at the University of Kentucky, is a past president of the Appalachian Studies Association.

**Kathleen M. Blee** is a professor of sociology and the director of women's studies at the University of Kentucky. She is the author of *Women of the Klan* and editor of *No Middle Ground: Women and Radical Protest.*

**Rodger Cunningham,** author of *Apples on the Flood: The Southern Mountain Experience,* is a visiting professor in General Studies at Berea College.

**Finlay Donesky,** currently living in Minneapolis, Minnesota, became familiar with the history of eastern Kentucky while teaching drama at the University of Kentucky in the early 1990s.

**Ronald D Eller,** an historian and the author of *Miners, Millhands, and Mountaineers: Industrialization of the Appalachian South, 1880–1930,* is the director of the University of Kentucky Appalachian Center.

**Stephen L. Fisher,** Hawthorne Professor of Political Science and director of the Appalachian Center for Community Service at Emory & Henry College, served as president of the Appalachian Studies Association in 1998–99.

**Denise Giardina** is the author of two historical novels set in Appalachia, *Storming Heaven* and *The Unquiet Earth*. Her most recent novel, *Saints and Villains,* narrates the life of Dietrich Bonhoeffer.

**Eula Hall,** an activist and health care advocate, is social director of the Mud Creek Clinic, which she founded in 1973 in Appalachian Kentucky.

**Fred Hobson** is Lineberger Professor of English at the University of North Carolina at Chapel Hill. He is the author, most recently, of *Mencken: A Life* (Random House).

**John C. Inscoe,** associate professor of history at the University of Georgia and editor of the *Georgia Historical Quarterly*, is author of *Mountain Masters: Slavery and the Sectional Crisis in Western North Carolina* and editor of *Appalachia in Black and White.*

**Katherine Ledford,** a doctoral candidate in American literature at the University of Kentucky, is writing a dissertation investigating the relationship between geography, class, and national identity in the early nation using Appalachian travel narratives from 1750 to 1850 as primary texts.

**Ronald L. Lewis,** Eberly Professor of history at West Virginia University, is a past president of the Appalachian Studies Association and author, most recently, of *Transforming the Appalachian Countryside: Railroads, Deforestation, and Social Change in West Virginia, 1880–1920.*

**Sally Ward Maggard,** research associate of the Regional Research Institute and associate professor of sociology at West Virginia University, is editor of the *Journal of Appalachian Studies.*

**Kenneth W. Noe,** an associate professor of history at the State University of West Georgia, is author of *Southwest Virginia's Railroad* and coeditor of *The Civil War in Appalachia.*

**Gurney Norman,** associate professor of English at the University of Kentucky, is the author of *Divine Right's Trip, Kinfolks,* and *Ancient Creek.*

**Phillip J. Obermiller,** visiting professor of urban affairs at the University of Cincinnati and a faculty associate of the University of Kentucky Appalachian Center, is the author of numerous articles and books on the experience of migrants from Appalachia in urban America.

**Herbert Reid** is a professor of political science at the University of Kentucky.

**Anne Shelby,** a writer and storyteller in Appalachian Kentucky, is the author of five books for children and *Lines from Home,* a collection of poems.

**Crystal Wilkinson,** a poet, short-fiction writer, and arts administrator who grew up on Indian Creek in Casey County, Kentucky, is a founding member of the Affrilachian Poets and the Bluegrass Black Arts Consortium.

**Darlene Wilson** is the director of institutional planning and research at Southeast Community College in Appalachian Kentucky. She is also completing a doctorate in history at the University of Kentucky.

# Index

**Anne Shelby,** a writer and storyteller in Appalachian Kentucky, is the author of five books for children and *Lines from Home,* a collection of poems.

**Crystal Wilkinson,** a poet, short-fiction writer, and arts administrator who grew up on Indian Creek in Casey County, Kentucky, is a founding member of the Affrilachian Poets and the Bluegrass Black Arts Consortium.

**Darlene Wilson** is the director of institutional planning and research at Southeast Community College in Appalachian Kentucky. She is also completing a doctorate in history at the University of Kentucky.

# Index